A Treatise on the

Law of
Lis Pendens

A Treatise on the

Law of Lis Pendens

or The Effect of Jurisdiction upon Property Involved in Suit

John I. Bennett, LL.D.

BeardBooks

Washington, D.C.

TO THE

HON. WALTER Q. GRESHAM,

JUDGE OF THE SEVENTH JUDICIAL CIRCUIT OF THE UNITED STATES, THE
BRAVE SOLDIER, WISE STATESMAN, LEARNED AND JUST JUDGE,
THIS WORK IS RESPECTFULLY DEDICATED BY

THE AUTHOR.

PREFACE.

The Bench and Bar have long felt the necessity of some elementary work on the law of Lis Pendens. The labor to the practicing lawyer of collecting for application in daily practice, from the many decisions on that subject scattered through the books, eliminating general principles from a mass of apparently conflicting and irreconcilable cases, and deducing correct conclusions from them, is by no means inconsiderable.

Many of the States have adopted what are known as Lis Pendens Statutes. While these statutes are in some respects similar, in others they differ materially. The courts of last resort of the various States where they are in force have, moreover, each given local construction to them by a series of decisions.

In other States the common law is in force on this subject, while, in still others, statutes merely modifying more or less the common law have been adopted. Under these circumstances the decisions of the courts on the law of Lis Pendens have been often made with more special reference to local laws than to general rules or principles of universal application. The growing importance of modern litigation also has added to the importance, if not to the necessity, of a better understanding of this branch of the law.

Cases are often brought involving judicial proceedings in sister States, and in the Federal courts—cases in which are called in question the judicial determinations of the courts in the different States.

In such cases it becomes necessary to know what the law
of Lis Pendens is in the various States of the Union.   Moreover, the general practitioner, in the absence of some elementary work on the subject, unless he has had occasion in
some special case to consult the decisions with something
more than ordinary care, is likely to have confused or erroneous views upon the law of Lis Pendens.   The same thing,
it is true, may be said of other subjects in these times of
multiplicity of reports and of jarring and conflicting decisions, often made by the same courts; but that makes the remark none the less applicable to the present subject.

These are some of the considerations which have induced
the author to write the present work.   He has endeavored
in the execution of his plan to reduce the text to as small a
compass as was possible, in order to properly treat all subjects legitimately falling within the perview of the work,
and to keep within the line of the decided cases; but he has
occasionally yielded to his original judgment and exercised
the right to question the correctness of decisions, which, as
it seemed to him, were vicious and without the support of reason.   In no other way, in his judgment, could an acceptable
Treatise be produced upon this, or in fact, upon any other
subject.   In order, however, to meet the wants of the profession, where the Reports of the numerous cases referred to
are not within the reach of the practitioner, he has added
succinct and copious notes of the more important decided
cases.

In the execution of his plan the author was entirely without a model.   It is believed that no work was ever before
written upon this subject.   In the treatment of the subject
the work has been divided into Seventeen Chapters, treating
in the order named, upon the early history and origin of
Lis Pendens; the principle upon which it is based; the com-

mencement, continuance and close of Lis Pendens; what property is subject to it; the necessary elements to create and make it valid; what constitutes a full prosecution of a case to maintain its validity; the general application of the rule to cases as they occur in practice, classified according to subjects; the Lis Pendens statutes of the various States; their construction by the courts in those States where they have been enacted; and, Lis Pendens as a defense. The author has added, in an Appendix, the Ordinances of Lord Bacon, adopted in 1618, with references to the early English Chancery cases construing them. The Ordinances of Lord Bacon lie at the foundation of almost the entire system of Equity Jurisprudence, and will be of interest to the profession for ready reference.

The author can scarcely hope to have avoided all errors and imperfections in carrying out the plan of his work. It is some satisfaction to him, however, that his work is to be submitted to the appreciation and judgment of the members of that profession which is the least biased and most conservative of all the learned professions. If his effort shall result in the better understanding, among his professional brethren and the courts, of a subject which has seemed to him worthy of a general Treatise, and in a more intelligent and uniform application in the future than in the past, of this branch of the law, in the administration of justice, he will be content.

J. I. B.

Chicago, Jan. 1, 1887.

TABLE OF CONTENTS.

CHAPTER I.

THE ORIGIN AND HISTORY OF THE DOCTRINE OF LIS PENDENS.

CHAPTER II.

THE PRINCIPLE UPON WHICH LIS PENDENS IS BASED.

CHAPTER III.

COMMENCEMENT, CONTINUANCE AND CLOSE OF LIS PENDENS.

CHAPTER IV.

COMMENCEMENT, CONTINUANCE AND CLOSE OF LIS PENDENS, CONCLUDED.

CHAPTER V.

AS TO WHAT PROPERTY THE RULE LIS PENDENS APPLIES—WHAT MAY BE RES LITIGIOSA.

CHAPTER VI.

WHAT ELEMENTS NECESSARY TO CONSTITUTE THE RES LITIGIOSA.

CHAPTER VII.

WHAT CONSTITUTES A "FULL PROSECUTION."

CHAPTER VIII.

APPLICATION OF THE RULE LIS PENDENS.

CHAPTER IX.

DOCTRINE OF LIS PENDENS IN ITS APPLICATION TO PURCHASERS.

CHAPTER X.

DOCTRINE OF LIS PENDENS IN ITS APPLICATION TO PURCHASERS, CON-
TINUED.

CHAPTER XI.

PARTIES TO ACTIONS INVOLVING THE RULE LIS PENDENS.

CHAPTER XII.

THE APPLICATION OF LIS PENDENS TO ANTECEDENT LIENS.

CHAPTER XIII.

DOCTRINE OF LIS PENDENS APPLIED UNDER REGISTRY LAWS.

CHAPTER XIV.

LIS PENDENS STATUTES.

CHAPTER XV.

CONSTRUCTION OF LIS PENDENS STATUTES BY THE COURTS.

CHAPTER XVI.

LIS PENDENS AS A DEFENSE.

CHAPTER XVII.

LIS PENDENS AS A DEFENSE, CONTINUED.

APPENDIX.

The Rules or Ordinances adopted by Lord Bacon, in 1618, being 101 in number, for the government of proceedings and the better administration of justice in the Court of Chancery.

For a statement of the contents of these Rules or Ordinances, see pages 437 to 474, *post.*

TABLE OF CASES CITED.

A.

C.

D.

E.

F.

French v. Royal Company, 5 Leigh, 680.
Freeman v. Shreve, 5 Norris, 135.
Freeman v. Howe, 24 How. 450.
Friswell v. King, 15 Sim. 191.
Frissell v. Haile, 18 Mo. 18.
Frost v. Beekman, 1 Johns. Ch. 288.
Frost v. Raymond, 2 Cain's R. 188.
Frogg v. Long, 3 Dana, 157.
Fuller v. Haughton, 5 Conn. 424, 416.

G.

Galketh v. Ester, 38 Ark. 599.
Gamsby v. Ray, 52 N. H. 513.
Garcias v. Ricardo, 14 Sim. 205
Garth v. Ward, 2 Atk. 174.
Garth v. Crawford, Barn. 450.
Gartside v. Ishenwood, 2 Dick. 612.
Gardner v. Peckham et als., 13 R. I. 102.
Garr v. Gomey, 9 Wend. 649.
Gardner v. Buckbee, 3 Cow. 120.
Garretson v. Brien et al., 3 Heisk, 534.
Gaskell v. Durdin, 2 Ball. & Beat. 167.
Gates v. Bushnell, 9 Conn. 529.
Gelpche v. Dubuque, 1 Wal. 520.
George, Exr. et al. v. Cooper Trustee, 15 W..Va. 666.
Getcheel v. Clark, 5 Mass. 309.
Gibler v. Trimble, 14 Ohio, 323.
Gibbons, Admr. v. Dougherty et als., 10 Ohio St. 365.
Gilman v. Hamilton, 16 Ill. 225.
Gilmore v. Gilmore, 5 Jones's Eq. 284.
Gillespie et ux. v. Bailey et al., 12 W Va. 70.
Gilbert v. Lynch, 17 Blatchf. 402.
Gist v. Davis, 2 Hill Ch. (S. C.) 258.
Gist v. Hawley, 33 Ark. 233.
Goldson v. Gardiner, 1 Vern. 459.
Goodale v. Marshall, 11 N. H. 88.
Goodwin et al. v. McGehee et al., 15 Ala. 232.

H.

I.

J.

Jackson v. Stone, 13 Johns. 447.

Jackson v. Hill, 8 Cow. 290.

Jackson v. Rightmyre, 16 Johns. 314.

Jackson v. Warren, 32 Ill. 331.

Jackson v. Losee, 4 Sandf. Ch. 407.

Jackson v. Dickinson, 15 Johns. 309.

Jackson v. Bowen, 7 Cow. 13.

Jackson v. Raney, 3 Cow. 75.

Jackson v. Wilson, 9 Johns. 94.

Jackson v. Centreville M. & A. Co. et al., 64 Iowa, 292.

Jackson v. Andrews, 7 Wend. 152.

James, Exparte, 3 Harl. & C. 294.

James v. Morey, 2 Cow. 246.

Jeffres v. Cochrane, 48 N. Y. 671.

Jenks v. State, 39 Ind. 1.

Jenkins v. International Bk. et al., 111 Ill. 462.

Jenks v. Phelps, 4 Conn. 149.

Jenkins v. Stevens, 60 Ga. 216.

Jenner v. Joleffe, 6 Johns. 9.

Jerome v. McCarter, 94 U. S. 734.

Jernigan v. Carter, 51 Ga. 232.

Jewett v. Locke, 6 Gray, 233.

Johnson v. Robinson, 20 Minn. 170.

Johnson v. Farwell, 7 Greenleaf, 370.

Johnson v. Stark Co., 24 Ill. 75.

Johnson v. Stone, 13 Johns. 447.

Johnson v. Storey, 1 Lea, 114.

Johnson v. Holdsworth, 1 Sims Ch. (N. S.) 106.

Johnson et al. v. Irby et al., 8 Humph. 654.

Jones v. Chiles, 2 Dana, 25.

Jones, etc. v. Lusk, etc., 2 Met. (Ky.) 359.

Jones v. Smith, Walker's Ch. 115.

Jones v. Bonner, 2 Ex. 229.

Jones v. Turnbull, 2 Mee. & W. 601.

Jones v. Martin, 5 Blachf. 278.

Jorgenson et al. v. M. & St. L. R'wy Co., 25 Minn. 206.

K.

L.

P.

Q.

R.

Y.

Z.

ADDITIONAL CASES CITED.

A.

Aldrich v. Woodcock, 10 N. H. 99.
Allen et al. v. Mayor et al., 9 Ga. 286.
Anderson et al. v. Wanzer, 5 How. (Miss.) 587.
Andrews v. Ludlow et al., 5 Pick. 28.

B.

Bades v. Harris, 20 Eng. Ch. & I. Y. & C. 230.
Badger et ux. v. Daniel et al., 77 N. C. 251.
Badger v. Badger, 1 Cliff. 237.
Baker v. Bird, 2 Ves. Jr. 672.
B. & O. R. R. Co. v. Gallahue, 14 Gratt. 562.
Barrisford v. Done, 1 Vern. 98.
Barter v. Tomlinson, 38 Barb. 641.
Baylie v. Brickall, 2 H. & M. 371.
Behrens v. Sieveking, 2 Myl. & Cr. 602.
Behrens v. Pauli, 1 Keen, 456.
Berry v. Whitaker, 58 Me. 422.
Billing v. Flight, 1 Mad. 230.
Bingham v. Lanping, 26 Penn. St. 340.
Bishop v. Young, 17 Wis. 46.
Blake v. Hatch, 25 Vt. 555.
Boardman v. Cushing, 12 N. H. 105.
Bowles v. Orr, 1 Y. & Coll. 464.
Bower v. Hadden & Co., 3 Stew. Eq. (N. J.) 171.
Boyd v. Weil et als., 11 Wis. 60.
Branch Bk. v. Poe, 1 Ala. 396.
Brinkerhoff v. Brown, 4 Johns. Ch. 671.
Bromley v. Holland, 5 Ves. 2.
Brooks v. Mills Co., 4 Dillon, 524.
Browne v. Poyntz, 3 Madd. 24.
Buckley v. Echert, 3 Penn. St. 368.

Ensworth v. Lambert et al., 4 Johns. Ch. 605.
Ennson v. Healey, 2 Mass. 32.
Exparte Howe, 1 Paige, 125.
Exparte Kyle, 1 Cal. 331.
Exparte Mobley in re McAfee v. McAfee, 19 S. C. 337.
Exparte Nesbit, 2 S. & L. 279.
Exparte Pemberton, 18 Ves. 282.
Exparte Price, 2 Ves. Sr. 407.
Exparte R. R. Co., 95 U. S. (5 Otto,) 221.
Exparte Sterling, 16 Ves. 258.
Exparte Watkins, 3 Pet. 193.

F.

Fay et al. v. Smith et al., 25 Vt. 610.
Fischer v. Hudson R. R. R. Co., 15 Barb. 37.
Fitch v. Waite, 5 Conn. 117.
Fleming v. Prior, 5 Madd. 423.
Forte v. Thompson, 12 C. & L. 568.
Forsythe v. Beverage, 52 Ill. 268.
Foster v. Jones, 15 Mass. 185.
Fowler v. McClelland, 5 Ark. 188.
Fox v. Reeder, 28 Ohio, 181.
Fulweiler v. Hughes, 17 Penn. St. 440.
Frisbee v. Langworthy, 11 Wis. 375.
Frothingham v. Haley et al., 3 Mass. 68.
Fuller v. Jewett, 37 Vt. 473.

G.

Gage v. Stafford, 1 Ves. Sr. 544.
Gage v. McLaughlin et al., 34 Wis. 551.
Gaines v. Chew, 2 How. 619.
Garrigan v. Carter, 51 Ga. 232.
Gillis v. McRay, 4 Dev. 172.
Glanton v. Griggs, 5 Ga. 424.
Godden v. Pierson, 42 Ala. 370.
Gordon v. Gilfoil, 99 U. S. 168.
Gossom v. Donaldson, 18 B. Mon. 231.
Grain v. Aldrich, 38 Cal. 520.
Grant et al. v. Shaw, 16 Mass. 344.

Gregg v. Berthea, 6 Port. (Ala.) 9.
Gridley v. Harraden, 14 Mass. 497.
Grider, etc., v. Apperson & Co., 32 Ark. 332.
Griffiths v. Hamilton, 12 Ves. 307.
Grosvenor v. F. & M. Bank, 13 Conn. 104.

H.

Hale v. Langdon's Heirs, 60 Tex. 561.
Hall v. Page, 4 Ga. 428.
Hardford v. Storie, 2 Sim. & Stu. 196.
Hanington v. DuChatel, 1 Bro. C. C. 124.
Harris v. Aiken, 3 Pick. 1
Harrell v. Whitman,19 Ala. 135.
Haven v. Wentworth, 2 N. H. 93.
Henderson v. Henderson, 3 Hare, 100, 113 to 115.
Hitt v. Lacy, 3 Ala. 104.
Hogue v. Curtis, 1 Jac. & W. 449.
Holt v. Kirby, 39 Me. 164.
Hopper, etc., v. Hopper, etc., 5 Ala. 442.
Houldtich v. Donegall, 1 Sim. &. Stu. 491.
House v. Mullen, 22 Wall. 42.
Howard v. Card & Co., 6 Me. 353.
Howell v. Freeman et al., 3 Mass. 121.
Hoyt v. Swift et al., 13 Vt. 129.
Hoyt v. Jones, 31 Wis. 397.
Hudson v. Hunt et al., 5 N. H. 538.
Huff v. Mills et al., 7 Yerg. 42.
Hughes v. Corey, 20 Iowa, 399.
Huggins v. York Bldg. Co., 2 Atk. 44.
Hunter v. Stewart, 10 W. R. 176.

I.

In re G. W. Tel. Co., 5 Biss. 363.
In re Paschal, 10 Wal. 493.
Ins. Co. v. Brune, 96 U. S. (6 Otto) 588.
Irving v. Smith, 17 Ohio, 226.

J.

Jennings v. Bond, 2 Jones & L. 720.
Jones v. Thomas, 3 P. Wms. 244.

Jones v. Nickson, Younge, 359.
Jones v. Segueira, 1 Phill. 82.
Jones v. Frost, 3 Madd. 8.

K.

Kergin v. Dawson, 1 Gilm. 86.
Kettle v. Harvey. 21 Vt. 301.
Kidd v. Shepherd, 4 Mass. 238.
King v. Dupine, 2 Atk. 603 and 604, note 2.
King v. Ray, 11 Paige, 239.
Kirkpatrick et al. v. Means et al., 5 Ir. Eq. 220.

L.

Lackland v. Garesche, 56 Mo. 267.
LaFramboise v. Grow, 56 Ill. 201.
Lane v. Felt, 7 Gray, 491.
Law v. Rigby, 4 Bro. Ch. 60.
Lawrence v. Blatchford, 2 Vern. 458.
Leaving et al. v. Brinkerhoff et al., 5 Johns. Ch. 329.
Leiber v. St. Louis, etc., 36 Mo. 382.
Locke v. Tippets, 7 Mass. 149.
Londonderry v. Baker, 7 Jur. N. S. 811.
London v. Liverpool, 3 Anst. 738.
Long v. Burton, 2 Atk. 218.
Lord Newbury v. Wren, 1 Vern. 220.
Lowry et al. v. Wright et al., 15 Ill. 95.
Loring et al. v. Marsh et al., 2 Cliff. (U. S. C. C.) 311.
Lyons v. Houston, 2 Harring. (Del.) 349.

M.

Mann v. Rogers, 35 Cal. 315.
Matherson v. Fitch, 22 Cal. 86.
Maule v. Murray, 7 T. R. 470.
May v. Baker, 15 Ill. 89.
McCaffrey v. Moore, 18 Pick. 492.
McMeekin et al. v. State, 9 Ark. 553.
Meadows v. Kingston, Ambler, 756.
Miller, etc., v. Hall et ux., 1 Bush. 229.
Mitchell v. Harris, 2 Ves. Jr. 135.
Moor v. Booth, 3 Ves. 350.

Rundle v. Schutz, 2 Miles, 330.
Russell v. Clingan et al., 33 Miss. 535.

S.

Saddler's Heirs v. Kidd's Exrs. et al., 3 Ohio, 541.
Saltus et al. v. Tobias et al., 7 Johns. Ch. 214.
Sanders v. McDowell, 63 Md. 509.
Savage et al. v. Hussey, 3 Jones, (N. C.) 179.
Sayles v. Tibbitts, 5 R. I. 79.
Sayward v. Drew, 6 Me. 263.
Scofield v. White et al., 29 Vt. 330.
Scott v. Rand et al., 118 Mass. 215.
Scotland Co. v. Hill, 112 U. S. 183.
Sears v. Carrier et al., 4 Allen, 339.
Selleck v. Phelps, 11 Wis. 380.
Sharon v. Hill, 22 Fed. R. 28.
Shearer v. Hardy, 22 Pick. 417.
Sheriff v. Buckner, 1 Litt. 127.
Ship Robert Fulton, 1 Paine (C. C.) 621.
Shotwell v. Lawson et al., 30 Miss. 27.
Sims v. Ridge, 3 Meriv. 458.
Skowhegan Bk. v. Farrer et al., 46 Me. 293.
Smith v. Barker et al., 10 Me. 458.
Smith v. Atlantic Mut. Fire Ins. Co., 2 Foster, (N. H.) 21.
Smith v. Wiley et al., 41 Vt. 19.
Smith v. Brittenham, 109 Ill. 549.
Spark v. Spicer, 1 Ld. Raymn. 738.
Spraggon et al. v. McGreer, 14 Wis. 439.
Staneils v. Raymond, 4 Carl. 314.
Stewart v. West, 1 H. & J. 536.
Stillman v. Isham, 11 Conn. 124.
Stoddard's Lessee v. Myers, 8 Ohio, 203.
Strout v. Clements, 22 Me. 292.
Sweeney v. Allen, 1 Penn. St. 380.

T.

Taber v. Nye et al., 12 Pick. 105.
Taylor v. The Royal Saxon, 1 Wal. Jr. (C. C.) 311.
Taylor v. Cornelius, 60 Penn. St. 187.

CHAPTER I.

THE ORIGIN AND HISTORY OF LIS PENDENS.

Lord Bacon adopted the rule into chancery.

SEC. 1. Lord Chancellor Bacon adopted certain ordinances or rules, "for the better and more regular administration of justice in the chancery, to be daily observed, saving the prerogative of the court."(1)

The twelfth of these ordinances or rules provided in these words, viz: "No decree bindeth any that cometh in bona fide, by conveyance from the defendant before the bill exhibited, and is made no party, neither by bill, nor the order: but, where he comes in pendente lite, and, while the suit is in full prosecution, and without any color of allowance or privity of the court, there regularly the decree bindeth; but, if there were any intermissions of suit, or the court made acquainted with the conveyance, the court is to give order upon the special matter according to justice."

(1) For Lord Bacon's Rules see Vol. 2, pp. 479 and 480 of Lord Bacon's Works, by B. Montague; also Beames' Orders in Chancery, p. 7. See Appendix *post.*

It is, probably, on account of the origin of the rule lis pendens, that it is so often called a "rule" in the books.

Definition of terms.

SEC. 2. The words lis and pendens, lite and pendente, mean precisely what their Latin significations are:

Lis means an action, a suit, a cause, a controversy.

Pendens is the present participle of *pendo*, meaning continuing or pending.

Pendente lite is the ablative absolute of lis pendens.

Bouvier, therefore, very properly defines lis pendens to be a pending suit, viz: "pending the continuance of an action while litigation continues."(1)

Pendente lite means during the pendency of a suit.(2)

Lis is defined as a suit, action, controversy or dispute.

Res is the subject matter, or the thing involved in the suit.

It usually is tangible property; but it may be a property or a personal right.

The commencement of lis pendens is the initial point of time at which the court first acquires jurisdiction of the res.

The end of lis pendens is that terminal point of time at which the court ceases to have jurisdiction of the res.

From the commencement to the end of lis pendens the res may be said to be res litigiosa, which denotes the litigated or contested condition or quality of the

(1) Bouv. Law Dic., p. 76; Rapaljes and Lawrence' Law Dic., tit. Lis Pendens, p. 765.

(2) Beames' Orders in Chancery, p. 7. Rapaljes and Lawrence' Law Dic., p. 945.

res. This character of the res remains fixed during the pendency of the suit.

Lis pendens, notice lis pendens, the rule lis pendens and notice of lis pendens are synonymous terms.

How some of these terms came to be used is explained hereafter.(1)

Early judicial history of lis pendens.

SEC. 3. Lord Bacon formulated the rule lis pendens, but its application, as a principle of practice in the courts, in all judicial proceedings, was very general long before and certainly immediately after its formulation by him.(2)

It is generally, therefore, claimed to be of common law origin. The consideration of a few of the older cases will tend to sustain this position. In the case of Hill *v.* Worsley and Rogison,(3) which was decided in 1663, Worsley had mortgaged to his co-defendant, Rogison, the land which constituted the res, and then agreed to sell the same land to the plaintiff, Hill, free of incumbrance, and partial payment was made upon the contract. Afterwards Worsley released to Rogison the condition and power of redemption in the mortgage, and, subsequently, while the property was res litigiosa, released to him all his right in the res. The court held, that neither of these releases ought to obstruct Worsley's conveyance to the plaintiff, Hill, because one of them was given pending the suit.

The earliest reported case in which the rule is announced is believed to be Arundel *v.* Arundel.(4)

(1) Sec. 17, *post.*

(2) Beames' Orders in Chancery, p. 7. See *post* appendix.

(3) Hardie's R., 320, (14 and 15, Chap. 2.)

(4) Arundel *v.* Arundel, Cro. Eliz. 677; 40 Eliz.

Early decision of Lord Keeper Finch.

SEC. 4. In Culpepper v. Aston,(1) Sir Robert Aston, the defendant, had purchased certain property after it had become res litigiosa.

The cause was heard, in the first instance, by Lord Chancellor Ashley; but was finally determined by Lord Keeper Finch, who held, that the purchase was not good, saying: "When the bill was exhibited against Henry Culpepper, the trustee, it will find him and all claiming under him pendente lite."

In Baens v. Cunning et al.,(2) decided in 1677, the court refers to Culpepper v. Aston, and states that Sir Robert Aston, though purchasing the same day the bill was exhibited and paying for his land without notice, yet he lost his land.(3)

Early decisions of Lords Nottingham and Camden.

SEC. 5. In the case of Fleming et ux. v. Page et al.(4) Lord Nottingham held a purchase made pendente lite to be subordinate to the decree, and that the purchaser took nothing by the purchase, and that the defendants be decreed to convey.

In Walker v. Smallwood,(5) decided in 1768, Lord Chancellor Camden said: "The question is, where a bill is filed by a creditor for sale of an estate to pay debts, and all the parties have put in answers and submitted to the jurisdiction, whether the heirs at law or devisee can sell without the privity of the court or creditors." * * * "I hold it a

(1) Culpepper v. Aston, 2 Ch. Cas. 115-222.

(2) Baens v. Cunning et al., 1 Ch. Cas. 300.

(3) See remarks of Kent, Chancellor, in Murray v. Ballou, 1 Johns. Ch. R. 576.

(4) Fleming et ux. v. Page et al., Finch, R. 320, 321, (29 Cas. 2.)

(5) Walker v. Smallwood, Amb. 677, 678.

general rule, that an alienation pending suit is void."

Early decisions of Lords King and Hardwicke.

SEC. 6.   Again in Sorrel v. Carpenter,(1) decided in 1728, Lord Chancellor King in deciding the case said: "Where there is a conveyance made pendente lite, without any valuable consideration, and to avoid and exclude a decree, it is to be highly discountenanced, and even though the alienation be for never so good a consideration, yet, if made pendente lite, the purchase is to be invalid."

In Garth v. Ward,(2) decided in 1741, where pending a bill filed to establish a will, a purchase had been made of a portion of an estate res litigiosa, from one of the devisees, Lord Hardwicke said: "In bills of this nature, for establishing a will and perpetuating testimony of witness, the advantage ought to be mutual, and the heir at law is at as much liberty to invalidate the will as the devisees are to establish it, and must be considered to all intents and purposes as a lis pendens."   *   *   *   "So in the case of a mortgagor who comes here for redemption of a mortgage, if, during such suit, he should assign the equity of redemption, and in the final hearing of the cause there should be a decree against the mortgagor, will not the assignment of the equity of redemption be barred by the decree?"

Other early cases.

SEC. 7.   There are numerous other early cases, prior to the adoption of Lord Bacon's rules, in which the rule lis pendens is recognized and enforced.

(1) Sorrel v. Carpenter, 2 P. Wms.   (2) Garth v. Ward, 2 Atk. 174.
482.

It was applied by Lord Hardwicke in Worsley *v.* The Earl of Scarborough;(1) by Lord Chancellor Cranworth in Bellamy *v.* Sabine,(2) and by Sir Wm. Grant, in The Bishop of Winchester *v.* Paine.(3) It was recognized and incorporated into a compilation of chancery rules, and causes in equity, called Prolegomena of equity.

Supposed to be adopted by analogy.

SEC. 8. By some the rule lis pendens is supposed to have been adopted by analogy, from proceedings at law.

Thus, in Sorrel *v.* Carpenter,(4) Lord Chancellor King said: "This in imitation of the proceedings in a real action at common law, where, if the defendant aliens, after pendency of the writ, the judgment in the action will overreach such alienation."

Following this suggestion, perhaps, other courts have assigned the origin of the rule lis pendens, as enforced in these early cases, and formulated in Lord Bacon's rule to its adoption into chancery from analogy to proceedings at law.

Rule lis pendens derived from the civil law.

SEC. 9. The better opinion would seem to be, that the remote derivation of the rule lis pendens, is from the civil law, whatever may have been the immediate origin of it.

The civil, or Roman law, is the great fountain from which flows most of the principles which make up the

---

(1) Worsley *v.* Scarborough, 3 Atk. 392.

(2) Bellamy *v.* Sabine, 1 De G. & J. 578.

(3) Winchester *v.* Paine, 11 Ves. 194. See also, Goldon *v.* Gardner,

cited in Self *v.* Madox, 1 Vern. 459; Finch *v.* Newnham, 2 Vern. 216; Culpepper *v.* Aston, 2 Ch. Cas. 116; Preston *v.* Tubbin, 1 Vern. 286.

(4) Sorrel *v.* Carpenter, 2 P. Wms. 482.

great body of equity jurisprudence, as administered, not only in England and among all English speaking peoples, but among other peoples also. By the Roman, or civil law, it was provided that: "A thing concerning which there is a controversy is prohibited, during the suit, from being alienated." "*Rem de qua controversia prohibemur in acrum dedicare.*"

This is the precise doctrine of lis pendens, as formulated by Lord Bacon and practiced in the court of chancery, before and since that time.

From the commencement of lis pendens, by the Roman law, the res or subject of litigation was converted into what was called res litigiosa,(1) which neither the plaintiff nor defendant could alienate.

The law of lis pendens in other countries.

SEC. 10.   The Spanish law has derived the principle of lis pendens from the Roman, and it is known in that law, under the term litis pendenica.

In the jurisprudence of Continental Europe, it is known by the designation, vitium litigiosum.

Bell, in his commentaries on the laws of Scotland, states the Scotch law on this subject thus: "It is a general rule which seems to have been recognized in all regular systems of jurisprudence, that during the dependence of an action, of which the object is to vest the property or obtain the possession of real estate, a purchaser shall be held to take that estate as it stands in the person of the seller, and to be bound by the claims which shall ultimately be pronounced." It is grounded on the maxim: "*Pendente lite nihil innovandum.*"(2)

---

(1) Mackenzie's Roman law, (3 Ed.) 329.

(2) 2 Bell's Com. on Laws of Scotland, p. 144.

Conclusion upon the subject.

SEC. 11. My conclusion, from the examination which I have made, is, that lis pendens is remotely derived from the Roman law; that it was in force, with slight modification, as a part of the body of the civil or Roman law, the same in substance as it is practiced in England and the United States; that it is an essential principle in any efficient judicial system; and has, also, been transplanted from the civil or Roman law into the jurisprudence of the countries of Continental Europe; but that it is also true that, while the germ of the law of lis pendens was inoculated into the jurisprudence of England from Roman stock, before that time, Lord Bacon by his twelfth rule, for the government of courts of chancery, first gave it efficiency and precision, as a part of the body of the common law of England.

Being a rule of the English Chancery Courts, it is in force in the United States, wherever statutes have not been passed modifying the common law on the subject.(1)

(1) 1 Story's Eq. Jur., § 57 and § 58.

CHAPTER II.

THE PRINCIPLE UPON WHICH LIS PENDENS RESTS.

The object of lis pendens.

SEC. 12. The underlying principle upon which lis pendens rests, as stated by Bouvier, is that, during the pendency of the suit, an alienee may be bound by the proceedings therein, subsequent to the alienation, and that such a purchaser may be bound by the judgment or decree in the suit, without being made a party. *Pendente lite nihil innovetur*, is a maxim of the common law.(1)

The sole object of lis pendens is to keep the subject in controversy within the power of the court, until the judgment or decree shall be entered, and thus make it possible to give effect to the decrees and judgments of courts of justice.(2)

Importance of correctly understanding it.

SEC. 13. It is of the greatest importance to have a

(1) Bouv. Law Dic., 120.   (2) Coke Litt. 344, *b*.

correct understanding of the rule itself and of the reasons for its adoption and enforcement, before proceeding to a discussion of the authorities bearing upon its application in special cases; because a misapprehension of the nature of the rule lis pendens will certainly lead to an erroneous application of it. It will be seen, in the course of this treatise, that on this account courts have frequently used language which tends to mislead and confuse rather than enlighten. Where the rule has not been erroneously applied, the reasons assigned for it have not always been the correct ones.

The sole object of the rule.

SEC. 14. It should always be borne in mind that the primary object—it might almost be said the sole object—to be attained by the rule lis pendens, is to make it possible for courts to execute their judgments and decrees. As is well said in the leading case of Newman v. Chapman:(1) "It is founded upon the

(1) Allen v. Poole, 54 Miss. 333; Fenwick's Adm. v. Macey, 2 B. Mon. 486.

In the leading case of Newman v. Chapman, 2d Rand. 93, a bill was filed to effectuate a former decree. The facts were that the land involved was the property of James Armstead, who died in 1788, having devised the property to his children, among whom William Armstead was allotted a portion. December 3, 1794, William Armstead mortgaged the portion allotted to him to Abraham Morehouse, and the latter assigned the mortgage to Jesse Simms. Before the mortgage was recorded and on the 11th day of

September, 1797, William Armstead and wife conveyed by deed dated September 26, 1793, to Thomas Newman. Simms filed a bill against William Armstead to foreclose the mortgage on the 12th day of May, 1797. A decree of foreclosure was entered, sale made by commissioners thereunder, and a commissioner's deed executed to Simms, July 13, 1804, and thereafter Simms conveyed to George Chapman. Simms having died, the present bill was filed to execute the decree against Newman and others. As this is a case so often referred to in the books, it is proper that a more extended notice than is usual should

necessity of such a rule, in order to give effect to the proceedings in courts of justice. Without it the administration of justice might in all cases be frustrated by successive alienations of the property which was the object of litigation, pending the suit, so that every judgment and decree could be rendered abor-

be given it in this connection. The court, in deciding the case, say at page 102: "The rule, as to the effect of lis pendens, is founded upon the necessity of such a rule, to give effect to the proceedings of courts of justice. Without it, the administration of justice might, in all cases, be frustrated by successive alienations of the property, which was the object of litigation, pending the suit, so that every judgment and decree would be rendered abortive, where the recovery of specific property was the object. This necessity is so obvious, that there was no occasion to resort to the presumption that the purchaser really had, or by inquiry might have had, notice of the pendency of the suit, to justify the existence of the rule. In fact it applied in cases in which there was a physical impossibility that the purchaser could know, with any possible diligence on his part, of the existence of the suit, unless all contracts were made in the office from which the writ issued, and on the last moment of the day. For, at common law, the writ was pending from the first moment of the day on which it was issued and bore teste, and a purchaser, on or after that day, held the property subject to the execution upon the judgment in that suit as the defendant would have held

it, if no alienation had been made. The court of chancery adopted the rule, in analogy to the common law; but relaxed, in some degree, the severity of the common law. For, no lis pendens existed until the service of the subpœna and bill filed; but, it existed from the service of the subpœna, although the bill were not filed until long after; so that a purchaser, after service of the subpœna and before the bill was filed, would, after the filing of the bill, be deemed to be a lite pendente purchaser, and as such be bound by the proceedings in the suit, although the subpœna gave him no information as to the subject of the suit. A subpœna might be served the very day on which it was sued out, and there is an instance in the English books of a purchaser who purchased on the day the subpœna was served, without actual notice, and who lost his purchase by force of this rule of law. This principle, however necessary, was harsh in its effects upon bona fide purchasers, and was confined in its operation to the extent of the policy on which it was founded; that is to the giving full effect to the judgment or decree which might be rendered in the suit depending at the time of purchase. As a proof of this, if the suit was not prosecuted with effect, as if the

tive, where the recovery of specific property was the object."

The necessity of the rule is inexorable, tempered by little or no consideration of conscience, because a relaxation of the rule, to avoid harsh applications in special cases, would defeat the object of the rule itself. Within certain limits, its enforcement is as imperative

suit at law was discontinued, or the plaintiff, suffered a non-suit, or if a suit in chancery was dismissed for want of prosecution, or for any other cause not upon the merits, or if at law or in chancery a suit abated; although, in all these cases, the plaintiff or his proper representative, might bring a new suit for the same cause, he must make the one who purchased pending the former suit, a party; and, in this new suit, such purchaser would not be at all affected by the pendency of the former suit, at the time of his purchase. In the case of an abatement, however, the original suit might be continued in chancery, by revivor, or at law, in real actions, abated by the death of a party by journies' accounts, and the purchaser still be bound by the final judgment or decree. If a suit be brought against the heir, upon the obligation of his ancestors binding his heirs, and he alienates the land descended, pending the writ, upon a judgment in that suit, the lands in the hands of the purchaser would be liable to be extended, in satisfaction of the debt."

In this case the court held that the lis pendens so pending was binding upon Armstead, Simms and Newman, although the mortgage to Morehouse had not been recorded, on the principle that a lis pendens would have force as between Armstead, Morehouse, and Simms, his assignee, on account of actual knowledge or notice on their part, and would be binding on Newman, because the deed to him was made pending the suit, and none the less binding, although it might be that Newman had no actual knowledge of the pendency of the suit.

That the rule lis pendens is based upon necessity and not upon constructive notice, see also the following authorities:

Jackson v. Andrews, 7 Wend. 152; Harrington v. Slade, 22 Barb. 166; Hersey v. Turbett, 27 Pa. St., (3 Casey,) 418; Diamond v. Lawrence Co., 37 Pa. St. 353; Fessler's Appeal, 75 Pa. St. 483; Loomis v. Riley, 24 Ill. 307; Jackson v. Warren, 32 Ill. 332; Green et als. v. White, 7 Blackf. 242; Gowan v. Donaldson, 18 B. Mon. 231; Inloe's Lessee v. Harvey, 11 Md. 519; Blanchard et al. v. Ware, 43 Iowa, 530; Farmers' Nat. Bk. v. Fletcher, 44 Iowa, 253; Bennett v. Williams, 5 Ohio, 461; Hunt v. Haven, 52 N. H. 162; Tilton v. Cofield, 93 U. S. 163; County of Warren v. Marcy, 97 U. S. (7 Otto,) 96.

as the demands of military necessity. The very existence and perpetuation of the courts depend upon its enforcement.

Chancellor Kent's views.

SEC. 15.   Chancellor Kent said in the case of Murray *v.* Ballou,(1) "I am bound to apply it and it is not in

(1) Perhaps there is no case so often cited on the law of lis pendens as that of Murray *v.* Ballou, 1 Johns. Ch. R. 566. The eminence of the Chancellor who delivered the opinion of the court, and the learning displayed in the opinion itself, have alike contributed to make it a leading case upon the questions involved. As the case will so frequently be referred to in the subsequent pages of this work, it is thought proper to reproduce it here for ready reference. The material facts of the case are, that one William Green purchased the land involved, together with other lands in 1792 ; that in 1796 and 1798 Green sold these lands to divers persons and took purchase money mortgages; that the mortgagees became insolvent ; that, in consequence, Green became embarrassed and in 1803, to secure advances made by one Patrick Heatly, a brother of Green's wife, assigned the bonds, notes and mortgages, to Joseph Winter as trustee for Heatly; that these mortgages were subsequently foreclosed and the lands bid in by Winter as trustee of Heatly under the decree of foreclosure ; that on August 13, 1805, after acquiring title, at the foreclosure sale, Winter executed a deed of trust, reciting the indebtedness of

Green to Heatly, the assignment of the mortgages aforesaid, and declaring his trust,and among other things providing for reimbursement of his own charges and expenses. On the 3rd of August, 1806, Heatly assigned to Temperance Green, his sister and wife of William Green, all his interests in the trust, and in June, 1809, she and others filed their bill against Winter—to which in October and December following supplemental and amended bills were added—charging defendant Winter with the facts above recited, and praying an injunction, which was issued and served on Winter. Subsequently Winter was superseded in his trust, and Robert Murray was appointed a receiver, with authority to use Winter's name in litigation. Notwithstanding these proceedings, in August, 1810, Winter sold to Ballou the premises involved in the case of Murray *v.* Ballou, and took his bond and mortgage for the consideration money, which were afterwards assigned to Hunt, who subsequently cancelled the bond and mortgage, and took a new bond and mortgage directly to himself from Ballou. Ballou and Hunt both claim to be ignorant of the proceedings in the chancery suit of Green *v.* Winter, above referred to, and to have been bona

my power to dispense with it. I have no doubt the
rule will sometimes operate with hardship upon a pur-

fide purchasers for value. Upon
this state of facts Chancellor Kent
gave the following opinion: "The
purchase, by Ballou, of Winter, was
made in August, 1810. The lot
purchased was held, at the time, by
Winter, in trust, for Temperance
Green; and a suit was then, and
for a year preceding, had been,
pending in this court by Mrs.
Green against Winter, charging
him with a breach of trust, and
praying that his authority, as trustee, might cease; and an injunction
had been issued and served, enjoin-
ing him from any sale, disposition,
or use of any of the lands or securities held by him in trust. The
plaintiff, Murray, was, afterwards,
appointed receiver, with authority
to sue; and upon a reference and
report, which took place in the progress of the suit, Winter was found
in arrear to the amount of $20,510;
and the amount of the above sale
to Ballou, as being invalid, and not
binding on the cestui que trust,
was not allowed as a charge to
Winter. By the final decree, Winter was ordered to convey and surrender to Mary Green and Henry
Green, the persons for that purpose
appointed by Mrs. Green, all the
property and interest whatever
held by him in trust. The suit so
commenced against Winter, having
been in a course of continued and
diligent prosecution, and having
been finally conducted to a decree
by which the charges in the bill
were established, a question arises,
and has been discussed in this case,

whether the purchase by Ballou, of
part of the trust property, pendente
lite, is binding on the cestui que
trust. Ballou has, in his answer,
denied any knowledge of the suit
at the time of his purchase. There
is no proof to contradict the answer,
and it is to be taken for true. But
though he had no knowledge of the
suit, it is not pretended that he was
ignorant of the existence of the
trust; and it is to be presumed,
from his silence, that when he purchased from Winter, he knew that
Winter held and sold the land, not
in his own right, but as trustee.
The bill charges, that it was generally known, at the time of the sale
that Winter's authority was questioned. The answer goes no further than to deny any knowledge of
the chancery suit or of the injunction, or of any suspension or defective power in Winter to sell. The answer of Hunt is to the same limited
extent; and the probability is, that
it was a matter of public notoriety
at the time, that Winter held the
large real estate in his possession as
a trustee. It has been said by
counsel for the plaintiffs, that Ballou was chargeable with notice of
the trust, by means of the registry
of the deed from Heatly to Mrs.
Green, which recited the declaration of trust executed by Winter.
This deed, containing this recital,
was registered on the 9th of April,
1810, but I cannot perceive any
justice in obliging Ballou to take
notice of the contents of that deed.
By what clew was he to be directed

chaser without actual notice, but this seems to be one of the cases in which private mischief must yield to

to look into the deed from Heatly to Mrs. Green ? He was dealing with Winter ; and supposing Winter's trust to be, otherwise, totally unknown to him, he might as well be required to examine the contents of every deed on record. If there had been any deed on record to which Winter was a party, he would have had a specific object and guide for inquiry; *caeca regens filio vestigia.* I have therefore, not thought it reasonable to charge Ballou with a knowledge of the existing trust, by reason of the registry of Heatly's deed, but rather to infer that knowledge from what is charged in the bill, and from the silence and strong implied admission in the answer. The inference from the answer is decisive. If a party means to defend himself, on the ground that he was a bona fide purchaser for a valuable consideration, without notice of a trust, he must deny the fact of notice, and of every circumstance from which it can be inferred. * * * And if notice of the trust existed when the purchase was made, then the general rule is, that the purchaser becomes himself the trustee, notwithstanding any consideration paid ; (Saunders *v.* DeHew, 2 Vern. 271; 2 Fonb. 152, 153,) and, though he may not, perhaps, be bound, in most cases, if the sale is fair, to look to the application of the moneys, yet, if the trust be suspended by process of the court, and the sale be made, as it was here, in contempt of that process, the purchaser, with notice,

ought not to be allowed to defeat it. The question of notice of the trust is also material, in as much as the purchaser's knowledge of it goes to lessen or destroy the hardship, if any there should be, in the application of the maxim, caveat emptor. If every man purchases at his peril, and is bound to look to the title and the competency of the seller, the duty is the stronger if he knowingly purchases of one acting as agent or trustee for others; for then he is bound to look into the validity and the continuance of the authority, and to call for an explanation of the nature and existing circumstances of the trust. But it will not be necessary to rest the cause on this ground. The other point, which has been pressed for consideration, appears to be altogether conclusive. Admitting that Ballou had no knowledge, in fact, of the suit of Mrs. Green against Winter, when he made the purchase, he is nevertheless, chargeable with legal or constructive notice, so as to render his purchase subject to the event of that suit.

The established rule is: that a lis pendens, duly prosecuted, and not collusive, is notice to a purchaser so as to affect and bind his interest by the decree; and the lis pendens begins from the service of the subpœna after the bill is filed. The counsel for the defendants have made loud complaints of the injustice of this rule, but the complaint was not properly addressed to me; for if it is a well

general convenience." * * * "We may be assured
the rule would not have existed and have been sup-

settled rule, I am bound to apply it, and it is not in my power to dispense with it. I have no doubt the rule will sometimes operate with hardship upon a purchaser without actual notice; but this seems to be one of the cases in which private mischief must yield to general convenience; and, most probably, the necessity of such a hard application of the rule will not arise in one out of a thousand instances. On the other hand, we may be assured the rule would not have existed, and have been supported for centuries, if it had not been founded in great public utility. Without it, as has been observed in some of the cases, a man, upon the service of a subpœna, might alienate his lands, and prevent the justice of the court. Its decrees might be wholly evaded. In this very case, the trustee had been charged with a gross breach of his trust, and had been enjoined by the process of the court, six months before the sale in question, from any further sales. If his subsequent sales are to be held valid, what temptation is held out to waste the trust property, and destroy all the hopes and interest of the cestui que trust? A suit in chancery is, in such cases, necessarily tedious and expensive and years may elapse, as in this case, before the suit can be brought to a final conclusion. If the property is to remain all this time subject to his disposition, in spite of the efforts of the court to prevent it, the rights of that helpless portion of the community, whose property is most frequently held in trust, will be put in extreme jeopardy. To bring home to every purchaser, the charge of actual notice of the suit, must, from the very nature of the case, be in a great degree impracticable. The only safe and efficient means of preventing such fraud and injustice, is to charge the purchaser with dealing with the trustee at his peril. The policy of the law does, in general, cast that peril upon the purchaser. Caveat emptor is the settled maxim of the common law. It is his business to inquire and to look to the person with whom he deals. If he knows him to be a trustee, then let him inquire of the cestui que trust, or let him ask at the register's office, whether there can be any suit pending against such trustee. He can always be safe if he uses due diligence; but the other party has no means of safety beyond his application to the court. Whatever may be thought of the rule, it appears to me to be less severe than that acknowledged rule of the common law, on which our courts have repeatedly acted, that a conveyance of land, without any warranty or covenant of title, will not enable the purchaser to resort back to the seller, even if the title should fail; (Frost v. Raymond, 2 Cains R. 188,) and if he has covenants to secure his title, he can seek for no more than the consideration which he has paid, without any allowance for the rise in

ported for centuries if it had not been founded in great public utility." This view, as to the object of the law of lis pendens, has been uniformly held by the courts of both the United States and Great Britain, notwithstanding occasional expressions which are

the value of the land, or the value of the improvements. (Pitcher *v.* Livingston, 4 Johns. Rep. 1.) I have said that the lis pendens was, of itself, notice to the purchaser, and it will now be proper to show that this rule is well established in our law. It is no more than an adoption of the rule in a real action at common law, where, if the defendant aliens after the pendency of the writ, the judgment in the real action will overreach such alienation. It was one of the ordinances of Lord Bacon, laid down for the better and more regular administration of justice in the court of chancery, that 'no decree bindeth any that cometh in bona fide, by conveyance from the defendant, before the bill exhibited and is made no party, neither by bill nor order; but where he comes in pendente lite, and while the suit is in full prosecution, and without any color of allowance or privity of the court, there regularly the decree bindeth.' (Lord Bacon's works, Vol. 4, 511.) Here we find the rule declared above two centuries ago, and by the highest authority to which we can appeal; and it will appear to have received support and application down to this day." The learned Chancellor then proceeds to review all of the leading English cases as well as some in our own country upon the subject

under consideration. The opinion then proceeds: "It would be impossible, as I apprehend, to mention any rule of law which has been established upon higher authority or with a more uniform sanction; and I should have thought it necessary to apologize for wasting so much time on the point, if I had not found the rule, ancient and stable as it is, questioned and resisted by plausible considerations addressed to my feelings. I may, also, be permitted to add, that as I am without the aid of any public reports, or any distinct knowledge of the decisions of this court during the time of my predecessors, I am obliged, in almost every case, to reassert, expound and vindicate the principles of our equity jurisprudence. Many a point is now raised which would, probably, never have been disturbed, if the means had been afforded to learn the doctrines of the court; and it cannot be too often repeated, and too deeply impressed, that established principles in equity can no more be dispensed with than the rules of law, and for this plain reason, that I am not clothed with a dispensing power. The persons in whose behalf this suit was instituted are, consequently, entitled to a conveyance of the land sold to Ballou, equally as if the title had remained in Winter."

sometimes claimed to assign other grounds for the
rule.(1)

Rule should not be promotive of fraud.

SEC. 16. Necessity being the sole ground for the
enforcement of the rule lis pendens, courts should not
adopt and enforce such a rule as would defeat this
object, and invite fraudulent practices, tending to defeat the jurisdiction of the court by alienation of the
subject matter of litigation, pending the suit. In the
court of chancery, proceedings being always administered in the light of conscience, the tendency naturally and rightly is to temper the administration of
that court with considerations of equity. Hence, in

(1) Sorrel v. Carpenter, 2 P.
Williams, 482; Bellamy v. Sabine,
1 De Gex and Jones, 577; Sedg-
wick v. Cleveland, 7 Paige, 287;
Van Hook v. Thockmorton, 8
Paige, 33; Cook v. Mancius, 5
Johns. Ch. 93; Murray v. Lylburn,
2 Johns. Ch. 441, 445; Hoxie v.
Carr, 1 Sumner, 183; Brandon v.
Cabiness, 10 Ala. 155; Lawrence v.
Lane, 4 Gilm. 354; Kern v. Hazelrigg, 11 Ind. 443; Boulden v. Lanahan, 29 Md. 200; Haven v. Adams, 3 Allen, 367; Barrowscale v.
Tuttle, 5 Allen, 377; Leitch v.
Wells, 48 Barb. 637; Edwards v.
Banksmith, 35 Geo. 213; McGregor
v. McGregor, 21 Iowa, 441; Knowles
v. Rablin, 20 Iowa, 101; 1 Dan. Ch.
Pr. (4th Am. Ed.) 280, 281 and notes,
400, 401; 1 Story's Eq. Jur., Sec.
406; 2 Story's Eq. Jur., Sec. 908.
Upon the general proposition
that purchasers from parties to a
suit, of the subject matter of the litigation, after the court has acquired
complete jurisdiction, are bound by
the judgment or decree which shall
be rendered in the case; whether
they paid value or not; or whether
they had actual notice of the suit
or not, the authorities are all one
way, and numerous:
Randall et al. v. Lowe, 98 Ind.
261; Eyster v. Gaff, 91 U. S. 521;
Daniels v. Henderson, 49 Cal. 242;
Harlock v. Barheiger et al., 30 Ind.
370; Kern v. Hazelrigg, 11 Ind.
443; Green et al. v. White, 7 Blackf.
242; Truitt et al. v. Truitt, 38 Ind.
17; Ferrier v. Buzick et al., 6 Iowa,
258; Blanchard et al. v. Ware, 37
Iowa, 305; Blanchard et al. v. Ware,
43 Iowa, 530; Tredway v. McDonald,
51 Iowa, 668; Carr v. Lewis & Co.,
15 Mo. App. R. 551; Currie v. Fowler, 5 J. J. Marsh. 145; Grider et
al. v. Payne, 9 Dana, 188; Grant v.
Bennett, 96 Ill. 513; Chanley v.
Ld. Dunsany, 2 Sch. & Lef. 690;
Hiern v. Mill, 13 Ves. 120.

some cases, expressions have been used from which it may be inferred that, the rule lis pendens ought to be so modified, in particular cases, as to regard the effect upon pendente lite claimants, as a duty paramount to that of the enforcement of an iron rule, essential to the maintenance of the jurisdiction of the court. These, however, are mistaken views. Firm adherence to a uniform rule, tending to conserve the rights and interests of litigants, will always result in the greater equity and the least mischief.

Why sometimes termed "Notice."

SEC. 17. Lis pendens is often spoken of as notice of lis pendens, and, in many of our digests of reports, the cases are placed under the head of "Notice." This is not correct. In the case of Bellamy v. Sabine,(1)

(1) The doctrine of the above case of Bellamy v. Sabine, is thus stated in the syllabus of that case. 1 De Gex and Jones, 566:

"The doctrine as to the effect of lis pendens on the title of an alienee is not founded on any principles of courts of equity with regard to notice, but on the ground that, it is necessary to the administration of justice that the decision of the court in a suit should be binding, not only on the litigant parties, but on those who derive title from them pendente lite, whether with notice of the suit or not. A person who, without notice of a suit, purchases from one of the defendants property which is the subject of it, is not in consequence of the pendency of the suit affected by an equitable title of another defendant, which appears on the face of the proceedings, but of which he has no notice and to which it was not necessary for any of the purposes of the suit to give effect."

The learned Lord Chancellor further on in his opinion (p. 580) says:

"The language of the court in these cases, as well as in Worsley v. The Earl of Scarborough, certainly is to the effect that lis pendens is implied notice to all the world. I confess, I think that is not a perfectly correct mode of stating the doctrine. What ought to be said is, that pendente lite, neither party to the litigation can alienate the property in dispute so as to affect his opponent. The doctrine is not peculiar to courts of equity. In the old real actions the judgment bound the lands, notwithstanding any alienations by the defendant pendente lite, and certainly that did not depend on any principle arising from implied notice."

Lord Chancellor Cranworth said, "It is scarcely correct to speak of lis pendens as affecting the purchaser through the doctrine of notice, though undoubtedly the language of the courts often so describes its operation. It affects him not because it amounts to notice, but because the law does not allow litigant parties to

Lord Justice Turner, in the same case (page 584), used the following language:

"The doctrine of lis pendens is not, as I conceive, founded upon any of the peculiar tenets of a court of equity as to implied or constructive notice. It is, as I think, a doctrine common to the courts both of law and equity, and rests, as I apprehend, upon this foundation, that it would plainly be impossible that any action or suit could be brought to a successful termination, if alienation pendente lite were permitted to prevail. The plaintiff would be liable in every case to be defeated by the defendant's alienating before the judgment or decree, and would be driven to commence his proceedings *de novo*, subject again to be defeated by the same course of proceeding. That this doctrine belongs to a court of law no less than to courts of equity, appears from a passage in 2nd Inst. 375, where Lord Coke, referring to an alienation by a mesne lord pending a writ, says, that the alienee could not take advantage of a peculiar provision in the Statute of Westminster the 2nd, because he came to the mesnality pendente brevi, and in judgment of law the mesne as to the plaintiff remained seised of the mesnalty, for

pendente lite nihil innovetur; and though Lord Bacon's orders which give the rule in equity are very generally expressed, the language of the order upon this subject being: 'No decree bindeth any that cometh in bona fide by conveyance from the defendant before the bill exhibited, and is made no party, neither by bill nor order; but where he comes in pendente lite, and while the suit is in full prosecution, and without any color of allowance or privity of the court, there regularly the decree bindeth;' this order must, I think, be understood to mean that the decree binds so far as the title of the plaintiff is concerned, for the context of the order seems to me to show that it was the title of the plaintiff only which was contemplated by it."

While the principal question, in the case of Diamond v. Lawrence County, was whether the bonds of a municipal corporation, issued in payment of a corporate subscription to the stock of a railroad company, were subject to the rule lis pendens upon a bill filed to enjoin their sale by the company, the court held the same general doctrine, that a lis pendens in equity, not collusive and duly prosecuted, is notice to a purchaser so far as to affect and bind his interest by the decree,

give to others pending the litigation rights to the property in dispute so as to prejudice the opposite party." * * * "The necessities of mankind require that the decision of the court in the suit shall be binding not only on the litigant parties, but also on those who derive title under them by alienation made

and that it is no more than the adoption of the common law rule in a relation where, if the defendant alienate after the pendency of the writ, the judgment will overreach the alienation. Diamond *v.* Lawrence Co., 37th Penn. St. 353.

The principle decided in the case of Hersey *v.* Turbett, 27 Penn. St. (3 Casey) 418, is stated in the syllabus of that case to be that where a party purchases at sheriff's sale, pending an action of ejectment for the premises, in which the persons whose title he purchases are parties, he is affected with notice of it, and bound by the judgment in the case, as much as if he had been an actual party to it. In passing upon the question, the court say, at page 428 : "When Mr. Oliphant purchased the interest of Blocher & Co., pending the ejectment, he was bound to take notice of it, as lis pendens. It was his duty to prosecute his rights in that action."

In the case of Bennett's Lessee *v.* Williams, 5th Ohio, 461, the facts were, that Jeremiah Williams, in 1824, was the owner of the land involved and being such, conveyed them to Salsbury by valid deed. Jeremiah Williams filed his bill in February, 1826, to vacate this conveyance and reclaim the title. Publication was completed May 10,

1826. On the 24th of May following, after the completed publication, Salsbury conveyed by deed to alienees, who conveyed to the plaintiff. In 1828, Jeremiah Williams conveyed to Miah Williams, the defendant. In 1828 a decree was entered in the chancery case, divesting Miah Williams of the title so acquired and revesting it in Jeremiah Williams. The possession had always remained either in Jeremiah Williams or Miah Williams, the defendant. Upon this state of facts the court say:

"No rule is better established than, that during litigation, no change shall be made in the title, affecting the right of the parties. Hence arises the principle at law, that the judgment in a real action, shall overreach an alienation after writ. The doctrine was adopted in chancery, by Lord Bacon, in analogy with this, and has since been constantly adhered to, that a decree binds all persons coming into the title, during the pendency of the suit, without leave of the court. The rights of Salsbury, and his vendees are affected by the operation of this rule; and in respect to Jeremiah Williams, and all who claim through the decree, it invalidates the sale made by Salsbury, during the pendency of the bill, in

pending the suit, whether such alienees had or had
not notice of the pending proceedings. If this were
not so there could be no certainty that the litigation
would ever come to an end."

The foundation for the doctrine of lis pendens does
not rest upon notice, actual or constructive; it rests
solely upon necessity—the necessity, that neither
party to the litigation should alienate the property in
dispute so as to affect his opponent.

which Williams was pursuing his
legal interests. A doubt is stated
in the argument, whether a purchase made, during a suit in equity
will be holden void, except in a
court of equity; but we entertain
the opinion, that in our State, where
decrees in chancery by statute of
themselves convey the land, the
rule will work its effects not only in
chancery, but at law."

The case of Inloe's Lessees v.
George C. Harvey, 11th Md. 519,
was an ejectment. John Zell and
Alexander Hopper being seized of
the title to the property in question, on the 24th of September,
1850, conveyed to Thomas W. Virguirs, who took possession March
10, 1854. Virguirs conveyed to the
plaintiff, as trustee. Before this
conveyance was made; and, on the
21st day of February, 1854, a bill in
chancery had been filed against
Virguirs, which had become a lis
pendens on the 28th of the same
month. On the 30th of November,
1854, a decree was entered in the
chancery case annulling the title of
Virguirs. Upon this state of facts,
Le Grand, (C. J.) delivering the
opinion of the court, says: "There

is but one question involved in this
case, and we think the Superior
Court decided it correctly. It is,
whether a purchaser pendente lite
is bound by the judgment rendered
against the party from whom he
makes the purchase? This was an
action of ejectment brought by the
appellant to recover certain property of which he had been dispossessed under a writ of *habere facias
possesionem.* The defence was,
that in an equity proceeding against
the person under whom he claimed,
to set aside a conveyance alleged to
have been made fraudulently, a decree was passed in conformity with
the prayer of the bill, and the property secured to the complainant, and
that during the pendency of this
proceeding, the appellant purchased
the property in question from defendant. The Superior Court, in
fact, decided that the appellant,
being a purchaser pendente lite,
was concluded by the decree in the
equity proceedings, and, notwithstanding the very ingenious argument of the counsel for appellant,
we are of opinion, decided correctly."

Constructive notice lis pendens.

SEC. 18.   While it is not true that the doctrine of
lis pendens rests in any degree upon constructive
notice, as a ground for its enforcement; and while,
as has been seen, it is enforced as well where there is
no notice, or presumption of notice, and in the absence
of any fraud on the part of the alienee, as where there
is actual and constructive notice, or actual fraud; yet
courts of equity indulge in, what is often a mere fiction, the doctrine of constructive notice of lis pendens.
In the absence of statutory or other regulation, requiring the filing of the bill with the clerk, before the
issue of the subpœna, or the requirement of the
filing, or recording of notice lis pendens, independent of the bill, it can hardly be claimed that there
are any such means provided for the acquirement of
knowledge by any person dealing with the property
which is about to become the subject matter of litigation, as would justify the use of the term "constructive notice."   In the ordinary case, where for want of
statutory requirement or some rule of court, having
the force of law, the subpœna may issue before the
bill, or any other paper in the case, disclosing its scope,
has been filed with the clerk, the public are in no
wise advised in reference to the subject matter of the
threatened litigation.   Even the service of the subpœna on the defendant, fails to furnish this information, either to the public or the defendant himself.   It
is not until the bill is afterwards filed, that the scope
of the litigation can be ascertained by the public.
Where the statute requires, as a prerequisite, and in
order to give the court jurisdiction, the filing of the
bill with the clerk, as is the case in some of the

States, there is a warrant for using the terms, "notice
lis pendens," and "notice of lis pendens;" but under
an unrestricted practice, such as has generally prevailed, while it is a pleasing fiction—it might be added,
delusion—there is little foundation in fact or practice
to justify the use of those terms, until the bill is filed.

Notice of court proceedings presumed.

SEC. 19.   After the bill is filed, and thus becomes a
public record, and ample means are afforded for the public to become advised as to what property is involved
in the litigation, there is much propriety in referring
to the pending litigation as "notice lis pendens" or
"notice of lis pendens."   It does not matter that few
persons, ordinarily, acquire actual knowledge of the
record of the suit, and, thus, of what property is involved in it.   The opportunity is afforded, by use of
diligence, of acquiring that knowledge, and a sound
public policy will not thereafter excuse the purchaser
of the property for not ascertaining the facts spread
out upon the records.   And this is upon the same
grounds of public policy, which sternly deny to the
citizen any advantage, excuse from liability, or discharge of duty, arising from an ignorance of the law,
a principle which is of such universal application as to have been crystallized into a maxim,
"*Igornantia juris neminem excusat.*"(1)   And so, all
men are presumed to take notice of proceedings in the
courts of justice.   This is a favored view of the English Court of Chancery, and from it has arisen the
doctrine of constructive notice of lis pendens, a doctrine which satisfies the conscience of the Chancellor,

(1) Broom's Legal Maxims, 232.

and seems to soften the harshness of the common law when applied in chancery, not by abrogating the rule by means of numerous exceptions, or making its application materially different in chancery and at law, but in some cases by giving weight to equitable circumstances bearing against its operation. Thus, in the case of Sorrel *v.* Carpenter, decided by Lord Chancellor King, in 1728, while the doctrine of lis pendens was fully recognized, and held to otherwise have barred the defendant, as having dealt with the subject of litigation; yet, as it was a hard case, the rule was not applied on account of a slight defect in the plaintiff's proof in deraigning his title.(1)

This doctrine of constructive notice lis pendens received recognition by the distinguished Chancellor Hardwicke, in the case of Worsley *v.* The Earl of Scarborough, in which he said that the suit "creates the notice," and assigned as the reason, that: "As it is a transaction in a sovereign court of justice, it is supposed all people are attentive to what passes there, and it is to prevent a greater mischief that would arise by people purchasing a right under litigation and then in contest."(2)

John Newland's views.

Sec. 20. John Newland, in his work on Contracts, written in 1806, speaks of the "pendency of a suit in one of the superior courts of justice" as "presumptive notice," and says, "the rule is founded on the idea, that as the pendency of the suit, is a transaction in a sovereign court of justice, all people are supposed to

(1) Sorrel *v.* Carpenter, 2 P. Williams, 482.   (2) Worsley *v.* The Earl of Scarborough, 3 Atk. 392.

be attentive to what passes there."(1) The doctrine of constructive notice of proceedings in courts of justice, as well as that of lis pendens itself, is founded, as has been said, upon sound public policy. The application of the principle in practice, as well as the indulgence in the presumption that all men know the law, is attended with severity in special cases; but where a hardship must exist, it is better that it should fall upon him, who, by diligence and intelligent research, might have avoided it, and is, hence, responsible for it, than upon the general public, who must preserve their right, through legal proceedings in the courts. The adoption of the rule, based upon the presumption of constructive notice in the courts of justice, is promotive, likewise, of intelligence, industry and fair dealing. It falls within the spirit and letter of that other wholesome maxim, "*vigilantibus, non dormientibus, jura subveniunt.*"(2)

Caveat emptor as applied to lis pendens.

SEC. 21. The application of this doctrine is also in accordance with the general policy of the law, in cases of purchase, which generally casts the peril upon the purchaser to know that he is getting a good title. Caveat emptor is the settled policy of the common law.(3) It is the purchaser's business, as a rule, to inquire of the person with whom he deals, with respect to the title to the property purchased. He can always be safe, if he uses due diligence, but the real owner often has no means of safety, beyond his application to the court.(4) The doctrine of constructive no-

---

(1) Newland on Contracts, p. 106.

(2) Broom's Legal Maxims, 799.

(3) Broom's Legal Maxims, 690.

(4) Murray *v.* Ballou, 1 Johns. Ch. R. 566, et seq.

tice of lis pendens, therefore, without regard to actual notice, is firmly established by repeated adjudications, both in England and the United States.(1)

(1) Worsley v. The Earl of Scarborough, 3 Atk. 392 ; Griffith v. Griffith, 1 Hoff. 153; Jackson v. Ketchum, 8 Johns. 479; Harris v. Curtis's Admr., 3 Stew. 233; Tongue v. Morton, 6 Harris and Johns. 21; Owings v. Myers, 3 Bibb. 279; Jackson v. Andrews, 7 Wend. 152; Chapman v. West, 17 N. Y. 125; Walker v. Batz, 1 Yates, 574; Hersey v. Turbett, 3 Casey, 428; Chandron v. Magee, 8 Ala. 573; Centre v. The Bank, 22 Ala. 743; Ashley v. Cunningham, 16 Ark. 163; Gilman v. Hamilton, 16 Ill. 225; Inloe's Lessee v. Harvey, 11 Md. 519; Harrington v. Slade, 22 Barb. 166; Pratt v. Hoag, 12 How. Pr. 215.

The case of Fleming et al. v. Page et al., decided in 1677, and reported in Finch at page 320, is so often referred to upon the subject of lis pendens, that I here subjoin a condensed statement of the facts of the case, and the opinion of the court, as reported. The land involved was originally the property of George Bland. Thomas Bland was a son and heir at law of George Bland. Margaret Fleming, the wife of Edward Fleming, the plaintiff, was the heir and sole daughter of Thomas Bland. George Bland, in June, 1635, purchased the property of Anne Page, but took a conveyance in the names of Revell and Hart, in trust for himself and his heirs. By his own appointment in writing, Revell, the surviving trustee of George Bland, conveyed the premises to John Whitlock and Elizabeth Cooper. Whitlock dying, Elizabeth married one Bayly, who at the time held all the writings of George Bland relating to the property. George Bland died in 1648, leaving the said Bayly and his wife in possession of those writings. Both Bayly and his wife, at the time of the commencement of this suit, had died; but it was claimed, that Bayly in his life time forged a will purporting to be the will of George Bland, whereby he devised an interest in the estate to his son Thomas, with a provision in favor of an Alms House; and made Bayly and Surman who, it is alleged, was a party to the forging of the will, executors, and they took possession of the premises. Whereupon Thomas Bland, the son, sued the executors, in chancery, for the benefit of the Alms House charity. Subsequently Bayly, having discovered the deed from Revell to Whitlock and Elizabeth Cooper (Whitlock having died) and he having married Elizabeth, waived his title as executor under the will, and set up title under the deed for himself in the right of his wife. Thereupon, Surman, his co-executor, in the year 1650, exhibited a bill against him, in the court of chancery, which was tried upon the issue of whether or not the conveyance to Whitlock and Elizabeth was in trust for George Bland and his heirs, and the jury found the fact to be that it was in trust; whereupon the court decreed that

Territorial scope of lis pendens.

SEC. 22.   Although the rule lis pendens, whether applied where the jurisdiction of the court attaches to the property before any means whatever of ascertaining what the suit involves exists, or after record notice has been made in the case, by the filing of the bill or otherwise, so as to advise the public in respect to the subject matter of litigation, has been held with great

Bayly and his wife held the property in trust, and that they convey the premises in execution of the trust. But before the decree was made, and pendente lite, Bayly conveyed the premises to one Blaker, the defendant. Surman died before any execution of the decree, and it was not revived against Bayly and his wife. Subsequently Blaker entered upon the premises and received the rents and profits, and thereafter Thomas Bland, being still ignorant of the forgery of the will, exhibited another bill against Bayly and his wife and others, in behalf of the charity. Blaker set up that he was a purchaser for a valuable consideration paid to Bayly and his wife, without notice of any incumbrance. But it appearing that the purchase was made pendente lite, the defense was overruled, and a decree passed against him, to re-convey the premises to Thomas Bland, and, deliver up the writings of George Bland, then deceased. Blaker, to evade this decree pretended that he had previously conveyed the premises and delivered the writings to one Page, who set up title, under color of a conveyance from one of his ancestors, of whom George Bland purchased the same, and filed several bills, but never discovered his pretended title from Bayly or Blaker until after the death of Thomas Bland. Subsequently one Wright obtained a decree upon the pretended will of George Bland, and obtained possession. The plaintiffs having discovered the forgery, a trial was directed upon the issue whether the writing produced was the real will of George Bland, and the jury found that it was not. In May, 1675, upon a further hearing, the former decree sustaining the will was reversed, and the plaintiff restored to possession. Page, having brought ejectment upon his pretended purchase from Blaker, the plaintiffs exhibited their bill to be relieved against him, that their title might be quieted, and to compel a conveyance to Margaret and her heirs, and to execute the trust. Page pleaded purchase, as before, for valuable consideration without notice, and answered, that Blaker had conveyed the premises to Fletcher and Hobson and their heirs, in trust for him and his heirs, and that he was holding possession under said title. Upon this state of facts the report says: "The court declared, that the conveyances to Revell and Hart, and from them to

uniformity, both in this country and in England, to subject the title of a pendente lite purchaser to the final determination of the suit, though not a party to it; yet the question has sometimes arisen as to the territorial prevalence of the rule. Does the rule apply to "all the world" without reference to the residence of the pendente lite purchaser? Or is it only efficient within a limited territorial jurisdiction? Is the pendency of a suit in one State efficient to defeat the title of a pendente lite purchaser residing in a State other than that where the suit pends? Or, where such a

Bayly and Elizabeth Cooper, were only in trust for George Bland and his heirs, whose grandchild and heir the plaintiff Margaret is; and that the several pretended purchases by Blaker and Page, being made pendente lite, were on purpose to defraud the plaintiff Margaret, they being made with full notice of the trust; and that the pretended purchase from Bayly and his wife had been made, and contrived in reference to the setting up the said forged will, and carried on by fraud and practice to the prejudice of the plaintiff's inheritance and her just title. Therefore it was decreed, that Page shall convey and shall cause Hobson and his trustee to convey the said manor and premises (by such deed as the master shall approve) to the plaintiff Margaret and her heirs, discharged of all incumbrances by them, etc., and that she and her heirs, and the said Edward Fleming her husband, in her right, shall hold and enjoy the same against Page, and all claiming under him, by virtue of his pretended purchase from Blaker, or by

and under the title of Bayly or his wife."

In the old case of Finch v. Newnham, decided in 1690 and reported in 2nd Vern. 216, a devisee obtained a decree against the heir, who, it was supposed had suppressed the will. Pending the suit, a third person got an assignment of a mortgage made by the testator, and then purchased the equity of redemption from the heir, with notice of the will. The will had been decreed valid. Upon a bill filed to redeem from the mortgage, and insisting that the former decree, to which the complainant was not a party, was unjust, in decreeing the lands to be enjoyed according to the will.

The court says: "But in regard that he purchased pendente lite, and with notice that there was a will, the court would not admit him to examine the justice of the former decree, nor to try at law, whether such will was canceled or destroyed by the testator; but declared he should be bound by the former decree, and accordingly decreed the redemption of the mortgage to the plaintiff."

purchaser resides in a foreign country? Strange as it may seem, the question has not been conclusively settled by the decided cases.

The Supreme Court of Tennessee, in the case of Shelton et al. *v.* Johnson et al.,(1) where slaves were the subject matter of litigation, held that lis pendens could only have force within the jurisdiction of the court or State where the suit was pending. The argument in favor of this conclusion is that the extent of constructive notice as to what is transpiring in the courts is limited by State lines or the territorial jurisdiction of the court; that it would seem to be against public policy to enforce the doctrine of lis pendens when applied to personal property which had been taken beyond the limits of the State, because it would interfere with commercial transactions, and overturn in practice the presumption that the title to chattels passes upon delivery; that as to such property, if the rule lis pendens were enforced in foreign States, it would require a purchaser to search the records of the courts in all the States before being assured that he was acquiring a title, or purchase at his peril this species of property, thus placing an embargo on sales, and requires purchasers to take risks which no prudent buyer would assume and pay full value for property. It is urged against this position, that if such were the law, chattel property involved in suit in one State could be fraudulently and collusively taken into another State, and there sold for value to bona fide purchasers, and subsequently in pursuance of a collusive arrangement recovered from the innocent buyer by the rightful owner. It must be conceded

(1) Shelton et al. *v.* Johnson et al., 4 Sneed, 680.

that there is much force in the argument, and that it stands upon very much the same ground which makes commercial paper an exception to the rule lis pendens.

In all cases where local courts must have exclusive jurisdiction, where the rights of such property must be determined in pursuance of law where the property is situated, and, also in all cases where the property is retained in the custody of the court, this objection can not have force. There can be no good reason assigned why the binding force of lis pendens, in such cases, should not be efficient everywhere. On the other hand text writers would seem to favor the view that where courts have jurisdiction, and the lis pendens binds personal property the binding force of the jurisdiction is efficient everywhere.

Extent of jurisdiction further considered.

Sec. 23. Mr. Story, in his work on Equity Jurisprudence, speaks of lis pendens as being: "A general notice of an equity to all the world."(1) Other text writers and courts often use similar language. The Court of Appeals of the State of Kentucky, in the case of Fletcher v. Ferrel,(2) went the whole length of applying the doctrine lis pendens to chattels, to the full extent of its conceded application to real estate. A bill had been filed in a Tennessee court for the proper division of slaves among heirs and an injunction had been issued in the case. Pending the suit in the Tennessee court one of the defendants removed some of the slaves into Kentucky and sold them to Fletcher and Sharp. Ferrel acquired title to the same slaves under the decree of the Tennessee court, and afterwards commenced sup-

(1) 1 Story's Eq. Jur., § 406.   (2) Fletcher v. Ferrel, 9 Dana, 372.

plemental proceedings in the State of Kentucky to have the Tennessee decree executed. The Kentucky court held that, where purchases are made in one State within the United States, pending a suit in another State, the purchasers must be treated as purchasing pendente lite, and be subjected to the rule applicable to such purchases. The decision was based upon the clause of the Constitution of the United States which provides, "that full faith and credit shall be given in each State to the public acts, records and judicial proceedings of other States;" and acts of Congress passed in pursuance of that provision, and the court concluded that in pursuance of this clause of the constitution and the laws passed thereunder the lis pendens of proceedings in each State must be given effect throughout the United States; that the proceedings in Tennessee had validity and effect and conclusive operation in the State of Kentucky upon parties, privies and pendente lite purchasers, that comity between the States, the letter of the constitution, and the acts of Congress, as well as the spirit and policy which dictated its adoption, require that the same credit and effect should be given it in each of the States that is given the proceedings in the State where they are had.

A recent case in the Court of Appeals of Missouri(1) maintains this position with force and clearness. If it is said that, innocent purchasers in sister States will suffer, if this rule is enforced, it is no more than occurs frequently in the common application of the rule lis pendens, or in the recovery of stolen property from those who have purchased in good faith and for value. If the court acquires jurisdiction over

(1) Carr v. Lewis & Co., 15 Mo. App. 551; Sec. 1, Art. IV, Const. U. S.

chattel property at all, if lis pendens becomes efficient anywhere, it would seem logical that its efficiency should be maintained so that the decrees of the courts may be executed everywhere. It would be better to enlarge the exceptions to the application of the rule lis pendens, always having those exceptions well defined, than to leave the question unsettled, in cases where the court clearly has jurisdiction over personal property in suit, as to whether decrees may or may not be enforced in different localities. It must be conceded, however, as we have above said, that the authorities are by no means in accord upon this question.

No reason is, therefore, perceived why the force of a lis pendens should be evaded merely by absence from the sovereignty where the suit is pending, and it is quite clear that, as to real property located within the jurisdiction of the court where its judgments and decrees may become or be made liens upon the property, all men must take notice and be bound by lis pendens without regard to residence. If, although the ultimate object should be to affect title to real estate, a suit purely in personam is commenced in a foreign State, as a bill to compel execution of a deed, it ought not to be held as lis pendens, as against a bona fide purchaser of the property without notice. And so, if the proceeding relate to personal property, not of a character to fall within the exceptions to the rule lis pendens, and the property should continue to remain within the custody of the court or litigating claimant, until the final determination of the cause, and without delivery to a purchaser, it is clear, that the doctrine of lis pendens should be effective, without regard to the residence of one attempting to deal with it pendente lite.

Conclusion.

SEC. 24.   It must be concluded, therefore, from this review of the authorities, that the primary and essential object and ground of the rule lis pendens is to enable courts of justice to maintain, notwithstanding pendente lite alienations by parties to the suit, jurisdiction over the subject matter of litigation so as to be able to enforce their decrees and judgments when they are rendered; that when, however, the quality of the res litigiosa will not be impaired thereby, a secondary ground or object, specially in courts of chancery, may be to administer the rule so as to preserve the equities of the parties, and place some stress upon actual and constructive notice, but that while many courts have taken an erroneous view, notice is never a primary object or ground for lis pendens.   That, so far as relates to the territorial scope of lis pendens, authorities are in conflict; but that the better rule would seem to be, that lis pendens, in any of the States, should be binding in other States of the Union.

CHAPTER III.

COMMENCEMENT, CONTINUANCE AND CLOSE OF LIS PENDENS.

Importance of the subject.

SEC. 25.   In order to determine how the rights of parties litigant, or of third persons, are affected by lis pendens, it often becomes necessary to know at what precise point of time the suit may be deemed commenced, so as to take effect upon property as a lis pendens. It is manifest, that there is some danger of confounding the various cases which may arise, in which it may become necessary to enquire as to the commencement of suits and their lis pendens. Lis pendens, or notice lis pendens, might seem to necessarily have the same meaning, when relating to the rights of the parties themselves involved in the case, when having reference to the running of the statutes of limitation and when referring to the rights of third parties, acquired pending the cause, in the subject matter of litigation. This is not, however, the case. The commencement of a suit, and of notice lis pendens may or may not be at the same point of time. In many, if not in all of the States, it is provided by statute when causes at common law and in chancery are deemed to be commenced. In the absence of any such provision, a suit at common law is commenced by the issuing of the writ by the clerk, and, unless governed by statutory provisions, the same would be true in chancery. But with regard to the defense of the statute of limitation, the suit in some States is regarded as commenced from the issuing of the writ, in others, from the delivery of the writ to the officer, and in others again, from the service of the process. With regard to the commencement of constructive notice of lis pendens, it may be said, that neither of these periods is necessarily the same.

Former practice as to filing bills.

Sec. 26. In former times it was not necessary, in chancery, to file the bill before issuing the writ. Process was frequently issued upon praecipe.(1) The

(1) Prior to 1705, the evils arising from the loose practice of issuing subpœnas in chancery upon praecipe, before filing the bill, became

same loose practice prevailed for a long time in the older States of the Union. In consequence of this practice, which prevailed at the time Lord Bacon adopted in chancery the rule lis pendens, the effect of notice lis pendens was postponed from the real commencement of the cause, until the service of subpœna upon the defendant. The manifest reason for this postponement was that there was not necessarily, on the files in the court of chancery, any bill which by its allegations would disclose to the world the subject matter of litigation. Although the mere service of subpœna upon the defendant would of itself furnish no notice to a purchaser of the subject matter of litigation, and would not necessarily inform the defendant even on that subject; yet, as the defendant would be presumed to have the means of ascertaining what the suit was about; and, thus acting honestly, avoid dealing with the property without disclosing to the purchaser the fact, that it was involved in litigation, in order to give the public an opportunity to learn facts not thus disclosed by any record; and in the supposed interest of justice and fairness the commence-

---

so great, that Parliament passed the statute of 4th Anne, Chap. 16, Sec. 22, which provided that:

"No subpœna, or other process of appearance, do issue out of any court of equity, till after the bill is filed with the proper officer in the respective court of equity, except in case of bills for injunctions to stay waste, or stay suits at law commenced, and a certificate thereof brought to the subpœna office or to him who usually makes out subpœna, or other process in the sev-

eral courts of equity, under the hand of the six clerk or other clerk in office who usually files bills in equity, for which certificate he shall receive no fee."

For further information upon the subject of the issuance of subpœnas in chancery before the bill was filed, see Sugden's Law of Vendors, (8th London Ed.) 745; Pigott v. Nower, 3 Swanst. 535, (note); and Anon. 1 Vern. 318. As to the practice in the time of Henry the VI, see 1 Spence's Eq. Jur. 349 and 367.

ment of the lis pendens was thus postponed until service of subpœna and the filing of the bill.(1)

Statutes upon the subject.

SEC. 27. More recently, however, in England(2) and in many of the States of the Union, lis pendens statutes have been passed, requiring the filing or recording of notices lis pendens, prescribing what they shall contain and, in most instances, declaring their legal effect. In those States where this has been done, the provisions of these statutes will prevail, so far as relates to the commencement of lis pendens.

In other States, statutes have been passed requiring the filing of bills in chancery with the clerk of the court, before the issuing of the subpœna, and in such terms that a subpœna issued without the previous filing of a bill would necessarily be declared void, thus insuring that there should appear upon the public records a pleading, containing full and specific allegations in respect to the subject matter of litigation. It

(1) Murray v. Ballou, 1 Johns. Ch. 576; Harrington v. Harrington, 27 Mo. 562; Metcalf et al. v. Smith's Heirs, 40 Mo. 575; Fenwick v. Gill, 38 Mo. 525; Shaw v. Padley, 64 Mo. 522; Banks et al. v. Thompson, 75 Ala. 531; Skeel v. Spraker, 8 Paige, 182; Heatly v. Finster, 2 Johns. Ch. 158; Green v. Slayter, 4 Johns. Ch. 38; Hale v. Warner's Admr. et al., 36 Ark. 217; Scudder v. Van Amberg, 4 Edw. 29; Hayden v. Bucklin, 9 Paige, 512; Grant v. Bennett, 96 Ill. 513; Lytle's Exr. v. Pope's Admrs., 11 B. Mon. 318; Lytle v. Bradford, 7 T. B. Mon. 112; Wickliffe's Exr. v. Breckenridge's Heirs, 1 Bush. 443; Metcalfe v. Larned, 40 Mo. 572; Sam-

uels v. Shelton et al.,48 Mo.445; Bailey v. McGinness, 57 Mo. 362; Herrington v. Herrington, 27 Mo. 560; Hirshizer v. Tinsley, 9 Mo. App. 339; Youngman v. Elmira, etc., R. R. Co., 65 Penn. St. 275; Mason et al. v. Saloy, 12 La. An. 776; Fash v. Ravesies, 32 Ala. 451; Steele v. Taylor, 1 Minn. 274; Hall v. Jack, 32 Md. 253; Hersey v. Turbett, 27 Penn. St. (3 Casey) 418; Cooley v. Brayton, 16 Ia. 10; Hart et al. v. Marshall, 4 Minn. 294; Crocker v. Crocker, 57 Me. 395; Berry v. Whitaker, 58 Me. 422; McPherson v. Housel, 2 Beas. Ch. 299.

(2) Sec. 7, Chap. II, 2d and 3d Victoria.

will thus be seen that the commencement of lis pendens will vary, according to the prevalence of statutory provisions, or the non-existence of any statutes upon the subject.(1)

The common law rule as to commencement of lis pendens.

SEC. 28.   Where no lis pendens statutes are in force, and in those States where there is no statutory requirement that the bill should be filed before the subpœna may issue, the common law rule as to the commencement of lis pendens is in force.   The law in such States undoubtedly is, that the lis pendens begins from the service of the subpœna after the bill is filed.   This has been the rule for over three hundred years, established by a long series of well considered cases, and while, as a new question, very strong reasons may be assigned for a different rule, it is too well established to be now shaken.(2)

(1) Sec. 4, Chap. 22, R. S. of Ill.; Hodgen v. Guttery, 58 Ill. 431.

(2) Story's Eq. Jur. § 405 and 406; Murray v. Ballou, 1 Johns. Ch. 566; Murray v. Lylburn, 2 Johns. Ch. 566; Green v. Slayter, 4 Johns. Ch. 38; Hopkins v. McLaren, 4 Cow. 667; Murray v. Blatchford, 1 Wend. 583; Jackson v. Andrews, 7 Wend. 152; Parks v. Jackson, 11 Wend. 442; Griffith v. Griffith, 1 Hoff. Ch. 153; White v. Carpenter, 2 Paige, 217, 252; Hayden v. Bucklin, 9 Paige, 512; Jackson v. Losee, 4 Sandf. Ch. 381; Com. Dig. Chancery, Tit. lis pendens. Allen v. Poole, 54 Miss. 325; Allen v. Mandeville, 26 Miss. 397; Sugden on Vendors, (7th Am. Ed.) 544; Centre v. The P. & M. Bank et al., 22 Ala. 757; Goodwin et al. v. McGhee et al., 15 Ala. 241; Miller v. Kershaw, 1 Bailey Ch. 471; Boynton v. Rawson, 1 Clark Ch. 584; Coulter v. Herrod et al., 5 Cush. (Miss.) 685; Wickliffe's Exrs. v. Breckenridge's Heirs, 1 Bush. 443; Lytle v. Bradford, 7 T. B. Mon. 112; Lytle's Exrs. v. Pope's Admr., 11 B. Mon. 318; Harrington v. Harrington, 27 Mo. 562; Fenwick v. Gill, 38 Mo. 525; Metcalf et al. v. Smith's Heirs, 40 Mo. 575; Bailey et al. v. McGinnis et al., 57 Mo. 371; Shaw v. Padley, 64 Mo. 522; Grant v. Bennett, 96 Ill. 513; Banks et al. v. Thompson, 75 Ala. 531; Skeel v. Spraker, 8 Paige, 182 ; Heatly v. Finster, 2 Johns. Ch. 158; Scudder v. VanAmburg, 4 Edw. 29.   See also note 2, sec. 26 *ante*.

The rule lis pendens of ancient origin.

SEC. 29. We have already seen that, the rule lis pendens, while probably not derived from, is analogous to, the rule which prevails in real actions at common law, where, if the defendant alienates after the pendency of the writ, the judgment will overreach such alienation, and that whatever its remote origin may be, it was adopted into chancery by one of the ordinances of Lord Bacon.(1) Chancellor Kent says, in the leading case of Murray v. Ballou, that at the time of the decision of that case, which was in 1815, the rule had then been declared, above two centuries, by the highest authority, and had received continuous support and application down to that time.(2)

Service before bill filed.

SEC. 30. As to whether, where the subpœna was issued and service had without bill filed, and the bill was filed after service, the lis pendens will or will not relate back and take effect from the service of the subpœna, the cases are not in harmony. The cases which hold that lis pendens relates back to service, at a time prior to the date of filing, are believed to rest upon the authority of an anonymous case decided in 1685, before the statute of 4th Anne, Ch. 16, Sec. 22, was passed.(3) Unless the subpœna then in use disclosed the matter in litigation with sufficient definiteness to enable the defendant to make alienation, that case furnishes no reason in support of the doctrine of relation, as applied to lis pendens.(4)

(1) Sec. 1, *ante.*

(2) Murray *v.* Ballou, 1 Johns. Ch. 576.

(3) See Sec. 26, note 1, *ante.*

(4) Anon. 1 Vern. 319; Pigott *v.* Nower, 3 Swanst. 536; Hopkins *v.*

The common law rule unsatisfactory.

SEC. 31. Although there are cases holding that, when the subpœna is issued and served before bill filed, after filing lis pendens will relate back to service, the rule is not supported by satisfactory reasons, and should not be followed, except where the subpœna points out the property involved in litigation. No record was kept of the issuing of the subpœna, and it was not required to be filed, at least until after service. It might not be possible for a stranger to the suit, by any degree of diligence, to learn that it had been issued or served and, if he did, it would give him no notice whatever of the subject matter of litigation. It seems monstrous to hold that as to a stranger a suit should be deemed pending from the time of such service so as to be constructive notice when actual notice was impossible of acquirement.(1)

When amendments are filed.

SEC. 32. Where the original bill or petition does not involve the property, but, pending the suit, an amendment or amended petition or bill is filed alleging new matter, and involving property not before in litigation, the lis pendens created by the amendment will commence from the filing of the amendment or amended pleading, and will not relate back to the com-

McLaren, 4 Cow. 667; Murray v. Blatchford, 1 Wend. 583; Jackson v. Andrews, 7 Wend. 152; Parks v. Jackson, 11 Wend. 442; Griffith v. Griffith, 1 Hoff. Ch. 153; White v. Carpenter, 2 Paige, 217, 252; Hayden v. Breslin, 9 Paige, 572; Jackson v. Losee, 4 Sandf. Ch. 407; Comyn's Digest Chancery, Tit. lis pendens; Allen v. Poole, 54 Miss. 325; Allen et al. v. Mandeville, 26 id. 397; Sugden on Vendors, (7th Am. Ed.) 544; Centre v. The P. & M. Bank et al., 22 Ala. 757; Goodwin et al. v. McGhee et al., 15 id. 241; Miller v. Kershaw, 1 Bailey Ch. 471; Boynton v. Rawson, 1 Clark Ch. 584; Coulter v. Herrod et al., 5 Cush. (Miss.) 685.

(1) Leitch et al. v. Wells et al., 48 Barb. 637.

mencement of the action so as to affect intervening rights. So when creditors filed a bill alleging that defendant had attempted to dispose of her interest for the purpose of defrauding her creditors, but did not allege in their pleading a judgment and, subsequently and pending the suit, filed an amended petition in the same case, alleging that they had obtained a judgment for the debt, on which an execution had issued and been returned *nulla bona*, it was held that the plaintiffs were entitled to no relief on the original petition, and that a purchaser of the interest in contest, having bought pending the litigation under the original petition, and before the amendment, held only subject to the result of that litigation: that as the plaintiffs had not shown themselves entitled to a decree upon matters then in litigation, the rights of the purchaser could not be affected by a different and distinct ground of relief subsequently asserted in an amended petition, and that the new lis pendens created by the amendment, did not relate back to the commencement of the action so as to affect intervening rights.(1)

Where no bill filed—no lis pendens.

SEC. 33. It has always been held that where there was no bill or petition filed, mere service of the subpœna in chancery would not create lis pendens, affecting third persons, not parties to the bill, and that the filing of the complaint, petition or bill, was necessary for that purpose.(2)

(1) Clark *v.* Havens, Clark's Ch. R. 563; Curtis *v.* Hitchcock, 10 Paige, 399; Mitford Pl. 400; Dudley *v.* Price's Adm., 10 B. Mon. 88.

(2) Leitch et al. *v.* Wier et al., 43 Barb. 637; Murray *v.* Ballou, 1 Johns. Ch. 566; Murray *v.* Lylburn, 2 id. 441; Hayden *v.* Bucklin, 9 Paige, 512; Anon. 1 Vern. Ch. 318; Bouvier's Law Dict. Tit. lis pendens (14th Ed. vol. 2-76); Olson *v.* Paul, 56 Wis. 30; Flood *v.* Isaac,

And so, also, under lis pendens statutes, the filing of the notice before the bill is filed creates no lis pendens, the filing of the notice under these statutes taking the place and performing the office of service.

Analogous rule in attachment.

SEC. 34.   And so, in a suit by attachment at law, it has been held, in analogy with the rule that a suit in chancery is not lis pendens as to strangers, until bill filed and service upon the defendant, that a garnishee is not bound by notice of the suit until service of garnishee process upon him, and that he would be protected in the bona fide sale and transfer of trust property, held under a deed made before service of the garnishment.(1)

Rule in ejectment.

SEC. 35.   In ejectment, under the old common law practice, unless the declaration is filed at the time of the service of notice, there is no lis pendens until it is filed, with proof of previous service.   If the declaration with proof of service endorsed is filed upon or before the appearance day, the suit will, by relation, be considered as having been commenced at the time of the service.   But in this action the writ necessarily discloses to the defendant the subject matter of litigation.   If the declaration and proof of service shall not be filed on the first day of the appearance term, there will be no lis pendens until an appearance and defense of the suit or a confession of judgment.(2)

34 Wis. 423; Butler *v.* Tomlinson, 38 Barb. 642; Stern *v.* O'Connell, 35 N. Y. 104; Cordon et al. *v.* Tyle et al., 53 Mich. 623.

(1) Hazard's Admr. *v.* Franklin, 2 Ala. 349.

(2) Sidwell et al. *v.* Worthington's Heirs, 8 Dana, 761.

In bill filed against partnership.

SEC. 36. Where a bill is filed by a creditor of a partnership against a surviving partner to enforce the lien of a firm creditor, and compel payment out of the firm assets, but does not allege that the surviving partner is insolvent, there is no lis pendens, even from the date of the service of process, so as to affect the choses in action sought to be subjected, or to over-reach, on that ground, settlements made between the surviving partner and the debtors of the firm, and the court will refuse a decree against the survivors and debtors who are made defendants, and have made settlements, on the ground that there was no lis pendens created binding the subject matters of settlement.(1)

Service upon one member of the firm.

SEC. 37. Where a bill is filed against the members of a co-partnership to enforce rights against specific property, in a State where service of process is necessary before lis pendens commences, service upon one of the members of the defendant firm will create lis pendens so that an intervening purchaser will be bound by it.(2)

Where service is accepted.

SEC. 38. As notice lis pendens is considered a hard rule as to strangers, it is held that, where a defendant accepts service of the subpœna and the acceptance is antedated, lis pendens shall not take effect prior to the actual time of the acceptance of service, as to any person acquiring an interest before that time. It may be said, in general, that the doctrine of lis pendens is one of *strictissimi juris*.(3)

(1) Pearson et al. *v.* Keedy, 6 B. Mon. 130.

(2) Dresser *v.* Wood, 15 Kan. 344.

(3) Cockrill *v.*Maney et al., 2 Coop. (Tenn.)59; Shelton et al.*v.* Johnston, et al., 4 Sneed, 672; Adam's Eq. 157

Where cases are remanded.

Sec. 39.   Where parties are once brought into court and, after judgment or decree, the case is prosecuted to an appellate court, by appeal or writ of error, and remanded, the defendant is still in court and new notice or service is unnecessary. This is true in attachment as well as in other cases.(1)

Where writ of error is sued out.

Sec. 40.   Where a bill had been filed to compel a conveyance, and a decree had been entered, operating under the statute as a conveyance to complainant, from which the defendant had sued out a writ of error and given a bond, but, before service of citation, and without knowledge that the writ of error was pending, the complainant conveyed to a bona fide purchaser for value, without notice, it was held, that a writ of error is a new suit, and that until the service of the citation, a writ of error is not to be considered as pending so as to affect strangers as a lis pendens, but that as between the parties where the writ of error is successfully prosecuted and a reversal ensues, it may be regarded as a continuance of the original suit, and the court would have power to revest titles and administer justice in accordance with the final determination of the Appellate Court.(2)

Where sheriff is instructed.

Sec. 41.   Where a writ is filled out and given to an officer, with instructions not to serve it until after a certain time, or the happening of a certain event, the suit will not be deemed to have been commenced until

(1) Reaugh *v.* McConnell et al., 36 Ill. 375; Murray *v.* Whitaker, 17 Ill. 230; Haywood *v.* Collins, 60 Ill. 340.

(2) Lessees of Taylor *v.* Boyd, 3 Ohio, 352; Woolridge *v.* Boyd, 13 Lea, 154.

the service of the writ.(1)   It is said that it is the
intention and the act combined, which, in fact, constitutes the commencement of the suit, because a writ
filled out without intention of service, is altogether
inoperative, as it may be filled out before the cause of
action commences or be antedated.(2)

Where clerk is instructed.

SEC. 42.   Where a declaration or petition is delivered to the clerk of the court, with instructions not to
issue process until further instructed, it is held, that it
is left with the clerk in his individual capacity as bailee,
and that it is no commencement of a suit, so as to
prevent the running of the statute of limitation, and
that the writ would not be considered as being legally
sued out, until delivered to the sheriff, with authority
to serve it on the defendant.(3)

Where one of several defendants dies without service.

SEC. 43.   Where a suit is brought against two, upon
a cause of action which is joint, and not joint or several, and after it is instituted, but before service, one
of the defendants dies, upon a plea in abatement setting up these facts, it will be held that no service of
process having been had upon the deceased defendant,
and no service having been had upon the surviving
defendant until after the death of his co-defendant,
the action cannot be said to have been commenced,
and as in that case service upon both is necessary, the
suit will abate.(4)

(1) Seaver *v.* Lincoln, 21 Pick.
267; Badger *v.* Phiney, 15 Mass. 359.

(2) Johnson *v.* Farwell, 7 Greenl.
373; Bronson *v.* Earle, 17 Johns. 65.

(3) McClelland *v.* Slanter, 30 Tex.
496.

(4) Clark *v.* Helms et al., 1 Root,
487.

Where sole defendant dies before service.

SEC. 44. As has already been shown, there is a substantial difference between the commencement of an action, and its being a suit depending between the parties, the first having reference only to the act of the plaintiff, but the second to the position of the defendant also. So if a defendant dies before service or appearance, it seems, the suit could not be revived against his personal representatives, nor could it be continued by supplemental bill against them.(1)

Commencement of suit in Connecticut.

SEC. 45. In an action at law it was held in Connecticut that, in that State, a suit is not considered as commenced until the service of the writ on the defendant.(2) The reason assigned, in Jenks v. Phelps,(3) for this ruling, is that it harmonizes with the practice, common in that State, of taking out blank writs signed and tested, with the privilege of alteration before service, the legal propriety of which has been recognized by the same court.(4) This practice really lies at the foundation of the rule which postpones the lis pendens until after service. The reason assigned in the case above referred to, greatly impairs the authority of these cases, and tends to unsettle the propriety of enforcing the rule in those States where neither this practice prevails, nor is its propriety recognized by the courts.

(1) Allen et al. v. Mandeville et al., 4 Cush. (Miss.) 399; 3 Danl's Ch. Pr. 1663 and 1698.

(2) Allen et al. v. Mandeville et al., 4 Cush. (Miss.) 399; 3 Danl's Ch. Pr. 1663 and 1698.

(3) Jenks v. Phelps, 4 Conn. 149.

(4) Spalding v. Butts, 6 Conn. 30; Gates v. Bushnell, 9 Conn. 535; Sanford v. Dick, 17 Conn. 215; Ward v. Curtis, 18 Conn. 291; Clark v. Helms et al., 1 Root, 486; Parsons v. Ely et al., 2 Conn. 377; Fuller v. Haughton, 5 Conn. 424.

It is, also, held in Connecticut that, under the statute of that State, a suit in attachment is not commenced by the mere delivery of a writ to an officer, but that the attachment of property under the writ is also a necessary incipient step in order to create a lis pendens in a suit in attachment.(1)

Commencement of suit in Arkansas.

SEC. 46.　Where the statute provided, that suits at law may be commenced by filing in the office of the clerk of the court a declaration, petition or statement, in writing, setting forth the plaintiff's cause of action, and suing out thereon a writ against the defendant, it is held in Arkansas, that unless the defendant makes his appearance voluntarily, the issuing of the writ is a necessary element in the institution of the suit, and that the joint act of filing the declaration and the issuance of the writ constitute the commencement of the suit.(2)

Commencement of suit in Vermont.

SEC. 47.　It is held in Vermont, where the language of the statute is, "the action shall be commenced and sued," that the time when the writ actually issues is to be considered the commencement of the suit; that the prima facie evidence of the time when the writ issues is usually the date; that there must be a delivery to an officer for service in season to be served and returned to the court to which it is made returnable, but that if the writ is abandoned, or if it is issued with no intention to have service of it, there is no commencement of a suit.(3)　A like rule as to presumption,

(1) Gates v. Bushnell, 9 Conn. 534.　White, 18 Cal. 639.
(2) State Bank v. Cason et al., 10　(3) Allen v. Main, 1 D. Chipman,
Ark. 481 ; see, also, Flandeau v.　95; Day v. Lamb, 7 Vt. 429; John-

as to the time of service is held in Maine, Massachusetts, New York and Arkansas.

Commencement of suit in Mississippi.

SEC. 48.   In Mississippi, although by rule of court authorized by statute, a suit in chancery, as between the parties, was deemed to be commenced by filing the bill merely, yet as to purchasers of the property in litigation during the pendency of the suit the doctrine has always been regarded as a hard one, and hence service of the subpœna, as well as its issuance, is deemed requisite to constitute such pendency.(1)

Commencement of lis pendens and suit in Missouri.

SEC. 49.   It is held in Missouri, that lis pendens is not notice to a purchaser so as to affect and bind his interests by the judgment till the service of the writ after the bill or petition is filed; but as between the parties, and as having application to the statute of limitation, the time of the filing of the declaration, and not the service of the writ, is regarded as the commencement of a suit at law.(2)

Commencement of suit in W. Virginia.

SEC. 50.   Where the subpœna was issued on the 3rd day of January, 1872, and was served on the 6th, but the bill was not filed until February following, it was held in West Virginia, that the subpœna served was not a sufficient lis pendens, and that

son v. Farwell, 7 Greenleaf, 372; Ford v. Phillips, 1 Pick. 202; Burdick v. Green, 18 Johns. 14; McLaren et al. v. Thurman, 8 Ark. 316; State Bank v. Brown, 12 Ark. 94; State Bank v. Cason et al., 10 Ark. 479; Fowler v. Boyd, Hemp. R. 214.

(1) Bacon et al. v. Gardner et al., 1 Cush. (Miss.) 62.

(2) Dougherty v. Downey, 1 Mo. 482, (side p. 675); Harrington v. Harrington, 27 Mo. 562; Fenwick v. Gill, 38 Mo. 525; Metcalf et al. v. Smith's Heirs, 40 Mo. 575.

when the bill was filed, the lis pendens, as to third parties, related back to the service of the subpœna.(1)

This was carrying the idea of the supposed efficiency of the service of the subpœna as notice to an absurd, not to say a ludicrous, extreme. It is not surprising that the legislature afterwards, and in 1877, enacted a lis pendens statute.

Commencement of suit in Kentucky.

SEC. 51. It is held in Kentucky, that a suit in chancery, brought against absentees, could not be deemed lis pendens, so as to be presumed notice to a purchaser, until the complete execution of the order to advertise. The rule seems to be followed in that State, that the filing of a bill is not notice of the pendency of a suit, before the subpœna is served. Completed publication is deemed equivalent to the service of a subpœna issued. So far as relates to the parties themselves and, hence, also, so far as concerns the running of the statute of limitation, the date of the issuance of the subpœna in chancery is the commencement of the suit. The date of the suing out of process at law and of the service of notice in the action of ejectment is also the commencement of suits at law in that State.(2)

When generally chancery suits commenced.

SEC. 51a. It may be said generally, that, at the present day, the filing of a bill, the taking out of the subpœna thereafter and making a bona fide attempt to serve it, is, in equity, the commencement of a suit, as against the defendant himself.

(1) Harmon v. Byram's Admr. et al., 11 W. Va. 521; Newman v. Chapman, 2 Rand. 93; see, also, 3 Sugden on Vendors, 459.

(2) Prindill v. Maydwell, 7 B Mon. 314.

Where the question is not regulated by statute, this may be said to be the law in all of the States.

This has been the rule in England also, since the statute of 4 Anne, C. 16, Sec. 22, requiring the filing of the bill before the issuance of the subpœna. Before that act was passed, it was not necessary to file the bill before the issuance and service of the subpœna, to appear and answer; it being sufficient if the bill were afterwards filed; the suit, as against the defendant himself, being then considered as commenced from the teste of the subpœna, as in suits at law commenced by original writs.(1)

When service by publication.

SEC. 52. The statutes of the different States provide for constructive service in certain cases, usually where personal service can not be had, by publication. These statutes vary in the different States. When such service is had the lis pendens is not in force until the publication is completed. The suit may be regarded as commenced before that time, according to the rule established by statute or otherwise in the various States.

The defendant might also, doubtless, under statutory provisions and authority, be brought in by the service of copies of orders directing the appearance of defendants. In such cases probably, the lis pendens would commence from the service of the order to appear.(2)

(1) Angell on Limitations, 330; Hayden v. Bucklin, 9 Paige, 512; Pigott v. Nower, 3 Swanst. 530; Webb v. Pell, 1 Paige, 564; Purcell v. Blennerhasset, 3 J. & L. 24; Forte v. Thompson, 2 Cr. & L. 568; Morris v. Ellis, 7 Jur. 413.

(2) Carter v. Mills, 30 Mo. 441; Hayden v. Bucklin, 9 Paige, 513; Clevinger v. Hill, 4 Bibb. 499 ; Prindill v. Maydwell, 7 B. Mon. 314; Chandron v. Magee, 8 Ala. 573.

CHAPTER IV.

COMMENCEMENT, CONTINUANCE AND CLOSE OF LIS PENDENS CONCLUDED.

When service upon defendants differently made.

SEC. 53. Thus it may occur that in a suit in chancery, where there are several defendants, some of whom are served with subpœna, and others by publication, lis pendens will commence in the same cause at different times with respect to different parties defendant. Again, it may often occur, where there are numerous defendants, that the service of subpœna upon different individual defendants may be had at different times, and that, from various causes different publications may be made as to other several defendants, and it is easy to suppose a case where, however numerous the defendants are, the commencement of lis pendens may differ as to each one of them. This often leads to much perplexity in the investigation of titles, and is necessarily attended with great risks to the purchaser, for very often the rights of parties as to the property involved in litigation may depend upon the ability to prove the precise time at which process was served, or service accepted. The lapse of a few minutes, or at most a few hours, with reference to the time when the purchase was made, may often be conclusive in favor of or against the purchase, and as the return of the officer will seldom show the hour or minute of service, and thus there will be no record evidence upon the question, the rights of the purchaser will be made necessarily to depend upon parol evidence.

Publication in attachment.

Sec. 54.   But the rule, it seems, is different in some States as to the commencement of an attachment, so far, at least, as relates to the defendants themselves. It was held, in Missouri, that where an attachment is issued against non-residents, their lands attached and an order of publication made, the suit is so far pending, before the completion of publication, that depositions taken upon notices posted in pursuance of the statute, before the order for publication had been completely executed, were held to have been taken pending suit.(1)

(1) Lewin v. Dille et al., 17 Mo. 68.

This would seem to be a departure from the general rule that, a party can not be bound until he has been brought into court either by personal service, or constructive notice. Generally the defendant is not in court until publication is complete.

When statute express.

SEC. 55.   Where a statute expressly provides when a suit shall be deemed to be commenced, for a declared purpose, the terms of the statute will control.   So, in California, where the statute provides that a suit shall be deemed to be commenced by the filing of complaint for the purpose of preventing the running of the statute of limitation, the time of the filing of complaint merely shall be a sufficient commencement of suit for that purpose; and no other proceeding in the case is necessary.(1)   The suit, however, must be commenced in good faith.

Where two writs issued.

SEC. 56.   Where a party attempts at law to avoid the running of a statute of limitation, by showing that the first writ was sued out in time for this purpose, it was held necessary to show that the first writ was not only issued, but was returned by the proper officer; and although it was shown that a second writ was issued in the cause, at a date too late to prevent the bar of the statute, and returned served, it was held not sufficient, in the absence of proof that the first writ was returned, to avoid the statute.(2)

Where no writ issued.

SEC. 57.   And so, the filing of a bill in chancery

(1) Sharp v. Maguire, 19 Cal. 577.   (2) Harris v. Woolford, 6 Term
R. (Danf. & E.) 617.

without suing out process thereon, or similarly in case of a cross-bill, where process is necessary to issue, in the absence of any provision of the statute to that effect, will not be regarded as the commencement of a suit. It follows that, in such cases, where a party files a bill in chancery, and neglects to take out process, the statute of limitation still continues to run, and cannot be avoided by showing that a bill was lodged in the clerk's office, or even filed in open court before the time had expired. It is obvious that, although it might remain in that condition for any length of time, there would be no suit pending against the defendant.(1)

Issuance of writ will not relate back.

SEC. 58. If, where process issues at any subsequent time, it should be considered as relating back to the time when the bill was filed, such a doctrine would have the effect of encouraging negligence on the one hand, and of defeating, on the other, the object of the statute of limitation, which was intended to obviate any injustice that might arise from the absence of testimony supposed to have been lost or forgotten through the operation of time. Hence, for the purposes of defense under the statute of limitation, after service in such case, the commencement of the suit will not relate back to the filing of the bill.(2)

Commencement of suit in England.

SEC. 59. It is held, in England, that it is not sufficient to show that a writ was sued out in time, in order to avoid the statute of limitation. The plaintiff

(1) Prindill *v.* Maydwell, 7 B. Mon. 315.   (2) Prindill *v.* Maydwell, 7 B. Mon. 315.

must also show that it was returned, for it is said that there must be some evidence of the intention of the plaintiff to pursue the action, and that, after the writ was sued out, it might be kept in plaintiff's pocket; and, that a record of the return must be made before an alias writ could issue.(1)

When limitation barred.

SEC. 60.   It was held, in Kentucky, where a bill was filed in October, 1830, and subpœna issued and returned, but not served, and where there had been no appearance by defendant, who died in 1831, and no steps to revive the suit were taken until March, 1838, that there was lis pendens between the parties barring the running of the statute.(2)

Where bill required to be filed before subpoena.

SEC. 61.   In those States where the legislatures have prescribed that, before the subpœna shall issue, the bill must be filed with the clerk, and the terms of such statutes are so far mandatory that, the courts are compelled to hold, that the issuing of subpœna without bill previously filed, is nugatory and the writ void, it should be held that lis pendens commences from the filing of the bill.   The statutes now in force in Illinois, Iowa and Texas may be taken as samples of the character of legislation referred to.   It would seem, that where general statutes are the same in terms as lis pendens statutes in States where such statutes are adopted, the former should receive the same construction as the latter.(3)

(1) Harris, qui tam, v. Woolford, 6 Danf. & E. 617; Atwood v. Barr, 7 Mod. 3; Brown v. Babbington, 2 Ld. Raym. 883.

(2) Lytle's Exrs. v. Pope's Admr., 11 B. Mon. 309.

(3) Hodgen et al. v. Guttery, 58 Ill. 435; Board, etc., v. T. & P. R'y Co., 46 Tex. 326; Haverly v. Alcott, 57 Iowa, 173.

Statute of Illinois

SEC. 62.   The fourth section of the chancery act of the State of Illinois provides that, "the mode of commencing suits in chancery shall be by filing a bill of complaint with the clerk of the proper court, setting forth the nature of the complaint."(1)   That statute has been in force for over forty years, having been embraced in the revision of 1845, and yet the Supreme Court of that State have not decided until recently in any case where the question was necessary to the decision of the cause, what construction should be placed upon it, as to the commencement of lis pendens.   They had held that a subpœna issued under the statute, without the previous filing of a bill, is absolutely void, and should be quashed.(2) They had, in numerous decisions, used language which seemed to imply that the true construction of that statute is that lis pendens commences at the time the bill is filed with the clerk.   In one case they had said, "the bill itself is sufficient notice to all the world so as to defeat any transfer subsequent to its filing."   In other cases they had used language equally as pointed upon this question.   The bar of the State and the judges of the circuit courts had, with great unanimity, been of the opinion that the rule of lis pendens in the State of Illinois was, that it commenced from the filing of the bill, and not from the service of the subpœna upon the defendant thereafter.   No case is found in the judicial history of the State where any other rule was intimated or declared.   But in a recent case the Supreme Court of that State have held that,

(1) Hurd's R. 'S. of Ill., 1877, p. 184, (Sec. 4, Ch. 22.)

(2) Hodgen et al. v. Guttery, 58 Ill. 435.

there is no lis pendens in chancery in that State until
service of subpœna after bill filed.(1)

Statute of Texas.

SEC. 63. The statute in force in the State of Texas,
upon the question of the commencement of suits in
chancery, provides that "all civil suits in the District
and County Courts shall be commenced by petition
filed in the office of the clerk of such court."

Under this statute, the Supreme Court of that State
have intimated that the statute should be construed
that, as to strangers, lis pendens commences from the
filing of the bill.

The court say: "It may, however, be well questioned whether there was a lis pendens, such as
operated as constructive notice of the purchase, at
the time these bonds were transferred. The determination of this point depends upon whether lis pendens begins from the filing of the petition or the service
of the citation." After stating the rule as laid down
by Chancellor Kent in Murray *v.* Ballou, the court
proceed: "It should be observed, however, that in
some of the courts, where it is held that constructive
notice of lis pendens dates from the service of the subpœna and filing of the bill, the suit or action is begun by
issuing the subpœna or other process, and not, as with
us, by the filing of the petition or bill setting forth
the cause of action. Hence, a stranger to the action
would have an opportunity of informing himself of
the existence and nature of the suit by the filing of
the bill, which would not be afforded merely by the
service of a subpœna. And it may be that public

(1) Grant et al. *v.* Bennett et al., 96 Ill. 513.

policy, from which this rule springs, should give it effect with us from the filing of the suit."(1)

Simplification of rule.

SEC. 64.   To hold that such statutes as those of Illinois, Iowa and Texas should be construed to mean that, lis pendens commences from the filing of the bill, would greatly simplify the law.   Under that rule, lis pendens, as to all defendants, would commence at the same time; whereas under the common law rule, as we have seen, there may be a different lis pendens as to every defendant.

Reasons for the rule as above.

SEC. 65.   We have seen that no rule of lis pendens should be adopted which would tend to the encouragement of fraud.(2)   It is quite manifest, that if the commencement of lis pendens were postponed, where the bill is required to be filed before the service of process, until after service, great opportunity would be afforded defendants to alienate the property which is the subject matter of the suit, before service.   Upon the filing of the bill, it becomes a record, as permanent, as open to inspection, as much the subject of notice to the whole world, as any other record.   If the suit involves the title to real estate, the allegations of the bill pass at once into abstracts showing the condition of title, and in most instances the public press notices the subject matter which is involved in suits commenced in courts.   The presumption that the public are attentive to proceedings in the courts of record, in these modern times, has passed from presumption to fact.   Opportunity, therefore, under the common law

(1) Board, etc., *v.* Texas & Pacific   (2) Sec. 16, *ante.*
R. W. Co., 46 Tex. 326-7.

rule, is given a defendant, without necessarily involving moral turpitude, on his part, to convey the subject
matter of litigation to a purchaser against whom it
can not be proven that he had actual knowledge of
the suit. This may occur in various ways. Officers
may neglect to promptly serve process, or the necessary delay of making publication, so as to secure completed service, gives ample time for the disposition of
the property involved. If the property in suit is personal, a transfer and delivery beyond the limits of the
State, or even within the State, before service or
completed publication, would defeat the jurisdiction
of the court.(1)

No reason for postponement to service.

Sec. 66. The making the bill a full record previous
to the issuance of process, avoids the force of the
reason for the postponement of the commencement of
lis pendens until service. That reason is far from
satisfactory, where the writ is liable to precede the
filing of the bill; for, as we have seen, service of
the process gives no intimation whatever to strangers,
or even to the defendant himself, as to what precise
property is involved, and the alleged reason that
conscientious scruples will impel the defendant to a
disclosure to his purchaser of the fact of the pendency
of the suit and of the property involved therein, have
been found, in practice, not to justify the presumption. By the filing of the bill the purchaser is afforded
an equal opportunity to know the contents of it, and
the scope of the litigation, as the defendant himself.

(1) The practice of suppressing
bills in the clerk's office before service, would seem to warrant the conclusion that the rule leading to such
a practice is wrong.

He is much more likely to avail himself of that opportunity, and learn the fact and what the bill involves before service, than he would be from the service, if no bill were filed until after service.

Hence, the reason for postponement of the taking effect of lis pendens until after the service of the subpœna upon the defendant ceases to have force, where the bill from the date of filing becomes a matter of public record. When the reason of a law ceases to exist, the law itself ceases; for reason is the soul of the law. *Cessante ratione legis cessat ipsa lex.*(1)

The Iowa statute.

SEC. 67. In the case of Haverly *v.* Alcott,(2) the Supreme Court of Iowa has decided "that third persons are charged with notice of the pendency of the action when a petition has been filed" with the clerk; that "notice of the pendency of an action is imparted by the filing of the petition."

Section 2628 of the Code, which the court construes or interprets in this decision, is as follows: "When a petition has been filed affecting real estate, the action is pending so as to charge third persons with notice of its pendency: and while pending no interest can be acquired by third persons in the subject matter thereof, as against the plaintiff's title." In that case the petition was filed July 3, 1879. The defendant Alcott and wife conveyed to Landis, July 16; Landis conveyed to Edmundson, who was an innocent purchaser for value and had no knowledge of the suit, July 18th. Service of process was not made until after this last conveyance. The latter was held bound by the lis pendens.

(1) Broom's Legal Maxims, 113.   (2) Haverly *v.* Alcott, 57 Iowa, 173-4.

The court should exercise discretion.

Sec. 68. We have seen that the doctrine of lis pendens rests solely upon necessity.(1) It is, therefore, a subject over which the courts are vested with greater discretion and power, in the adoption of the rule, than upon other questions. It is a law of self-preservation for the courts, and in the absence of mandatory directions from the legislative department, they are compelled, in the interest of self-preservation and their own integrity and power over their own decrees and judgments, to adopt such a rule as will be conservative of these objects.

Question of fact sometimes involved.

Sec. 69. In determining at what time a suit commences to pend as to strangers, it often becomes the duty of the court to ascertain facts, as well as to apply the law. We have seen that the commencement of notice lis pendens is that point of time at which the effect of the suit commenced attaches to the subject matter of litigation.(2) It often becomes necessary to determine, as a fact, whether the claimant of the property involved, at and before that point of time, had acquired a complete or established equitable or legal right to the property. Whether he should be classed as an ante litem claimant, or a pendente lite purchaser, may depend upon that fact.

A writ of error a new lis pendens.

Sec. 70. In all cases where judgments and decrees have been rendered, and neither appealed from nor superseded, and a writ of error is afterwards sued out, the writ of error is a new suit, and a new lis pendens

(1) *Ante*, Sec. 14.   (2) Sec. 2, *ante*.

commences to run. The lis pendens of the writ of error, however, will not relate back to the time of the rendition of the judgment or decree.(1)

Under lis pendens statute.

SEC. 71. As we shall see hereafter, in States where lis pendens statutes are in force, the commencement of lis pendens, so far as relates to suits affecting real estate, is fixed by filing a notice of lis pendens in some public office designated by statute, or recording the same, which notice is required to give full information in regard to the character and identity of the suit.(2)

No lis pendens until bill filed.

SEC. 72. But in analogy with the common law rule which required the bill on file, as well as the service of subpœna in order to constitute lis pendens, so under lis pendens statutes the notice is not effective to create valid lis pendens until the bill or petition is filed.(3)

Common law authorities not uniform.

SEC. 73. The common law authorities, as to when notice lis pendens in suits in chancery commences, are by no means uniform in holding that lis pendens does not commence until subpœna is served after bill filed. Thus, in the case of Drew v. Lord Norbury, where, in 1774, certain creditors filed a bill against certain persons interested in lands of a deceased testator, of whom B. was one of the defendants, to subject

(1) Ludlow's Heirs v. Kidd's Exrs. et al., 3 Ohio, 541; Sec. 40, *ante.*

(2) Sec. 307, *post.*

(3) Bensley v. The Mountain Lake Water Co., 13 Cal. 307; Corwin v. Bensley, 43 Cal. 263; Arnold v. Casner, 22 W. Va. 459 ; Burroughs v. Reiger et al., 12 How. Pr. R. 171; Tate v. Jordan, 3 Abbott Pr. R. 392; Sec. 314, *post.*

the property to sale for satisfaction of the debts of the estate; B. never appeared and there was no evidence, that he was ever served with subpœna until 1783, when an amended bill was filed. In 1782 certain leases of the property were made and recorded. There was a decree for an account and sale of the lands in 1784. It was held that, the suit was lis pendens before the service of the subpœna on B., who was a necessary defendant, and that those holding under the lessees were pendente lite purchasers.(1)

Proof of publication.

Sec. 74. The certificate of the printer or publisher of a newspaper, as to the fact of publication, and as to the time when it was completed, is not the only evidence competent to prove that fact. The newspaper containing the publication, accompanied by parol evidence as to the publication having been in fact made, are, also, competent evidence. Where the publication is made in pursuance of an order of court, recited in the notice, the order should also be produced.(2)

In Pierce v. Carleton, 12 Ill. 358, and in subsequent cases in that State, it has been ruled, that parol evidence may be introduced, in connection with the certificate of the publisher of a paper, to establish the fact of publication, and the pendency of the suit and that it will be presumed in the Supreme Court, in the absence of a showing in the record to the contrary, that that was done.

Continuous for some purposes until decree executed.

Sec. 75. But although it is true, in a general sense,

(1) Drew v. Lord Norbury, 9   (2) Chandron v. Magee, 8 Ala. 573;
Irish Eq. R. 171.   Haywood v. Collins et al., 60 Ill. 332.

that lis pendens ceases with the rendition of judgment or entry of final decree, yet, in the case of a
foreclosure of a mortgage on real estate, it cannot be
said that lis pendens ceases upon the making of the
master's deed after sale under the decree. Where
something remains to be done by the court, in the
execution of its judgments and decrees, other than
can be done without order of court, by the merely
ministerial officers of the court, lis pendens continues
until the decree is executed. So, in the case of the
foreclosure of a mortgage, it continues until the purchaser has been put into possession of the property.
Until then the power of the court is not *functus
officio*.(1)   It seems that, in such cases, the whole public is a party to the decree, because it is of a public
nature, and of record, of which all persons are bound
to take notice.(2)

Effect of orders of dismissal in chancery.

SEC. 76.   A dismissal of a libel for divorce in Massachusetts, stands on the same footing as the dismissal
of a bill in equity, and unless it appears on its face to
be made " without prejudice," will be a bar to another
libel for the same cause.(3)   Where the plaintiff did
not in his bill show an interest or liability, requiring
the aid or interference of a court of equity, and it was
dismissed on that ground, he will be estopped from
bringing a new bill stating matters sufficient to
authorize the action of the court.(4)   If a bill does
not bring before the court all the parties necessary for

(1) Lomax Dig. 534.
(2) Jackson *v.* Warren, 32 Ill.
340; Sugden on Vendors, 281,
285.

(3) Thurston   *v.* Thurston, 99
Mass. 39.
(4) Gist *v.* Davis, 2 Hill Ch.(S.C.)
*335.

a proper determination of the suit, but the bill, instead of being dismissed on that account, is dismissed *for want of equity*, this is a bar to any future bill seeking relief.(1) A bill to redeem was filed. The defendant having answered, the plaintiff failed to reply, and, without the knowledge of the defendant, dismissed the suit. The defendant afterwards had judgment entered in his favor for costs. It was held, the bill being dismissed without any restriction, that this was a judgment on its merits, and as such it was a bar to any future bill for the same cause.(2) If a bill by a vendor seeking a specific performance of a contract to purchase, be dismissed on account of some defect in his title, the doors of courts of equity are, and ought to be, forever closed upon him, though he may afterwards be able to make a good title. If the court intended to grant the complainant further time, it should have continued the cause, and thereby have given him an opportunity to complete his title, or should have dismissed the bill without prejudice.

Where order of dismissal final, lis pendens conclusive.

SEC. 77. It follows as a necessary conclusion from the relation which lis pendens bears to the final judgment or decree; and, may be stated as a general rule, that wherever the dismissal of a bill in chancery may be set up in bar for the same cause of action, the lis pendens becomes conclusive upon the property involved. Mr. Freeman, in his work on Judgments, says: "The dismissal of a bill in chancery stands nearly on the same footing as a judgment at law, and will be presumed to be a final and conclusive adjudi-

---

(1) Curtis *v.* Trustees of Bardstown, 6 J. J. Marsh. 536.

(2) Barrowscale *v.* Tuttle, 5 Allen, 377.

cation on the merits, whether they were or were not heard and determined, unless the contrary appears on the face of the pleadings, or in the decree of the court.(1)   Only one case has come under my observation, in which the decree dismissing a bill has not been considered as necessarily final and conclusive,(2) while the cases are numerous sustaining the view that, such dismissal is a bar to any subsequent bill, unless it appears on the record to have been made without prejudice, or otherwise not on the merits.(3)   If in fact a decree be rendered dismissing a bill, because of some defect in the pleadings, or for want of jurisdiction, or because complainant has an adequate remedy at law, or on any other ground, not involving the merits, it is the general practice, both in England and in the United States, to state in the decree that the dismissal is without prejudice; and the omission of these words is an error which will be corrected upon appeal.   In case it dismisses the bill generally, the right of the vendor to compel a specific performance is thereby conclusively and *perpetually* negatived.(4) A section of the law of the United States in relation to patents provides that, where two patents interfere, any person interested may apply in equity, on notice to the adverse parties, and the court may *adjudge and declare* either of the *patents void* in whole or in part, or *inoperative and invalid* in any particular part of the United States.(5)   The effect of a decree entered, gen-

(1) Smith's Leading Cases, vol. 2, p. 667; Wilcox v. Balger, 6 Ohio, 406.
(2) Wright v. DeKlyne, 1 Pet. C. C. 199.
(3) Kelsey v. Murphy, 26 Penn. St. 78; Perine v. Dunn, 3 Johns. Ch. 508; Neafie v. Neafie, 7 Johns Ch. 1; Foote v. Gibbs, 1 Gray, 412; Parish v. Ferris, 2 Black, U. S. 606; Durant v. Essex Co., 7 Wall. 107.
(4) Hepburn et al. v. Dundas, 1 Wheat. 179.
(5) Patent Act 1836, 5 U. S. Stat. at Large, 122.

erally dismissing a bill brought before the court under this act, is not equivalent to a judicial declaration that the patent of the complainant is either inoperative or void. In announcing this conclusion, the court, after suggesting that the dismissal may have been ordered because the plaintiff did not show that defendant violated his rights, or because the defendant may have shown a license from the plaintiff, said judgment or decree under this statute cannot be accepted as determining that point, unless it be direct and affirmative in terms, and in the words of the statute. The court must *adjudge* the patent *void* in whole or in part, or inoperative and invalid in some particular part of the United States. Had the decree asserted the interference of the patents, and declared either of them void, that decree would have been conclusive.

When lis pendens ends.

SEC. 78. The general rule is that notice of lis pendens ends with the final decree in chancery or judgment at law,(1) but the decree or judgment must be final.

They must be of such a character as puts a conclusion to the matters in question in the suit. Interlocutory decrees or orders cannot have that effect, although they may purport to settle the rights of the parties. The court, however, still would have power to modify or vacate them, and for all purposes of notice or binding force, lis pendens will continue, notwithstanding such orders or decrees. The principal ground upon

(1) Newland on Cont. 507; Worsley v. Scarborough, 3 Atk. 392; 1 Ch. Cas. 35; see also, Gore v. Stacpoole, 1 Dow. 30; Kinsman v. Kinsman, 1 Russ. & Mylne, 617; Price v. White, 1 Bailey's Eq. (S. C.) 233; Blake v. Heyward, 1 Bailey's Eq. (S. C.) 208; Turner v. Crebill, 1 Ohio, 174.

which this rule is based, so far as relates to the rights or interests of third parties, is, that the public have cognizance of what is taking place in courts of record, within their jurisdictions. When, therefore, the court ceases to act in a cause, the reasons requiring vigilance cease to exist. While the final judgments and decrees are not, after their rendition, notice lis pendens, they still continue, however, to be notice of their contents as matters of record, and binding upon the property involved as judgments and decrees. Where an appeal is prayed and allowed, as a part of the judgment or decree, and the terms of the appeal are complied with by the appellant, the judgment or decree becomes suspended, and lis pendens is continued.

When, however, the final judgment or decree is rendered by the appellate court or the trial court, upon a remand of the cause, lis pendens ends. So, also, if a writ of error be made a supersedeas by terms prescribed while the court retained jurisdiction, lis pendens will, in like manner, continue until final judgment or decree.

If, however, no appeal from the judgment or decree in the trial court shall be perfected, and no writ of error be sued out, so as to be a stay of execution of the judgment or decree, lis pendens ends at the time of the judgment or decree in the trial court.

CHAPTER V.

Whether applicable to personal property.

SEC. 79. In many cases the courts have intimated grave doubts as to the propriety of applying the doctrine of lis pendens to personal property of any character. These have ordinarily been cases where the property involved has fallen within the conceded exception to the general rule; and the decision of the question was not necessary, or involved in the disposition of the particular case. Thus, in Winston v. Westfeldt,(1) where the property involved

(1) Winston v. Westfeldt, 22 Ala. 760.

As an illustration of the loose manner in which the subject of lis pendens is often treated by the courts, the case of Miles v. Lefi, 60 Iowa, 168, is an example. The court decided the case upon the question of estoppel, as effective to destroy the lis pendens of the case. It was a case where the plaintiff had purchased the property involved in the suit, at a chattel mortgage sale, at which the defendant was present and also purchasing property other than that in question. It appears he represented and advised the plaintiff to make the purchase, and

was commercial paper, which is a generally conceded exception to the rule, the Supreme Court of Alabama went beyond the requirements of this particular case, and argued that Lord Bacon's ordinance can only be properly construed to apply to real estate, contending that the use of the word "conveyance,"(1) in that ordinance, necessarily compels that conclusion. To sustain this position, the court, in that case, cites Powell on Mortgages, in saying, "There is no case in which equity has determined the property in goods to be affected by means of a lis pendens, when possession is the principal evidence of ownership, as of personal chattels."(2)

In the case of Chase v. Searle, the Supreme Court of New Hampshire approved the general conclusions of the court in Winston v. Westfeldt.(3)   The New Hampshire case was a creditor's bill, for the discovery of equitable assets, in which there was no receiver, and no specific allegations as to particular property. There are doubtless other cases in the books, where a doubt is cast upon the propriety of applying the rule lis pendens to chattel property of any character, unless the property is in the custody of the court in some way.

afterwards purchased the same property at an execution sale, which could have no force, except upon the hypothesis that the chattel mortgage sale was invalid. Under these circumstances he was held to be estopped. The court, however, after deciding all there was in the case to decide, adds, "the doctrine of lis pendens has no application to personal property." This language was clearly *obiter dictum*, and can not be regarded as a binding declaration of the court in the case. As we have seen, the weight of authority is very largely the other way, and the declaration of the Iowa court is the exception rather than the rule.

(1) Sec. 1, *ante.*
(2) 2 Powell on Mort. 618.
(3) Chase v. Searle, 45 N. H. 517.

English authorities.

SEC. 80.   In order to reach a proper conclusion with respect to some general rule, or rules, as to the application of the doctrine, to chattel property, a more particular review of the authorities would seem proper. It may be remarked, in passing, however, that the argument, that Lord Bacon's rule when framed does not seem, by its terms, to have been intended to apply to chattels — should not be conclusive of the question; for while the rule originated with Lord Bacon, the reason and necessity for its adoption, lying back of the rule itself, would of themselves have established the doctrine, had Lord Bacon never drafted the ordinance — and, the same rationality and necessity would have fixed the extent and scope of its application.   This necessity is no more nor less than the demand of a sound public policy—that an application of the rule be made, whereby the least detriment and the greatest good will result to the general public.

One of the earliest English cases bearing upon the question is that of Taylor v. Jones, decided by Lord Hardwicke in 1743.   It was a bill filed by creditors to reach certain stocks of the defendant debtor, which were vested in trustees, for the benefit of his wife and children, after the death of the debtor.   The learned Chancellor said: " I must decree for the plaintiffs, the creditors, against the wife and children; for though I have always great compassion for wife and children; yet on the other side, it is possible if creditors should not have their debts, their wives and children might be reduced to want."(1)

In the case of King v. Dupine, where it was sought

(1) Taylor v. Jones, 2 Atk. 600.

by a creditor to reach annuities of a debtor, defendant, vested in trustees, by a bill in chancery, Lord Hardwicke, again, subjected the annuities to the payment of the debt, although orders had been given to third persons for the annuity fund pending the bill.(1)

The case of Edgell v. Haywood was a creditor's bill, and involved chattels. The same learned Chancellor, in deciding the case, said: "After a bill brought, and lis pendens created as to this thing, such assignment could not prevail."(2)

In the case of Self v. Madox et al., Madox had been decreed to pay the plaintiff a sum of money, or deliver up possession of a house and lands. Madox, pending the suit, assigned his interest to a creditor. The report states that, the court decreed the possession of the house and lands to be delivered to the plaintiff, without regard had to this conveyance; and the case of Goldson and Gardiner, in 1680, was cited, where the court had made the like decree in the case of a conveyance made by the father to the son prior to the decree, but pending the suit.(3) In Gaskell v. Durdin, Lord Manners said: "The rule of this court undoubtedly is, that any interest acquired in the subject matter of a suit, pending the suit, is so far considered a nullity that it cannot avail against the plaintiff's title; and if this rule were not attended to there would be no end to any suit; the justice of this court would be evaded, and great hardship and incon-

(1) King v. Dupine, 2 Atk. 603–4, note (2).

(2) Edgell v. Haywood, 3 Atk. 352.

(3) Self v. Madox, 1 Vern. 459. In Irvin v. White, 7 Vesey, 413,

Lord Eldon expressed a doubt whether lis pendens applies to personal property, and later, in Hood v. Aston, 1 Russ. 412, he again expressed himself in like manner.

venience to the suitor necessarily introduced. It is extremely difficult to draw any line, and very danger- ous to allow of the rule being frittered away by excep- tions."(1) The case of Horn v Horn, was a creditor's bill, after judgment and Fi. Fa. returned nulla bona, to reach public stocks in the name of trustees. The body of the defendant debtor had been taken on a Ca. Sa. after the bill was filed. Lord Hardwicke, in deciding the case, held, that where there is an equitable demand and the party is taken in execution on a decree, this court will notwithstanding issue all its process against his lands and tenements and effects, and the body being detained is not in this court a satisfaction; the reason is, because he is detained for the contempt; but at law the detaining of the body is a satisfaction, and you cannot afterwards take his goods. This bill is not founded on an original equitable demand, but is brought in order that this court may extend its power to reach what the common law cannot. The stock to be sure is not liable on the Fi. Fa., but supposing it had been in the defendant's own name, the taking his person in custody had certainly protected the stock. This is matter merely at law, and the plaintiff has taken defendant's body by Ca. Sa. after the bill was filed.(2) The court dismissed the bill. This case

(1) Gaskell *v.* Durdin, 2 Ball. & B. atty, 169.

(2) Horn *v.* Horn, 1 Ambler, 79. The cases of Dundas *v.* Deutens, 2 Cox, 240 (more fully reported in 1 Vesey, Jr. 196), M'Carthy *v.* Goold; 1 Ball. & Beatty, 390, and Grogan *v.* Cooke, 2 Ball. & Beatty, 233, are cited as in conflict with Horn *v.* Horn, *ante.* In Grogan *v.* Cooke, *ante,* Lord Thurlow is reported as

saying: "The opinion in Horn *v.* Horn is anomalous and unfounded, that forty such opinions would not satisfy me."

In Dundas *v.* Deutens, *ante,* it appears that the case of Horn *v.* Horn was cited to the court, by counsel for the plaintiff, and, that upon reading the case Lord Thur- low observed "that there was noth- ing in the case applicable; but only

was criticised by Lord Thurlow in Dundas v. Deutens, and by Lord Manners in McCarthy v Goold,(1) but Lord Ellenborough, in the case of Scott v. Scholey,(2) upon the same question of the power of the chancery court, held the same view as Lord Hardwicke. Chancellor Kent, in the case of Reade v. Livingston, referring to the opinion of Lord Thurlow in the case of Dundas v. Deutens, said: "A case so uncertain and variously reported can be of no material use or authority."(3)   Much of the confusion and apparent conflict in these cases has clearly arisen from want of proper attention to the precise question which Lord Hardwicke decided. In that case the bill was dismissed, as appears from the opinion above, on the ground that the plaintiff, having taken a Ca. Sa., upon his judgment at law, and caused the debtor to be arrested on it, it was a satisfaction at law, and a court of chancery would not aid the plaintiff beyond his legal rights. The court, though the question was not necessarily involved in the decision of the case, adds,

the *nota bene* at the bottom, which only contained the private opinion of the reporter." (See Dundas v. Deutens, 1 Vesey, Jr. 197, note 1).

In the case of M'Carthy v. Goold, *ante*, Lord Manners is reported as saying : " I listened very attentively to Lord Thurlow in the case of Dundas v. Deutens, which was heard upon decree, and not upon motion, and he was clearly of opinion that *choses in action*, of which description is stocks, could not be reached by the process of this court."

In Otley, Admx. v. Lines et al., 7 Price's Exch. R. 274, Baron Graham is reported as saying : " I own the determination of the case of Edgell v. Haywood very much surprised me. * * * I never recollect an instance of that decision having been followed as an authority in a court of equity in point of practice by the adoption of a proceeding so exceedingly strong. The authority of Lord Hardwicke is very great, and any case founded upon it requires some answer."

(1) M'Carthy v. Goold, 1 Ball. & Beatty, 389.

(2) Scott v. Scholey, 8 East. R. 467.

(3) Reade v. Livingston, 3 Johns. Ch. R. 490.

that, if the arrest had been made in the chancery case, upon its process, the arrest would not have been a satisfaction of the debt, and the court would not have retained the bill. The terms of the trusteeship, or trust, does not seem to have been reached in the decision of the case. It was upon this latter question that the adverse criticisms in Dundas *v.* Deutens,(1) M'Carthy *v.* Goold, and Grogan *v.* Crooke,(2) seem to have proceeded. It may be added, also, that when these subsequent cases, adverse to the views of Lord Hardwicke, as to the power of the court of chancery— in 1790—the English Bankrupt Laws had been established, after which it became less necessary to maintain the general power of the court of chancery over this species of property, as the policy of the bankrupt law was adverse to special liens.

Authorities in this country.

Sec. 81.   On the other hand, the views expressed by Lords Hardwicke and Ellenborough have been generally adopted in this country. In Scudder *v.* Van Amburg et al., a creditor's bill had been filed. The judgment debtor sold pendente lite to Van Amburg. A supplemental bill was afterwards filed. No receiver had been appointed, and the question was, on the effect of the filing of the bill as notice. It was held, that the lis pendens operated as constructive notice to Van Amburg, the pendente lite purchaser, and defendant to the supplemental bill; and that he could not hold the furniture, which was the subject of litigation, as against a judgment creditor of his vendor;

(1) Dundas *v.* Deutens, 1 Vesey,   Beatty, 389; Grogan *v.* Cooke, 2
Jr. 196; 2 Cox, 240.   Ball. & Beatty, 233.
    (2) M'Carthy *v.* Goold, 1 Ball. &

and that the creditor, by the bill, acquired a lien from the moment of the filing of the bill.(1) Hadden et al. v. Sprader et al. was a creditor's bill, which alleged that the debtor, Davis, had fraudulently conveyed to Hadden. The property consisted of choses in action, money and stocks; and pending the bill, assignments were made of the property involved, or some of it.(2) Judge Woodworth, in a very able opinion concurred in by Chief Justice Spencer, reviewed all of the English authorities, followed the cases of Taylor v. Jones;(3) Horn v. Horn;(4) Patridge v. Gopp;(5) and Scott v. Scholey,(6) and reached the conclusion that after the filing of the bill, and service of the subpœna, the trustee would be affected with notice, and would not pass title to a purchaser from him pendente lite. The adverse cases of Dundas v. Deutens;(7) Caillard v. Eastwick,(8) and Lord Eldon's decisions in 9th Vesey, 369,(9) and 10th Vesey, 368,(10) are regarded as *dicta*. The like view was taken by Chancellor Walworth, in the case of Edmunton v. Lyne,(11) and again in Corning et al. v. White,(12) and Farnham v. Campbell.(13) In the latter case, the court refers to Hadden et al. v. Spader et al., and approves of it as right, independent of the statute of the State then in force. The same views are held in the

(1) Scudder v. Van Amburg et al., 4 Edw'd Ch. 31.

(2) Hadden Impl. etc. v. Sprader et al., 20 Johns. R. 553.

(3) Taylor v. Jones, 2 Atk. 600.

(4) Horn v. Horn, 1 Ambler, 79.

(5) Patridge v. Gopp, 1 Ambler, 596.

(6) Scott v. Scholey, 8 East. 435.

(7) Dundas v. Deutens, 1 Vesey Jr. 196; 2 Cox, 240.

(8) Caillard v. Eastwick, 2 Anst. 381.

(9) Rich v. Cockell, 9 Vesey, 369.

(10) Rider v. Kidder, 10 Vesey, 368.

(11) Edmunton v. Lyne, 1 Paige Ch. R. 640.

(12) Corning et al. v. White, 2 Paige Ch. R. 567.

(13) Farnham v. Campbell, 10 Paige Ch. R. 601.

case of Brinkerhoff *v.* Brown.(1)   The case of
Leitch *v.* Wells(2) involved bank stock, in the name

(1) Brinkerhoff *v.* Brown, 4 Johns. Ch. 671.

(2) Leitch *v.* Wells, 48 Barbour, 649 to 653.

The opinion in this case is deemed of such practical utility and importance that I subjoin the following extract from it:

"It is, therefore, clear that the express company could not acquire the title, legal or equitable, to the Tompkins Co. bank stock against these plaintiffs; because, not only was the action above mentioned pending when it took the assignment of the stock, but the complaint which had been filed and served, specifically claimed that stock as a part of the trust fund; and as to that stock, the decision in the case, which held that the stock vested in and belonging to the plaintiffs, concluded the express company.

It is not so perfectly clear in regard to the seventy-three shares in the Bank of Syracuse; for at the time of the assignment of it to the express company, although the action was pending, the complaint did not specifically claim it as equitably belonging to the plaintiffs. But I have come to the conclusion that the action, as it then stood, was notice to the express company as to anything which was part of the trust between the plaintiffs and John Kellogg, on account of which the action was commenced, whether specifically stated or not, provided it could be brought into that action as constituting part of the trust. And yet it must be conceded that there is no lis pendens, so as to charge strangers, until after the filing of the bill or complaint, as well as the service of the subpœna or summons, upon the defendant. (Anonymous case, 1 Vern. 318; Supplement to Vesey, Jr., Vol. I, 284; Hayden *v.* Bucklin, 9 Paige, 514, 515; Bouvier's Law Dic., title Lis Pendens, 2.)

I have said that the original complaint in that action did not specifically claim the shares of stock in the Bank of Syracuse; but it did claim among other things, that in or about the year 1849, John Kellogg received from Leitch his co-executor, 300 shares of the capital stock of the Bank of Syracuse; 100 shares of the Onondaga County bank; 127 shares of the Tompkins County bank; together with other property belonging to the estate of Daniel Kellogg. That afterwards he had transferred the same to his wife, without consideration, and for the purpose of defrauding the plaintiffs. The complaint also averred that the plaintiffs were not informed whether the whole of said legacy of $25,000 was ever set apart and invested by the executors as directed by the will; but that they were informed and believed that the 127 shares of the Tompkins County bank were set apart as a portion of the said legacy, and so kept till transferred to his wife as aforesaid. It is also claimed that he was insolvent, but that he had the charge and control of a large amount of property held ostensibly

of trustees, and the court held that the pendency of
the bill was notice and binding upon Kellogg who re-

in the name of his wife, consisting
of bank stocks, bonds and mortgages, and real estate amply sufficient to satisfy the legacy and the
interest and income thereof; and
that the same was a portion of the
estate of Daniel Kellogg, etc. The
complaint demanded an account by
John Kellogg of his trust; and also
an account by his wife of the money,
choses in action, or other property
then in her hands, being the proceeds of the estate of Daniel Kellogg; and that she be compelled to
convey to the plaintiffs a sufficient
sum, or amount, to make up any de-
ficiency; and that John Kellogg be
removed from his trusteeship, and
for further relief.

As between the plaintiffs in that
suit and John Kellogg and his wife,
it was not necessary to insert in the
supplemental complaint the allegations that the Syracuse Bank stock
was also a trust, as part of the fund
of $25,000. In the original com-
plaint, enough had been alleged to
require John Kellogg and his wife
to account as to all things concerning the original legacy of $25,000,
and to enable the plaintiffs to follow it through any mutations or
changes which had occurred, unless it had become the property of
a bona fide owner; and if upon the
accounting in that action it appeared that the seventy-three shares
had become a trust fund, then,
without any amendment of the original complaint, (which contained a
general prayer for relief,) the court
would have given the same judg-

ment that it did, to-wit, that it belonged in equity to the plaintiffs,
and was vested in them at the
death of their mother.

It was not therefore a collateral
matter, but was within the original
issue, and was really as much a part
of the subject in issue then, as it
was afterwards under the supplemental complaint. And the far-
thest that any case has gone
(which has come to my knowledge,)
in deciding that a lis pendens is not
notice to a stranger, who becomes
a purchaser of personal estate, in
good faith, and for valuable consideration, during the continuation of
the action, is that of Worsley v.
The Lord of Scarborough, (3 Atk.
392,) where, while it is expressly
held that all persons who purchase
a right in litigation are bound to
take notice of what is transacting
there, and are bound by the result,
it is said, 'Thirdly : no case has
gone so far, and it would be inconsistent if, where money is received
upon an estate, and there is a question depending in this court upon
the right of, or about that money,
but no question relating to the estate upon which it is received, but
is wholly a collateral matter, that a
purchaser of the estate, pending
that suit, should be affected with
notice, by such implication as the
law creates by the pendency of a
suit.' (And see Vesey's Supplement, 284; Self v. Madox, 1 Vern.
459.) And it is quite as reasonable
that a person who purchases pendente lite a chose in action not

ceived stock from Leitch pending the suit, and that
the title to the stock was acquired subject to the determination of the pending suit. In Blake v. Bigelow
et al.(1) the Supreme Court of Georgia, held, that
a specific lien was acquired upon equitable assets by
the commencement of a suit in equity. And so the
Supreme Court of Indiana held in The Bank of the
United States et al. v. Burke et al.(2)   Bolling
v. Carter et al.(3) was a bill filed by Carter &
Womack against Skanes, to foreclose an unrecorded

negotiable, (and when a purchaser
ordinarily has to look to his vendor
as his security for title,) which is
in litigation in the action, should
carefully inquire into the right of
his vendor or assignor, as it would
be to require of a cestui que trust,
who commences a suit to recover
the trust fund, that he should know
and set out with precision, in his
complaint, the changes which his
trustee has fraudulently made of
the trust fund. It is sufficient that
he commences his suit to recover
the fund, and sets out enough to
enable those who desire to do so,
to ascertain how far the litigation
may extend; and what property, or
rights to property, may be involved
in the decision. All this was done
in that action, and it was the duty
of the express company, as between
it and the plaintiffs, to learn what
were the real rights of Mrs. Kellogg to the stock which she assigned
to it. And it will be recollected
that in the action against Kellogg
and wife, there was no dispute
about the legacy of $25,000, nor but
that the mother and the present
plaintiffs were entitled thereto; nor

but that it came to the hands of
John Kellogg in some form; nor
but that he was responsible for it;
but the real and only issue under
the original complaint, was what
he had done with the fund, and
how invested it; and to what property or persons could the plaintiffs
resort for its recovery.

The express company was also
bound to take notice that the action
was brought to remove John Kellogg as trustee, and for an accounting, and that he could not, therefore, while the action was pending,
dispose of the trust fund, and was
bound to inquire into the equities
of himself and wife. And there is
the more reason why it should be
so, as the loans, to secure which the
notes were given, and the stock assigned, were made to him. (Murray v. Ballou, and Murray v. Lylburn, *supra*.")

(1) Blake v. Bigelow et al., 5 Ga.
439.

(2) The Bank of the United States
v. Burke et al., 4 Blackf. 144.

(3) Bolling v. Carter et al., 9 Ala.
921.

chattel mortgage, made by defendant upon a slave, and which had been foreclosed, and a decree of foreclosure entered. Pending the suit, Skanes made a second mortgage to Bolling, and upon this latter mortgage a sale was made, and Bolling claimed title under it. The court held that the property was subject to the decree, by virtue of notice lis pendens of the suit, saying, "It would be impossible, in the nature of things, after the omission to register the mortgage, to give notice so general that all the world should know it, and unless the suit affected the title in the possession of Skanes it would at all times be in his power to defeat the mortgage by sale to another." The court refers, disapprovingly, to Newman v. Chapman,(1) so far as relates to the conclusions of the court, as to the property involved in that suit. The Supreme Court of Mississippi(2) in the case of McCutchen et al. v. Miller, which involved the title to slaves, sold pendente lite to Miller, while in the State of Louisiana, gave the subject of the application of the doctrine of lis pendens to chattels careful consideration, and Justice Fisher, in delivering the majority opinion of the court, says: " The rule had its origin in controversies touching real estate; but it may be conceded, that at this day it applies with equal force to controversies in regard to personal property." The able dissenting opinion of Justice Handy is in accord with the opinion of the majority of the court on this question; and after referring to Lord Hardwicke's decision in Edgell v. Haywood, he says: "It is well settled by authorities in this country that, if a creditor files

(1) Newman v. Chapman, 2 Rand.   (2) M'Cutchen et al. v. Miller, 31
102.   Miss. 66.

a bill," etc., * * * "he acquires a specific lien by filing the bill," etc. But the Court of Appeals of Kentucky in the case of Fletcher et al. v. Ferrel(1) went the whole length of applying the doctrine of lis pendens to chattels, to the full extent of its conceded application to real estate. Certain slaves were originally the property of Mary Norvell, of Virginia, the title to which, charged with certain restrictions, was vested in her children, after they had become citizens of Tennessee. A bill was filed in a Tennessee court for the proper division of the slaves. It was filed May 7, 1828, and passed to decree, upon the merits, in 1831. An injunction was issued against the defendants, soon after the filing of the bill, prohibiting the removal of the slaves. Pending the suit, and in violation of the injunction, one of the defendants removed some of the slaves into Kentucky, and sold them there to Fletcher & Sharp, who claimed to own them. Ferrel acquired the title to the slaves, accruing under the decree of the Tennessee court, and filed the bill referred to against Fletcher & Sharp, setting up the proceedings in Tennessee, to execute the decree. Upon this state of facts the court held, that where purchases are made in one State, within the United States, pending a suit in another State, purchasers must be treated as purchasing pendente lite, and be subjected to the rule applicable to such purchases. That Sec. 1, Art. IV., of the Constitution of the United States, providing that, "Full faith and credit shall be given in each State, to the public acts, records, and judicial proceedings of every other State, and that Congress may by general laws prescribe the manner in which such acts, records,

(1) Fletcher et al. v. Ferrel, 9 Dana, 373; Acuff v. Rice et al., 3 Head, 296.

and proceedings shall be proved and the effect thereof," and the act of Congress of 1790, providing that,
"The said judicial proceedings, authenticated as aforesaid, shall have such faith and credit given to them in
every court within the United States, as they have
by law or usage, in the courts of the State from
whence said records are or shall be taken," are to be
construed as giving effect to lis pendens throughout
the United States; that in the case before the court,
the "judicial proceedings" in Tennessee, had in Kentucky "validity and effect, and conclusive operation,
not only upon parties and privies but also upon pendente lite purchasers." That comity between the
States, the letter of the constitution, and act of Congress, as well as the spirit and policy which dictated
its adoption, requires that the same conclusive credit
and effect should be given to it, in each of the States,
upon the rights of "all persons and all matters involved in the litigation," and that the claimants by
purchase in the State of Kentucky acquired no title
to the slaves.(1)

Authorities not all in harmony.

Sec. 82.   Courts are not entirely in accord upon the
question as to how far the doctrine of notice lis pen-

(1) That lis pendens applies to personal property as well as real estate, see: Buford v. N. L. Packt. Co., 3 Mo. App. 159; Bolling v. Carter, 9 Ala. 921; Lewis v. Meux, 1 Strobh. Eq. 182; Scott v. McMillen, 1 Litt. 309; Edgell v. Haywood, 3 Atk. 357; Watson v. Wilson, 2 Dana, 413; Scudder v. Van Amburg, 4 Edw. 29; Newman v. Chapman, 2 Rand. 93; McCutchen v. Miller, 31 Miss. 88; Carr v. Lewis & Co., 15 Mo. App. R. 551; Tyler v. Hyde, 2 Blatchf. 308; Tabb v. Williams, 4 Jones's Eq. 352; Fletcher v. Ferrel, 9 Dana, 376; Diamond v. Lawrence Co., 37 Pa. St. 353; Kellogg v. Fancher, 23 Wis. 1; McIllwrath v. Hollander, 73 Mo. 112; Wills et al. v. Whitmore et al., 9 Baxt. 193; Dovey's Appeal, 97 Pa. St. (1 Out.) 153; Kinberling v. Hartley, 1 McCrary, 136; McCanley v. Rogers, 10 Bradf. 562.

dens will apply, when the subject matter of litigation is personal property, or rather as to how many and what exceptions there are to the general rule. Some cases, as we have seen, have gone so far indeed, as to hold that the rule should be strictly confined to real estate, while others seem to deny the existence of any or but a single exception to the general rule as applied to personal property. McCutchen *v.* Miller,(1) decided in the Supreme Court of the State of Mississippi, was a case where a creditor's bill had been filed and a receiver appointed to take charge of slaves, alleged to have been fraudulently sold on execution against the defendant; and, before the slaves were seized by the receiver, delivered by the execution purchaser to a third party. There was some question as to the lien of the judgment upon which the creditor's bill was based, it being contended that the pending of the creditor's bill was not binding upon the property; so that the facts of that case should constitute an exception to the general rule of notice lis pendens. It would seem that the decision of the majority of the court is not sound; and, that the dissenting opinion of Justice Handy, of the same court, in the same case, declares the law as it is.

The conclusion seems warranted that after the bill is filed and lis pendens commences, the specific property involved in the litigation becomes subject to the claim or demand of the complainant; and, that if the claim should turn out to be of such a nature, that the property ought to be subjected to it under the rules prevailing in a court of equity, the power of unrestricted disposition in the defendant

(1) McCutchen et al. *v.* Miller, 31 Miss. 83.

would be suspended or lost, and a purchaser from him, pendente lite, would take the property subject to the lien which attached upon it by the institution of the suit; that in the case of personal property, it would be immaterial whether the judgment were a lien or not when the suit was commenced, for in such case it is the execution and not the judgment which would become a lien, and that if its collection had been obstructed so that the levy could not be made by reason of fraudulent conveyances of the defendant, to remove which the bill was filed, and the execution remained in full force and capable of enforcement against the property but for the obstacles created by the fraudulent conveyances, the court would have jurisdiction over the property; and, hence, it would be bound by lis pendens. The authorities go even farther than that; and it is well settled in this country, that if a creditor files a bill to set aside fraudulent conveyances, and to have the property applied, by the aid of a court of equity, to the payment of his judgment, although no lien has been or can be acquired at law, he acquires a specific lien or power over the property by filing the bill, and is entitled to priority over other creditors; and that any party purchasing the property sought to be subjected to the claim is a purchaser pendent lite.(1)

The scope of lis pendens as to chattels.

SEC. 83. From this review of the cases, it will be seen that, while the application of the rule lis pendens

(1) McDermott v. Strong, 4 Johns. Ch. 687; Edmunton v. Lyne, 1 Paige, 637; Corning et al. v. White, 2 Paige, 567; Farnham v. Campbell, 10 Paige, 598; United States Bank v. Burke, 4 Blackf. 141; Hadden v. Sprader et al., 20 Johns. R. 554; Blake v. Bigelow et al., 5 Ga. R. 437.

to personal property is established by the weight of authority, especially in this country, yet, that the decisions of the courts, as to the extent of its application, are far from harmonious. While the majority of cases warrant the conclusion of its general application, as between citizens of the same jurisdiction where the cases pend, yet one respectable court(1) has denied the application of the doctrine altogether; others(2) have held, that it cannot have force beyond State lines; while still others(3) hold, that it is efficient upon purchasers throughout all of the States of the Union. Under this state of the decisions, the question arises—how ought the rule, where chattels are involved, to be declared and enforced by the courts? Some uniform rule ought certainly to be adopted. The adoption of either rule, expressed in any one of the cases, can be hardly less mischievous than the existence of no rule, with the necessarily resultant jarring decisions. Such a rule ought to be adopted as will be productive of the least mischief and the greatest benefit. From the nature of things, hardships must result from the adoption of any rule.

After a careful consideration of the subject, I am inclined to think that, subject to the acknowledged exception in favor of commercial paper, the adoption of the rule established by the Kentucky, Missouri and Mississippi(4) cases, will be less productive of mischief than that of the Virginia and Tennessee(5) cases, viz:

(1) Secs. 22 and 23, *ante*, and notes 1 to 15 inclusive.

(2) Shelton et al. *v.* Johnston et al., 4 Sneed, 680; Newman *v.* Chapman, 2 Rand. 102.

(3) Fletcher et al. *v.* Ferrel, 9 Dana, 373. Note to Sec. 22, *ante.*

(4) McCutchen et al. *v.* Miller, 31 Miss. 66; Fletcher et al. *v.* Ferrel, 9 Dana, 373; Carr *v.* Lewis & Co., 15 Mo. App. R. 551.

(5) Shelton et al. *v.* Johnston et al., 4 Sneed, 680; Newman *v.* Chapman, 2 Rand. 102.

that a lis pendens, involving personal property, commenced and prosecuted with due diligence to a decree, in any of the States, should have full force and conclusive effect as well upon pendente lite purchasers as upon the parties and privies, throughout all of the United States. Such a rule would have a uniform application everywhere, and would have the salutary effect of defeating all attempts to deprive the courts of jurisdiction and successful litigants of the fruits of their litigation. The hardships resulting from such a rule are not of an unavoidable character. The seller would be held to a more rigid accountability as guarantor of title; the doctrine of caveat emptor would soon compel caution on the part of buyers, and possibly indemnity in cases of dealings between strangers, against failure of title and loss thereby. Such a rule might somewhat retard the freedom of commercial exchanges; but dealers of responsibility and commercial character would be little affected by it. When it became well understood, in consequence of uniform decisions of the courts or congressional legislation in pursuance of the provision of the constitution,(1) people would deal with respect to the rule; and requirements of bills of sale with covenants of title, and written guarantees of title would, in case of careful dealers, avoid in great measure the hazards assumed by buyers.(2)

(1) Sec. 1, Art. IV., Const. U. S.

(2) Mr. Freeman in his valuable work on Judgments, Sec. 194, says: "Every consideration of necessity and public policy which demands and justifies the law of lis pendens as applied to real estate, also demands and justifies the application of the same law to personal property. In fact, the ease with which personalty could be transferred to parties having no notice of the litigation, is much greater than in the case of real estate. The probabil-

Notice lis pendens as applied to slaves.

SEC. 84. It is held that litigation involving title to slaves is notice lis pendens.(1) In order that such should be the case, however, the property must be specifically described in the pleadings. There has been a disposition on the part of some courts to hold that notice lis pendens should be confined to litigation involving real estate, and, as we have before seen,(2) exceptions have been made in the cases of municipal bonds and coupons and negotiable promissory notes, on grounds of public policy. The courts of the Southern States, where slavery formerly existed, have generally applied the rule to litigation involving that species of property, and so, in a case where a bill was filed to foreclose a mortgage upon slaves, and, pending the case, another mortgage was made upon the same slaves, it was held that the pending suit was notice to the

ity of the defendant's entirely defeating the object of the suit, by a transfer of the property pendente lite, is rather greater in the case of personal than of real estate. and the necessity of some law prohibiting such transfer, to the prejudice of the prevailing party, is therefore greater in the former case than the latter." Freeman on Judgments, Sec. 194. On the other hand Powell states, in his work on Mortgages, (2 Powell on Mortgages, 618, note 1,) that: "There is no case in which equity has held the property of goods to be affected by reason of a lis pendens where possession is the principal evidence of ownership, as of personal chattels."

In Powell v. Williams, 14 Ala. 476, it is said: "Lis pendens is notice to all persons, at least within the jurisdiction of the State, of the matters litigated, and will prevent a third person from acquiring an interest by purchase, which can affect the plaintiff's rights." Among the cases which imply that lis pendens does not apply to chattels are Winston v. Westfeldt, 22 Ala. 570; McClaurine v. Monroe's Adms., 30 Mo. 469. These cases related to negotiable paper

(1) Newman v. Chapman, 2 Rand. 93; Howard et al. v. Kennedy's Exr., 4 Ala. 593; Montgomery v. Middlemus, 21 Cal. 103; Montgomery v. Byers et al., 21 Cal. 107; Watson v. Dowling et al., 26 Cal. 125.

(2) Bolling v. Carter et al., 9 Ala. 921.

second mortgagee, and that, as against the parties to the former suit which proceeded to decree, the second mortgagee had no rights, but was bound by that decree. In that case the court held that the registry of a chattel mortgage was notice to the same extent and in the same manner as the registry of deeds to real property, and, so also, that litigation in regard to the personal property involved in a chattel mortgage would be like notice lis pendens as litigation involving title to real estate. In the case of Newman *v*. Chapman a contrary opinion was intimated,(1) but the courts of Alabama, Kentucky, and other Southern States hold as above stated.

Lis pendens will apply to steamboats.

SEC. 85. In the case of Thomas *v*. Southard,(2) Thomas had filed a bill to enforce a pledge of the steamboat Columbia, plying on the Ohio river between Cincinnati and New Orleans He subsequently filed

(1) Newman *v*. Chapman, 2 Rand. 93.

(2) Thomas *v*. Southard, 2 Dana, 480. The above case is of interest on account of other questions than that directly involved in the text. After the bill was filed, which occurred while the Columbia was within the jurisdiction of the Circuit Court of Jefferson Co., Kentucky, it was libeled in the port of New Orleans, in the District Court of the United States, upon lawful claims against the boat, other than those involved in the bill or those acquired by Southard on execution sale of an interest on a judgment rendered in State courts. Thomas and Southard intervened and set up their claims in the admiralty case, in which a decree was entered, and the boat was sold and the proceeds were distributed. Thomas became the purchaser.

The bill continuing to pend in the State courts, and a cross-bill having been filed by Southard, the court held, that the lis pendens of the bill did not affect the maritime jurisdiction of the District Court of Louisiana, which attached at New Orleans, nor the decree pronounced by it; and that that decree became res adjudicata upon Southard's rights; and that notwithstanding the pending injunction against Southard not to sell his interest in the boat.

a supplemental bill for an injunction against a sale by the sheriff of an interest in the boat claimed by Southard. It was held that a levy made by Southard subsequent to the commencement of the lis pendens of the bill could only attach pendente lite.

Does not apply to negotiable paper.

Sec. 86. The authorities are uniform in this country, however, with the exception of a few Pennsylvania(1) cases, that the doctrine of lis pendens does not apply to negotiable paper before due. The various reasons assigned in support of this exception to the rule of lis pendens are such as to satisfy the judgment. It is said in support of this exception that Lord Bacon, in using the word "conveyance" in the rule of lis pendens, had in view its application to real property only, and that it would be a violent extension of the rule to apply it to commercial paper. Again, it is said that commercial paper represents almost all civilized nations, and a very large proportion of the commercial operations of the world; serves, to a great extent, as the representative of money; is justly a favorite of the law, and should, on the ground of public policy, enjoy immunities and privileges which are extended to no other species of property; that the credit and confidence due to it must necessarily be impaired, if the buyer were required to examine the records of the courts before he could be sure of his purchase. The tendency of the courts has therefore been to uphold this description of property, in the hands of the bona

(1) Keiffer v. Ehln, 13 Penn. St. 388; Diamond v. Lawrence Co., 37 Pa. St. 353; Day v. Zimmerman, 63 Penn. St. 72; Matheny v. Hughes, 10 Heisk. 405; Bond v. T. & P. R. W. Co., 46 Tex. 328; Lindsley v. Diefendorf, 43 How. Pr. R. 357; Edward v. Banksmith et al., 35 Ga. 213; Mims et al. v. West, 38 Ga. 19; 1 Parsons on Notes and Bills, 260.

fide holders, against defenses which might exist as between the original parties. The bonds and coupons of municipal corporations, expressed in negotiable words, have been held in numerous cases to be negotiable paper, and not to be subject to the rule of lis pendens. Whatever doubt there may be as to the proper line of limitation, for the application of the doctrine of lis pendens to personal property, it is quite clear that it should not be applied where money, bank bills, or any of the various species of commercial paper are involved, and where bona fide holders have acquired title thereto before due and are not chargeable with actual notice.(1)

(1) Powell on Mort. 618; Hood v. White, 7 Vern. 413; Winston v. Westfeldt, 22 Ala. 770; Goodwin et al. v. McGehee et al., 15 Ala. 241; Miller v. Kershaw, 1 Baily Ch. 471; Boynton v. Rawson, 1 Clark's Ch. 584; In re Great Western Tel. Co., 5 Bissell, 363; Board etc. v. T. & P. Railway Co., 46 Tex. 328; Murray v. Lylburn, 2 Johns. Ch. 441; Myers Ass. v. Hazzard, 4 McCrary, 107; Falkner v. Warren, Tex. Court of App., (Cir. Cas.) Sec. 660; Leitch et al. v. Weir et al., 48 N. Y. 613; Freeman on Judgments, Sec. 194; Mims et al. v. West et al., 38 Ga. 18.

In the case of Winston v. Westfeldt, ante, Goldthwaite, Justice, said: "Negotiable paper representing as it does in almost all civilized nations a very large proportion of the commercial operations, and serving to a great extent, as the representative of money, is justly a favorite of the law, and enjoys immunities and privileges which are extended to no other species of

contract. The tendency of the courts has been to uphold this description of paper in the hands of the bona fide holder against every species of defense which might exist as between the original parties. The credit and confidence due to it must be impaired if the buyer was required to examine the court of every county in the State before he could be sure of his purchase; and such would necessarily be the case if the doctrine of lis pendens applied to it. There are no adjudications to force us to this extremity; the strongest considerations of public policy seem to forbid the extension of the rule to money or bank bills, and we think that commercial paper, as the representative of money, should stand on the same footing in this respect."

Mr. Freeman, in his work on Judgments, says: "The necessity of preserving the negotiable character of negotiable paper not due, so as to require no inquiry beyond the inspec-

Municipal bonds commercial paper.

SEC. 87.   It has been determined, in numerous cases in applying the rule lis pendens, that municipal bonds and the coupons to such bonds detached, expressed in negotiable words, are commercial paper, and hence that they fall within the exception to the operation of the rule lis pendens, unless brought into the custody of the court, or transferred after due, or with actual notice of some defense thereto, or other infirmity invalidating the bonds or coupons. It was said in Mercer Co. v. Hacket that this species of bond was "intended to pass by manual delivery, and to have the qualities of negotiable paper," and that, "their value depended mainly upon this character." In Weith et al. v. Wilmington, the Supreme Court of North Carolina, referring to this language, say, "we follow the decision, as establishing a convenient and useful principle." In the case of Spooner v. Holmes,(1) Justice Gray, delivering the opinion of the court,

tion of the paper itself in relation to its ownership has properly been considered paramount to the necessity of avoiding transfers pendente lite, and that class of paper therefore is the only property not liable to be affected by the doctrine of lis pendens."—Freeman on Judgments, Sec. 194.

It is said in Jeffres v. Cochrane, 48 N. Y. 671, that lis pendens should not be extended to money, bank bills or commercial paper. Holbrook v. N. J. Zinc Co., 57 N. Y. 617, holds that, certificates of stock of joint stock companies are not subject to lis pendens. Durant v. Iowa City, 1 Wool. 73, and Stone v. Eliott, 11 Ohio State, 252, hold that,

the doctrine of lis pendens does not apply to commercial paper.

(1) Weith v. City of Wilmington, 68 N. C. 25; San Antonio v. Lane, 32 Texas, 405; Bank of Rome v. Village of Rome, 19 N. Y. 24; Seybel v. National Currency Bank, 54 N. Y. 288; White v. Vermont & Mass. R. R. Co., 21 How. 575; Moran v. Com'rs of Miami County, 2 Black. 722; Mercer County v. Hacket, 1 Wallace, 83; Gelpche v. City of Dubuque, 1 Wal. 519; Meyer v. Muscatine, 1 Wal. 564; Murray v. Lardner, 2 Wal. 857; Thompson v. Lee County, 3 Wal. 177; Supervisors v. Schenck, 5 Wal. 772; Aurora City v. West, etc., 7 Wal. 82; Arent v. Commonwealth, 18 Gratt.

said, "in the opinion of the majority of the court, the coupons in question do not stand upon the same ground as chattels.   They are negotiable promises for the payment of money issued by the government, payable to bearer and transferable by mere delivery, without assignment or endorsement.   They are therefore not to be considered as goods, but as representatives of money, and subject to the same rules as bank bills or other negotiable instruments payable in money to bearer."   "The rule of caveat emptor does not apply to them."   "And according to the great weight of authority, the same rule applies to bills of exchange or promissory notes payable to bearer."(1)

773; Railway *v.* Clenery, 13 Ind. 161; Clark *v.* Janesville, 10 Wis. 136; Mills *v.* Jefferson, 20 Wis. 50; Clapp *v.* The County of Cedar, 5 Clarke, 15; Barrett *v.* County Court, 44 Missouri, 197; Johnson *v.* County of Stark, 24 Ill. 75; Craig *v.* City of Vicksburg, 31 Miss. 216; Chapin *v.* Vermont & Mass. R. R., 8 Gray, 575; Nat. Exchange Bank of Hartford, etc., 8 R. I. 379; Virginia *v.* Ches. & Ohio Canal Co., 32 Md. 501; Conn. Mut. Life Ins. Co. *v.* Cleveland, etc., R. R. Co., 41 Barb. 9; Spooner *v.* Holmes, 102 Mass. 505; Morris Canal, etc., *v.* Fisher, 1 Stocer, 667; Goodman *v.* Simonds, 20 How. 343; Raphael *v.* Bank of England, 17 C. B. 161; Commonwealth *v.* Emigrant Industrial Savings Bank, 98 Mass. 12; Worcester Co. Bank *v.* Dorchester & Milton Bank, 10 Cush. 488; Wyer *v.* Dorchester & Milton Bank, 11 Cush. 51.

(1) The decisions in Pennsylvania are in conflict with the other cases on this question. In Diamond *v.*

Lawrence Co., 37 Penn. St. Woodward, J., said: "We have said on several former occasions that we will not treat bonds like these as negotiable securities. On this ground we stand alone. All the courts, American and English, are against us. Be it so. We are not insensible to the importance of this fact, nor are we wanting in deference to the learning and wisdom of the judge who differs from us. But we are a Pennsylvania tribunal sitting in judgment on an occasional and extraordinary accounting for money created under Pennsylvania statutes. We know the history of these municipal and county boards, how the legislature, yielding to popular excitement about railroads, authorized this issue; how grand juries and county commissioners, and city officers were moulded to the purposes of the speculators; how recklessly railroad officers abused this overwrought confidence, and what burdens of debt

Does not apply in tax proceedings.

SEC. 88.   The doctrine of lis pendens does not apply
as against taxes assessed and levied by the taxing
power.   The general power of taxation is a govern-
mental power.   It is an indispensable ingredient in
every constitution.   Without such a power, either the
government must perish for want of revenue, or the
people must be subjected to continual plunder, and
thus civil, organized society be overthrown.   The
power to levy and collect taxes, is, therefore, an incident of sovereignty, without which no government
could long exist.   It is an expressed grant of power in
the Federal constitution.   In State constitutions, it
passes under the general designation of "legislative
power," and is implied upon the principle that a
grant of legislative, judicial and executive powers carries with it, by construction, all of the means necessary for their execution.   This being the nature of the
taxing power, whether exercised by the Federal States
or municipal governments—organized within the
State and exercising the power of the State—it is
manifest that taxes, when levied in pursuance and under the forms of law, must constitute primary liens,
inherent in the property,—efficient as against all rights
of individuals to the property taxed—whether those
rights relate to the title or liens upon the title to the

and taxation have resulted to the
people." The opinion then points
out that these bonds are local, dependent on statutory law; and, in
that respect, differ from ordinary
commercial paper; that they recite
the authority upon which they were
issued; that they were under suit
and bills of exchange cannot be;
that they only resemble bills of
exchange in being payable to bearer; that the constitution of the State
since this issue had been amended
so as to prohibit future issue, and
that these distinctions justify the
court in refusing to treat these
bonds as commercial paper.

property.(1) It follows that a lis pendens, in any litigation between citizens or other litigants, does not affect in any manner subsisting and efficient, primary liens for taxes, created and existing under the taxing power of the Federal and State governments. This, however, is not the case, if the taxes are merely personal and by provisions of law do not become a lien upon property, except as other judgments become liens. In those States where there are general statutes declaring a lien for taxes, it is said the assessment of land and the lien which it creates are public matters of record, of which all purchasers are bound to take notice. Where a purchaser buys land, which is subject to an existing lien for taxes, he must see, at his peril, that the taxes are paid, and if he neglects this duty, he takes the hazard of the judgment against the land, the lien of which, by operation of law and by relation, will antedate his purchase.(2)

Does not apply in condemnation proceedings.

SEC. 89. In proceedings for the condemnation of land for public use, there is no lis pendens. This proceeding is based upon and conducted in virtue of the right of eminent domain, and is justified upon the ground that the interest of individuals must yield to the imperative demands of the general public, exercised for the public good. The exigencies liable to arise, requiring the prompt seizure and appropriation of private property for the public use, are so great that the rules and usages adopted in other legal proceedings are in some measure departed from, the primary object of the exercise of this power being the securing of

(1) Blackwell on Tax Titles, p. 8. 654; Wright v. Walker, 30 Ark. 44;
(2) Reeve v. Kennedy, 43 Cal. Bigelow on Eq. 189.

the property for the public use. The determination
of the rights of individual owners to the property
seized, is a matter allowing of more deliberation.
This contest usually occurs over the fund held in *cus-
todia legis*. In order, however, to subserve public
ends, it becomes necessary that property should be
taken discharged of all liens, and hence this species of
legal proceedings does not allow the property itself to
be dealt with, so far as relates to contest in regard to
the title to the property or liens upon it, and is an exception to the rule lis pendens. It seems, however,
that where the legislatures of the several States have
provided by express statutes for the filing of notices
lis pendens in condemnation proceedings that practice
is allowable.

**The right to an office, when real parties contestants,
the subject of lis pendens inter-partes.**

SEC. 90. In an action by mandamus, where the relator is the real party contesting the right to an office,
although prosecuting in the name of the State, as
against another person contesting for the same office,
is the subject of lis pendens inter-partes. Nor is any
reason perceived why the final determination in such
a cause should not be conclusive upon the contestants, as between the parties and other persons in any
suit where such party is a litigant. And, so, it was
held in Louisiana that a proceeding by mandamus
brought in the name of the State, by one contestant,
as relator, against another contestant, although carried on nominally in the name of the State to determine the right to the office of mayor of the city of
Jefferson, was the subject of lis pendens.(1)

(1) State of La. *v.* Kreider, 21 La. An. 482.

CHAPTER VI.

WHAT ELEMENTS NECESSARY TO CONSTITUTE THE RES LITIGIOSA.

General statement—res litigiosa.

SEC. 91. It may be stated generally that in order that what we term the res litigiosa may exist, three things must concur: first, the property must be of a character to be subject to the rule lis pendens; second, the court must acquire jurisdiction both of the person and the res, and third, the res must be sufficiently described in the pleadings. If these three things do not concur there is no res litigiosa.

Notice of facts averred in pleadings.

SEC. 92. As a general rule lis pendens is, in law, notice of any fact averred in the pleadings, pertinent to the matter in issue or the relief sought, and of the contents of exhibits filed and made a part of the pleadings, or proved.(1) But in order that the notice

(1) Allen v. Poole, 54 Miss. 333; 343; Marshall v. Shephard, 23 Kas.
Centre v. The Bank, 22 Ala. 743; 326.
Turner et al. v. Babb et al., 60 Mo.

may attach, the property involved must be so pointed out in the proceedings, as we have before seen, as to warn the public that they intermeddle at their peril.(1)

As to the description of property required.

SEC. 93.　It is proper to enquire, in this connection, what character of description in the bill, or other pleading, is essential to the existence of lis pendens. The doctrine of constructive notice lis pendens is subject to the limitation that the specific property sought to be bound must be so pointed out by the proceedings as to warn the whole world.　Unless this is done there is no binding lis pendens.　In the case of Lodge v. Simonton,(2) the rule was stated to be that a purchaser should be bound, whenever there was enough in the proceedings to lead a vigilant mind to the knowledge of the truth.　It is said that the property must be so pointed out by the proceedings as to warn the whole world that they intermeddle at their peril.(3) This statement, however, hardly defines the character and definiteness of the description of the property, which will constitute notice lis pendens.　It may be said in general that a lis pendens will be created where the property involved in suit is described, either by such definite and technically legal description that its identity can be made out by the description alone, or where there is such a general description of its character, or status, and by such reference that, upon inquiry, the identity of the property involved in litigation can be ascertained.　Descriptions falling with-

(1) Miller v. Sherry, 2 Wal. 237.
(2) Lodge v. Simonton, 2 P. & W. 448.
(3) Lewis v. Mew, 1 Strob. Eq. 180.

in the latter, as well as the former class, are efficient to create lis pendens. And so it has been held that where a trustee was restrained from "selling any more of the trust negroes," it was not a lis pendens. And so, also, a general bill for an account of real or personal property, without any specific description, does not create such a lis pendens as will affect purchasers.

Where the bill, however, seeks to charge a particular estate with a particular trust, a lis pendens is created. In the case of Miller v. Sherry, the Supreme Court of the United States say: " To have that effect a bill must be so definite in the description, that any one reading it can learn thereby what property is intended to be made the subject of litigation."(1)   In Griffith v. Griffith the court say the bill should have described particular lots or charged an equity upon all of the real estate of the defendant, in a prescribed territory, or some other allegation or charge of such a character as to enable purchasers to see by an examination of the bill itself that the complainants claimed some right to or equitable interest in or lien on the premises.(2)   Where, however, there is nothing in the proceedings except the simple description of the property, which will tend to put the public upon inquiry, or give a clue where further and more definite knowledge can be acquired, the description must be so definite that any one reading it can learn thereby what property is intended to be made the subject of litigation.(3)   On the other hand, if enough appears in the

(1) Sugden on Vendors, 1045.
(2) Griffith v. Griffith, 1 Hoff. Ch. 153.
(3) Miller v. Sherry, 2 Wall. 237. In the case of Miller v. Sherry, *ante*,

the court say, "the original bill was in the form of a creditor's bill. * * It contained nothing specific, except as to the transactions between Miller and Richardson. There was

proceedings to put a purchaser on guard, although they do not in themselves describe the property with that particularity which amounts of itself to complete identification, lis pendens would be created. Thus, in the case of Green *v.* Slayter,(1) where the bill described the property as "divers lands in Crosby's manor," and as held in trust for the complainant by defendant Winter — and it was shown in the case that

no other part of the bill upon which issue could have been taken as to any particular property. It was effectual for the purpose of creating a general lien upon the assets of Miller,—as the means of discovery, and as the foundation for an injunction,—and for an order that he should convey to a receiver. If it became necessary to litigate as to any specific claim, other than that against Richardson, an amendment to the bill would have been indispensable. It did not create a lis pendens, operating as notice, to any real estate. To have that effect, a bill must be so definite in the description, that any one reading it can learn thereby what property is intended to be made the subject of litigation. * * It is evident that the premises in controversy were not in the mind of the pleader when this bill was drawn." In the above case of Griffith *v.* Griffith, *ante*, the court say, "to have made such a bill constructive notice to a purchaser from the defendant therein, it would have been necessary to allege therein that these particular lots, or that all the real estate of the defendant in the city of New York, had been purchased

and paid for either wholly, or in part, with the funds of the infant complainant, or some other charge of a similar nature should have been inserted in the bill, to enable purchasers, by an examination of the bill itself, to see that the complainant claimed the right to, or some equitable interest in, or lien on the premises." In Boshear *v.* Leahy, 6 Heisk. 163, it is said that in order to bind by lis pendens the property involved must be specifically pointed out in the pleadings; the courts say, that "the specific property must be so pointed out by the proceedings as to warn the whole world that they intermeddle with it at their peril." Referring to Shelton *v.* Johnston, 4 Sneed, 672, this decision is claimed not to be in conflict with that. 2 Kents' Com. 101 (note); Adams' Eq. Pl. 157 (note). For further insufficient descriptions see: Gardner *v.* Peckham et al., 13 R. I. 102; Almond *v.* Almond, 4 Rand. 662; Brightman *v.* Brightman, 1 R. I. 112; Gilmore *v.* Gilmore, 5 Jones' Eq. 284; Isler *v.* Brown, 66 N. C. 556; Baird *v.* Baird et al., Phil. Eq. 317.

(1) Green *v.* Slayter, 4 Johns. Ch. 39.

Winter's trusteeship in the lands was matter of public notoriety—Chancellor Kent said: "It is true there might have been divers lands in ' Crosby's manor ' held in trust by Winter, and yet the lots sold to defendant have been held by him in his own absolute right. But though this was possible it was an improbable fact; and if every bill contained sufficient matter to put a party upon inquiry the bill in 1809 answered that purpose. The doctrine of lis pendens is indispensable to right and justice in the cases and under the limitations in which it has been applied; and according to the observation of Lord Chancellor Manners, we must not suffer the rule to be frittered away by exceptions. Was it too much to have required of a purchaser charged with notice of all the facts in the bill to have called upon Winter to discover the source of his title? The general rule is, that what is sufficient to put the party upon inquiry is good notice in equity. The least inquiry, even of Winter himself, would have satisfied the purchaser that the lots he purchased were parcel of the trust lands mentioned in the bill."

When description sufficient to put upon inquiry.

Sec. 93a. So, if the description is such as that the purchaser is reasonably put upon inquiry, and such as to raise a presumption of probability that the property may be included in that which is involved in the litigation, there is a lis pendens, efficient to charge the property in the hands of a pendente lite purchaser with the results of the litigation. In determining whether legal proceedings are sufficient to constitute notice lis pendens, all of the pleadings including exhibits made a part of them are to be considered. If a chancery proceeding, the bill, answers and replications, including

the exhibits to any of them, referred to and identified
in the pleading itself, are to be considered. In such
case they are as much a part of the record as the
pleading itself. But parties should not be required to
look beyond the pleadings and exhibits. Evidence
taken and filed in the case, after it is commenced,(1)
ought not to be construed as constituting notice lis
pendens. If the rule were extended thus in its application, it would often prove a snare to innocent
parties. Evidence and depositions are not records until incorporated into a bill of exceptions or certificate
of evidence; and it would be a great hardship to require the public to read voluminous evidence, and
know as matter of law just when such evidence or the
exhibits thereto became files of the courts. This limitation upon the doctrine of notice lis pendens would
seem to be a reasonable one, because it is supported
by the same reasons which recommend the doctrine of
constructive notice itself. The further application of
the rule to special cases is reserved for consideration
in its proper place hereafter.

Thus it will be seen that although it is necessary
in order to constitute lis pendens that the proceedings should, directly or indirectly, designate
specific property, yet, where the description is so
definite that any one reading it can learn thereby,
either by the description or reference, what property
is intended to be made the subject of litigation,
it is sufficient. As in the case cited, where the
description was "divers lands in Crosby's manor,"
held in trust by the defendant, it was held to be the
duty of the public to inquire of the defendant, and

(1) Centre v. P. & M. Bank et al., 22 Ala. 743.

thus ascertain that the property involved was covered by the description. It is sufficient, if the information thus furnished a purchaser is of such a character that it becomes probable that the property is the same as that involved in the litigation. That is to say, it becomes the duty of the purchaser to avail himself of the information given by the pleadings, by the use of reasonable diligence, to ascertain at his peril whether the property he is about to purchase is the same involved in the suit.(1)

When description insufficient for lis pendens.

SEC. 94.   The mere mention in a creditor's bill, filed for the purpose of reaching the interest of a debtor as devisee of an estate, of the existence of a mortgage, and making the mortgagee a defendant, without any allegation in the bill as to the validity of the mortgage, or asking any relief in regard to it, does not create such a lis pendens as will affect the validity of a sale under the mortgage.(2)   If the validity of the mortgage were assailed by a proper allegation in the bill and prayer for relief, there would be a lis pendens; and perhaps so when the prayer is deficient.(3)

(1) Hamlin v. Bevans, 7 Ohio, 316. The petition did not describe the particular property, and was held not to subject the property of the defendant generally, during the pendency of the case, to lis pendens. In Russell et al. v. Kirkbridge, 62 Tex. 459, it is said, that the specific property must be so pointed out in the proceedings, as to inform the whole world in order to be a lis pendens. Jaffray v. Brown, 17 Hun. 576. The notice of lis pendens in an attachment suit described the property as, "all the real estate of the defendant Brown, or in which he may have an interest in Chenango County." It was held a nullity.

(2) Cockrill v. Maney et al., 2 Cooper, 49.

(3) Shelton v. Johnston, 4 Sneed, 672. It is said in Spencer v. Spencer, 9 R. I. R. 162, that the only ground on which a lis pendens is created in a divorce suit is where by the allegations of the bill some property is so put in litigation and

Created by amendments.

SEC. 95. Although the original pleadings or proceedings may not be efficient to constitute notice lis pendens, amendments may be subsequently filed, setting up new matter, or so stating the subject matter intended to have been covered by the original pleadings or proceedings as to create a lis pendens as to the matter so described in the amendments. The same rules, however, as to the character of description of property, will apply to amendments, which apply to the original proceedings. If the original proceedings were insufficient to constitute lis pendens, there will be none in the case prior to the filing of the amendment. Every such amendment, showing a new equity, and properly pointing out the property involved by it, creates a new lis pendens. Thus, it was said in Dudley *v.* Price's Admr.,(1) "If, during the pendency of a suit, any new matter or claim, not before asserted, is set up and relied upon by the complainant, the defendant has a right to insist upon the statute (of limitation) until the time that the new claim is presented, because, until that time, there was no lis pendens, as to that matter, between the parties."

In order to bind a purchaser by lis pendens, the statements contained in the pleadings should be so specific that no subsequent amendments will be neces-

brought under the jurisdiction of the court as to be bound to abide the decree of the court; when this is done public policy requires that no alienation be made or lien acquired to defeat or embarrass the litigation. As a general rule bills filed for alimony and maintenance merely do not constitute lis pen-dens. Brightman *v.* Brightman, 1 R. I. 112; Almond *v.* Almond, 4 Rand. 662; Gilmore *v.* Gilmore, 5 Jones' Eq. 284; Baird *v.* Baird et al., Phil. Eq. 317.

(1) Dudley *v.* Price's Admr., 10 B. Mon. 88; Long *v.* Barton, 2 Atk. 218.

sary. If amendments are made, and new matters are brought in thereby, as to the new matters brought in issue by such amendment there will be no lis pendens anterior to the filing of the amendment. Every such amendment, showing a new equity, creates a new lis pendens.(1) And where lis pendens statutes are in force and new parties are brought in by amendment, it is indispensable that there should be a new notice of lis pendens as to such parties.

Property described in interrogatory.

SEC. 96. Where an interrogatory, attached to the bill, describes property, but there is no allegation in the bill with respect to it, of such a character as to charge an equity in favor of the complainant upon it, there will be no notice of lis pendens. The language of the bill must be such as to lead any one reading it to believe or suppose that it was the intention of the pleader to charge an equity upon the property. And so where a bill for discovery merely was filed, containing no allegation of any kind in reference to the land subsequently brought into the suit, except an interrogatory enquiring whether the land was not held by one of the defendants in trust, and there was subsequently filed a supplemental bill, making distinct allegation that the land was held in trust, and asking relief, it was decided that a purchaser, before the filing of the supplemental bill, did not take pendente lite, and that the lis pendens as to the land could not antedate the filing of the supplemental bill.(2) But the case would be different if the allegations of the bill,

(1) Stone v. Connelly et al., 1 Met. (Ky.) 653; Cromwell v. Clay, 1 Dana, 579; Kennedy v. Adams, 11 B. Mon. 105.

(2) Low et al. v. Pratt et al., 53 Ill. 440.

referring to the interrogatory, charged in any form an equity upon the property described in the interrogatory, and the interrogatory constituted a part of the bill. In such case the description in the interrogatory would be just as efficient to create notice lis pendens as if it were embraced in the body of the bill.

The claimant of the res must be impleaded.

SEC. 97. If, although a suit is pending, the person holding the title to the property has not been made a party to the suit, so that there is a lis pendens as against him, a purchaser from the person so holding the title, without actual notice of the claims of the complainant in the bill, will not be bound by the determination of the suit. To affect a purchaser, who comes in pendente lite, under the holder of the legal title, with constructive notice of the equity claimed against it, such holder of the legal title must have been impleaded at the time of the purchase. It is not sufficient that there is a claim made in the pleadings to the property. If he should be made a party after the purchase, the lis pendens would not take effect by relation, so as to charge the purchaser with notice, although the property may have been specially designated in the bill.(1) It would be a great hardship, and public policy would not justify a requirement that a purchaser make investigation outside of the parties to the record, in pending suits, to ascertain the possible rights in the property of persons other than the parties to the litigation, or that the purchaser should deal with the property, at the peril of subsequently having the title of such other persons drawn into the

(1) Carr v. Callaghan, 3 Littell, 365; Macey v. Fenwick's Admr., 9   Dana, 198; French v. The Loyal Company, 5 Leigh, 680.

pending litigation. If, however, one should hold the legal title by an unrecorded deed, and the person holding the recorded title were made a party, the fact that the holder of the title not of record was not a party would not protect a purchaser from him.(1)

The court must have jurisdiction.

Sec. 98. Unless the facts set forth in the bill, petition or other pleading, on behalf of the complainant or plaintiff, present a case for the jurisdiction of the court, it is clear that the proceedings will not operate as a lis pendens so as to affect the property sought to be subjected by the proceeding, or to overreach a subsequent sale or disposition of it.(2) If, however, enough appears from the pleadings to show that a proper case can be made, and they were subsequently amended so as to show a case for the exercise of the jurisdiction of the court, it might be a question of doubt whether, when lis pendens did attach by amendment, it would not so far relate back as to affect the good faith of an antecedent sale or disposition of the property.

The primary object of suit not material.

Sec. 99. The primary object for which the suit is brought is not material, provided the court has jurisdiction of the property for secondary purposes; and

(1) Norton v. Birge, 35 Conn. 250; Hoyt v. Jones, 31 Wis. 397.

(2) Jones, etc. v. Lusk, etc., 2 Met. 389; Caldwell's Heirs v. White, 4 Mon. 569.

In Carrington's Heirs v. Bonts et al., 1 McLean, 167, it is held that where there is no jurisdiction there can be no lis pendens.

In Pearson v. Keedy, etc., 6 B. Mon. 130, it is held that, if there be any equity in a bill, and its allegations are not sufficient to give jurisdiction, although process may be served, there shall be no such lis pendens against debtors of a firm against whom such a bill is filed, as to overreach settlement thereafter made between a surviving partner and his debtors.

so it would seem that where a bill for divorce and alimony is filed by the wife against the husband, and there is no special allegation in it pointing out any particular property which is sought to be charged with the payment of the alimony, there will be no lis pendens as to either real or personal property of the defendant. Such a case cannot be distinguished from those where the action is professedly in personam, and where the contention in the case is entirely independent of any particular property. The same results of the advantage to the public—the same argument founded upon public policy—would exist in the one class of cases as in the other. If, however, the bill should contain special allegations—should point out particular real or personal property,—and within the limits of the manifest jurisdiction and powers of the court to grant the relief should seek to have alimony assigned out of such specific property, there would be constructive notice of the lis pendens.(1)

(1) In the case of Brightman v. Brightman et al., the Supreme Court of Rhode Island said: "The complainant says, in the next place that though the said deed was made and received bona fide, and upon a fair consideration, yet, being made pending her petition for divorce and alimony, the purchaser took the estate subject to a decree subsequently passed on said petition. We apprehend it is well settled, that he who purchases property pending a suit in which the title to it is involved, takes it subject to the judgment or decree that may be passed in such suit against the person from whom he purchases. That he purchased bona fide, and paid full consideration for it, will not avail against such a judgment or decree. Nor will he be permitted to prove that he had no notice of the pendency of the suit. The law infers that all persons have notice of proceedings of courts of record. This rule has been adopted from motives of public policy. Without it, the effect of every judgment and decree might be avoided, by a mere transfer of the defendant's title, as a decree of judgment was about to be passed against him. 11 Ves. R. 197. A party might always be in pursuit of his rights without being able to overtake them. 2 Peere Wms. R. 264. But the rule only relates to

Conclusion.

SEC. 100.   Thus it is manifest that there can be no lis pendens, unless the court has acquired in some

suits involving the title to property, and is not to be extended beyond the property involved in the suit. 1 McCord's R. 264. The suit must relate to the estate, and not to any thing collateral, such as money secured on it. 3 Atk. 392. The rule applies where a third person attempts to intrude into a controversy by acquiring an interest in the matter in dispute, pending suit. 4 Cow. 667; 2 Johns. Ch. Cases, 445. We do not apprehend that the rule of lis pendens is applicable in this case. The prayer of complainant's petition was for divorce and for alimony out of her husband's estate. It did not affect the title to his real estate, or necessarily seek to put any incumbrance on it. Alimony is to be granted out of the personal or real estate, and (is) not necessarily a charge on either. Had the prayers in this case been for alimony to be assigned her out of this particular farm, the case would somewhat resemble some of the cases in the books, where the rule has been applied. But it is not so; it is general for alimony out of his estate. If such a prayer locks up the real, it equally does the personal estate of a respondent to such a petition, and each and every part of it. The instant such a petition is filed, the respondent's business, however extensive it may be, must stop. Purchasers and dealers with him, by the policy of the law, are bound by the decree of alimony that may be passed; although they do not ever know that they are dealing with a married man. Alimony will be claimed and must be allowed to attach to any and every part of the personal property that the husband had at the filing of the petition. We do not think the case falls within the rule of lis pendens, nor within the reason of that rule." Brightman v. Brightman et al., 1 R. I. 112.

Where it was alleged in a bill for a divorce, brought by the wife, that the husband owned a city lot in the city of Atlanta, and pending the suit, the defendant sold and conveyed the lot, it was held that the purchase was subject to the decree in the case.

Venable v. Craig, 44 Ga. 437. When no land is described in the bill, and the defendant conveys, for the purpose of defeating a decree for alimony to a grantee, who takes with a knowledge of the purpose, the conveyance would be invalid.

Where the court has ordered the defendant not to dispose of his property, and the defendant sells, in order to impeach the sale, it must be shown that the purchase was made with actual knowledge.

Venable v. Craig, 44 Ga. 437. In another case it was held, that when in a bill for a divorce the defendant's lands were merely described, but the bill was not so framed as to seek relief against the lands, there was no lis pendens as to the lands.

manner jurisdiction(1) of the thing involved in the suit. This arises from the very nature or essence of lis pendens itself. It is the binding effect of the suit upon the property or thing involved, which holds it within the power of the court, so as to enable the court to render efficient judgment or decree upon it in the case. The court can have no such power, either anterior to or at the time of judgment or decree, unless it has jurisdiction. It matters not in what way the jurisdiction fails. It may be for want of general jurisdiction in the court over the form of action, or the class of property involved. It may be for manifest want of equity in the form of the bill. It may be on account of defective or insufficient description in the pleadings or proceedings of the particular property or thing, or it may be for want of proper service. Whatever the ground of failure to acquire jurisdiction may be, the result must inevitably follow, that as to the particular property or thing, there can be no lis pendens in that case. The elements are wanting to constitute res litigiosa.

Sapp *v*. Wightman, 103 Ill. 150. But if, pending the suit, the bill had been amended so as to seek relief against the lands, there would have been a lis pendens from the time of the filing of the amendment.

(1) Carrington *v*. Bents, 1 McLain, 167; 9 Pet. 86.

The author is aware that he might with propriety very much enlarge this discussion upon the jurisdiction of the court, as properly falling within the scope of this work; but the subject has been ably and exhaustively treated, in separate treatises upon this special subject, by Mr. Freeman and other able writers, to whose works the reader is referred.

It has been the design of the author to confine this treatise within the limits of substantial originality, as related to a practical discussion of the subject of lis pendens.

CHAPTER VII.

WHAT CONSTITUTES A "FULL PROSECUTION."

Rule requires full prosecution.

SEC. 100½. Lord Bacon's rule provided that in order that it should have full force upon pendente lite purchaser, purchasing without notice, the suit involving the res should be in "full prosecution," and that "intermission of suit" should not occur. It becomes important to determine what constitutes a close and continuous prosecution of suit within the meaning of the rule lis pendens.(1)

Lord Bacon's rule does not mean that the suit must

(1) See Sec. 1, *ante*.

be brought to a close within any limited time, or that steps shall be taken in the course of the prosecution of the cause within any limited period. Such a construction of the rule would be disastrous to the rights of litigants and would tend to the defeat of justice. It evidently means a constant prosecution — a prosecution of the suit without such negligent intermission as may be shown to be inexcusable or as shall not be satisfactorily explained.(1)

A reasonable excuse for delay may be shown.

SEC. 101. In order that lis pendens shall retain its vitality the suit must, as we have seen,(2) be duly prosecuted, and the failure to prosecute will destroy its force and legal effect; but while a lis pendens may be lost by neglecting to prosecute, a reasonable excuse for the delay complained of is always available to keep the lis pendens in life. And so where a bill was filed in September, 1811, and a decree was not entered until February, 1859, a period of more than forty-seven years, the court accepted as a satisfactory excuse for the delay the fact of the successive deaths of parties and the necessary substitution for them of their representatives.(3)

Lord Nottingham's construction.

SEC. 102. Lord Nottingham gave a construction to Lord Bacon's rule, which ought to have great authority, coming as it does from " the father of equity."

(1) Ferrier v. Bazick et al., 6 Iowa, 258.

(2) *Ante*, Sec. 1.

(3) Wickliffe's Heirs v. Breckenridge's Heirs, 1 Bush. 443. Where the parties to a decree leave the case off the docket for the purposes of the decree, it is a lis pendens though left off of the docket. Moore v. Ogden, 35 Ohio St. 430; Beumont v. Herrick, 24 Ohio St. 445; Hunter v. Hopeton, 4 McQueen, 972.

That illustrious judge held that "full prosecution" existed so long as the cause continued to pend and the court continues to have complete jurisdiction over the res and person. He understood that the only real ground for destroying lis pendens was an "intermission" in a cause for an undue period without any reasonable excuse. Where there was no intermission it was considered the "common case."

In his Prolegomena of Equity, a compilation of chancery rules and causes in equity, occurs this passage: "The Lord Bacon in his twelfth rule seems to direct that if a purchase is made pendente lite after some long intermission the case shall differ from the 'common case.' But the rule, though reasonable, is not always observed; for in Martin v. Stiles, 1663, the bill filed in 1640, abated by death in 1648; a bill of revivor was filed in 1662; and the purchase was in 1651, and yet the purchaser was bound; because now, by relation of the bill of revivor, it was pendente lite."(1)

Early decision of Lord Brougham.

SEC. 103. The doctrine of lis pendens received strong endorsement in the case of Landon v. Morris.(2)

The plaintiff had received an ante-nuptial promise from his wife's father, that certain property was entailed upon his daughter, who was an only child. Sub-

---

(1) The authorities for what is called "close and continuous prosecution," and "reasonable diligence," are: McGregor v. McGregor, 21 Iowa, 441; Herrington v. Herrington, 27 Mo. 560; Myrick v. Selden, 36 Barb. 22; Watson v. Wilson, 2 Dana, 413; Clarkson et al. v. Morgan, etc., 6 B. Mon. 441. On the o her hand, in Gossom v. Donaldson, 18 B. Mon. 238, it is said it is only unreasonable and unusual negligence which will cause the benefit of lis pendens to be lost.

(2) Landon v. Morris, 5 Sims. 248.

sequent to her marriage to plaintiff, her father having died, the representation made to the plaintiff proved untrue. Plaintiff and his wife filed a bill against the widow of the testator praying conveyance of the property. The bill was filed in 1816. The widow answered, and an injunction having been granted, it was continued in 1818. The same year the widow mortgaged the property, and in the following year, 1819, sold her interests to divers persons having no knowledge of the suit. In November, 1822, the bill was amended. In December following plaintiff learned of the conveyance made by the widow and the persons to whom she had conveyed, but did not make them parties to the suit and opposed her grantee of the fee in his attendance in the case before the master. In 1831 plaintiff filed an original bill against the widow's grantee of the fee, stating the foregoing proceedings and praying conveyance of the property to the wife and for a receiver. The widow's grantee answered, and relied on the delay in the proceedings in the former suit, the want of notice when he purchased, and on the plaintiff not having made him a party to that suit. A motion was made and order entered by the Vice-Chancellor for a receiver. The case afterwards coming up before Lord Chancellor Brougham, in deciding the case, he said: "The general doctrine of lis pendens is not contested. The principle of the decision in The Bishop of Winchester v. Paine is admitted, that a purchaser pendente lite is bound by the decree made against the person from whom he purchases; and, accordingly, a decree of foreclosure was held to bind the subsequent mortgagees of an equity of redemption, though they had not been made parties. And that case, it may be observed, was stronger than this, inasmuch as an exception was taken to the title on this ground, by a purchaser, and was disallowed and a specific performance decreed.

Such being the acknowledged rule, is there anything in the circumstances of the purchase here in question which can create an exception in favor of the party making it? I have adverted to some of the alleged peculiarities, in stating the facts of the case, and have disposed of them. It is further said, and mainly urged, that the plaintiff knew there was another party, and purposely went on in his absence, and without bringing him into court, in order that he might be bound in his absence; and it is observed that there is no case of lis pendens which goes so far. It would, however, be a direct innovation of that doctrine and quite unwarranted, either by the principle on which it rests or by anything to be found in the cases which have been decided upon it, if we were to allow an exception of this description, and to enable a purchaser to escape from the effects of the suit by showing that his purchase became known to the party suing the vendor, and that this party afterwards went on without calling upon him or letting him in to defend the suit. That the case is not here on the merits is certain; and that payment into court, and change of possession by appointing a receiver, would not be ordered if there seemed to be anything very doubtful now upon its merits, may be admitted. Possibly, if the case were such as made it probable that the purchasers * * * could disclose merits which she has not brought forward, things might be left to stand as they now do until the hearing; but this is, in the highest degree, unlikely, from the relation in which the parties stand to each other; nor can we, in reviewing the circumstances of the case, entertain any great doubt which way it is likely to turn. In making the order, then, I take for granted that the whole of the facts to which I have adverted entered into His Honor's view, and they appear to me sufficient to justify that order.''

Delays in chancery proceedings.

Sec. 104.   In determining what is a continuous and close prosecution of a suit, the court will take notice that in chancery proceedings delays are necessary and sometimes great.(1)   In England this was notoriously so, and became the subject of notice.   A cause was before Lord Nottingham that had been pending thirty years.(2)   By the civil or Roman law the *litis contestatio*, which is our res litigiosa, was not destroyed by inaction until a period of forty years had elapsed.(3)

Chancellor Kent, in Murray *v.* Ballou,(4) says: "A suit in chancery is necessarily tedious and expensive, and years may elapse   *   *   before the suit can be brought to a conclusion."

(1) In Watson *v.* Wilson, 2 Dana, 413, the court says: "As to the negligence objected to in this case we are not prepared to say, nor does our experience in the ordinary progress of a chancery suit in this State authorize us in saying, that from May, 1825, till 1828, when Wilson obtained his deed, there was a lapse of time which, unexplained, would of itself amount to laches, such as to deprive the complainant of the benefit of the sale." In Gossom *v.* Donaldson, 18 B. Mon. 237, the court held that a delay of three years were not negligence in prosecuting a suit, and would not destroy lis pendens.

(2) Lives of Eminent English Judges, by Welsby, 75.

(3) Code 7, Chap. 7, Sec. 39.

(4) Murray *v.* Ballou, 1 Johns. Ch. R. 576.

Presumption in favor of continuance.

SEC. 105. When jurisdiction has attached to the res, the general rule should be that the suit will pend, so long as it is not dismissed by the court, sua sponte, or for want of prosecution, or upon the motion of the parties, or be brought to a close by reason of some statutory provision or rule of court having force of law. This presumption would be overcome by manifest evidence of neglect to prosecute and the burden of explanation would be thrown upon the plaintiff. If the cause finally went to decree or judgment, it should fairly be presumed, in the absence of a showing of intermission upon any of the grounds above stated, that there had been a binding lis pendens, and that intervenors pendente lite, are bound by the judgment or decree. After the lis pendens has attached and the *litis contestatio* is established, however great the delay in prosecution may be, the discontinuance of the cause must be left to the discretion of the court. So long as the court in the exercise of its sound discretion retains the case, the lis pendens ought to be held valid. If, however, by reason of the plaintiff's neglect to prosecute, the court shall lose its power over the cause, it will be otherwise.

Otherwise a dangerous discretionary power.

SEC. 106. To hold to the contrary would vest the court with a discretionary power which would be perilous to the rights of litigants. When the elements of a valid lis pendens exist, and the court in the enforcement of its acknowledged jurisdictional power shall proceed to judgment or decree and its execution, if it were permissible for the same or another court in a collateral proceeding to say that there had not been a valid lis pendens binding upon the res, it would amount to the nullification of a judgment or decree where the court had acknowledged jurisdiction. Such a result would be most disastrous and ought never to occur.

The only instance where in a collateral proceeding a court ought to have power to declare the invalidity of the res litigiosa is where one or more of its essential elements—the res, jurisdiction or a proper description are wanting, or where the conduct of the plaintiff has been so misleading, by reason of negligence or other conduct, as to estop him. Even this latitude leaves the vital question of the validity of the lis pendens very much at large, and the powers of the court in collateral proceedings ought not to be further extended. The doctrine that the judgments and decrees of courts, however erroneous, are valid until reversed or otherwise annulled, and can not be attacked collaterally, is a wholesome one which ought not to be relaxed.(1)

Loose language of some of the courts.

SEC. 107. Cases are found in the books where the language used by the courts would seem to import that lis pendens may be declared invalid in a collateral proceeding from mere negligence without respect to its degree, or from the mere lapse of time, without regard to the circumstances of the case. A close examination of

---

(1) Erroneous judgment valid until reversed. Freeman on Judgments, Sec. 135; Wimberly v. Hurst, 33 Ill. 166; Cloud v. Eldorado Co., 12 Cal. 128; Ex parte Watkins, 3 Pet. 193; Preston v. Clark, 9 Ga. 246; Blakely v. Calder, 1 Smith, (N. Y.) 621; B. & W. R. R. Co. v. Sparhawk, 1 Allen, 448; Cailleteau v. Ingouf, 14 La. An. 623; Balgiano v. Cooke, 19 Md. 375; Savage v. Hussey, 3 Jones (N. C.) 159; Hathaway v. Hemmingway, 20 Conn. 190; Feaster v. Fleming, 56 Ill. 457; Chase v. Christianson, 41 Cal. 253.

these cases will show that such language is generally dictum and that the case was decided upon other grounds.

Obiter dicta of this import was used in the case of Gibler v. Trimble,(1) and Trimble v. Boothbey, where the suit had been dismissed twelve years and was not pending when the purchase was made, and where the contract of purchase was made before the suit was commenced. So in Harrington v. McCollum(2) where after a general dismissal there had been a bona fide purchase, and two years had passed before the case had been reinstated. In Watson v. Wilson(3) the purchase was made after the suit abated and there was a delay of two years in reviving the suit. In Harrington v. Harrington(4) the purchase was made before the lis pendens commenced. In Clarkson v. Morgan,(5) where the court uses the language "reasonable diligence in prosecution of suit," the purchase was made before the lis pendens, and there had been twenty-seven years' adverse possession.

Not a continuous prosecution.

Sec. 107½. But the case must pend continuously. If it comes to an end and another is commenced the suit is not continuous. So where a bill was filed, one of the purposes of which was to obtain an account of

---

(1) Gibler v. Trimble, 14 Ohio, 323 and 109.

(2) Harrington v. McCollum, 73 Ill. 483.

(3) Watson v. Wilson, 2 Dana, 411.

(4) Harrington v. Harrington, 27 Mo. 562.

(5) Clarkson et al. v. Morgan, etc., 6 B. Mon. 443. See, also, Haughtwout et al. v. Murphy, 7 C. E. Green, (N. J.) 535; Newman v. Chapman, 2 Rand. 103; Fenwick, Adm. v. Macey, 2 B. Mon. 470; French v. Royal Co., 5 Leigh, 729; Diamond v. Lawrence Co., 37 Pa. St. 353; Green et als. v. White, 7 Blackf. 243–4; Feighley v. Feighley, 7 Md. 563.

rents and profits, and after it had proceeded to a master's report and its approval by the court, the suit was allowed to rest, until it abated by death of a party. A supplemental bill was afterwards filed to charge the estate with an alleged balance upon the accounting. Prior to the filing of the supplemental bill conveyances had been made. Lord Chancellor Lyndhurst held that there was not such a continuous prosecution as to keep the lis pendens of the original suit in force.(1)

(1) Kinsman v. Kinsman, 1 Russ. and Myl. 623. Lord Lyndhurst said: "The single question was, not whether lis pendens was notice to a purchaser, for of that there could be no doubt,—but whether there was or was not a lis pendens in this case? He took it to be perfectly clear that, in order to constitute *litis pendentia*, there must be a continuance of *litis contestatio;* and without going so far as to say with Lord Bacon, that there must be a constant and vigorous prosecution of the suit, still something should be done to keep it alive and in activity. It was unnecessary to go through the authorities which had been adverted to, the rather as, with the exception of Worsley v. Earl Scarborough, where Lord Hardwicke drew the acknowledged distinction between a pending suit and a decree, they would not be found to lay down any distinct principle upon the subject. He was ready to admit that a decree for an account in a creditor's suit would not determine a lis pendens. But when the proceedings went a great deal further than the account; when the cause had been referred to the master, to see what proportions of a given encumbrance two estates should respectively bear; when the master had made his report; when that report, unobjected to and unexcepted to, had been fully confirmed; when the whole of the equities between the parties had been adjusted and adjudicated upon; when everything had been obtained under the decree which the suit had contemplated, and nothing remained but to carry the decree into effect, the case was most materially changed. After the decree, and before execution, it was not pretended that lis pendens could any longer exist. If that were in substance the case here, to what did the difference in form amount? It might be true that no general decree had been made upon the cause coming back for further directions. And why was it so? In all probability because no further directions were required; the rights of the parties having been ascertained and decided by the report, that report confirmed, and still unappealed from, was in

Benefits lost by laches, questioned.

SEC. 108. Some of the courts hold that the party who claims benefits arising from a lis pendens, must, in order to be entitled thereto, as against bona fide purchasers, show that the suit has been duly prosecuted.

A mechanic's lien case was brought in 1852. The suit was ready for hearing in 1853. In 1856 a mortgage was made upon the property involved. In 1857 a petition was filed to foreclose the mortgage. The owners of the mechanic's lien claim, and of a prior mortgage, were made parties to the foreclosure suit and set up and relied upon the prior mortgage and lien suit. No steps were taken in the mechanic's lien suit from 1853 to 1857. It was held in that case that a failure for four years to prosecute the mechanic's lien claim, without an excuse for the delay, was such gross negligence as to deprive the lien claimants of the right to enforce it against subsequent mortgagees, who, it appeared, had no notice of the suit. This and like cases, it seems to me, push the doctrine of loss of lis pendens by negligence too far. The terms which are used are not so material, but it seems to me that in order to invalidate lis pendens the negli-

truth the final judgment in the case. How many years had elapsed after that decree had been pronounced? Upwards of a quarter of a century; and matters might have gone for a century longer, because nobody had any motive to interfere. If the supplemental bill were considered as growing out of the former suit, that might, in a certain sense, be held to be, and perhaps his honor had so held it, a continuance and prosecution of the original cause; but it would be an abuse of the plain meaning of the term lis pendens to apply it to a case like the present, where the supplemental bill was not filed till after the sale had taken place.

Upon these grounds, his lordship was of opinion that at the time when the purchase was made, there was no *litis pendentia* of which the purchaser was bound to take notice."

gence must be so great, and the circumstances such, that a court can say that a party who is deprived of the force of lis pendens ought to be estopped, by reason of the circumstances of the case. Those facts and circumstances ought to be such that a court can say, having in mind that Lord Bacon's rule required a full prosecution, that persons complaining have been misled and induced to act in such manner that those causing such acts should be bound by estoppel.(1)

Estoppel as applied to lis pendens.

SEC. 109.   The ground upon which to place the invalidity of lis pendens for a failure to take action in

(1) Ehrman, etc., v. Kendrick, 1 Met. 146; Watson v. Wilson, 2 Dana, 406; Clarkson, etc., v. Morgan's Dev., 6 B. Mon. 447. It is said in Petree et al. v. Bill, 2 Bush. 62, that a delay of two years without a step taken in the case, or a motion made indicating an intention to prosecute the suit, in the absence of any excuse or satisfactory reason for the delay, is such gross and culpable negligence as to destroy the force of the lis pendens. It is said in Hawes, etc., v. Orr, etc., 10 Bush. 437, that "one who claims the benefit of lis pendens against a bona fide purchaser, must show that the suit was prosecuted with some diligence, and that there was no unreasonable delay. Ehrman v. Kendrick, 1 Met. 149; Watson v. Wilson, 2 Dana, 406; Clarkson v. Morgan, 6 B. Mon. 447." It is said in Ferrier v. Busick, 6 Iowa, 258, that a suit must be duly, constantly and continuously prosecuted in order that it may be treated as a lis pendens.

In Bybee v. Summers, 4 Ore. 261 it is said that to give effect to lis pendens the suit should be prosecuted with such diligence as to give the proceedings some degree of notoriety, and that a delay of five years to prosecute a suit was such unreasonable delay as to invalidate lis pendens. It was held in the case of Mann v. Roberts, 11 Lea, 57, that the lis pendens created by filing papers for condemnation in the Circuit Court and the order of condemnation was lost as against an innocent purchaser for value, by the failure to prosecute for nearly five years. It is said in that case that the rule lis pendens is strictissimi juris. That there must be a close and continuous prosecution. That it is not lost by ordinary diligence and will only be lost by unusual and unreasonable delay, and that the delay may be explained. It is said also in that case that "the doctrine of lis pendens does not depend upon notice at all."

pending suits, for want of "full prosecution," as provided in Lord Bacon's rule, is not, as in many cases
seems to be supposed, negligence merely as such, but
estoppel as warranted by such negligence, and other
conduct on the part of those seeking the enforcement
of lis pendens. Were the invalidity of lis pendens
based upon the ground of negligence alone, power
would be left in the courts to say in each instance
what is and what is not such negligence as should invalidate lis pendens. It would thus in effect make it
a question, the decision of which would rest in the
discretion of the court. It is the province of the
court to declare what the law is and not to make the
law. It is wise to establish rules for judicial determination, rather than to require the court to decide
every case upon its own facts and without reference
to any rule. If the principle of estoppel by conduct
is applied to all of these cases of failure to make "full
prosecution," the court will have for a rule of decision
the well established doctrine of the law of estoppel.
It is established by writers on this subject, that in order to constitute estoppel by conduct, there must concur, *first*, a false representation or concealment of
facts; *second*, that it must be with the knowledge of
the person making the one or concealing the other;
third, that the person affected thereby must be ignorant of the truth; *fourth*, that the person seeking to
influence the conduct of the other must act intention-
ally for that purpose, and *fifth*, that persons complaining shall have been induced to act by reason of such
conduct of the other. In passing upon this question
of negligent prosecution, the courts may well, in applying these elements, assume it to be the duty of

every complainant to make full prosecution of suits, and that third parties have a right to expect and believe that such diligence has been used; and in the absence of information to the contrary treat the facts of non-prosecution of suits as fraudulent concealment on the part of plaintiffs, with their knowledge and intention. Thus a rule may be applied to all these cases which will enable the courts to say, in accordance with established rules of law, when lis pendens claimants are estopped and when they are not.(1)

Affected by estoppel further considered.

SEC. 110.   Then the doctrine of estoppel may sometimes be invoked to bar the enforcement of the rule lis pendens against a pendente lite purchaser. This, as we have seen, may occur when a complainant makes such disposition of the case that it may be inferred that the right to enforce the lis pendens, as to the property involved, has been abandoned, and a decree is taken in the case warranting the conclusion that the complainant looks to a relief entirely independent of, and without regard to, an application of the rule. So, where a moneyed decree was taken against the defendant, for the value of chattels involved in suit, and failing to obtain satisfaction of the moneyed decree, the complainant subsequently invoked the aid of the rule lis pendens, in order to reach the chattels which had been sold pending the suit for full value, it was held that the complainant was estopped.(2)   And

(1) Bigelow on Estoppel, 480.

(2) In the case of Smith *v.* Browne's Admr. et al., 9 Leigh, 293, which was a bill in chancery, involving the title to a slave, the complainant took a decree against the defendant for the value of the slave, which he had sold pending the suit; and failing to collect the amount of the decree, afterwards attempted to enforce his claim to the title of the slave, as acquired in virtue of the rule lis pen-

so, a pendente lite purchaser is estopped from raising any questions which are adjudicated in the pending suit, however warrantable the position would have been but for the relation assumed by such a purchaser. Thus also where an action was brought against a corporation to foreclose a mortgage purporting to have been executed by it, and a decree was rendered enforcing the mortgage, one who had bought the mortgaged property at sheriff's sale on a judgment at law which became a lien subsequent to the commencement of the lis pendens in the foreclosure case, during the pendency of the suit, was estopped from claiming that the mortgage was not the act of the corporation.(1) In such case the court having acquired jurisdiction of the corporation, it was estopped by the decree, and the purchaser at sheriff's sale, having taken pendente lite, was bound as effectually by the decree as was the party defendant in the foreclosure case.

Application of estoppel.

SEC. 111.   In a recent case in Iowa the doctrine of

dens, and the court, in deciding the case, said: "The plaintiffs in equity, by proceeding to take a decree against Fox for the value of the slave James, abandoned their proceedings in rem, and could not afterwards proceed for the specific property against the purchaser pendente lite, as the title of the slave was changed by a decree for his value."

The case of McConnell v. Hanley, 7 J. J. Marsh. 528, is one where the doctrine that lis pendens may be waived or lost by estoppel by conduct, is clearly stated. A plaintiff had proceeded by attachment and acquired an attachment lien upon slaves. After the attachment suit had become a lis pendens, another creditor levied upon and sold some of the slaves upon execution, and the plaintiff in the attachment suit purchased at the sale, and gave a sale bond for the purchase price. He afterwards filed a bill in chancery to enjoin the collection of the bond, relying upon the facts above stated. It was held that the purchase at the sheriff's sale was a waiver of the lis pendens of the attachment.

(1) Horn v. Jones et al., 28 Cal. 194.

estoppel was applied and held to nullify lis pendens. It was an action brought to recover the value of two horses. The owner had executed a chattel mortgage upon the property which had been recorded, to secure his bondsmen upon an injunction bond. A suit was instituted upon the bond, and pending the suit the bondsmen seized the property upon the chattel mortgage, and foreclosed the mortgage. The plaintiff was present at the sale, made no objection thereto, bid off other property covered by the mortgage and recommended the defendant to buy the horses. At that time plaintiff had no interest in the horses. Subsequently judgment was recovered upon the bond against the bondsmen in the suit which was pending at the time of the chattel mortgage sale, and a special execution was issued on this judgment and levied upon the horses. The plaintiff became the purchaser at the execution sale, and brought suit to recover the value of the purchase. The Supreme Court of Iowa properly held, that by reason of his conduct at the sale, inducing the defendant to make the purchase, under the circumstances shown in the case, he was estopped from claiming title himself, which could be based only upon the assumption that the chattel mortgage sale was invalid. The rule undoubtedly is as stated in Gregg v. Wells, that "A party who negligently or culpably stands by and allows another to contract, on the faith and understanding of a fact which he can contradict, can not afterwards dispute that fact in an action against the person whom he has himself assisted in deceiving." It seems to me that there can be little difficulty in placing most cases where parties have negligently prosecuted suits upon this ground of estoppel. Lord Bacon's rule itself provided against any intermission of suit and for full prosecution.(1)

Estoppel further considered.

SEC. 112. In a recent case in Illinois, where the subject was very elaborately discussed by counsel of ability, and carefully considered by the court, the application of the doctrine of estoppel to lis pendens as affecting its efficiency was very fully and clearly considered and announced. In the case under consideration, there had been a delay of four years and two days between the date of the reversal of the case in the Supreme Court and the filing of the mandate in the Superior Court. In that case the court say: "The suit must be kept upon the docket, and there should be no such delays in taking the ordinary steps in bringing it to a final hearing as to lead the opposite party or the community at large to suppose the suit had been abandoned. More especially one will not be heard to invoke this doctrine who has deliberately made false representations to his adversary, for the express purpose of throwing him off his guard, and surreptitiously obtaining a decree against him, as was done in this case, especially when there is good reason to suppose his adversary might and otherwise would have successfully resisted the decree." The matter of leaving a cause off the docket, when in the regular course of the business of the court it would be expected to be there, is a circumstance which may be regarded as tending very strongly to mislead the other side into the belief that the case is abandoned. When to this is added the fact that statements were made to induce a false belief and corresponding action, in neglect of the case,

(1) Miles *v.* Lefi, 60 Iowa, 168; Gregg *v.* Wells, 10 Ad. & E. 90.

and advantages are taken of those circumstances, it is a clear case of estoppel by conduct, and the Supreme Court of Illinois, in so holding, has, it seems to me, placed the question upon the right ground.(1)

The true ground of decision.

SEC. 113. Thus the true ground for decision, in collateral proceedings, in determining as to whether a lis pendens which has been pursued to judgment or decree is or is not invalid, is whether or not under all of the circumstances of the case the prosecution has been attended with such negligence as to have fraudulently induced third persons to believe that the prosecution has been abandoned or will be abandoned, and to have authorized them, in good faith, to deal with the property, or has induced such an assumption of a relation to the res, that it is more equitable that one who has acted with such fraudulent negligence should suffer than that the pendente lite purchaser should be deprived of his purchase. It ought always to require a strong case thus to annul a lis pendens. Upon this ground most of the decided cases may be placed.

Further application of the principle.

SEC. 114. Thus, in the case of Fox v. Reeder,(2) where a bill was filed in 1842 to foreclose a mortgage, the case went to a decree, was referred to the master to report, and an order of sale was made; but no step was taken in the case for twenty-seven years, when the suit was dismissed for want of prosecution and reinstated. The purchaser had been in possession under

(1) Durand et al. v. Lord, 115 Ill. 621; Freeman on Judgments, Sec. 202; Harrington v. McCollum, 73 Ill. 476.

(2) Fox v. Reeder, 28 Ohio St. 181.

his purchase, holding adversely for twenty-one years, and had made valuable improvements.

In Gossom v. Donaldson,(1) the purchaser went into adverse possession after final decree, had continued there more than twenty years, and had made valuable improvements.   In Kinsman v. Kinsman(2) there had been a decree which was substantially final, but some act remained to be done to carry it into execution.   No attempt was made to execute the decree for more than twenty-seven years, during which time the purchasers held adverse possession and had erected valuable improvements.

Close and continuous prosecution.

SEC. 115.   It has been supposed by some that the use of the phrase "close and continued prosecution," which has, doubtless, led to much loose *dicta* on this subject, is an improper deduction from Preston v. Tubbin,(3) due to a statement of the reporter and not of the court.   All that that case decided is that the pendency of the suit at the time of purchase does not affect the purchaser with notice *in any new suit*, the first having been dismissed or discontinued.

Mere lapse of time.

SEC. 116.   Where no "intermission" has occurred, and no other circumstance exists in the case tending to induce the belief that the suit is ended, mere lapse of time will not destroy lis pendens.   In Hunter v. Earl of Hopeton,(4) where the suit had remained dormant eighteen years, Lord Chancellor Westbury said:

(1) Gossom v. Donaldson, 18 B. Mon. 237.

(2) Kinsman v. Kinsman, 1 Rus. & M. 617.

(3) Watson v. Wilson, 2 Dana, 412; Preston v. Tubbin, 1 Vern. 486.

(4) Hunter v. Earl of Hopeton, 4 McQueen, 972.

"This action never has been disposed of, no further step having been taken since the defense was lodged. It has been asleep since 1847, but it is still lis pendens." Lord Kingsdown said: "The suit which, although it had fallen asleep, was, when the notice should have been given, and, I imagine, *still is*, lis pendens." In the case of Wickliffe's Heirs *v.* Breckenridge's Heirs,(1) as we have already shown, there had been a delay of forty-seven years, and the court held the lis pendens not impaired. It is there said not to be necessary that the prosecution should be "with even ordinary diligence."

The rule of the civil law.

SEC. 117. Unlike the common law, the civil or Roman law prescribed a limit to the vitality of *litis contestatio;* but it was a long period. Prior to Justinian, if an interval of *thirty years* intervened after any act of the judge or one of the parties relating to the cause, this was equivalent to the lapse of the right to proceed, or a bar to the further prosecution.(2) Justinian extended the period to forty years. The same period was fixed as a limitation of actions.(3) Al-

(1) Wickliffe's Heirs *v.* Breckenridge's Heirs, 1 Bush. 443; Gossom *v.* Donaldson, 18 B. Mon. 238.

(2) Cod. Theod. 4, 14, 1.

(3) Cod. Lib. VII. Tit. 39, 9.

Saepe quidam suos obnoxios in judicum vocantes et judiciariis certaminibus ventilatis, non ad certum finem lites producebant; sed taciturnitate in medeo tempore adhibita propter potentiam forte fugientium, vel suam imbecilitatem, vel allos quoscunque casus (quam sortis humanae multa sunt) quae nec dici nec enumerari possunt, deinde jure suo lapsi esse videbantur eo, quod post cognitionem novissimam triginta annorum spatium effluxerit, et, hujusmodi exceptione opposita suas fortunas ad alios translatas videntes merito quidem sine remedio autem lugebant.

"Often parties to suits, after commencing judicial proceedings (*i. e.,* after *litis contestatio*) do not carry on their causes to a final end, but in the meantime adhere

though the cause might lie dormant during this period, there was still, *litis contestatio*, lis pendens.(1)

Analogy to period of limitation.

SEC. 118. As, in the civil law, the period during which a cause might lie dormant and lis pendens remain in force, is in analogy to the prescribed period of limitation. So in many cases courts have given force to the circumstance that purchasers have been in possession holding adversely for a sufficient time to have barred the right of recovery but for the pendency of the suit. The fact that a purchaser is thus in open, notorious and adverse possession, and that litigation is allowed to lie dormant, especially when the occupant has no actual knowledge of the suit, constitutes strong ground for impairing the lis pendens, especially when the period of bar by limitation has run.(2)

Dismissal after purchase.

SEC. 119. Where a case is dismissed after a purchase is made pendente lite, and the suit is again reinstated, it will depend upon the terms of the dismissing order and the circumstances of the case, whether the lis pendens will be restored and the purchaser be bound by the judgment or decree.

If the dismissing order is absolute and unconditional,

to silence, either on account of their weakness or other causes (of which humanity are subject to a great number) which cannot be enumerated, so they would seem to let their right lapse, which, after the space of thirty years has elapsed, in the course of varying events, they would be without remedy."

Justinian extended this period to forty years, namely, "*quod nos corrigentes,* etc." See Cod., 7-39, latter part of section 9.

(1) Const. of Justinian, 9, 7, 39; Savigney's System, Vol. 5, Secs. 237-252.

(2) Fox *v.* Reeder, 28 Ohio St. 181; Gossom *v.* Donaldson, 18 B. Mon. 237; Kinsman *v.* Kinsman, 1 Rus. & Mylne, 617.

the title will vest and the lis pendens be destroyed; but if the dismissing order is with leave to restore within a time limited, and the restoration takes place, or is without prejudice, or with general leave to reinstate, and the case is reinstated within a reasonable time, the lis pendens is preserved.(1)

(1) Ferrier *v.* Bazick et al., 6 Iowa, 258; Harrington *v.* McCollum, 73 Ill. 483; see, also, on the subject of the effect of dismissals: Thurston *v.* Thurston, 99 Mass. 39; Gist *v.* Davis, 2 Hill Ch. 335; Curtis *v.* Trustees, etc., 6 J. J. Marsh. 536; Barrowscale *v.* Tuttle, 5 Allen, 377; Smith's Leading Cases, 667; Wilcox *v.* Balger, 6 Ohio, 406; Wright *v.* De Klyne, Pet. C. C. R. 199; Kelsey *v.* Murphy, 28 Penn. St. 78; Perine *v.* Dunn, 3 Johns. Ch. 508; Neafie *v.* Neafie, 7 Johns. Ch. 1; Foote *v.* Gibbs, 1 Gray, 412; Parrish *v.* Ferris, 2 Black. 606; Durant *v.* Essex Co., 7 Wal. 107; Hepburn *v.* Dundas, 1 Wheat. 179.

In Drayson *v.* Pocock, 4 Sim. 284, it appeared that a testator devised his real and personal estate to trustees to be sold for the benefit of his children. They filed a bill to have the will established and trusts performed. At the hearing the bill was dismissed as against the heir, and the court did not establish the will, but made a decree affecting the personal estate only. The suit afterwards became abated and was not revived.

On the death of the surviving trustee, another suit was instituted for the appointment of new trustees, which was done. The new trustees then sold a part of the testator's real estate to the plaintiff, who filed a bill for specific performance.

In deciding the case, the Vice-Chancellor said: " When the case was heard, the court dismissed the bill, as against the heir, and did not establish the will, but made a decree which regarded personal estate only; and therefore there was no general lis pendens with respect to the real estate."

CHAPTER VIII.

APPLICATION OF THE RULE LIS PENDENS.

Preliminary statement.

SEC. 120.   Having shown the origin and character of the rule lis pendens; the principles upon which it rests for support; when it commences; how long it continues, and when it ends; what may be the subject of it; what are the elements necessary for its existence; what is necessary to constitute the quality or state of res litigiosa; what is meant by full and continuous prosecution, we are prepared to enter upon the discussion of cases in which it has been applied.

The importance of this branch of the subject.

SEC. 121.   The consideration of the question as to how the rights of third parties, strangers to the litigation, except as involved in it by their relation to the subject matter of suit and without being parties thereto, is important.   The amount and value of properties involved in this manner, the title and right to which is established or defeated daily in our courts of justice by its application, is very great, and it becomes important to litigants and courts that uniform rules should be eliminated from the mass of decisions upon this branch of the law, so that less confusion and greater certainty in the law upon this subject may prevail.   The great variety of cases, and the changed and varied facts of each, have rendered this branch of the subject one which requires diligent investigation and careful discrimination.

Binding character of lis pendens.

SEC. 122.   It can hardly be inferred that Chancellor Kent, in his opinion in the case of Murray v. Ballou, intended, in his statement that the rule lis pendens had been in force and in continuous application for above two centuries, to emphasize that part of the rule which relates to the commencement of lis pendens; on the contrary, the argument of the learned Chancellor would indicate that the emphasis was particularly intended to be placed upon the nature and binding force of the rule itself without reference to the time of its commencement.(1)

Lis pendens a common law doctrine.

SEC. 123.   The doctrine of lis pendens is applicable as well at law as in chancery.   It was originally applied in actions at law, especially in real actions, where it was always held that the judgment should overreach an alienation by the defendant after the suit was commenced.(2)   Some courts seem to have

(1) Murray v. Ballou, 1 Johns. Ch. 577; Newell v. Newton, 10 Pick. 470; Holman v. Patterson's Heirs, 29 Ark. 358; Garretson v. Brien et al., 3 Heisk, 535; Exch. Bank v. Andrews, 12 Heisk, 306; Talbot's Exrs. v. Bell's Heirs, 5 B. Mon. 323; Hale v. Warner, Admr., 36 Ark. 217; Moon's Admr. v. Crowder, 72 Ala. 79; Jackson v. Andrews, 7 Wend. 152; Harrington v. Slade, 52 Barb. 166; Hersey v. Turbett, 27 Casey, 418; Diamond v. LawrenceCo. 37Casey,353; Fowler's

Appeal, 75 Casey, 483; Loomis v. Riley, 24 Ill. 307; Green et al. v. White, 7 Blackf. 242; Gossam v. Donaldson, 18 B. Mon. 231; Inloe's Lessee v. Harvey, 11 Md. 519; Blanchard v. Ware, 37 Iowa, 308; Farmers' Nat. Bank v. Fletcher, 44 Iowa, 253; Bennett v. Williams, 5 Ohio, 461; Tilton v. Cofield, 93 U. S. 163; Hunt v. Haven, 52 N. H. 162; County of Warren v. Marcy, 92 U. S. 96.

(2) Chandron v. Magee, 8 Ala. 573.

expressed a different view and to suppose that the doctrine is applicable only in chancery (1) But the fact is it was adopted into chancery, as shown in a former chapter,(2) by Lord Bacon, in analogy with the rule as enforced in real actions at common law. The strictures of Mr. Freeman in his work(3) on Judgments, upon the opinion in the case of King v. Bill, upon this point, although severe, are well deserved. There are other cases in which the loose and unguarded language of courts have tended to a like erroneous conclusion upon this question.(4)

Not peculiar to a court of chancery.

SEC. 124. As has just been stated the doctrine of lis pendens is not peculiar in its application to courts of chancery. In the old real actions a judgment at law was conclusive upon the title to the lands involved, although the defendant had conveyed pendente lite.(5) According to the opinion of Lord Justice Turner it is said, "that this doctrine belongs to a court of law, no less than to courts of equity, appears from a passage in 2d Inst., 375, where Lord Coke, referring to an alienation by a mesne lord pending a writ, says that the alienee could not take advantage of a particular stat-

(1) King v. Bill, 28 Conn. 593.

(2) Sec. 1, *ante.*

(3) Freeman on Judgments, Sec. 192.

(4) Jackson v. Dickinson, 15 Johns. 309; Doe v. Howland, 8 Cow. 277; Jackson v. Bowen, 7 Cow. 13; Bissell v. Payne, 20 Johns. 3; Jackson ads. Raney, 3 Cow. 75; Roberts ads. Jackson, 1 Wend. 486.

(5) Newman v. Chapman, 2 Rand. 102; Murray v. Ballou, 1 Johns. Ch. 566; Bellamy v. Sabine, 1 De Gex and Jones, 580; Diamond v. Lawrence Co., 37 Penn. St. 353; Hersey v. Turbett, 27 Penn. St. (3 Casey,) 423; Johnson v. Stone, 13 Johns. 447; Bennett's Lessee v. Williams, 5 Ohio, 461. Where a purchaser pendente lite makes improvements upon lands purchased, he subjects the improvements which he may make, as well as the lands, to the result of the suit. Patterson v. Broom et al., 32 N. Y. 95.

ute of Westminster, because he came to the mesnalty pendente brevi, and in judgment of law the mesne as to the plaintiff remains seized of the mesnalty, for *pendente lite nihil innovetur*." And so now, a purchaser from a defendant in ejectment takes his title pendente lite, and though not a party, is bound by the judgment at law which may be rendered against his grantor after conveyance. In the case of King against Bill et al. language is used which implies that lis pendens applies solely to chancery proceedings. This is not correct.(1)

(1) In King *v.* Bill, referred to in the text, the court uses the following language: "Whatever may be the extent to which the doctrine of lis pendens is carried elsewhere, or is to be adopted here, it being now for the first time brought before our courts, we are of the opinion that it is not necessary for us to examine it, because it is purely an equitable doctrine, adopted, recognized and enforced in courts of equity alone, and cannot be rendered available in proceedings in courts of law; and therefore in an action at law in which the legal title only of the plaintiff should come in question, that title could not be met or impaired by an application to it of a merely equitable principle, the cognizance of which is confined to courts of chancery. And if, in the present controversy, the defendant can avail himself of that principle on his petition against Mason, he can do so, not in an action at law between himself and the plaintiff, but only by a petition in chancery founded on a claim for equitable relief which is cognizable in that court alone."

Mr. Freeman, in his valuable work on Judgments (Sec. 192), uses the following severe, but well merited, language, with reference to this case: "In the case of King *v.* Bill (28 Conn. P. 593) the statement is made that lis pendens is a purely equitable rule, recognizable only in equity. This case is, however, chiefly, if not exclusively, remarkable for the clearness and precision with which it misstates the law of lis pendens. It has no force as an authority, being overruled by the case of Newton *v.* Birge, 35 Conn. 250." Freeman on Judgments, Sec. 192.

In the case of Jackson *v.* Stone, 13 Johns. 447, the facts were, that actions in ejectment had been brought in 1810 for the same lands against Samuel and Benjamin Baldwin, and judgments recovered in October, 1813. Pending the ejectment suits, the defendant Stone purchased from one Scott, who had also acquired his title from the

Not favored by presumptions.

SEC. 125.   As the rule of lis pendens is often attended with hardship, it is not a favorite with the

Baldwins, pendente lite. Upon this state of facts the court in their opinion say: "The defendant, as respects the title to the premises, stands in the same situation as the Baldwins, from whom he took the possession of the parcel of land for which the action of ejectment was brought. The defendant in an action of ejectment cannot by giving up the possession to a third person, after the commencement of the suit, defeat the effect of the recovery. It is perfectly well settled that a recovery in an ejectment, as far as respects the right to mesne profits, is conclusive of the title, as to the land possessed by the defendant when the action was brought, into whose hands soever it may subsequently pass by transmutation of the possession from the defendant in ejectment."

The case of Jackson ex dem. Hendricks *v.* Andrews et al., 7 Wend. 152, was an ejectment. Title was in Abraham Franklin. Judgment was recovered against him and docketed May 21, 1808. Execution was issued and the property in question sold on the judgment by the sheriff and sheriff's deed was issued to Hendricks November 15, 1821. Abraham Franklin had conveyed to Henry Franklin the same premises, March 29, 1800, but the deed was not acknowledged until March 29, 1808, nor recorded until April 21, 1808, and the latter had conveyed to Abraham. It was further shown

that Hendricks had filed a bill in chancery against Abraham Franklin, Henry Franklin and others, attacking the deed last above referred to, on June 3, 1809. That a decree had passed in that case on the 20th day of January, 1817, declaring said deed null and void. Upon this state of facts the court say:

"The first inquiry in this case is as to the effect of the proceedings in chancery instituted by the lessor of the plaintiff upon the rights of the parties. It is not pretended that Henry Franklin had any other title to these premises than such as he acquired by the deed from Abraham Franklin; and that deed was expressly adjudged and pronounced to have been void on the ground of frauds not incidentally and collaterally, but in a proceeding instituted in proper form and with proper parties for the express purpose of testing its validity. Again: The conveyance from Henry Franklin to Cushman was made in November, 1810, while the suit in chancery against the grantor, calling in question his title to this identical property was pending and in a course of active and persevering litigation. This conveyance was void on the ground of lis pendens. A lis pendens duly prosecuted is notice to a purchaser so as to effect and bind his interest. The conveyance is so far a nullity, and it cannot avail the party against the title established by the pending suit."

courts; and a party claiming the benefit of it must clearly bring his case within it. The rule will not be helped out by the presumption of essential facts so as to give it effect. In the absence of proof, therefore, it will not be presumed that the bill was filed prior to the service of the writ or the entry of the judgment;(1) nor will the court presume service of the writ,(2) or any other fact material to make out a lis pendens.(3)

And so where a bill was filed by C against A, February 13, 1818, to avoid a deed to him from a grantor, through which alone A claimed title; but it did not appear when the subpœna was served; judgment was rendered against A on the 17th day of February, 1818; a deed was made to B on the 16th day of May, 1818, in pursuance of a sale made on execution, the decree in the chancery suit being entered on June 16th, 1818. It was held that B was not a pendente lite purchaser, and that he took a valid title by the sheriff's deed.(4)   It is a doctrine *strictissimi juris*.

Lis pendens not strictly a lien.

SEC. 126.   Although often referred to for convenience, as a lien, lis pendens is strictly not a lien. It is simply the power or force of jurisdiction of the court. When brought to enforce a lien, it may be said to energize or give efficiency to the lien, and thereby itself, in connection with the lien which it enforces, be treated as a lien. But of itself it is simply the power of the court, taking effect upon the subject matter of

(1) Leitch et al. *v.* Weir et al., 48 N. Y. 609.

(2) Roberts ads. Jackson, 1 Wend. 486.

(3) Sorrel *v.* Carpenter, 2 P. Wms. 482; 3 Sugden on Vendors, 460.

(4) Roberts ads. Jackson, 1 Wend. 486; Sanders *v.* McDonald, 63 Md. 509.

the suit, so as to hold it within the grasp of the court for the execution of final judgment. And so it has been held that a bill filed to enforce an equity against a fund vested in real estate, and not based on a judgment and execution, can not strictly be said to be a lien. In such case the lis pendens merely disables the defendant from conveying, pending the suit, except subject to the final judgment or decree; and so in North Carolina, where the defendant in a pending cause of the character above described was vested with the legal title to real estate, and pending the suit went into bankruptcy, and an assignee was appointed under the bankrupt law, the title to the real estate was held to vest in the assignee, and the complainant was compelled to go into the bankrupt court to prosecute his claim, or in default of so doing be barred by the action of that court. While the main doctrine of that case as to the lien of lis pendens is correct, it would seem to be more in accord with the authorities had the complainant filed an original in the nature of a supplemental petition, and brought the assignee in bankruptcy into the case, and thus to have maintained the jurisdiction of the chancery court, and have taken decree in accordance with the rights of the parties in that court.(1)

The courts may prescribe a rule lis pendens.

Sec. 127. By the act of Congress, passed in pursuance of the provisions of the constitution of the United States, March 2, 1793,(2) it is declared to "be lawful for the several courts of the United States from

---

(1) Dixon v. Dixon, 81 N. C. 329; Blum v. Ellis, 73 N. C. 293; Withers v. Stenson, 79 N. C. 341.

(2) Act of March 2, 1793, Ch. 22, (1 Stat. L. 333).

time to time, as occasion may require, to make rules
and orders for their respective courts, directing the
return of writs and process, the filing of declara-
tions and other pleadings, the taking of rules, the entering and making up of judgments by default, and
other matters in the vacation; and otherwise, in a
manner not repugnant to the laws of the United
States, to regulate the practice of the said courts
respectively, as shall be fit and necessary for the ad-
vancement of justice, and especially to prevent delays
in proceedings." Under this and other congressional
legislation, rules have been prescribed by the Supreme
Court of the United States, and the District and Circuit Courts, regulating the practice in these courts;
and the question arises, how far the provisions of
State statutes, regulating the practice in suits prosecuted in the State courts, and in reference to their becoming notice lis pendens, are binding upon the Federal Courts. It was determined by the Supreme Court
of the United States, in Wayman et al. *v.* Southard et
al., and The Bank of the United States *v.* Husted,(1)
that Congress possesses the power, exclusive of the
State legislatures, to regulate the proceedings of the
Federal Courts, and might constitutionally confide the
power to the courts themselves.

That court accordingly held, in those cases, that
the laws of Kentucky compelling plaintiffs to receive
certain bank notes in satisfaction of their executions,
or upon the refusal so to do, compelling the acceptance of replevin bonds from defendants, staying
the payment two years, were held not to be binding

(1) Wayman et al. *v.* Southard,   States *v.* Husted, 10 Wheat. 61.
10 Wheat. 40; Bank of the United

upon the Federal Courts; and so likewise a statute
of Kentucky, forbidding the sale of property upon execution for less than three-fourths of its appraised
value. The Supreme Court of California, in the case
of Majors *v.* Cowell,(1) has recently held that statutes
passed by the various State legislatures, regulating
the filing of notices of lis pendens, do not apply to
actions commenced or pending in the Federal Courts
of the United States, unless such statutes, or the substance of them, have been adopted as rules of practice
by the Supreme Court of the United States, or by the
rules of the Circuit Courts, made in pursuance of the
39th rule of the Supreme Court. So it would seem
that the Federal Courts have power to establish by
rule, or probably by judicial determination, what
shall constitute notice lis pendens in the Federal
Courts, and are not bound by the provisions of legislative enactments upon the subject of lis pendens in
the several States. They may, however, adopt such
legislation as the rule for the Federal Courts. In
passing upon and giving legal effect to proceedings
which have been had in the State courts, the
Federal Courts will, however, give effect to such proceedings, in accordance with the rule lis pendens, as
provided by the State legislatures.

**Essentials where lis pendens applies to personal prop-
erty.**

SEC. 128. I am thoroughly satisfied from a review
of the authorities, that at the present time the doctrine
is well established that, with the exception of negotiable paper, lis pendens applies to personal property as
well as real estate.

(1) Majors *v.* Cowell, 51 Cal. 482.

In order, however, that there may be an efficient
lis pendens, where chattels are involved in the suit,
it is necessary that the property be exactly identified
by specific description in the bill; that the suit be
continuously and energetically prosecuted; that the
vendor be a party at the time of the sale, and that the
court to which the summons is returned have complete jurisdiction of the property in dispute.   The
decree will not affect holders of equitable interests or
contingent rights, and taking judgment or decree for
the proceeds of the property involved during the suit,
or its value, will be construed as a waiver of the right
to enforce lis pendens.   In the case of Fletcher *v.*
Ferrel, 9 Dana, 372, the doctrine was maintained that
lis pendens involving personal property would have
effect in other States than that in which the proceedings were had, and in a recent case in Missouri the
court, referring to that case, say: "We have no doubt
that within the United States, purchasers in one State
pending suit in another must be treated as pendente
lite purchasers and subject to the rule applicable to
such purchasers, when the suit has been prosecuted
with due diligence to a decree, process has been personally served on defendant, and the subject matter
of the controversy is within the jurisdiction of the
court."   While this rule, thus broadly held and apparently maintained by the text writers, may in some instances work hardship, the position taken in the cases
above referred to would seem to be a logical conclusion.   If the lis pendens is efficient as well upon personal property as upon real estate, shall it not be
treated as efficient and binding everywhere, as well as
in the State where the proceedings are had?   If not,

where shall the line be drawn to which its efficiency shall reach, and where it shall end? If the action were replevin there could be no question that the judgment of the court would be binding everywhere.(1)

Doctrine of lis pendens in Supreme Court of the United States.

SEC. 129. The decisions of the Supreme Court of the United States have been in conformity with the weight of the authorities on all questions involved in the law of lis pendens. In the case of the Mechanic's Bank of Alexandria v. Setons,(2) decided in 1828, the doctrine that a pendente lite purchaser is bound by the judgment or decree which may be entered in the cause, was fully sustained. In Miller v. Sherry(3) they held that a bill in chancery which does not describe the property with sufficient definiteness to identify it would not be constructive notice of the lis pendens, and that lis pendens does not commence until service upon the defendant after the bill is filed. In the case of the County of Lee v. Rogers(4) they held that the rule lis pendens did not apply, because of the discontinuances which had occurred in the cause. In the case of the County of Warren v. Marcy,(5) decided in 1877, Justice Bradley, delivering the opinion of the court, went into a very learned and elaborate discussion upon the whole subject of the law of lis pendens. That was a case brought by Marcy against the county and its officers, to enjoin the issuance or delivery of railroad aid bonds, and the principal question in the case

(1) Carr v. Lewis & Co., 15 Mo. App. R. 551; Fletcher v. Ferrel, 9 Dana, 372.

(2) Mech. Bk. of Alex. v. Setons, 1 Pet. 299.

(3) Miller v. Sherry, 2 Wal. 337.

(4) County of Lee v. Rogers, 7 Wal. 181.

(5) County of Warren v. Marcy, 97 U. S. 96.

was whether the law of lis pendens applies to such bonds or negotiable paper. The learned Justice, speaking for the court, refers to the leading case of Murray v. Ballou, and concurs with the conclusions of Chancellor Kent, in respect to the doctrine of lis pendens, as elaborated in that and other cases decided by that learned Chancellor. He also discussed other leading cases in various States of the Union, and reaches the conclusion in accord with all the authorities that the rule lis pendens does not apply to negotiable paper, and affirming the doctrines of the law of lis pendens generally upon other questions. This case of Warren County v. Marcy may be regarded as a leading case upon this branch of the law in this country.

Again, the binding force of lis pendens upon a purchase, pending the suit, was declared in 1883, in Whiteside v. Hazelton.(1) Finally, in the case of Scotland County v. Hill,(2) Justice Waite, delivering the opinion of the court, declared the doctrine as sustained by the authorities generally, that actual notice to a purchaser of county bonds, before the purchase, of their invalidity, or an injunction against their issuance or delivery, would have the effect of a lis pendens upon the purchase, although in that particular case the property involved was negotiable paper. It will thus be seen that the decisions of the Supreme Court of the United States are in accord with the general doctrines promulgated by other courts, upon the various branches of the law of lis pendens.

The court will not presume service to sustain lis pendens.

SEC. 130.   The doctrine held in the early cases that

---

(1) Whiteside v. Hazelton, 110 U. S. 296.

(2) Scotland County v. Hill, 112 U. S. 183.

the court will not presume the existence of a material fact, in order to sustain a lis pendens, was applied in a case in Maryland.

Pending a suit to foreclose a mortgage, the mortgagor and his wife conveyed the property.

It did not appear from the record in the foreclosure suit whether at the time of the conveyance the defendant had been served with process. The court held, first, that there could be no lis pendens until the bill was actually filed and the subpœna served upon the defendant; second, that if the deed was made before the subpœna was served, the legal title passed to the assignee, unaffected by the subsequent decree in the foreclosure case; third, that as the record in the foreclosure case did not show when the subpœna was served, the court would not presume that the conveyance was made after the service, and consequently held that there was no lis pendens when the deed was made.(1)

Where the decree is merely for money.

Sec. 131.   Where a bill was filed to enforce a lien for purchase money, but was not prosecuted with that view, but, on the contrary, when it came to decree, the decree was so framed as merely to determine the amount of the purchase money, without any provision with respect to the lien, one who had purchased the land pending the bill, although with full knowledge of the equitable lien, was held not bound by lis pendens.(2)

Does not apply in actions in personam.

Sec. 132.   It may be stated as a general rule that

(1) Sanders v. McDonald, 63 Md.   (2) Briscoe v. Bronaugh, 1 Tex.
509.   326.

where the litigation relates merely to a moneyed indebtedness, or the contention is over a mere money demand—whatever the form of action is—there is no such lis pendens as will charge the property of the defendant with the final judgment or decree in the case.

This conclusion necessarily follows from the well settled principles which have already been considered. In such an action—whether it be an assumpsit, debt, trespass, trover, or case—or although in equity, it must be limited to a contention over a simple moneyed demand. There is never any issuable allegations in the pleadings which should be considered as constructive notice that any particular property of the defendant is sought to be charged with the judgment or decree which may be obtained against the defendant. All that may be inferred from the suit is that a claim may result against the defendant's estate generally, which, if maintained, may have to be satisfied out of his real or personal property, or possibly neither.

If the rule lis pendens were pushed to the extreme of an application in actions in personam—whether arising ex contractu or ex delicto—defendants would have to submit to any exactions which claimants, upon unfounded and unjust claims, might make against them, or quit doing business altogether.

If the pendency of a personal action were constructive notice lis pendens, it would be liable to be made efficient upon any of the property of the defendant of whatever character, and there would be a practical prohibition against dealing with the defendant pending the litigation. It would therefore be against public policy to apply the rule to personal actions.(1)

Lis pendens of amended bill.

SEC. 133.   A bill was filed in the name of one having

(1) St. Joseph Manf. Company v. Daggett, 34 Ill. 562; Ray et al. v. Rowe, 2 Blackf. 258; Shearon v. Henderson, 38 Tex. 250; Russell et al. v. Kirkbridge, 62 Tex. 459.

In the case of Ray et al. v. Rowe, 2 Blackf. 258, Scott, Justice, delivering the opinion of the court, said: "The only question referred to our adjudication is the correctness of the charge given by the court to the jury. The court instructed the jury that a transfer of property made by a defendant during the pendency of an action of slander against him, and before the rendition of judgment, is of itself fraudulent, unless it be made in pursuance of a prior contract, or in payment of a precedent bona fide debt; that all purchasers are bound to take notice of the pendency of said suit; and that if a purchase be made during the pendency of such action, whether with or without consideration, it is considered fraudulent in law, as to the judgment plaintiff, unless there is other property sufficient to satisfy the judgment. To this instruction the defendant excepts. On the broad ground that fraud vitiates all contracts, a conveyance made with a design to avoid the payment of a just debt, or to defeat the recovery of a pre-existing right, is void as it respects creditors, and the pendency of a suit is one of the many badges of fraud which would induce a court of equity to set aside

such conveyance or a jury to regard it as a nullity in a trial at law. The pendency of an action is constructive notice of the matters involved in that suit, and a purchaser of the property which is the immediate object of the pending action will be affected by it as a purchaser with notice. But a lis pendens is not even constructive notice of any other points than those which are in dispute between the parties to such action. 3 Atk. 392; Newell on Contracts, 506, 507. So much, then, of the instruction as states that a transfer of property made during the pendency of an action of slander is of itself fraudulent, whether with or without consideration; and that all persons are bound to take notice of such action in the unqualified manner expressed is unsupported by authority."

In the case of Worsley v. The Earl of Scarborough, 3 Atk. 392, so often referred to in the books as an authority, the court said: "No case has gone so far, and it would be very inconvenient if where money is secured upon an estate, and there is a question depending in this court upon the right of or about that money, but no question relating to the estate upon which it is secured but is wholly a collateral matter, that a purchaser of the estate pending that suit should be affected with notice by such implication as the law creates by the pendency of a suit."

no interest in the subject matter of suit; but in the exercise of a judicial discretion the real parties in interest were allowed to be substituted as complainants. There was no lis pendens, however, until after the amendment was made, substituting the real parties.

In all such cases the suit will be regarded as pendent only from the time of the amendments,(1) and a purchase made before the amendment will not be affected by the lis pendens.

Lis pendens statutes not binding on Federal Courts.

SEC. 134.   As we have seen, State statutes providing for the filing of notices lis pendens do not apply to suitors in the United States Courts.   The object of such statutes is to regulate the remedy and proceedings in court, and cannot be said to establish property rights by their entering into and becoming a part of contracts relating to the rights of property.

What rights will be secured or cut off by the operation of such statutes depends entirely upon what the parties involved shall do.   These statutes may therefore be said to relate to the remedy.   That being so it is clearly beyond the power of the legislatures of the several States, as we have already shown, in this mode to prescribe remedies in the Federal Courts.

(1) Clarkson et al. *v.* Morgan's Devisees, 6 B. Mon. 452; Mitford Pl. 400 (top p.) Mitford says: "In most of the cases the indulgence given by the court is allowed to the mistakes of the parties, and with a view to save expense; but when *injury* may arise to *others*, the indulgence has been more rarely granted, and so far as the pendency of a suit can affect others than the parties to the suit or strangers, matter brought into a bill by amendment *will not have relation* to the time of filing of the original, but the suit will be so far considered as pendent only from the time of the amendment."

The lis pendens of an amendment will not relate back prior to the filing of the amendment. Stone *v.* Connelly, 1 Met. (Ky.) 654; Dudley *v.* Price's Admr., 10 B. Mon. 88; Sec. 32, *ante.*

The Supreme Court of the United States in the exercise of clearly defined powers can alone prescribe rules of practice for the Federal Courts of the Union, subject to the right of the various inferior Federal Courts to adopt further rules not inconsistent or in conflict with those so prescribed. This position is not in conflict with the numerous cases which hold that the Federal Courts are bound by the construction of the Supreme Courts of the several States, construing the State statutes, and relating to the rights of persons and property.

When, however, the Federal Courts are called upon to pass upon proceedings had in State courts, where it would appear that notices lis pendens under State statutes had been filed, the Federal Courts will give force and the same effect to such lis pendens notices as would be given by the courts of the several States, but will not be compelled to adopt as rules of proceedure the practice of filing notices lis pendens in the Federal Courts, nor if filed in supposed pursuance of State statutes would any effect be given thereto.(1)

Money in hands of the law.

Sec. 135. Where an officer of court has in his hands moneys, collected in pursuance of court orders and process, and is made a defendant to a bill in chancery which seeks to reach such moneys, he will not be held bound by the lis pendens of the chancery suit, if he should pay over the moneys in his hands, in obedience to the orders and process of the court of which he is an officer.

(1) Wayman et al. *v.* Southard, 10 Wheat. 40; Bank of the U. S. *v.* Husted, 10 Wheat. 51; Majors *v.* Cowell, 51 Cal. 482.

His superior duty is to the court of which he is an officer and by which he would be liable to punishment for contempt if he should fail to pay over the money.

Such moneys are in the custody of the law, and public policy requires that they should not be involved in litigation. In such case public policy requires that the lis pendens should not be enforced.(1)

Notice to protect liability does not create lis pendens.

Sec. 136.   Where one carrier is sued for the loss of goods, and notifies the second carrier to. whom he delivered the same for transportation of the pendency of a suit against the first carrier, and requires him to defend, the judgment against the first carrier is not conclusive as to the question of liability of the second carrier.

It is only conclusive as to the fact that the judgment was recovered, and that it was for the value of the goods lost. Such notice does not create a lis pendens as against the second carrier, and is in no manner conclusive upon the question of privity.(2)

Nor where suit was brought upon the covenants of a deed could the defendant create a lis pendens, as against his covenanter, not a party to the suit, by the service of a notice and requirement of defense. Such notice has legal effect upon the rights of the parties upon other grounds than that it is a lis pendens.

(1) Turner v. Fendall, 1 Cranch. 116; Wilder v. Bailey, 3 Mass. 289; Freeman v. Howe, 24 How. 450; Lammon v. Feusier, 111 U. S. 17; Covell v. Heyman, 111 U. S. 176; Van Norden v. Morton, 99 U. S. (9 Otto) 378; Krippendorf v. Hyde, 110 U. S. 276; Buchanan v. Alexander, 4 How. 20; Gilbert v. Lynch, 17 Blatchf. 402; Clark v. Shaw et al., 28 Fed. R. 356; Carrington et al. v. Didier et al., 8 Gratt. 265.

(2) The C. & N. W. R. R. Co. v. The N. Line Packet Co., 70 Ill. 271.

It may be stated as a general proposition that notice
to defend or protect liability does not create or constitute lis pendens.

Lis pendens legislation and judicial construction.

SEC. 137.   Recently the legislatures of many of the
States have passed statutes in effect providing
that notice lis pendens shall commence from the time
of actually filing or recording a paper, denominated a
"notice of lis pendens," giving the title of the case
and describing the subject matter of the suit.

The importance of these statutes and the decisions under them is so great that the author has
deemed it proper to devote to them two chapters of
this work.(1)   But it may be remarked here that the
force and effect of these statutes are substantially the
same, so far as relates to the opportunity given to the
public to become advised as to the subject matter of
litigation, as the statutes of Illinois, Texas, Iowa and
some of the other States above referred to.(2)

The legislative direction that notices of lis pendens
filed under these statutes shall be regarded as constructive notice to strangers from the time of filing, is
one which the courts, where public policy under the
terms of the statute would require to be adopted,
should adopt without legislative direction.

In the absence of such legislative construction, the
courts should construe statutes in such a manner that
the conclusion reached will be promotive of the public
good.

Knowledge of entry of fiat equivalent to lis pendens.

SEC. 138.   In the case of Boils *v.* Boils et al., which

(1) See chapters XIV and XV,   (2) Secs. 62, 63 and 67, *ante.*
post.

was a divorce suit, a fiat had been entered by the court for an injunction against the defendant not to dispose of his lands pending the suit, but the injunction had not issued, nor had the subpœna been served.

A purchase was made from the defendant, with the full knowledge on the part of the purchaser that the fiat had been made. It was held that the conveyance by the defendant to the purchaser was invalid; that the knowledge that the fiat had been entered was equivalent, in effect, to the injunction itself.(1)

Amendatory bill filed without leave not lis pendens.

SEC. 139. Where a bill was filed which did not by its allegations involve the property in dispute, and an answer had been filed to it, and afterwards the complainant, without leave of court, filed an amendatory bill which alone involved the property in question, and the defendant during the progress of the suit, under this state of the pleadings, sold the property which was sought to be involved by the amendatory bill and which consisted of slaves. It was held that the amendatory bill was improperly filed without leave of court, and did not create a lis pendens as to the slaves, and that the sale made by the defendant would not be vacated as having been made pendente lite.(2)

Lis pendens does not affect with fraud.

SEC. 140. It was said in Meade v. Lord Orrery that "a lis pendens is only a general notice of an equity to all the world, but cannot affect any particular person with a fraud, unless there was a special notice of the title in dispute then to that person."

From this statement it has grown into a sort of

(1) Boils v. Boils et al., 1 Cold. 284.   (2) Baldwin v. Love et al., 2 J.J. Marsh. 490.

maxim, found frequently in the books, that a lis pendens does not affect with fraud.(1)

What is meant by this statement is that the moral turpitude and its consequent legal disability or the disqualification which attaches to a person who has committed actual fraud, and creates a disability to his or her assertion of rights which otherwise would attach to the property or thing in respect to which the fraud was committed, does not attach to any person who becomes a purchaser pendente lite, unless there was such special notice to the purchaser as would give the transaction the color of actual fraud.

That the notice of lis pendens in itself, by virtue of the proceedings alone, would not have the legal effect of casting an imputation of moral turpitude upon the pendente lite purchaser, nor otherwise bar his rights, than by the judgment or decree in the pending case. That it could not be said of such a purchaser, in opposition to his attempting to assert any right to the thing in suit not barred by it, that the court would not aid him because he had been a party to a fraud, because he did not come into court with clean hands, or for any other like reason prohibit his assertion of a right which may attach at law or in equity to a person who has committed a fraud, or to the property or thing in respect to which the fraud was committed.(2)

How lis pendens affects limitations.

SEC. 141. Cases may sometimes arise where, although the contention relates solely to a money

(1) Meade *v.* Lord Orrery, 3 Atk. Eq. B. 2, Ch. 6, 3, note (n); Idem B.
211.   3, Ch. 3, 1, note (b.)
    (2) 1 Story's Eq. Jur. 406; 2 Fonb.

demand, yet the judgment or decree may, when rendered, operate upon some lien or security upon property in such a manner as to affect it.

Thus, where a moneyed demand is secured by mortgage upon real estate, and a suit at law is brought upon the indebtedness in an action in personam, and pending the suit at law, which of itself would not be a lis pendens, a statute of limitation would have run against the mortgage as well as against the debt, but for the suit at law; and after the running of the statute, judgment in personam shall be rendered in the suit at law, what, if any, effect will the judgment and proceedings in the suit at law have upon the mortgaged property?

In cases where the defendant in the suit at law is the same person as the mortgagor, and the mortgaged property is sold for full value, after the statute of limitation would have run against the mortgage, but for the suit at law merging the mortgage debt into the judgment and proceedings in the suit at law, could it be claimed in a subsequent suit to foreclose the mortgage that the purchaser pending the suit at law was bound by the effect of the judgment upon the mortgage, and that by reason of the rendition of the judgment the mortgage debt had been revived—was not limited and could be foreclosed as against the purchaser—thus giving effect to the suit at law indirectly as a constructive notice lis pendens?

It may well be argued, in favor of such a result, that the mortgage is a mere incident of the debt; that the owner of the debt is necessarily the equitable owner of the mortgage; that therefore the revival of the debt, to which the mort-

gagor was a party, would operate as a revival of
the mortgage and prevention of the running of the
statute of limitation, and that the rendition of the
judgment at law, defeating the bar of the statute as to
the debt, would also defeat the bar of the mortgage,
and that a new limitation would commence to run on
the mortgage from the date of the judgment at law.
That it would be the duty of anyone dealing with the
mortgaged property to ascertain at his peril the condition of the obligations secured by the mortgage; and
thus to know that a personal action was pending on
them and that a judgment, with its legal consequences
upon the mortgage and the property secured thereby,
would follow.

Although this would be a harsh application of
the doctrine of notice lis pendens, in connection
with notice of the terms of the mortgage under
the recording laws, it would seem to be warranted by
the grounds upon which it rests. It is clear in the
ordinary case of a pendente lite purchaser of the subject of litigation that the statute of limitation cannot
be invoked as against the successful litigant, to avoid
the results of the application of the rule lis pendens,
however long a time may elapse after the purchase
until the final determination of the pending case.

It is true the bringing of suit arrests the running of
the statute of limitation. But if, at the time the
statute is arrested, it has not become a complete bar, it
cannot become so pending the suit, and so during the
progress of the suit, involving the title to real estate,
where the doctrine of lis pendens is applicable, the statute of limitation will not run in favor of the purchaser
so as to defeat the operation of the rule lis pendens.

Lis pendens applies to femme coverts.

SEC. 142. Where a creditor's bill was filed against a femme covert to subject her separate property to the payment of a debt, it was held that the doctrine *pendente lite nihil innovetur* applies to femme coverts as well as to other litigants, except as modified by local statutes.(1)

Proceedings in a State court by leave of a Federal Court in pending suit.

SEC. 143. Where a Federal Court has jurisdiction of a pending case before it and leave is given a party to the suit to institute proceedings in a State court, for any purpose which the Federal Court may deem germane to the pending suit, the proceedings so allowed by license of the Federal Court will be a lis pendens binding upon purchasers of the property involved in the suit in the Federal Court.

So, where one of the defendants in a proceeding to foreclose a railroad mortgage in a Circuit Court of the United States, by leave of the court, proceeded in a State court to establish a vendor's lien on the road, a purchaser of the railroad property at the foreclosure sale was held chargeable with notice of the proceedings in both the State and United States Courts and was bound by lis pendens.(2)

Filing of supplemental bill does not discontinue the prior lis pendens.

SEC. 144. Filing of a supplemental bill does not have the effect to discontinue the antecedent lis pendens of the original bill.

As we have seen, if other property is involved by

(1) Hughes & Co. *v.* Hamilton et als., 19 W. Va. 395.

(2) Loomis et al. *v.* Davenport et al., 17 Fed. R. 301.

the supplemental bill, the scope of the lis pendens is enlarged but not destroyed. The new lis pendens caused by the supplemental bill, if additional property becomes involved, will commence with the filing of the supplemental bill, except as to new parties, and as to them will generally commence from the service of the subpœna.(1)

Lis pendens an excuse for a trustee.

SEC. 145. Lis pendens is a good excuse for apparent laches of a trustee or other persons acting in a fiduciary character. And so it has been held in Delaware that where a testator died in 1812 and executors were appointed to administer under the will and shortly afterwards a bill in chancery was filed involving the estate and, in consequence of the pendency of this suit, the accounts of the executors were not determined by the Orphan's Court until 1841, the lis pendens was a sufficient excuse for the delay and apparent laches.(2)

Where a lis pendens injunction not necessary.

SEC. 146. Where a bill in chancery is filed seeking to affect real estate and has become a lis pendens, an injunction issued against the defendant to prevent his disposing of or incumbering the lands is unnecessary.

So soon as the suit becomes an efficient lis pendens the defendant is unable to dispose of the lands. Should he do so his conveyance would be invalid when overreached by the decree which would be rendered in the case. Lis pendens effectually prevents the alienation pending the suit.(3)

(1) Stoddart's Lessee v. Myers, 8 Ohio, 203; Sec. 133, *ante.*

(2) Colwell, Admr. v. Miles, 2 Del. Ch. 117.

(3) Smith v. Malcolm, 48 Ga. 346; Powell v. Quinn et al., 49 Ga. 529;

Where defendant disabled pendente lite.

SEC. 147. Where, at the time of the filing of a bill for specific performance of a contract, a defendant has power to fulfill his contract, but becomes unable to do so either wholly or in part during the pendency of the suit, the court having had jurisdiction of the subject matter, and having the power to afford partial relief by decreeing a specific performance so far as the defendant's ability extends, can give the plaintiff compensation in damages also.(1)

Lis pendens applies to the proceeding by scire facias to foreclose mortgage.

SEC. 148. In this country statutory provision is made in many of the States for the foreclosure of mortgages and for other purposes at common law by scire facias. This proceeding when brought for the enforcement of a lien is based upon the record of the instrument, the provisions of which are sought to be incorporated in judgment and enforced. In such cases the lien is enforced in accordance with the recorded instrument.

The rule lis pendens is applicable to this form of action, adopted in the foreclosure of mortgages, as well as to the suit in equity for the same purpose.

So in a case in Pennsylvania, under the statute of that State, a mortgage was executed by one Haven to Love. Stevenson purchased the mortgage and took an assignment to himself. He afterwards obtained a loan from Lewis and gave a mortgage on the same land and also agreed to assign the mortgage in ques-

Matthews et al. v. Cody et al., 60 Ga. 357; Snowdon & Co. v. Craig, 26 Iowa, 156; Mays et al. v. Wherry et al., 3 Cooper, 81; Tabb v. Williams, 4 Jones' Eq. 352.

(1) Wiswall v. McGowan, 2 Barb. 270; Kempshall v. Stone, 5 Johns. Ch. 193.

tion. This assignment was not made, but Lewis brought a scire facias thereon claiming to be the equitable owner of the mortgage.

Pending the suit Anderson bought at a sheriff sale the undivided interest of one Kelly, who was co-terre tenant with Stevenson when the mortgage was executed. Anderson afterwards intervened in the scire facias case. It was held that the proceeding by scire facias was a lis pendens so as to charge Anderson with the notice of the equitable ownership of the mortgage.(1)

When the court will not aid.

SEC. 149. Where a deed is set aside as fraudulent upon bill filed by creditors and a conveyance of the estate has been made pendente lite, the pendente lite purchaser will not be held to account upon a subsequent bill for rents and profits from the filing of the first bill. The court of chancery will go no farther than to remove the fraudulent conveyance and will leave the parties to their remedy at law as to rents and profits.

This is upon the familiar principle, constantly enforced in chancery, that where parties to a fraudulent transaction ask the Chancellor to relieve them from the consequences of their own fraudulent acts, such relief will be denied.

Nor will a court of chancery aid one who tortiously secures possession of property. A court of chancery will not allow the possession of property involved in suit to be changed, pending a suit, tortiously or collusively; and it was held where a party applied to the Chancellor to protect him in possession by an in-

(1) Anderson v. Love, 16 Reporter, 763.

junction that although he was rightfully entitled to the possession the court would not sustain him in tortiously, by his own act, securing it.

In such cases the court will not interfere to prevent the opposing party who has been put out tortiously from recovering if he can at law the possession of which he has been forcibly deprived.(1)

Interest on balance pending injunction suit.

SEC. 150. Where a party is prevented by the pendency of an injunction suit from establishing his right at law, it is the duty of the court to see that no injury arises to him in consequence of the court's interference and the pendency of the suit preventing him from asserting his rights at law. This principle was early decided by Lord Eldon, and afterwards by Lord Chancellor Manners.(2)

The doctrine of tacking.

SEC. 151. Where there were three mortgages on the same premises and pending a bill brought by the first mortgagee to foreclose the first mortgage, making the second and third mortgagees parties, the third mortgagee bought the first mortgage. It was held by the

(1) Higgins et al. v. The York Bldg. Co., 2 Atk. 107; Grafton v. Griffin, 1 Russ. & Myl. 336; Parkhurst v. Alexander, 1 Johns. Ch. 398; St. Andrew's Church v. Thompkins, 7 Johns. Ch. 14; 1 Story's Eq. Jur., Ch. 70, Secs. 412, 420; Chase v. McDonald, 7 Harr. & Johns. 160; Burnett v. Deniston, 5 Johns. Ch. 35.

In the above case of Higgins et al. v. The York Bdg. Co. it was further held that a mortgagor was entitled to the rents and profits for the years he was in possession of the mortgaged premises, even though they were received by him pending the suit to foreclose the mortgage.

(2) O'Donel v. Browne, 1 Ball. & Beat. 262; Pulteney v. Warren, 6 Ves. 73; Morgan v. Morgan et al., 2 Dick. 643. In the case of O'Donel v. Browne, *ante*, interest was allowed upon the balance found upon an accounting before the master from the time it was found pending suit.

High Court of Chancery of England, and in accord with the English rule, that the third mortgagee would thereby obtain a priority and should be paid his whole money before the second mortgagee. This was called the doctrine of tacking.(1)   But the English doctrine of tacking mortgages is generally exploded in this country.(2)

When bill against pendente lite holder demurrable.

Sec. 152.   Where one takes a conveyance of the subject matter of litigation pending the suit, and after the suit is prosecuted to final judgment or decree, the complainant files a fresh bill against the pendente lite purchaser, a demurrer to the bill will be sustained. This manifestly should be so, on the principle that the pendente lite purchaser takes subject to the final determination of the pending suit and is bound, although not made a party, whether he had or had not actual knowledge of the pendency of the suit at the time of purchase, or whether he paid a valuable consideration or not.

And so where a complainant had obtained a decree establishing title in himself, and pending the suit the defendant had conveyed to another, and after the commissioner appointed by the court had conveyed to the complainant, he filed a fresh bill against defendant's grantee to remove the pendente lite conveyance to him as a cloud, it was held that the bill would not lie, the title having passed by the com-

(1) Robinson *v.* Davison et als., 1 Bro. Ch. 63.

(2) Grant *v.* U. S. Bank, 1 Caine's Cas. in Eq. 112; Bridgen *v.* Carhartt, Hopk. 234; Hughes *v.* Worley, 1 Bibb. 200; Colquhoun *v.* Atkinson, 6 Munf. 550; James *v.* Morey, 2 Cow. 246; Loring *v.* Cooke, 3 Pick. 50; Coombs *v.* Jordan, 3 Bland. 284; Frost *v.* Beekman, 1 Johns. Ch. 298.

missioner's deed, and that complainant had a complete remedy at law.(1)

Lis pendens on cross petition.

SEC. 153. Where a defendant in a suit involving real estate having filed his answer filed a cross petition, alleging that he was the owner of an equitable interest in certain lands and that the legal title was in the wife of the plaintiff, and thereupon the court ordered that she be made a party to the suit, whereupon she answered the cross petition.

It was held that under this state of the pleadings, there was a lis pendens as to the lands described in the cross petition.(2)

Defective lis pendens validated.

SEC. 154. Where property was about to be sold upon a judgment and execution issued thereon which were subject to attack for irregularities, and the defendant in execution filed a bill to enjoin the sale, and the complainant in his pleadings asked the court to grant affirmative relief and validate the levy made by the sheriff, and the court so adjudicated in favor of the judgment creditor, dismissing the defendant's bill for injunction, it was held that the cross-claim of the judgment creditor to have his levy validated was a lis pendens which made valid the levy, and a sale thereunder and thereafter passed the title of the defendant in execution and those holding under him to the purchasers at execution sale.

Where another creditor of the common debtor procured a judgment against said debtor subsequent to the one which was so validated, and proceeded to sell

(1) Majors *v.* Cowell, 51 Cal. 479.   (2) Brundogo *v.* Briggs, 25 Ohio St. 652.

on such junior judgment the purchaser became a pendente lite purchaser, and was bound by the adjudication in the pending injunction case.(1)

Lis pendens of bill to partition.

SEC. 155.   The lis pendens of proceedings to partition land whether they occur in chancery or in pursuance of statutes at common law, do not interfere with the owners of undivided interests, although parties to the suit in dealing with the property.   Whatever conveyances occur pending such a proceeding will, like all other cases of pendente lite conveyances, be controlled by the decree or judgment in the partition case when it comes to be entered.   Such conveyances if made will be given effect by the court upon the interest in severalty finally apportioned to the party conveying or receiving conveyances, and the remaining interest apportioned to the adverse party in severalty will be discharged by the decree or judgment from the effect of such conveyances.

The same is true with respect to incumbrances made pendente lite.   They will be given effect by the court upon the interest in severalty which shall be awarded to the mortgagor or his assigns, and the other interest in severalty will be discharged therefrom.(2)

(1) Allen v. Halliday, 28 Fed. R. 261; Stoddard's Lessee v. Myers, 8 Ohio, 203; Turner et al. v. Babb et al., 60 Mo. 342; Wade on Notice, Sec. 377; Tilton v. Cofield, 93 U. S. 168.

(2) In the case of Speller v. Speller, 3 Swanst. 557, an injunction was allowed, but Lord Eldon said on granting it: "I wish it to be understood as my opinion that in general, on a bill for specific performance of an agreement to sell, the plaintiff is not entitled to restrain the owner from dealing with his property; a different doctrine would operate to control the rights of ownership." Echliff v. Baldwin, 16 Ves. 267; Curtis v. Marquis of Buckingham, 3 Ves. & Bea. 168.

Lis pendens of an appeal.

SEC. 156. When an appeal has been effected from a judgment rendered in a probate court, before a justice's court or other trial court to an Appellate Court, the lis pendens of the suit is continued and held in force. If the trial in the Appellate Court shall be de novo, the jurisdiction of the Appellate Court or the scope of the lis pendens in that court will be the same as it was in the trial court—that is, it will have jurisdiction to determine all issues which were triable in the court below.(1)

In cases of dismissal.

SEC. 157. It is said that even where a bill in chancery is dismissed without prejudice and re-instated, it is a debatable question, upon which respectable authority may be found on both sides, whether a purchaser of the subject matter in litigation, after the dismissal but before the case is re-instated, would take pendente lite.(2)

If the dismissal were with leave to re-instate within a time limited, and the case were re-instated within the time, it would seem that there should be a lis pendens; but if the order of dismissal were silent

(1) Washburne *v.* Van Steenwick, 32 Minn. 337.

(2) Harrington et al. *v.* McCollum, 73 Ill. 483.

In Harrington et al. *v.* McCollum, *ante,* 73 Ill. 483, the text of Freeman on Judgments, Sec. 203, is approved and it is said that, "If a suit were prosecuted with effect, as, if at law it were discontinued, or the bill suffered a non-suit; or if in chancery the suit were dismissed, for want of prosecution, or for any other cause, not on the merits; or if at law or in chancery no suit abated; although in all such cases a new action could be brought, it could not affect a purchaser during the pendency of the first suit." Still less, it is said, could a purchaser, after dismissal and before revival of the suit in such cases, be affected. Price *v.* White, 1 Bailey's Eq. 234; Blake *v.* Heyward, 1 Bailey's Eq. 208; Turner *v.* Crebill, 1 Ohio, 174.

as to the right to re-instate, the better opinion would seem to be that there would be no lis pendens. This should certainly be so after the term had passed or the period had elapsed within which the court would have power or the party a right to have the cause re-instated, and especially if the rights of third parties had intervened.

When note not set off in pending case.

SEC. 158.   Where, at the time a plaintiff brought a suit, the defendant held a note against him, upon which he had commenced a suit against plaintiff prior to the date of the plaintiff's writ, and before the trial term of the plaintiff's case defendant had recovered a judgment upon his note in his own suit, the question arose whether the note which the defendant had held could be set off in the plaintiff's suit.

It was held that it could not, because the note had become merged in the judgment, and the defendant's claim in that form was not a proper subject of offset.(1)

Bill against administrator.

SEC. 159.   Where a bill was filed against the administrator of an estate, in the course of administration, by a creditor of the estate, it was held that the suit was lis pendens and notice to all the world of the prior right of the claimant, a creditor of the estate, and that a purchase from the heirs, pending the suit, of property which would be affected by the result of the suit against the administrator, would be charged with the prior lien of the complaining creditor, and bound by the decree or judgment against the administrator.(2)

(1) Andrews *v.* Varrell, 46 N.   (2) Dunn, etc. *v.* Jones, Coke R.
H. 17.   (1 N. J.) 133.

But the pendency of a suit in a foreign county from that in which an executor resides and where the testator died and his estate was being administered, and to which suit the executor was not a party, is not a lis pendens as against such executor, nor is it presumptive notice of a claim against the estate involved in such suit, so as to render the executor liable personally.

When decision of Appellate Court final.

SEC. 160. And so it is held that where a case is appealed to the Supreme Court of a State, and that court has remanded the case with instructions to the inferior court, that such determination of the Supreme Court is a final adjudication of the rights of the parties, from which an appeal will lie to some court which has appellate jurisdiction.

As, where a federal question was involved in a case which was decided by the Supreme Court of a State, entitling the party to appeal to the Supreme Court of the United States, and the Supreme Court of the State remanded the case with directions to the inferior court, it was held that the order and adjudication of the Supreme Court of the State was a final order in the case, from which the parties could sustain their appeal to the Supreme Court of the United States.(1) That being so, it follows that parties acquiring an interest in the subject matter of litigation after such litigation has been determined by the Supreme Court of a State, and the case is remanded with instructions, but before a final decree is entered by the inferior court, will take pendente lite and be concluded by the decision of the Supreme Court. If this were not so there could be

(1) Comrs., etc. v. Lucas, 9 Legal News, 91.

no end to litigation, and the determinations and decisions of courts of last resort could be successfully thwarted.

Cost in pendente lite purchase.

SEC. 161. The vendee of a defendant in a foreclosure case takes the property subject to all the costs which may be made in the case, including those occasioned by an appeal prosecuted by the defendant subsequently to his conveyance.

It would seem the same rule should apply to any other character of case where at the time of conveyance or transfer the lis pendens binds the property.(1)

Assumption clause in conveyance.

SEC. 162. Where .there was a clause in a conveyance assuming the indebtedness secured by a mortgage upon the real estate, and there had been a verbal understanding before the commencement of a suit to foreclose the mortgage that the assumption clause contained in the deed should be released, but the agreement was not reduced to writing and filed until the foreclosure suit had become a lis pendens, it was held that the release having been made in pursuance of an ante litem agreement was valid, although reduced to writing pendente lite.(2)

Where recovery of judgment and return of execution waived.

SEC. 163. In the case of Carr v. Fearington et al.(3) it appeared that a State Convention of the State of North Carolina had passed "An ordinance to change the jurisdiction of the courts and rules of pleadings

(1) McPherson v. Hansel, 2 Beas. Ch. 299.

(2) O'Neill v. Clark, 6 Stewart,

(1) 445.

(3) Carr v. Fearington et al., 63 N. C. 561.

therein," which provided for retardation in the process of the collection of debts in the common law courts, and by Sec. 18 of that ordinance, that any "creditor attempted to be defrauded" might "without obtaining judgment at law file his bill in equity," and empowering the courts to direct proper issues to be made up and tried, and to make such orders and decrees as to right and justice might appertain.

Prior to this ordinance it was the settled law of the State that before a creditor could file his bill in chancery, either to subject equitable assets to his debt or to avoid fraudulent conveyances made by the debtor, he must have established his debt at law and that the creditor must show by the pleadings and proof that the debtor had no property liable to execution, in addition to showing that he had obtained judgment and taken out an execution thereon and had it returned nulla bona.

The Supreme Court of North Carolina held that the effect of the ordinance was to waive the necessity of procuring a judgment and issuing and causing to be returned nulla bona an execution thereon as preliminary to the right to file a creditor's bill. They held that such a bill, filed under the ordinance upon a claim not reduced to judgment, was a lien upon the assets of the defendant debtor.(1)

Other general applications of lis pendens.

Sec. 164. The examples of general applications of the rule lis pendens noticed in this chapter by no means embrace them all.

***

(1) Rountree *v.* McKay, 6 Jones' Eq. 87; Tabb *v.* Williams, 4 Jones' Eq. 352; Kirkpatrick *v.* Means, 5 Ir. Eq. 220; Wheeler *v.* Taylor, 6 Ir. Eq. 225; Carr *v.* Fearington et al., 63 N. C. 561.

In subsequent chapters, in the application of the rule to classes, all cases will be considered with respect to their respective classes.

But aside from these, the consideration of its application generally to individual cases might be extended to much greater length.

A striking illustration of this remark is the application of the rule lis pendens to proceedings by garnishment.

Scope of lis pendens in garnishment.

Sec. 165. Garnishment is generally considered a proceeding at law and, as a rule, the scope of its lis pendens extends to and embraces only legal rights and interests. It reaches legal assets of defendants in the hands of third persons or intercepts legal credits owing to debtors of plaintiffs invoking its aid.(1)

But property held by one as a custodian of the law, or as a disburser of public moneys, or in other official capacity, is not bound by the lis pendens of this proceeding.(2)

Property actually in the hands of a pledgee or mortgagee is not bound by it, as such person would be the trustee of the pledgor or mortgagor.(3)

(1) Thomas v. Hopper, 5 Ala. 442; Price v. Masterson, 35 Ala. 483; Lackland v. Garesche, 56 Mo. 267.

(2) Prindle v. Shutz, 2 Miles, 330; Corbyn v. Ballman, 4 W. & S. 342; Buckley v. Echert, 3 Penn. St. 368; Clark v. Boggs, 6 Ala. 809; Thorn v. Woodruff, 5 Ark. 55; Fowler v. McClelland, 5 Ark. 188; Stillman v. Isham, 11 Conn. 124; McMeekin v. State, 9 Ark. 553; Winchell v. Allen, 1 Conn. 385; Ward v. Hartford Co., 12 Conn. 404; Lyons v. Houston, 2 Harring, 349; Rollo v. Andes Ins. Co., 7 C. L. N. 63.

(3) Drake on Attachments, Secs. 538-540; Hudson v. Hunt, 5 N. H. 538; Patterson v. Harland, 12 Ark. 158; Budlam v. Tucker, 1 Pick. 389; Central Park v. Prentice, 18 Pick. 396; Whitney v. Dean, 5 N. H. 249; Howard v. Carl, 6 Me. 353; Callender v. Farbish, 46 Mo. 226; Kergin v. Dawson, 1 Gilm. 86; Rhodes v. Magomigal, 2 Penn. St. 39.

But the lis pendens of this process may be and is enlarged by statutes in some of the States.(1)

In order to extend the lis pendens of this process to property in the hands of a mortgagee or pledgee, there must be a tender or offer of payment of the mortgage debt.(2)

Constructive possession of the property will not authorize the execution of the process.(3)

The lis pendens will not bind where there is in possession of the garnishee property without his knowledge or consent.(4)

A chose in action is not subject to it except the proceeding be against the payor. It can not be enforced against a person holding such property merely for collection, or as collateral security, or for safe keeping.(5)

It cannot be invoked against equitable debts, nor unless the debts can be enforced in an action at law by the defendant against the garnishee.(6)

(1) Aldrich v. Woodcock, 10 N. H. 99; Boardman v. Cushing, 12 N. H. 105; Chapman v. Gale, 32 N. H. 421; Hughes v. Corey, 20 Iowa, 399; Carty v. Fuestermaker, 14 Ohio St. 457; Blake v. Hatch, 25 Vt. 555; Treadwell v. Davis, 34 Cal. 601.

(2) Cotton v. Marsh, 3 Wis. 221; Frisbee v. Langworthy, 11 Wis. 375; Cotton v. Watkins, 6 Wis. 629; Selleck v. Phelps, 11 Wis. 380.

(3) Andrews v. Ludlow, 5 Pick. 28; Willard v. Sheafe, 4 Mass. 235; Grant v. Shaw, 16 Mass. 344; Burrell v. Letson, 1 Stob. 239; Drake on Attachment, Secs. 482, 484.

(4) Staniels v. Raymond, 4 Carl. 314; Bingham v. Lanping, 26 Penn. St. 340.

(5) Grosvenor v. F. & M. Bank, 13 Conn. 104; Hall v. Page, 4 Ga. 428; Clark v. Viles, 32 Me. 32; Rundlet v. Jordan, 3 Me. 47; Skowhegan Bank v. Farrar, 46 Me. 293; Rhignel v. McConnell, 25 Penn. St. 362; Deacon v. Oliver, 14 How. (U. S.) 610; Morse v. Pillow, 3 Humph. 448; Fitch v. Waite, 5 Conn. 117; Fuller v. Jewett, 37 Vt. 473; Lane v. Felt, 7 Gray, 491; Scofield v. White, 29 Vt. 330; Ames v. Jackson, 35 Vt. 173; Smith v. Wiley, 41 Vt. 19; Ellison v. Tuttle, 26 Tex. 283; Tirrell v. Canada, 25 Tex. 455.

(6) Harrell v. Whitman, 19 Ala.

The process cannot be enforced upon debts which become due upon a contingency and which may therefore never become absolutely due.(1)

It is now generally held that, although a debt is not due at the service of the writ, yet that if it is absolutely payable at a future date it may be reached by garnishment.(2)

But the garnishee will not be compelled to make payment until it is fully matured in accordance with the terms of his contract. In such case the entry of the judgment will be delayed, or if not delayed, the execution will be stayed until the debt is due.(3)

The pendency of a suit for the collection of a debt will not place it beyond the reach of garnishment.(4)

135; Roby v. Labuzan, 21 Ala. 60; Godden v. Pierson, 42 Ala. 370; Grain v. Aldrich, 38 Cal. 520; Hoyt v. Swift, 13 Vt. 129; May v Baker, 15 Ill. 89; Lowry v. Wright, 15 Ill. 95; Patten v. Smith, 7 Ind. 438; Gillis v. McRay, 4 Dev. 172.

(1) Haven v. Wentworth, 2 N. H. 93; Burke v. Whitcomb, 13 Vt. 421; Tucker v. Clisby, 12 Pick. 22; Roberts v. Drinkhard, 3 Met. (Ky.) 309; Wentworth v. Whittemore, 1 Mass. 471; Taber v. Nye, 12 Pick. 105; Russell v. Clingan, 33 Miss. 535; Harris v. Aiken, 3 Pick. 1; Sayward v. Drew, 6 Me. 263; Frothingham v. Haley, 3 Mass. 68; Kettle v. Harvey, 21 Vt. 301; Bishop v. Young, 17 Wis. 46; Bates v. N. O. J. & G. N. R. R. Co., 4 Abb. Pr. 72; B. & O. R. R. Co. v. Gallahue, 14 Gratt. 562; Davis v. Ham, 3 Mass. 33; Wood v. Partridge, 11 Mass. 488; Clement v. Clement, 19 N. H. 460; Shearer v. Handy, 22 Pick. 417.

(2) Branch Bank v. Poe, 1 Ala 396; Cottrell v. Varnum, 5 Ala. 229; Fulweiler v. Hughes, 17 Penn. 440; Dunnegan v. Byers, 17 Ark. 492; Clanton v. Griggs, 5 Ga. 424; Place v. Jones, 3 Murph. 256; Stewart v. West, 1 H. & J. 536; Pursell v. Pappenheimer, 11 Ind. 327; Sheriff v. Buckner, 1 Litt. 127; Sayward v. Drew, 6 Me. 263; Willard v. Sheafe, 4 Mass. 235; Walker v. Gibbs, 2 Dall. 211; Fay v. Smith, 25 Vt. 610; Clapp v. Hancock Bank, 1 Allen, 394; Nichols v. Scofield, 2 R. I. 123.

(3) Wilson v. Albright, 2 G. Greene, 125; Anderson v. Wanzer, 5 How. (Miss.) 587; Gridley v. Harraden, 14 Mass. 496.

(4) Crabb v. Jones, 2 Miles, 100; Smith v. Barker, 10 Me. 458; Sweeney v. Allen, 1 Penn. St. 380; Jones v. N. J. R. R. Co., 1; Grant's Case, 457; Foster v. Jones, 15 Mass. 185; Locke v. Tippets, 7 Mass. 149; Hitt

But when the suit has arrived at such a stage that it is too late to interpose the garnishment of the debt, as a defense in the suit, the right to garnishee will be denied.(1)

v. Lacy, 3 Ala. 104; Huff v. Mills, 7 Yerg. 42; Leiber v. St. Louis, 36 Mo. 382.

(1) Erenson v. Healey, 2 Mass. 32; Howell v. Freeman, 3 Mass. 121; Kidd v. Shepherd, 4 Mass. 238; Mc-Caffrey v. Moore, 18 Pick. 492; Holt v. Kirby, 39 Me. 164; Strout v. Clement, 22 Me. 292; Caila v. Elgood, 2 Dow. & R. 193; Coppell v. Smith, 2 D. & E. 312.

CHAPTER IX.

DOCTRINE OF LIS PENDENS IN ITS APPLICATION TO PURCHASERS.

Preliminary statement.

SEC. 166. Having treated in the preceding chapter the subject of the application of the rule lis pendens generally in cases where that doctrine has been applied in the courts, we will next proceed to consider cases where the doctrine is applied in respect to purchases at sales occurring under circumstances involving the rule.

These, it will be perceived, may vary with each case. Purchases may be made from the parties to suits or their grantees, under trust deeds executed pendente lite, or prior to the initiation of lis pendens, under judgments and decrees of courts, and in various other ways.

Formerly a purchase pendente lite champerty.

SEC. 167.   In 1300, in the reign of Edward I, an English statute(1) was enacted providing, among other things, that no other officer or other person for and in consideration of a part of the thing involved in suit, should take upon him the business " that is in suit;" that no litigant upon any such agreement should give up his right in the thing in litigation to another, and declaring a forfeiture of the lands and goods of the litigant equal in value to the interest so given up as a penalty for so doing, and also declaring such interference with the subject of litigation champerty and maintenance.   Under this statute the English courts

(1) The statute referred to, 28 Edw. I, Chap. 11, is as follows: "And further, because the king hath heretofore ordered by statute that none of his ministers shall take no plea of maintenance by which statute other officers were not bounden before this time; (2) the king will, that no officer nor any other (for to have part of the thing in plea) shall not take upon him the business that is in suit; (3) not none upon any such covenant shall give up his right to another; (4) and if any do, and he be attainted thereof, the taker shall forfeit unto the king so much of his lands and goods as doth amount to the value of the part that he hath purchased for such maintenance.   (5) And for this attainder, whosoever will, shall be received to sue for the king before the justices before whom the plea hangeth and the judgment shall be given by them.   (6) But it may not be understood hereby that any person shall be prohibit to have counsel of pleaders, or of learned men in the law for his fee, or of his parents and next friends."

held(1) that conveyances by litigants of the subject matter of suit made lis pendens are void. This English statute was substantially re-enacted in the State of New York. The New York statute(2) in addition explicitly declared, "that every such conveyance and agreement should be void." In the case of Jackson ex dem. v. Ketchum et al.,(3) in which Chancellor Kent and Ambrose Spencer were of the Judges deciding it, this question came before the court under the New York statute for decision, and the court in a per curiam opinion held that the sale of the subject matter of that suit for a consideration was a violation of the statute and mala fides, following the decisions under the English statute.

It is believed that no such penal or prohibitory statute is now in force in any of the States, and the law now unquestionably is that such conveyances and agreements are voidable merely. In the case of Camp v. Forrest et al.,(4) the Supreme Court of Alabama, after referring to the English and New York statutes, say: "We find many cases in which the effect of lis pendens to impart notice of the matter in controversy is considered, but in none that has come under our consideration has the pendency of a suit for land been held to take from the defendant in possession the right to sell it in the absence of a statutory prohibition."

It may now be laid down as the uniform rule that a conveyance of real estate involved in litigation is not void, but that the grantee takes the title of his grantor

(1) Mowse et al. v. Weaver et al., Moore, 655.

(2) Laws of N. Y., vol. 1, p. 343; 2 R. S. 691, S. 56.

(3) Jackson ex dem. v. Ketchum et al., 8 Johns. 480.

(4) Camp v. Forrest et al., 13 Ala. 120.

subject to the pending litigation, but without the right necessarily to become a party. He succeeds to the interests of his grantor and is entitled to the fruits of the pending litigation and is bound by its determination adversely to him.(1)

Purchaser of legal title pendente lite.

Sec. 168. In Krebaum *v.* Cordell et al. the bill was filed by Delia B. Cordell and her husband against George W. Cordell, alleging that certain lands were purchased with the money of the wife and title taken without her knowledge in the name of her husband, that she had paid all taxes on the land, and that the husband without her knowledge had conveyed to the defendant without consideration and prayed a conveyance to the wife.

A supplemental bill was afterwards filed alleging conveyance pendente lite to Krebaum. The court held that appellant took pendente lite and must convey to Delia B. Cordell, the wife.(2)

Conveyances pendente lite are now voidable merely.

Sec. 169. The title acquired by a pendente lite

---

(1) In Metcalfe *v.* Pulverloft, 2 Ves. & Beam. 205, it is said: "The true interpretation of the rule is that the conveyance does not vary the rights of the parties in that suit; that it gives no better right, having no effect with reference to any beneficial result against the plaintiff in that suit." * * * * "The purchaser is in the same situation in which the vendor stood, upon this plain principle that the suit is to be decided according to the state of the case when it was instituted; and the rights, however they may be varied by death, bankruptcy, etc., cannot be affected by the voluntary act of either party."

(2) Krebaum *v.* Cordell et al., 63 Ill. 24. In Jaffrey *v.* Brown, *ante,* it was held that the purchaser of an antecedently acquired equity may perfect his title or claim by buying in legal title from those not connected with the suit as parties, privies or otherwise. See, also, Parks *v.* Jackson, 11 Wend. 442;

purchaser is only avoided by the judgment rendered or decree entered in the pending case. As between the parties to the sale the title is valid. It is merely voidable, not void.(1) Its validity is entirely dependent upon the result or outcome of the pending litigation. If the seller shall succeed in the suit and the lis pendens is ended by a decision in his favor and is not revived by appeal, or is ended by final determination on appeal, the purchaser's title becomes valid. If the title of the seller is divested by the adjudication of the court in the pending case the purchaser takes nothing.

Thus in the case of Cromwell v. Clay the principal question was, whether the deed of a purchaser pendente lite was absolutely void or merely voidable? Cromwell had instituted an action of detinue, founded on a bill of sale which Crear executed to him for a slave, at a time when Piper and Waugh had separate suits in chancery pending against Crear, for the purpose of subjecting the slave to the payment of his debt. Clay, as deputy sheriff, took the slave into his possession in virtue of an order from the Chancellor. The court held that " the bill of sale from Crear to Cromwell was not absolutely void." That "as the

Gibler v. Trimble, 14 Ohio, 323; Irving v. Smith, 17 Ohio, 226; Clarkson et al. v. Morgan's Dev., 6 B. Mon. 441; Fogarty v. Sparks, 22 Cal. 142.

(1) Norton v. Birge, 35 Conn. 250; Merrick et al. v. Hutt., 15 Ark. 344; Bayer v. Cockerill, 3 Kan. 282; Lee v. Salinaes, 15 Tex. 495; Meux v. Anthony, 6 Eng. 411; Shotwell v. Lawton, 30 Miss. 27; Lytle v. State, 17 Ark. 609; Walden v. Bodley's Heirs, 9 How. 34; Copenhagan v. Hoffaker, 6 B. Mon. 13; Jackson v. Warren, 32 Ill. 331; Loomis v. Riley, 24 Ill. 307; Inloe's Lessee v. Harvey, 11 Md. 519; Sharp v. Lumley, 34 Cal. 611; Barrelli et al. v. Delassus et al., 16 La. An. 280; Calderwood v. Tevis, 23 Cal. 335; Horn v. Jones, 28 Cal. 194; Montgomery v. Byers et al., 21 Cal. 107; Boulden v. Lanahan, 29 Md. 200; Hurlbutt v. Baleenop, 27 Cal. 50.

chancery suits had not been decided " (when the case at law was decided) "it could not be affirmed that the complainants would certainly obtain decrees subjecting the slave to the payment of their demands." That if the bill should be dismissed the title would be unquestionably good.   That the title to the slave would not lose its efficiency until final decree in favor of the complainants in the chancery case.   That in the meanwhile the title to the slave would vest in Cromwell.   That if a decree should be rendered in the chancery cases, subjecting the title of the slave to the payment of Crear's debts, the decrees, to the extent of the debts, would avoid the bill of sale, but that it would be good as to the equity above the amount decreed in the chancery cases.(1)

Sale on trust deed pendente lite.

SEC. 170.   Where the validity of a trust deed is not drawn in question by a bill in chancery, but the scope of the bill simply involves the question as to the amount due under the trust need, the trustees may proceed to sell under the trust deed pending the chancery suit, but the purchaser at the sale will take subject to the determination of the court in the pending case.   If the court shall hold that the entire amount claimed under the trust deed, or an amount equal to the amount bid at the sale, perhaps, is due, the purchaser's title will be valid notwithstanding the suit; but if, on the contrary, the court shall decide in the chancery case that there is nothing due, he would take nothing by the purchase.(2)

But where a bill was filed to redeem from a mort-

(1) Cromwell v. Clay, 1 Dana, 579.

(2) Jenkins v. International Bk. et al., 111 Ill. 460.

gage which contained a power of sale and, pending the suit, a sale was made under the mortgage in pursuance of the power, the trustee being a party to the bill to redeem, and the land was purchased by strangers to the suit, it was held that they were purchasers pendente lite and chargeable with notice of the rights of the complainant.(1)

A purchaser pendente lite of trust property.

Sec. 171.   But where a suit in chancery was pending, involving property alleged by the pleadings to be held by a defendant in trust, and a sale upon a judgment against the party so holding in trust was made without any actual notice to the purchaser of the trust property, it was held that the purchaser would take the property as trustee and subject to the rights of the cestui que trust, and that the pendency of the bill alleging the capacity in which the property was held would be notice to such purchaser.(2)

It is said that a person so purchasing at judicial sale acquires no better title than the defendant in execution had, and in the case referred to it was held that the familiar doctrine that one who purchases from a trustee with notice of the trust, either actual or constructive, should be charged with the same trust in respect to the property as the trustee from whom he purchases, would apply; and that, too, even though the purchaser pays a valuable consideration.

Pendency of suit involving consideration of note, not notice.

Sec. 172.   Where a note was given for purchase money of real estate, and a bill was afterwards filed al-

(1) Roberts et al. *v.* Fleming et al., 53 Ill. 204.

(2) Pindell et al. *v.* Trevor et al., 30 Ark. 250.

leging that no consideration was paid for the note, in that the title to the real estate had failed, and the note was transferred during the pendency of such bill, it was held in Vermont that the pendency of the chancery suit was not constructive notice to the party to whom the note was transferred of any defect or failure in its consideration, although the purchaser knew at the time he received the note that it was originally given for the real estate involved in the suit, but had no actual knowledge of the pendency of the bill.(1)

This case may be classed with others which hold that negotiable paper is not subject to notice lis pendens on the ground that, although the rule lis pendens is based upon grounds of public policy, yet that its enforcement in such cases would involve a greater injury to the public than the benefits which would result therefrom, and hence that stronger reasons grounded in public policy exist in favor of exempting commercial paper from the operation of the rule, than of enforcing the rule.

Decree dismissing bill where pendente lite purchaser.

SEC. 173.   In a case where a bill had been filed calling for a sworn answer, and after the filing of the answer the suit was dismissed, but pending the suit the defendant had conveyed the property, and the same complainant had brought a new bill, it was held that the decree of dismissal of the former bill was a conclusive bar to the second bill, and that the grantee of the property pendente lite was protected by that decree in his ownership of the property.

Had the decree of dismissal contained the express

(1) Sawyer v. Phaley, 33 Vt. 69.

provision that it was made without prejudice, or with leave to commence another suit, the effect of the decree would have been otherwise.

Rights of tenants taking lease pendente lite.

SEC. 174. Where a tenant takes a lease to property from a party to a pending suit, he is bound by the determination of the suit and cannot, as to the property, enforce the rights apparently secured to him by the terms of his lease. And so it was held in Massachusetts, where a mortgagor had leased the mortgaged property pending a suit to foreclose the mortgage, and had delivered possession of a portion of the property to the tenant, who retained the actual possession thereof under a claim of right by virtue of some provisions of the mortgage, after formal possession had been delivered to the mortgagee upon the execution issued upon the judgment recovered in his suit, that the tenant could not recover damages for buildings or improvements made by him on the premises, although he had reason to believe his title to be good.

It is said that the means of knowledge were open to the tenant; that it was his duty to have examined the records of the courts; that he was bound to know the allegations of the pending bill as well as of the registry of deeds involving the property; that therefore the tenant in such case must be treated as in possession by an act of disseizin, and although in that case the improvements were very valuable, they were held to belong to the owner of the soil.(1)

Lease pendente lite from executor under power in a will.

SEC. 175. But, although it is the general rule that

(1) Haven et al. v. Adams et al., 8 Allen, 363; Yates v. Smith, 11 Brad. 549.

a lease taken from a party to a suit, pending the suit, is subject to the decree which may be entered in the case, yet when the lessor is an executor, and the lease is made in good faith in pursuance of a power given in the will itself, it will be valid although made pendente lite.

And so, when a creditor came in by motion under a decree directing a sale of lands devised for the payment of debts, to set aside a lease obtained pendente lite from a devisee under the will, with a leasing power, the motion was denied.(1)

Collusive assignee pendente lite.

Sec. 176.   But where a decree of foreclosure was entered in October, 1858, a sale made by the master in December following, a master's deed executed in September, 1860, to the purchaser, and thereafter in November following the defendant to the foreclosure suit surrendered possession to a stranger to the suit, it was held, in Illinois, that the purchaser took pendente lite, that he was to all intents and purposes a party to the decree and that the same proceedings might be had against him that could have been had against the defendant, his grantor.

And it was so held in Kentucky, where, pending a suit in chancery involving real estate, a person wrongfully obtained possession from a party to the suit, that the Chancellor had power and it became his duty to restore possession to the rightful party, and that a stranger who thus intermeddles with the possession, pending the litigation, becomes subject to

(1) Moore *v.* MacNamara, 2 Ball. & Beat. 186. In the above case Lord Chancellor Manners distin- guished that case from Gaskill *v.* Durdin, 2 Ball. & Beat. 167.

the lis pendens of the suit by reason of his intrusion.(1)

When assignee in possession, not bound.

SEC. 177. Whether or not an assignee of real property involved in litigation is or is not bound by the determination of the case depends generally upon the fact whether the assignment was made before or after the commencement of the suit. The rule is general that the judgment or decree determines the rights of and is binding upon the parties and their privies only.

In all cases therefore where the interest was acquired before the suit and the person interested was not brought in as a party, the litigation would not bind such interest; and so, where the tenant is in possession of a distinct portion of the property at the time suit is brought involving the property and is not made a party, he would not be bound by the judgment or decree and could not be dispossessed by process issued thereon.(2)

When assignee in possession, bound.

SEC. 178. But in all cases where a defendant to a suit shall, pending litigation, transfer his possession pendente lite to a third party, in whatsoever form the transfer may be made, and such party goes into possession, the determination of the suit will be conclusive and binding upon the tenant or assignee, and process may issue upon the judgment or decree against the tenant, although he has not been made a party thereto, and he may be evicted thereon.

If the law were otherwise it would lie in the power

---

(1) Jackson *v.* Warren, 32 Ill. 343;   (2) Howard et al. *v.* Kennedy's
Turner *v.* Thomas etc., 13 Bush. 526.   Ex., 4 Ala. 593.

of a defendant to perpetually protract litigation by transferring his interest to a third party and yielding possession so as to compel a new action against successive defendants or assignees.

Condemnation proceedings not lis pendens.

SEC. 179.   In those States whose constitutions provide, in effect, that private property shall not be taken for public use without just compensation, proceedings for the condemnation of land for the use of the public or public corporations are not notice lis pendens of such condemnation proceedings, and so where, pending condemnation proceedings, the owner conveys to a third party, notice to the grantor will not be held to be constructive notice to the grantee of the property. In such case the proceedings will not bind the purchaser.

Ante litem contract of purchase and payment before suit.

SEC. 180.   An agreement had been made for the purchase of land upon which a payment of $1,000 had been made, when a bill was filed involving the land and service had upon the holder of the legal title. The balance of the purchase money amounting to $1,000 did not become due until after lis pendens commenced.   It was held that, although it was not such a bona fide purchase without notice as would protect the purchaser and avoid the lis pendens, the payment of the first installment was bona fide and should be refunded.

In such cases a court of equity will look to the effect of a decree and give it such shape as will do equity and prevent injustice.(1)

(1) Fessler's Appeal, 75 Pa. St. 502.

Purchase upon execution pendente lite.

SEC. 181. After a bill is filed to set aside alleged fraudulent conveyances of real estate and has become a lis pendens, a sale upon execution issued upon a judgment recovered after the bill became a lis pendens, will be subject to the pending suit and will be overreached by the purchase under the decree.

In such case the Chancellor will compel the pendente lite purchaser to surrender the possession on a petition in the chancery case.(1)

---

(1) Scott v. Coleman, 5 T. B. Mon. 73. The court in this case say: "According to the ancient chancery practice such a purchaser, though not a party to the suit, would upon petition be compelled to surrender the possession. If, after the merits of a contest are fully settled, and after the land which was the main matter of dispute is sold under the decree of the court, the purchaser should have to resort to his action at law to obtain the possession either from the defendant or one who gained possession while the suit was pending, it must be concluded that the powers of courts of quity must be inadequate to apply he remedy necessary to enforce their decrees. Such is not, however, the case. Chancellor Kent, of New York, with a perspicuity characteristic of his opinions, has laid down the rule upon this subject, and has proved from reason and by reference to many adjudged cases, that by petition the purchaser of property under a decree will be put into possession of his purchase. The course of proceeding as stated by him seems anciently to have been first, to obtain an order or decree on the defendant to deliver possession, which order was served on the defendant accompanied with a demand of the possession; and there was sometimes a formal writ of execution of the orders to deliver possession. An attachment then issued for disobeying this order, but that attachment, it seems, was only matter of form and was not to be served. The next act was an order for an injunction against the tenant to deliver possession, which issued, of course, on affidavit of the previous steps, and then on affidavit of the service of injunction and refusal, a writ of assistance to the sheriff or marshal to put the party into possession issued, of course, on motion without notice." Kershaw v. Thompson et al., 4 Johns. Ch. 609; Dove v. Dove, 2 Dickens, 617; Newland Pr. I, 98; Stribley v. Hawkie, 3 Atk. 275; Hugenim v. Basly, 15 Vesey, 180; Penn v. Lord Baltimore, 1 Ves. 444; Roberclean v. Rous, 1 Atk. 543; Jackson v. Warren, 32 Ill. 340.

Purchaser from trustee or agent bound to know the facts.

Sec. 182. And so under a defense of bona fide purchase without notice, if it should turn out that the purchaser had notice of a trust existing when the purchase was made, the general rule is that the purchaser becomes himself the trustee, notwithstanding any consideration paid.(1)

And though he may not perhaps be bound in most cases, if the sale is fair, to look to the application of the money, yet if the trust be suspended by process of the court and a sale be made in contempt of that process, the purchaser with notice ought not to be allowed to defeat it. If he knowingly purchase of one acting as an agent or trustee for others, he is bound to look into the validity and continuance of the authority and to call for an explanation of the nature and existing circumstances of the trust.(2)

A plea of bona fide purchase which states that the purchaser paid a good and valuable consideration, to-wit: a certain sum of money then advanced and paid without notice, etc., is not good.(3) The consideration ought to be set forth in amount in traversable form, so that the plaintiff can traverse it if he choose, or the court can see that it is adequately valuable if not traversed. There must be a denial of notice and of every circumstance from which it may be inferred.(4)

Equitable rights of pendente lite purchaser protected.

Sec. 183. We have also seen that conveyances pen-

(1) Saunders *v.* DeHew, 2 Vern. 271.

(2) Murray *v.* Ballou, 1 Johns. Ch. 574.

(3) Story's Eq. Pl. Sec. 805; Secombs' Adm. *v.* Campbell, 9 Re-

porter, 708.

(4) Bodimin *v.* Vandebendy, 1 Vern. 179; Anonymous, 2 Vent. 361; Jones *v.* Thomas, 3 P. Wm. 244, n; Lawrence *v.* Blatchford, 2 Vern. 458.

dente lite are not prohibited and held void, but that the interest of the grantor passes subject to the final determination of the pending cause. The administration of principles of equity requires therefore, in such cases, that whatever rights the grantor had should be decreed in favor of his grantee.

And so where a deed had been made by a father to his children, supported by a valuable consideration as to half the land, but voluntary as to the other half, upon a bill filed by creditors to reach the property the children were held seized of the legal title to one-half the land as trustees of their father's creditors, and were confirmed in their right to the other half.(1)

Conditional assignment pendente lite.

SEC. 184. Where a bill was filed against an assignee of a mortgage holding by a conditional assignment to have it delivered up and cancelled on the ground that it was paid, and alleging that the complainant had recovered in ejectment against the assignee upon the ground of its payment, it appearing that the assignment was conditioned to reassign to the assignor and that pending the suit the assignee had reassigned to him in pursuance of the conditions of the original assignment, and the assignor also having been made a party, it was held that the doctrine of notice of lis pendens did not apply; that it applies only where a third person attempts to intrude into a controversy by acquiring an interest in the matter in litigation, pending the suit, but that in the given case the assignor's interest existed before the suit was commenced and he might have been made an original party.(2)

(1) Sec. 167, *ante*.

(2) Newland on Cort. 507; Worsley v. The Earl of Scarborough, 3 Atk. 892; Churchill v. Grove, 1 Ch. Cas. 35; Hopkins v. McLaren, 4 Cow. 678.

Purchaser estopped by recitals.

SEC. 185. A purchaser is estopped by the recitals which appear in the deeds through which he claims title.

If these recitals show a purchase pendente lite the purchaser must abide by the decision of the case of his grantor.(1)

The lis pendens of a bill filed for the surrender of a mortgage.

SEC. 186. Where a bill was filed to compel the specific performance of an agreement to surrender a mortgage in the county where the land lies, after service of process, the suit becomes a lis pendens, and an assignee of the mortgage after the court has thus acquired jurisdiction is bound by the decree which may be entered in the case.(2)

Bona fide purchasers—relation.

SEC. 187. In a case where judgments were obtained against a person who was the apparent owner of the land, and it was apparently subject to the lien of the judgments, and after the lien of the judgments had attached, a bill was filed against the defendant in the judgments attacking the title of the judgment debtor, it was held that a purchaser of the property at sheriff's sale, upon executions issued on the judgments, was a bona fide purchaser for value and without notice, and that a title so acquired would relate back to the time when the lien of the judgments attached.

It may well be doubted whether the scope of the decision in that case ought not to be restricted to the facts of that particular case and not adopted as a general rule.

(1) Talbott's Exrs. *v.* Bell's Heirs, 5 B. Mon, 323.

(2) Sumner et al. *v.* Waugh et al. 56 Ill. 532.

The report of the case does not show for what amount
the sale was made, whether for an amount not in excess of the judgment liens or for a greater sum.   The
bill being a pending suit in a court of record at the
time of the purchase, the purchaser was bound to
know that record.   If therefore, with the knowledge
that the complainant claimed to be the owner of the
land, the purchaser should bid and purchase at a price
in excess of the liens of the judgments, it would seem
that it could hardly be said that the purchase was
bona fide and without notice.(1)

Incumbrances pendente lite.

SEC. 188.   The same reasons which led to the adoption of the rule lis pendens as applicable to pendente
lite purchasers apply with equal force to the application of the rule to pendente lite incumbrancers, and
all such incumbrances are bound by the decree or
judgment in the pending case.

Nor is it necessary that the parties to such pendente lite incumbrances should be made parties to
the pending suit, for they can claim no rights under
such incumbrance, except what belong to the person
under whom they assert title, since they purchase
with constructive notice.

If it were necessary to bring in all such parties,
there would be no end to suits ; for defendants would
have the power, by the repeated execution of such
incumbrances, to prolong the litigation ad infin-
itum.(2)

(1) Scarlett et al. v. Graham et al.,
28 Ill. 321.

(2) In Cooley v. Brayton, 16 Iowa,
19, Judge Dillon, in delivering the
opinion of the court, said: "We have
now reached the question whether
this decree was equally binding, or
binding at all on the appellant, he
not being a party thereto. He purchased pendente lite and is con-

Pendente lite judgments.

SEC. 189.   The question of the status of judgments rendered pending suits to forclose mortgages has often been the subject of judicial determination. In England the judgment did not become a lien until registration after it had been rendered, and the question often arose whether junior judgment creditors were necessary parties to foreclosure suits.

The same rule was applied in such cases as in the ordinary case of pendente lite alienations, and hence it was uniformly held that unless the creditor had made his judgment a lien prior to the initiation of the foreclosure suit, they were unnecessary parties, because the

structively bound. At the date of his purchase, not only had the Wahl foreclosure proceedings been commenced, but Smith Brayton (under whom appellant claims) had answered therein. Under these circumstances the appellant was not a necessary party upon the general principles of equity practice.

"Incumbrancers, who become such pendente lite, are not deemed necessary parties, although they are bound by the decree; for they claim nothing except what belonged to the person under whom they assert title, since they purchase with constructive notice; and there would be no end to suits if a mortgagor might, by new incumbrances created pendente lite, require all such incumbrancers to be made parties." Story's Eq. Pl. Sec. 194. Grounded upon the same reasons, the same rule would apply to purchasers pendente lite. In Youngman v. Elmira, etc. Railroad Company, 65 Penn.

St. 287, Judge Sharswood, delivering the opinion of the court, said: "It is perfectly well settled that incumbrancers who become such pendente lite are not necessary parties to a bill to foreclose, although they are bound by the decree, for they can claim nothing except what belongs to the person under whom they assert title, since they have constructive notice; and there would be no end of such suits, if a mortgagor might by new incumbrances created pendente lite require all such incumbrancers to be made parties." In Mason et al. v. Saloy et al., 12 La. Ann. 776, Justice Cole, delivering the opinion of the court, says: "As these mortgages were executed on property claimed by Mason pending his suit to recover the same, they were without effect so far as he is concerned." Story's Eq. Plead. 194; 1st Wash. on Real Prop., 593; Citizens' Bank v. J. E. Armor et al., 11th La. Ann. 468.

rights of the judgment creditors and their assigns were cut off by the decree which should be rendered in the case, without their presence in court, in the same manner that pendente lite alienations were over-reached and annulled by it.

Thus, in the case of Trye v. Earl of Aldborough, a bill was filed to foreclose a mortgage in 1833. Pending the bill a judgment was recovered against the defendant in the foreclosure suit which became a lien. A decree of foreclosure was entered in 1842. The judgment creditor made application to the court for the appointment of a receiver to extend over a portion of the mortgaged premises.

The Lord Chancellor denied the motion, on the ground that the rights of the judgment creditor as to the mortgaged property had accrued pendente lite and were bound by the decree.(1)

(1) Trye v. Earl of Aldborough, 1 Ir. Ch. R. 666; Lynch v. Nolan, 10 Ir. Ch. R. 57; Massey v. Batwell, 4 Dru. & War. 58; 5 Ir. Eq. R. 382; Leake v. Leake, 5 Ir. Eq. R. 361; The Bishop of Winchester v. Beavor, 3 Ves. 314; L' Estrange v. Robinson, 1 Hog. 262.

Johnson v. Holdsworth, 1 Sims, Ch. (N. S.) 106, is a bill filed by a judgment creditor against a mortgagee and the purchaser at the foreclosure sale to redeem from the mortgage. Subsequent to the foreclosure various judgments had been confessed against the mortgagor, and the question was whether in this bill to foreclose these subsequent judgment creditors were necessary parties. Under the English statutes then in force judgments did not become liens until they were registered, as required by statute. These judgments were not registered in time to be made liens before the commencement of the foreclosure suit, and it was held in this case therefore that these subsequent judgment creditors were not necessary parties to the bill to redeem. It was argued by counsel in that case that judgment creditors, registering their judgments pending suit, were subject to the rule lis pendens; but the point was not passed upon by the court, because the position was sufficient that these judgment creditors had no liens prior to the commencement of the foreclosure.

Pendente lite purchasers at sheriff's sale.

SEC. 190.   The question has often arisen in cases where judgments at law have been rendered, pending litigation against parties to such litigation, in whom the title to the property involved in suit was vested, whether purchasers at sheriff's sale, upon executions issued upon such judgments, were voluntary pendente lite purchasers and bound by notice lis pendens, or acquired title by operation of law in such manner that the purchase would be held intact and not so bound—as in the case of an investment of title by assignment in bankruptcy or insolvency.

The courts are uniform in holding that all such purchasers are voluntary pendente lite purchasers, and are bound by the determination of the pending suit precisely as if they had taken by voluntary conveyance from the party to the suit in whom the title was vested.   It is said that the purchase is wholly an act of volition on the part of the purchaser; that he acts for himself, is influenced and governed by his own judgment, directed by his own interests and not the interests of others.

That the fact that he acquires the title by operation of law, viz: by virtue of the judgment and execution sale, makes no difference.   That he takes the title of the judgment debtor *cum onore*—that is, charged with the lis pendens of the suit—and that it would be incompatible with well established principles to allow him the benefit of the rule which might be invoked by a trustee, succeeding by operation of law to the title.

Such purchasers are therefore held bound in the same manner and to the same extent by the judgment or decree as though they had acquired title by voluntary conveyance.(1)

(1) The language of the court in the case of Steele *v.* Taylor et al., 1 Minn. 273, is so well chosen and so much to the point upon the subject matter of this section, that I add the following extract from it. The facts of the case were that a bill was filed to enforce performance of a contract to convey land. Pending the bill, other parties obtained judgments against the defendant in a chancery suit, and purchased the lands at sheriff's sale. After the purchase an application was made by the purchasers to be made parties to the chancery suit, and an appeal from the order denying the application was taken to the Supreme Court, where it was held that they must be deemed voluntary pendente lite purchasers. In deciding the case the court say: "His purchase is wholly an act of volition on his part, and he receives and holds in his own right and not in trust for the use of others all the estate that he obtains by his purchase. He acts for himself wholly in making his bids and purchase, and is influenced and governed by his judgment of what under the circumstances his own interests, and not those of others, require or render advisable. He cannot be deemed other than a voluntary purchaser, though he receives his title by operation of law. The lis pendens is notice to him, and he takes the title *cum onore* precisely as he would by bona fide voluntary conveyance from the judgment debtor, and his position with reference to both of the original parties to the suit is the same as it would be under such voluntary conveyance. It seems to me that it would be inconsistent and incompatible with other well established principles to allow him, for the protection of his own private interests, the benefits of the rules applicable to the case of a trustee upon whom the title had, by operation of law, been cast for the use of others, as in the cases of assignees in bankruptcy or insolvency, and of receivers in chancery. He does not hold the position or rest under the responsibilities, nor is he subject to any of the duties of such trustee, who as such is always subject to the jurisdiction and amenable to the call of the court of chancery, and entitled to the benefit of its directory orders. Nor does he stand in a light like that of an heir at law upon whom there is a descent by the death of an ancestor pendente lite." * * * "The rule is that incumbrancers who become such pendente lite need not be made parties. They stand in no better position or more favorable light, relative to the parties, than voluntary bona fide purchasers pendente lite, nor is it proper or reasonable that they should. They are in the same manner and to the same extent bound by the decree."

The same court, in the case of Hart et al. *v.* Marshall, 4 Minn. 292, follows the doctrine of the case of Steele *v.* Taylor et al., *ante*, and approves of it. So also in the case of

Purchaser under a decree a pendente lite purchaser.

SEC. 191.   One who purchases at a sale of mortgaged property made in pursuance of the directions of the decree of foreclosure, by that act submits himself to the jurisdiction of the court, in the suit in which the sale is made, as to all matters connected with the sale or relating to him in the character of purchaser, and so, when the mortgaged property is converted into money pursuant to the directions of the decree of foreclosure and sale, the purchaser stands in the relation of a trustee, having in his possession a trust fund which it is the duty of the court to dispense according to the rights of the parties litigant.

Hence he must of necessity be subject to the jurisdiction of the court in all matters touching his relation as purchaser.   For otherwise the parties entitled to the fund might be delayed in the attainment of their rights and the primary jurisdiction of the court be baffled or defeated.(1)

When proceedings are in rem.

SEC. 192.   Where a suit is either, in whole or in part, in the nature of a proceeding in rem to recover, enforce a lien upon or subject to decree specific property, a sale of the subject matter of litigation after lis pendens has commenced, even to one who had no notice of the suit, will not change the rights of the parties to the litigation or the power of the court over the subject of the action.

Such an one is a pendente lite purchaser.   He is

Crocker v. Crocker, 57 Me. 396. In the case of Fash v. Ravesies, 32 Ala. 455, it is held that a purchaser at sheriff's sale, who buys the interest of a defendant to a bill in chancery after the same has become notice lis pendens, will be a pendente lite purchaser.

(1) Coulter et al. v. Herrod et al., 5 Cush. (Miss.) 690.

not a necessary party to the suit and must take the property *cum onore*.(1)   Although this is said with reference to a proceeding in rem, the principle should not be applied in any narrow sense.

In any case where, by the commencement of a suit, a lien is created or asserted and the court acquires jurisdiction over and the power to administer the property involved, it may be said that the suit is a proceeding in rem.

When sale under a trust deed made pendente lite.

SEC. 193.   Where, upon the sale of real estate a deed is made to the buyer, and at the same time a trust deed is given back to the seller to secure purchase money, the two conveyances will be treated as one transaction, and as having been made contemporaneously.   The deed and the trust deed in such case will both take effect at the same time.

Where a trust deed was made under such circumstances for the purchase money, and the trustee proceeded to sell in pursuance of the terms of the trust deed, the purchaser of the land who executed the trust deed filed a bill against the trustee, alleging that the indebtedness secured by the trust deed was usurious, and asked for an accounting and an injunction against the sale, which was granted.

Upon an appeal to the Supreme Court it was held that the injunction was improperly granted; that the suit, had it proceeded without the injunction, would have been a lis pendens and the purchaser at the trustee's sale a pendente lite purchaser, and therefore bound by whatever decree would be

(1) Wyckliffe's Exrs. *v.* Breckenridge's Heirs, 1 Bush. 443.

rendered in the case, although not a party to the proceeding.(1)

Assignment of goods and chattels made pendente lite.

SEC. 194.   Where a creditor of a corporation has filed a bill against the corporation and obtained service so that the suit becomes a lis pendens, and the corporation afterwards makes an assignment, the assignee will take subject to the pending suit.   And so, where at the suit of the creditor a receiver for the corporation was afterwards appointed, and he brought a suit against the assignee to set aside and vacate the assignment, it was held that the assignee took the property, which was goods and chattels, subject to the lis pendens, and the assignment was set aside.(2)

(1) George Exr. et al. *v.* Cooper Trustee, 15 W. Va. 666.

(2) Leavitt Receivers, etc. *v.* Tyler et als., 1 Sandf. Ch. 209.

CHAPTER X.

DOCTRINE OF LIS PENDENS IN ITS APPLICATION TO PURCHASERS CONTINUED.

When title of grantor divested pendente lite.

Sec. 195. In an action of ejectment, where the facts appeared in evidence that the plaintiff's title was derived through a deed made by the defendant in a chancery suit after the completion of publication against him and pending that suit, and that plaintiff's grantor was afterwards decreed in the suit to convey to the complainant, which decree itself operated as a conveyance, it was held that the plaintiff in eject-ment, although his grantor held the legal title when he conveyed to him, was a pendente lite purchaser and took nothing by his conveyance.(1)

Endorsee of a sued note.

SEC. 196. The endorsee of a note, who has no knowledge that a prior action is pending on it, may, notwithstanding the pendency of such action, main-tain a suit against the same defendant on the note.

If the endorsee, the plaintiff in the second suit, knew of the first suit and if the endorsement was for the purpose of oppression, it would be otherwise.(2)

Where note assigned pending suit.

SEC. 197. Where after a suit has been brought upon a promissory note and has become a pending suit it is assigned to a third party, the defendant can not set up as a defense to the note the assignment and change of ownership.

The name of the purchaser might be substituted for that of the plaintiff in most States, or if that can not be done, the purchaser may be permitted to prose-cute the suit for his use in the name of the original plaintiff upon indemnifying against costs.(3)

Release of mortgage pendente lite--effect of.

SEC. 198. The partial release of a mortgage pending litigation involving the mortgaged property,(4) where

(1) Bennett's Lessee *v.* Williams, 5 Ohio, 461.
(2) Colombier *v.* Slin, 2 Chit. 637.
(3) Ivey et al. *v.* Drake, 36 Ark.234.
(4) Scudder *v.* Van Amburg et al., 4 Edw. Ch. 31.

neither the mortgagee nor releasee are parties to the litigation, and where the mortgage was executed prior to the suit, and the release was made in good faith, does not constitute the releasee a pendente lite purchaser.(1)

This should be clearly so, on the ground that the rights of the mortgagee had attached and become completed before the commencement of the suit and before he was made a party. The mortgagee and the releasee would fall within the class of ante litem claimants.

When court record not notice—doctrine questioned.

SEC. 199. It was held in Indiana(2) that the record of a commissioner's deed made under a decree for specific performance in the case in which the decree was entered, was not notice to a purchaser of the lands pending the suit.

In that case, A obtained a decree in chancery against B for specific performance of a contract for the purchase of a tract of land, by which decree the land was ordered to be conveyed to him by a commissioner. The commissioner was appointed to make the deed, the deed was made, reported to the court, approved and recorded among the records of the court, but was not recorded in the recorder's office until five years after the decree.

Pending the suit, the defendant B sold and conveyed the land to C, who afterwards conveyed to D, who purchased for a valuable consideration and in good faith, and had his deed duly recorded.

It was held that the record of the chancery suit

(1) Styvesant v. Hone et al., 1   (2) Rosser v. Bingham, 17 Ind.
Sandf. Ch. 419.   542.

was not such constructive notice as was binding upon the purchaser subsequent to C.

It is difficult to reconcile this case with the other cases on this subject. Here was a purchase from a party to the suit pending the suit. It seems to me, with great respect for that court, that it is not a question of notice, but of the application of the rule lis pendens, simply because of its necessity.

How far a judgment evidence against pendente lite purchaser.

SEC. 200. Although a purchaser pendente lite is not made a party, he is not only bound by the judgment or decree finally entered in the pending case, but such judgment or decree is also evidence against him, with respect to the subject matter of litigation, to the same extent as if he were a party to the record.

This necessarily follows from the position that a pendente lite purchaser takes the place of his grantor, and from the fact that he is bound to know the proceedings, not only of the court in that particular case, but of all the courts of record within the jurisdiction where he resides, whenever he attempts to deal with the subject of litigation, to the same extent that he is bound to know the contents of recorded instruments of conveyance in pursuance of the registry laws.(1)

Lis pendens of bill to set aside sale.

SEC. 201. Where a bill is filed against an executor to set aside a sale of lands made to himself, it constitutes such a lis pendens as will overreach and annul a conveyance of the same lands made by the executor pending the suit.(2)

(1) Watson *v.* Dowling et al., 26 Cal. 125.

(2) Carmichael *v.* Foster, 69 Ga. 372.

Purchaser after dismissal and before revival.

SEC. 202. If a suit at law is dismissed, or the plaintiff suffers a non-suit, or in chancery the bill is dismissed for want of prosecution, or for any other cause not on the merits, although in all such cases a new action might be brought, it could not affect the purchaser during the pendency of the first suit.

Where the suit is dismissed and afterwards reinstated the doctrine of lis pendens is not applicable to one who purchases after the dismissal and before the revival of the suit—still less could a purchaser before the dismissal and before the revival of the suit be affected.(1)

Agent purchasing a tax title.

SEC. 203. A person who is in possession of real estate pendente lite and as the tenant of one of the parties to the suit, cannot acquire a tax title to the property involved and assert it as an independent title. In such cases the purchase will be held to inure to the benefit of the cestui que trust, when the suit shall determine who he really is.(2)

It is the duty of the owner to pay the taxes, and payment or purchase by the tenant will be presumed to have been in discharge of that duty. Hence the purchaser would be deemed to be the trustee of the owner.

This would seem to be the ground upon which the courts hold the doctrine which we have stated.

Conveyance after decree and before writ of error.

SEC. 204. Where a bill had been filed to compel

(1) Price v. White, 1 Bailey's Eq. 234; Blake v. Hayward, 1 Bailey's Eq. 208; Turner v. Crebil, 1 Ohio, 174.

(2) Whiting et al. v. Beebe et al., 12 Ark. 583; Burr v. McEwin et al., 1 Baldwin's R. 162.

a conveyance, a decree entered in pursuance of which the title had vested in the complainant and the complainant, after decree but before a writ of error had become a lis pendens, conveyed to an innocent purchaser for value and without notice of the contemplated writ of error, it was held that the grantee was a bona fide purchaser and that the validity of the title so acquired would not be affected by the reversal of the decree in the original suit.(1)

The ground of this decision is that the lis pendens

(1) Taylor's Lessee *v.* Boyd, 3 Ohio, 352; Mulvey *v.* Gibbons, 87 Ill. 367; Eldridge *v.*Walker et al., 84 Ill. 274; McJilton *v.*Love, 13 Ill. 487. It is said in Pierce *v.* Stinde et al., 11 Mo. Ap. R. 364, to be well settled that a writ of error is a new suit, and not merely a continuance of the suit, the judgment in which it is brought to reverse. Tidd's Pr. 1141; Bachelor *v.* Ellis, 7 Term R. 184; Ripley *v.* Morris, 7 Ill. 381; Allen *v.* Mayor, 9 Ga. 286;Gregg *v.* Berthea, 6 Port. 9; Robinson *v.* Magarity, 28 Ill 423. In the case of Pierce *v.* Stinde et al., *ante,* the court says: "Indeed this writ is now regulated in England and probably in most of the American States by statutes as with us. But these statutes, it is conceived, do not create a new remedy, they merely define and regulate a remedial process which existed at common law. This being so, it is clear that when a sale of land is made between the date of final judgment affecting the land and the date when the proceeding in error is commenced to reverse that judgment, it is not subject to a lis pendens, and the purchaser will get a good title by the purchase, notwithstanding the circumstance that the judgment is afterwards reversed in the proceeding under the writ of error." McCormick *v.* McClure, 6 Blackf. 466; Clarkson et al. *v.* Morgan's Dev., 6 B. Mon. 441. On the other hand the cases holding that a purchase after judgment and before writ of error is subject to lis pendens, are: De Bell *v.* Foxworthy's Heirs, 9 B. Mon. 228; Clary et al. *v.* Marshall's Heirs, 4 Dana, 95; Earle et al. *v.* Couch, 3 Met. 450; Gore *v.* Stackpoole, 1 Dow. 31; Ludlow's Heirs *v.* Kidd, 3 Ohio, 541. In Miller etc. *v.* Hall et ux., 1 Bush. 229, it is said that the theory of sales of real estate, made under the orders and judgments of courts, is that the court itself is vendor, and that the commissioner or master is the mere agent of the court in executing its will; that therefore the purchaser from a party who obtained his title by a decree which had been reversed, was a pendente lite purchaser, and stood no better than such vendor whose title was destroyed by the reversal.

ceases upon the rendition of the judgment or the entry of the decree and that the suing out of a writ of error is the commencement of a new suit.

Conveyance after a writ of error.

SEC. 205. But where a party to a suit conveys after the suing out of a writ of error and the Appellate Court determines the case adversely to the title of the grantor, his grantee will be a pendente lite purchaser.(1)

Where the statute provided for the filing of a writ of error bond and the writ was sued out and bond given but service had not been had, it was held that there was a lis pendens from the time of the suing out of the writ.

Lis pendens in ejectment.

SEC. 206. One who takes title or possession from a defendant in ejectment pending the suit is bound by the judgment and can be evicted by the process which shall issue therein, although he is not a party thereto.(2)

(1) Coulter et al. v. Herrod et al., 5 Cush. (Miss.) 690.

(2) Sampson v. Ohleyr, 22 Cal.201; Jackson v. Tuttle, 9 Cow. 233; Jones v. Chiles, 2 Dana,25; Smith's Lessee v. Tabue's Heirs, 1 McLean, 87; Howard et al. v. Kennedy's Exrs., 4 Ala. 592; Hickman v. Dale, 7 Yerg. (Tenn.) 149; Long v. Morton, 2 A. K. Marsh. 498; Hanson v. Armstrong, 22 Ill. 442; Wallen v. Huff, 3 Sneed, 82; Bradley v. McDaniel, 3 Jones, (N. C.) 128; Hersey v. Turbett, 3 Casey (27 Pa. St.) 428; Jackson v. Stone, 13 Johns. 447; Jackson v. Hill, 8 Cow. 290; Jackson v. Rightmyre, 16 Johns. 314; Fremont v. Crippen, 10 Cal. 211; Fogarty v. Sparks, 22 Cal. 142; Long et al. v. Neville et al., 29 Cal. 132. In Brown et al. v. Marzyck, 19 Fla. 840, it is said that a writ of assistance in a foreclosure case to put out one who came into possession pending the suit by collusion with the mortgagee for the purpose of causing delay, is proper. In Snively v. Hitechew, 59 Penn. State, 49, the binding force of the rule lis pendens is applied to an ejectment case. Thomas brought an ejectment against Anderson. Pending the suit Anderson sold to Smith. Thomas afterwards recovered the land in ejectment. Smith was held bound by notice lis pendens.

Where a bill was filed to enforce a lien for purchase money and there was a tenant in possession asserting an adverse claim, but the tenant was a pendente lite purchaser of one from whom the complainant had recovered the land in ejectment, the tenant was held bound by the judgment and a decree was entered for the sale of the interest claimed by him, and for the surrender of the possession.(1)

Lis pendens as to an unrecorded mortgage.

SEC. 207. Where a bill in chancery has been filed, the object of which is to reform a mortgage and then foreclose it, the lis pendens, as to the reformation of the mortgage, will bar the right of a grantee of the mortgagor receiving conveyance after the lis pendens becomes in force.(2)

Lis pendens of bill to correct title.

SEC. 208. And in such case as is mentioned in the preceding section where there was a mistake made in the pendente lite conveyance by the omission of a tract, it has been held upon bill filed to correct the mistake that, although the title was acquired pendente lite, the proof showing that the grantee acquired bona fide rights, the relief should be granted and the conveyance corrected.(3)

Lis pendens of bill to establish will.

SEC. 209. A bill filed to establish a last will and testament and perpetuate the testimony of witnesses, has been held to constitute a lis pendens affecting with notice a purchaser either under the devisee or under the heirs.(4)

(1) Henly *v.* Gore et al., 4 Dana, 135.

(2) Lebanon Savings Bank *v.* Hollenbeck et al., 29 Minn. 322.

(3) Willis *v.* Gettman, 53 Mo. 731; Newland on Contract, 506.

(4) Garth *v.* Ward, 2 Atk. 174; Garth *v.* Crawford, Barn. 450.

This is manifestly correct, because, if the devisee could lawfully convey pending such a bill, he might effectually defeat the title of the heirs as ultimately determined by the court in a case where the bill should be brought by the heirs, or vice versa if the bill were filed by the devisee.

In either case the jurisdiction of the court would be defeated, which is a sufficient if not the sole ground of the assertion and enforcement of the doctrine of lis pendens.

Pendente lite purchase by defendant from complainant.

SEC. 210.   Where in an action involving real estate the defendant pending the suit becomes the purchaser of the interest of some of the complainants in the property in dispute, and the case is appealed to an Appellate Court, the latter court will not disturb the judgment on that account, unless the appeal be taken by those complainants who have sold their interest.(1)

Assignment of decree between partners.

SEC. 211.   Where a bill is filed by a partner against his co-partners or co-partner and service is had, the lis pendens will not only protect against pendente lite purchasers, but all other equities of which it gives notice.

Where such a case results in a decree for the payment of a partnership balance, and an assignment of the decree is made pending the suit and in advance of such decree, the assignee will take his assignment subject to constructive notice of the equitable rights of the co-partners.   This is specially the case where the assignment is made to a solicitor in the case.(2)

(1) Drennen's Adm. et al. v. Walker et al., 21 Ark. 539.

(2) Lockwood v. Bates et al., 1 Del. Ch. 436.

A purchase pending foreclosure upon judgment not a prior lien estopped.

SEC. 212. Pending the foreclosure of a mortgage against a corporation, in a State where lis pendens statutes are in force, a notice of lis pendens having been filed under the statute, a purchase was made at a sale upon a judgment not a prior lien to the mortgage.

It was held that the purchaser was estopped from denying that the mortgage was an act of the defendant corporation, and that he was a pendente lite purchaser and was not a necessary party to the foreclosure. The title acquired by the sale upon the judgment was annulled by the force of the lis pendens of the forclosure case.(1)

Lis pendens where judgment executed in chancery.

SEC. 213. In a proceeding at common law a judgment was recovered which became binding upon certain property, and afterwards, for the purpose of the better execution of the judgment, a bill in chancery was filed with respect to the same property, and the sale of the property was made under the decree entered in the chancery suit.

A purchase was made of the property in suit pending the proceedings at law. It was held to be a pendente lite purchase, and as much so as if the sale had been made upon the judgment at law instead of upon the decree in chancery.(2)

Lis pendens of bill to subrogate.

SEC. 214. Where a bill was filed which alleged that the complainant had advanced money to the defendant

(1) Horn v. Jones et al., 28 Cal. 194.   (2) Smith v. Coker, 65 Ga. 461.

which was used by him to pay a note which was a lien on the land involved in the suit, and asking that the complainant be subrogated to the rights of a former holder of the note, there was held to be a lis pendens so far as relates to the real estate, and a purchaser of the land pendente lite was held to be bound thereby.

But a bill, seeking by its allegations to charge the estate of a married woman in lands, for family and plantation supplies, was held, under the married woman's act of Mississippi, not to constitute a lis pendens.

The reason probably was that she was not legally holden for the payment of such supplies, and if she were, that an action in personam was the proper remedy, at least until after judgment at law.(1)

Mortgage pending second trial in ejectment.

Sec. 215. Where in an action of ejectment after judgment on the first trial a new trial was taken under the statute, and pending the second trial a mortgage was made upon the land involved in the ejectment suit, it was held that the mortgagee took the property pendente lite, and was bound by the judgment which was rendered upon the second trial.(2)

So in England, where an appeal to the House of Lords was taken after an order of dismissal in the trial court, and pending the appeal there was a purchase, it was held to be pendente lite.(3)

So also where there was a temporary abatement of the suit without laches, and the suit was subsequently restored.(4)

(1) Chaffe v. Patterson, 61 Miss. 28.

(2) Smith et al. v. Cottrell, 94 Ind. 381.

(3) Gore v. Stacpoole, 1 Dow. 18, 31; 3 Sugden on Vendors, 459.

(4) White & Tudor Eq. Cases, 126.

A purchaser upon a judgment prior to service.

SEC. 216. One who purchases upon a judgment which became a lien upon the property subsequently involved in a chancery suit prior to the service of the subpœna, is not a pendente lite purchaser. A suit in chancery was commenced and an injunction issued, but before the service of the subpœna a judgment was confessed, which became a lien upon the property involved in the chancery suit.

A purchase was made upon the judgment by one having no notice of the chancery suit. It was held that such a purchaser at sheriff's sale was not a pendente lite purchaser, and that he acquired a good title to the property.

It is also held in the same case that another, who purchased through an agent who knew of the chancery suit, before the service of the subpœna, was a pendente lite purchaser.

Lis pendens did not bind the first purchaser, because it did not commence until the service of the subpœna and the purchaser had no knowledge of the suit. It did bind the other purchaser, because the knowledge of his agent was imputed to him.(1)

Notice presumed in pendente lite purchase.

SEC. 217. In all cases where purchases are made pendente lite, a presumption must be entertained that the purchasers purchased with full notice of the rights of the parties in the pending case.(2)

(1) Roberts ads. Jackson et al., 1 Wend. 486.
(2) Woodfolk v. Blount et als., 3 Hey. (Tenn.) 152; Sorrel v. Carpenter, 2 P. Wm. 482; Worsley v. Scarborough, 3 Atk. 392; Walker v. Smallwood, Amb. 677.

Statutes as to opening up judgments.

SEC. 218. Statutes exist in most of the States, providing for defendants who are not personally served with process appearing and opening up judgments and decrees after they have been rendered upon terms prescribed by such statutes.

While there are some decisions which seem to be in conflict with the view now expressed, the weight of authority is largely in favor of the position that judgments and decrees rendered under such statutes upon publication or other constructive notice are final and unconditional judgments and that the laws relating to opening up judgments are no part of the judgments themselves, and hence that sales made under such judgments to bona fide purchasers without notice are valid, notwithstanding these provisions of such statutes.

This question was carefully considered in the case of Scudder v. Sargent by the Supreme Court of Nebraska. The Code of Civil Practice of that State provides in substance that a party against whom a judgment has been rendered upon publication merely, may within five years after the date of the judgment or order be opened and the defendant allowed to defend upon proper application to the court, accompanied by a full answer, with an affidavit satisfactory to the court that during the pendency of the suit the defendant had no actual notice thereof in time to appear and make his defense.

That court decided that, notwithstanding this provision of the statute, the judgment sought to be opened was final and that the provisions of the statute in no manner affected its finality. That it fixed the rights of the parties and their privies, so long as it stood un-reversed by appeal or otherwise.

In that case a notice was served upon the plaintiff of a motion to admit the defendant to defend under this statute.

Before any rule was entered on the subject, a con-veyance was made by a party who had acquired title under the judgment to a purchaser in good faith and without notice of the proposed motion, and it was held that the grantee acquired a valid title.

The mere notice of the application did not consti-tute a lis pendens. The lis pendens of the former suit had ceased upon the entry of the judgment. A new lis pendens would not accordingly commence until the court in pursuance of the notice should make an order granting leave to defend.(1)

When lis pendens in bill for alimony.

SEC. 219.   The general doctrine undoubtedly is that a bill filed merely for alimony and maintenance is not a lis pendens so far as relates to the property of the de-fendant, yet, where specific property is described and shown to be the only or nearly the only property owned by the defendant and the residence of the pe-titioner, and the property is so described in the bill as to be drawn within the jurisdiction of the court, so to speak, there will be a lis pendens as to such property and a purchaser will be bound by the final decree in the case.

In a North Carolina case a certain lot was specifi-cally described in such a bill and by an order of court it had been assigned to the complainant, who was the wife of the defendant, for her residence. The final decree

(1) Scudder *v.* Sargent, 15 Neb. 103.

first rendered in the case was reversed by the Supreme Court of that State. The cause was remanded, but pending the suit in the Supreme Court after the reversal and before the case was redocketed, the defendant executed a trust deed on the premises and a sale was made in pursuance of the terms of the trust deed to a third party.

It was held that(1) the purchase was made pendente lite, and that the purchaser was bound by the final decree which was entered in the cause awarding the property to the complainant.(2)

Prior and junior lis pendens.

Sec. 220. Where there were two mortgages executed upon the same premises and after a suit to foreclose the prior mortgage had become a lis pendens, and those interested in the junior mortgage had been made parties, another suit was brought by the holder of the second mortgage, which latter suit was foreclosed pending the suit to foreclose the first mortgage, and the premises were sold under the decree foreclosing the junior mortgage, and the owner of the latter mortgage purchased at the sale.

(1) Daniel v. Hodges, 87 N. C. 97. In the case of Ulrich v. Ulrich, 3 Mackey, 290, the court follow the case of Daniel v. Hodges, and hold that while the rule is that in a bill for alimony and maintenance there is no lis pendens as to the property of the defendant generally, yet where as in that case a certain lot was described in the bill, and it is alleged that the lot constitutes the principal property of the defendant out of which the alimony should be decreed, there is lis pendens as to such property.

(2) The following authorities sustain the position that the general rule is that bills for alimony and maintenance do not bind the property of defendants with lis pendens: 1 Story's Eq. Jur., Sec. 196; Almond v. Almond, 4 Rand. 662; Brightman v. Brightman, 1 R. I. 112; Baird v. Baird et al., Phil. Eq. 317; Isler v. Brown, 66 N. C. 556; Tabb v. Williams, 4 Jones' Eq. 352; Gilmore v. Gilmore, 5 Jones' Eq. 284.

Upon a bill afterwards brought by him to redeem from the first mortgage, he was held to have become a pendente lite purchaser, the court holding that the doctrine of lis pendens should be enforced in the suit brought upon the senior mortgage, as against the lis pendens of the second suit, and that the lis pendens of the prior suit had the effect to annul it.(1)

Lis pendens no application without suit.

SEC. 221.   The doctrine of lis pendens can only apply where there is a suit where the purchaser derives title from a party to it and where the suit is duly prosecuted.   Nor can it apply unless a decree be entered in the case to affect it, nor until such a decree is entered.(2)

It can be enforced or invoked only against purchasers from parties to the litigation after suits are commenced.   And so when A purchased from B and was in possession before a suit was commenced by C, and A was permitted to be made a party defendant, it was held that there could be no lis pendens against A and his assigns.(3)

Insufficient description for lis pendens.

SEC. 222.   Pending a bill filed, affecting the title to a farm which contained a tract of timber land, timber was cut and carried off by parties other than those to the suit.   The land was described in the bill, but not the timber.   After a decree had been entered in the cause granting the relief prayed in respect to the land and the lis pendens of the case was ended thereby, another

(1) Murphy v. Farwell et al., 9 Wis. 103.

(2) Davis v. Christian et als., 15 Gratt. 11; Arnold v. Smith et al., 80 Ind. 422; Britz et al. v. Johnson et al., 65 Ind. 564.

(3) Clarkson et al. v. Morgan's Devisees, 6 B. Monroe, 446.

bill was filed against the persons who had cut and taken away the timber during the pendency of the prior suit for an account for its value. There was no allegation in this latter bill of collusion between those alleged to have cut and carried off the timber and the defendants in the former suit.

It was contended that the lis pendens of the former suit was notice to and binding upon the defendants in the latter suit. The court properly held that the defendants were not bound by the lis pendens of the former suit; first, because the description was not so specific as to the timber as to create lis pendens. The timber was not so pointed out and designated in the bill as to notify the world that it was involved in suit. The court held, secondly, that in such a case, as the defendants in the second suit were neither parties to the former suit nor purchasers from them, nor their privies, an allegation of collusion between them and the defendants in the former suit was necessary in order to give the court jurisdiction over them to compel them to account, and that as this bill was framed it was simply in effect an action of trover, and the bill was dismissed.(1)

(1) Gardner *v.* Peckham et als., 13 R. I. 102; see notes to Sec. 93, *ante.*

CHAPTER XI.

PARTIES TO ACTIONS INVOLVING THE RULE LIS PENDENS.

Preliminary statement.

Sec. 223. It is proper that we should consider in a separate chapter questions arising as to necessary or proper parties and relating to parties generally, in cases involving the rule lis pendens.

While at the same time the discussion will necessarily involve other questions, yet it would seem consistent with an orderly plan of the work that we should group together those cases which specially bear upon the parties to the litigation where the rule lis pendens has been applied or its application has been denied.

Pendente lite purchaser not a necessary party.

SEC. 224. It follows from these same principles that one who purchases the subject matter of litigation pending a suit is not a necessary party to the litigation.

This proposition is embraced within the elements of Lord Bacon's rule itself.

The party from whom he purchased continues as the representative of his interest and the purchaser is bound by the result.(1)　If admitted as a party he

(1) Watson v. Dowling et al., 26 Cal. 127; Young v. Cardwell, 6 Lea, 171; Eyster v. Gaff et al., 91 U. S. 521; Doe v. Childress, 21 Wal. 642; Yeatman v. Savings Inst., 95 U. S. 764; Jerome v. McCarter, 94 U. S. 734; Wickliffe's Exrs. v. Breckenridge's Heirs, 1 Bush. 443; Hale v. Langdon's Heirs, 60 Tex. 561.

While the complainant may either make a pendente lite purchaser a party, or may ignore the purchase and proceed to final decree against the original parties, such purchaser is not entitled to be made a party to the litigation either by publication or by supplemental bill in the nature of an original bill. 1 Story's

Eq. Jur. Sec. 405; Adam's Eq. 278 (note 2, p. 194); Story's Eq. Pl. 156 and note.

In Poston v. Eubank, 3 J. J. Marsh. 43, it is held that a pendente lite purchaser is not a necessary party.

In Clark's Heirs v. Farron, etc., 10 B. Mon. 451, the court holds that a purchaser from a successful party to a suit is not a necessary party to a bill of review, but is bound by the decision upon such bill or upon a writ of error, although not a party. The court say: "A writ of error upon a decree for title would be of little avail if the title could be placed out of the reach of

could only prosecute or defend in the shoes of his grantor. The court would not permit any new questions to arise in the cause in consequence of such purchase.

It is probable that, in the exercise of its discretionary power, the court might permit one acquiring an interest pendente lite to appear and prosecute or defend; but it is not a matter of right, nor does it become necessary to the efficiency of the final judgment or decree that the other parties to the litigation should cause such pendente lite claimant to be made a party.

Pendente lite purchaser no right to prosecute an appeal.

SEC. 225. It follows from the principle that a pendente lite purchaser is not only not a necessary party to a suit but not entitled upon his own motion to become such, that such a purchaser has no right to prosecute a writ of error or appeal from an adverse decision against his grantor. In a case where such a purchaser at the time of rendition of the judgment

the party or the court by a private sale immediately after the decree."

Lord Bacon's rule seems to imply that where the fact of a conveyance pendente lite is brought to the attention of the court, it might give order in the case in accordance with justice and that therefore a pendente lite purchaser may bring the fact of purchase to the attention of the court, and be allowed to defend in the name of his grantor. This has been expressly held in the State of Indiana. It has also been held repeatedly that a grantor by his deed authorizes his grantee to use his name for defense of the property conveyed by the deed.

12th of Lord Bacon's ordinances; Boszell v. Boszell, 105 Ind. 77; Steeple v. Downing, 60 Ind. 478; Vail v. Lindsey, 67 Ind. 528; Exparte R. R. Co., 95 U. S. 221.

In Lord v. Veazie, 8 How. (U. S.) 250, affidavits were allowed to be read in the Supreme Court of the United States upon appeal for the purpose of showing that the controversy between appellant and appellee was not a real one, but that one of the parties had disposed of his interest and the suit was collusive. Upon the showing made the appeal was dismissed.

against his grantor in the trial court was permitted to pray an appeal in the name of his grantor, upon motion made in the Appellate Court to dismiss the appeal, the motion was allowed.(1)

Whether assignee in bankruptcy a necessary party.

SEC. 226. There is some conflict of authority upon the question as to whether or not an assignee in bankruptcy, where the bankruptcy and appointment of assignee occurs pendente lite, is a necessary party to the suit. The weight of authority clearly is to the effect that he is not a necessary party; that where pending the suit a party to it files his petition in bankruptcy and an assignee in bankruptcy is appointed to administer upon the property involved in the pending suit, the assignee and purchasers from him at assignee's sale stand like other pendente lite purchasers and take title subject to the final determination of the pending case, and that if they desire to become parties to the suit they must apply to the court for leave. Otherwise the court may proceed as if no assignment in bankruptcy had ever been made.(2)

(1) Clarke et als. *v.* Koehler, 32 Tex. 679. In Baasen *v.* Eilers et al., 11 Wis. 277, the facts were that a mortgagor had sold the mortgaged premises pending a foreclosure suit for a certain sum, and the vendees agreed to pay off the mortgage but neglected to do so, and upon a bill filed to foreclose the mortgage a decree was entered against the vendor. The premises were sold upon the decree. The vendees appealed in the name of the mortgagor, their vendor, who himself had waived an appeal. It was held that the vendees were pendente lite purchasers and had no such right as would enable them to prosecute an appeal, but it appearing in the record that the court below had set aside a sale under the decree, the Supreme Court affirmed the decree.

(2) Young *v.* Cardwell, 6 Lea, 171; Eyster *v.* Gaff et al., 91 U. S. 521; Doe *v.* Childress, 21 Wal. 642; Yeatman *v.* Savings Inst., 95 U. S. 764; Jerome *v.* McCarter, 94 U. S. 724; Cleveland *v.* Boerum, 24 N. Y. 613; Zane *v.* Fink et al., 18 W. Va. 730.

In Williams *v.* Winans, however, it was held that a person who has acquired an interest in the controversy after the commencement of the suit as assignee or successor will in general be bound by the decree and proceedings and should properly be made a party by supplemental bill.(1)   There is a distinction between necessary and proper parties to a suit.   The assignee is a proper party and the character of the relief sought may make him a necessary party.

Where assignee a necessary party.

SEC. 227.   There is some conflict of authority upon the question whether or not or in what cases an assignee of an interest held at the commencement of a suit by either party to it must or should be made a party to the proceedings.   A careful examination of the authorities, however, on the subject will lead to a substantial reconciliation of the apparent conflict.

The general conclusion from all the authorities would seem to be that, where the interest is voluntarily assigned, the assignee or his grantee is an unnecessary party to the suit because such cases come squarely within the rule of pendente lite purchasers.   On the other hand the weight of authority seems to be that where the interest is divested compulsorily or by operation of law, while in most instances the presence of the assignee is not absolutely necessary to the validity of the proceeding, yet it is desirable and expedient where it becomes important that conveyances should be made or other personal acts done by the assignee which can not be enforced otherwise than by his presence in court as a party to the suit.

Thus where it is necessary to compel an assignee to

(1) Williams *v.* Winans, 5 Green, 393.

join in a conveyance, such assignee although not a necessary party for other purposes in the case is a proper party, at the election of the plaintiff. If the procurement of a conveyance for instance is necessary it may be said that he is a necessary party.

The case is somewhat different so far as relates to a complainant or a defendant, where a defendant goes into bankruptcy or otherwise loses by operation of law the interest which he had at the commencement of the suit. In such case it may be said that the suit, while it does not abate as to such defendant, is defective for want of the presence of the assignee in bankruptcy or other assignee. In that case the assignee should be brought in by an original in the nature of a supplemental bill.

The complainant has the right to perfect his case in this way so as to avail himself of the complete remedy which he would have had against the assignor.(1)

Equitable bona fide purchasers ante litem protected.

SEC. 228.   One who becomes a purchaser of real estate at sheriff's sale on execution made before a bill is

(1) Story's Eq. Pl., 156, 329, 330, 342, 349 and 351; Beame's Pl. in Eq. 299; 2 Danl. Ch. Pr. 957.

In the case of Smith v. Brittenham, 109 Ill. 549, complainant after the commencement of suit and before any hearing or disposition of the case upon the merits voluntarily transferred his interest to another, and it was held that thereby the suit had become defective for want of proper parties and that no valid decree could be entered in the cause until complainant's assignee by a supplemental bill or otherwise should make himself a party complainant to the cause. See, also, Mason v. York & Cumberland R. R. Co., 52 Me. 82.

In Daily et al. v. Kelly, 4 Dow. R. 440, Lord Eldon held that if pendente lite conveyances became vexatious, upon bringing the proper parties before the court they would be enjoined.

This was done in Echliff v. Baldwin, 16 Ves. 267, and Curtis v. The Marquis of Buckingham, 3 Ves. & Beat. 168.

filed to foreclose a mortgage upon the same premises, but who does not get his sheriff's deed until after the filing of the bill and commencement of lis pendens, although made a party to the chancery suit, is not a pendente lite purchaser.

It may be stated as a general principle that one who has acquired a complete equitable right to a legal title to property before lis pendens commences, will be protected as a bona fide purchaser, although the equitable should ripen into a legal title pending suit.

This is especially true where the delay in acquiring the legal title is in consequence of an omission of duty in a public officer.

And so likewise where a party has acquired an equitable title to property by contract entered into bona fide and without notice before suit, he will be protected, although he may acquire and perfect the legal title subsequent to the commencement of lis pendens. We have shown in a former chapter that these are not pendente lite purchasers.(1)

Purchase through prior equity not barred.

SEC. 229.   Where title to the property involved in suit is acquired through a prior equity existing before the commencement of lis pendens and in no manner by purchase from a party to a suit, the rule lis pendens will not apply.

Thus, where one had entered into an ante litem contract for the purchase of the property, but the contract had not been fully executed, and subsequently

(1) 1 Story's Eq. Jur., Secs. 64, c.; Story's Eq. Pl., Secs. 604, a.; Flagg v. Mann, 2 Sumner, 487; Haught- wout et al. v. Murphy, 7 Green, 548; Bassett v. Nosworthy, 2 Leading Cas. Eq. 1, and notes.

in pursuance of the terms of the contract had paid
for the property and received conveyance of it from
one holding the title at the time the contract was
made, but who subsequently had been made a party
to a suit—in which suit the contract was in no wise
assailed, it cannot be doubted but that the grantee
would receive the title to the property in no manner
charged with the lis pendens, although the conveyance were made pending the suit.(1)

In virtue of his prior equity through the ante litem
contract and not himself having been made a party,
the lis pendens should not be given effect as to him.

And so where the title is acquired by operation of law resulting from an ante litem and prior
equity—as where one purchases at sheriff's or master's sale upon a judgment or decree which had
become a lien prior to the taking effect of lis pendens.

Thus also where it appeared in an action of ejectment that after the issuance but before the service
of the subpœna—that is before lis pendens commenced
—the defendant made a mortgage, with power of sale
upon the property in litigation, upon which and after
the commencement of lis pendens a sale was made,
it was held that the mortgagee did not take pendente
lite, and the purchaser at the mortgage sale was not
bound by the judgment rendered in the ejectment

(1) Shaw v. Padley, 64 Mo. 519.
Hunt v. Haven's Adm., 52 N. H.
162, holds that to be bound by
lis pendens the purchase must be
from a party to the suit.

In Irvin's Lessee v. Smith, 17
Ohio, 226, it is decided that the doctrine of lis pendens does not apply
to one who has an interest in the
property involved in the suit, but
who is not a purchaser from a party
to the suit nor made a party himself.

That the holder of title, independent of a party to a suit and not derived from a litigant, is not bound
by lis pendens, see Davis v. Rankin
et al., 50 Tex. 279.

case commenced after the execution of the mortgage.(1)

In such case it is clear that the mortgagee and purchaser had a perfected right before lis pendens commenced, and for that reason were not subject to the rule (2)

(1) Watson v. Dowling et al., 26 Cal. 127.

(2) This subject will be found thoroughly discussed in the case of Parks v. Jackson, 11 Wend. 443. Chancellor Walworth in his opinion in that case adverts to the cases which hold that general judgments at law, liens on real estate generally will be so controlled by a court of equity as to protect the prior equitable right of third parties against the legal liens of judgments, and also against purchasers under execution thereon, who are chargeable with actual or constructive notice of these prior equities. Ex parte Howe, 1 Paige's R. 125; Hampton v. Edelin, 2 Har. and Johns. R. 64; 1 Atkinson on Cor. 512. That when the vendee of the judgment debtor is in actual possession of the premises under a contract of purchase executed prior to the judgment becoming a lien, the purchaser at sheriff's sale will have constructive notice of his equitable rights, and will take the legal title subject to those rights. Tuttle v. Jackson, 6 Wend. 213; Buck v. Halloway's Devisees, 2 J. J. Marsh. R. 180; Chesterman v. Gardner, 5 Johns. Ch. R. 33. That in such cases if the whole of the purchase money had been paid before the judgment, the purchaser at sheriff's sale would hold the legal title as the

trustee of the party in possession with prior equity, and that when only a portion of the money had been paid prior to judgment and sale, then the remaining payment may be made by the owner of the prior equity to the purchaser at sheriff's sale, and he be compelled in equity to convey the legal title. Farholts v. Reed, 16 Serg. & Rawle, 267.

But if the contract was executed after the lien of the judgment, the rule would be otherwise, because the equity would be junior and not prior.

Hampton v. Edelin, 2 Har. & Johns. R. 64; Butts v. Chinn, 4 J. J. Marsh. R. 641.

Senator Seward, in delivering a separate opinion in the case of Parks v. Jackson, ante, 11 Wend. 458, seems to labor under the impression that the case of one in possession, under a contract prior to suit or other prior equity, constitutes an exception to the rule lis pendens. Such is certainly a mistaken view, because a holder under an ante litem contract, or by other right acquired before suit, is in no sense a pendente lite purchaser or intermeddler. This case should not be classed with the well known exception in regard to commercial paper. The learned senator proceeds, however, to point

When treated as a party.

SEC. 230. Where in a creditor's bill a party went before the master and proved his claim and afterwards brought a bill in his own name bringing in the parties to the former suit and also the heirs at law, a plea of the pendency of the former action was held good, Lord Hardwicke saying that "A plaintiff who comes in before a master under a decree is quasi a party to that suit. The present plaintiff does not by his bill make any case to show it was absolutely necessary that the heir at law should be brought before the court."(1)

Statutory right to be a party.

SEC. 231. Although the general rule is that a purchaser pendente lite or one treated as such cannot of his own right be made a party to a pending suit, yet that rule may be varied by legislation.

The legislature of New Jersey passed an act which provides that in any suit for the foreclosure of a mortgage upon or which may relate to real estate or personal property in that State, all persons claiming an interest in or incumbrance on or lien upon such property by or through any conveyance, mortgage, assign-

ut that the reason of the rule lis pendens does not apply in the case of an ante litem purchaser, and that "this reason has no application to a third party whose interest subsists before the suit was commenced, and who might have been made an original party." Hopkins v. McLaren, 4 Cow. 678.

The learned senator, after showing that this should especially apply where the equitable owner was in possession of the property, says: "I consider myself well supported in the view I have taken of this case, by the circumstance that I have not found, nor has there been shown to the court, a solitary case in which the rule lis pendens has been applied to a person who purchased by contract and enters into possession, and in part performs his contract before suit commenced, and then pendente lite without actual notice fulfills his contract and takes a deed for the land."

(1) Neve v. Weston et ux., 3 Atk. 557.

ment or any instrument which could be recorded, registered or filed in any public office of that State and which was not filed at the time the suit was commenced, should be bound by the proceedings in the suit, so far as such property is concerned, as though such person were made a party and had appeared in the suit as defendant, and that all such persons upon causing their unrecorded conveyance, mortgage, assignment, lien or other instrument to be recorded or filed as provided by law would have the right to come in and be made a party to the record upon an application by petition.(1)

Lis pendens where one partner only is served.

SEC. 232. Where suit was brought against a partner by creditors to reach the partnership assets and but one of the partners was served with process, it was held that service upon one of the partners created a lis pendens so that intermeddlers with the partnership assets would be bound by the decree which should be entered in the case.(2)

Where purchasers pendente lite might appear.

SEC. 233. Although the general rule is that a pendente lite purchaser has no right to appear in the pending cause and be allowed to set up his rights acquired by the purchase, yet it has been held and would seem to be within the meaning of Lord Bacon's rule that the court would have discretionary power to allow a purchaser, where he could show he held equitable rights, to appear at least in the name of his grantor and present those rights.

Where a railway company had obtained its right

(1) Dinsmore *v.* Wescott, 10 Green, 304; Laws N. J., 1870, p. 40.   (2) Dresser *v.* Wood, 15 Kas. 344.

of way upon premises upon which a mortgage was
being foreclosed, and it was clear that it was
bound by the lis pendens to have known of the existence of the mortgage and was bound by the final decree which was rendered in the foreclosure suit, it was
said that it might have appeared and been made a
party to the proceedings and have had a decree so
framed that the right of way of the railway acquired
pending the suit should only be sold in case the residue did not sell for a sufficient amount to satisfy the
mortgage debt.(1)

Change of trustee pending suit.

SEC. 234.   Pending a suit in chancery against trustees, if other trustees are substituted in place of the
original ones after the court has acquired jurisdiction
of the defendants and the subject matter of the suit,
the lis pendens of the suit will bind the substituted
trustees and it is not necessary that they should formally be made parties.

Nor is an injunction against the new trustees necessary. The lis pendens of the suit will control and
nullify the acts of the new trustees without injunction.
As a matter of precaution, however, it may be the better practice to file a supplemental bill setting up the
simple fact of the substitution of trustees.

(1) Jackson v. Centreville M. &
A. Co. et al., 64 Iowa, 292; Severin
v. Cole et al., 38 Iowa, 463; Cooley
v. Brayton, 16 Iowa, 10; Crum v.
Cutting, 22 Iowa, 411.

This is a fair sequence from the
language of Lord Bacon's order
which is, "or the court made acquainted with the conveyance, the
court is to give order upon the
special matter according to justice."

It seems a fair construction of
Lord Bacon's ordinance therefore
that, where the fact of a conveyance
is brought to the knowledge of the
court, it may make such order with
reference to the party receiving
such conveyance as shall be according to justice.

In that case, however, there can be no new issue with the new trustees except as to whether they are substituted trustees. The pleadings and proofs in the original case will be treated as legally and regularly in the case after the substitution.(1)

Owner must be served in condemnation suit.

SEC. 235. Pending a bill to foreclose a mortgage proceedings were had by a railroad company to condemn the mortgaged lands for railroad purposes, but the mortgagee was not made a party. It was held that the railroad company would take the land pendente lite.

The railroad company had made valuable improvements upon the property and claimed that it should only pay for the value of the property unimproved, but it was held that it should pay for the property in its improved condition.(2)

Lis pendens does not apply to tax sales.

SEC. 236. The authority of the State to make sale of property for the non-payment of delinquent taxes is paramount to the right of the owner and all others, and where such sale is made in accordance with law, is conclusive against all persons; hence as against the rights of the State the pendency of suits involving the property has no force or effect.

This constitutes an exception to the rule that all

(1) Broraem v. Wood, 12 Green, 372.

(2) North Am. Coal Co. v. Dyett et als, 2 Edw. Ch. 115. It was held in King v. Donnelly, 5 Paige, 46, that in a partition case where the legal title to the estate as to an undivided share of the premises was in a trustee, and a new trustee was substituted pendente lite, that the new trustee should be brought in by supplemental bill. See, also, Osgood et al., Receivers, v. Maguire, 61 Barb. 59.

purchases during the pendency of a suit are held bound by the decree that may be made against the person from whom title is derived.

This exception is founded upon grounds of public policy. The enforcement of the rule of lis pendens in such cases would endanger the very existence of the State. The right of the State to its revenue is paramount. Nor is the State a party to the litigation.

Notice of lis pendens not necessary in tax cases.

SEC. 237. Hence in those States where lis pendens statutes are in force it is not necessary that the State or other taxing power should file notices of lis pendens under the statute in tax proceedings.(1)   A lien of the judgment against the property for the non-payment of taxes cannot be created by the filing of a notice of lis pendens.

The statutes of the various States determine at what point of time in the proceeding to collect taxes the tax shall become a lien upon real estate. These provisions vary in the different States. In most of the States the assessment creates the lien, and when further steps are taken in the collection of the tax, as the judgment, sale and deed, by operation of law they relate back to and take effect from the date of the assessment. The assessment and lien which it creates are public matters of record, of which all purchasers are bound to take notice, and when a purchaser buys land which is subject to an existing lien for taxes he must see at his peril that the taxes are paid, and if he neglects this duty he takes the hazard of a judgment against the land, the lien of which by operation of law

(1) Reeve v. Kennedy, 43 Cal.   Bigelow on Eq. 189.
653; Wright v. Walker, 30 Ark. 44;

and by relation will antedate his purchase. If the rule were otherwise the collection of taxes would be almost impossible.

Public necessity therefore requires that no notice of lis pendens should be required to be filed in this class of cases.

And so where a lot was listed in the name of A, to which B held an equitable title, and while so held C became the purchaser of the property at a tax sale, and it not having been redeemed, he received a tax deed for it.

Subsequently to the purchase at such tax sale C bought the property of B and paid full value for it, took a deed and went into possession without any actual notice of any pending suit or lien acquired prior to such conveyance by B. Subsequent to C's purchase at tax sale, but before he received the deed from B, an attachment had been levied upon the lot as the property of B, which attachment was afterwards prosecuted to judgment, sale and sheriff's deed. D and E who purchased and received the sheriff's deed, brought suit against C to recover the property. It was held that C was not a pendente lite purchaser. The grounds upon which this decision was based were that the tax sale was a prior proceeding to the attachment suit, and that therefore he had a right to prosecute his tax claim and obtain satisfaction of it as a first incumbrance; that to say that he was a pendente lite purchaser under the attachment proceedings would be to reverse the natural order and postpone the first to the second incumbrance and thus utterly destroy his tax claim acquired prior to and without regard to the subsequent lien.

That the law requires the owners of lots to see that the taxes are paid and that if they neglect it they or any one claiming under them have no right to complain of the consequences of their own negligence; that the payment of taxes is one of the first and highest obligations a citizen owes the State, and hence that any suit or lis pendens as between individuals cannot affect the right of the State to sell the lot for taxes or the rights of innocent third parties buying at such tax sales; that proceedings for the collection of taxes are in the nature of proceedings in rem, to which the whole world may be said to be parties.

So far, however, as relates to the purchase of B's equitable title without regard to the tax title acquired by C, the latter would have been held to have been a pendente lite purchaser and to have taken subject to the attachment lien upon the property.(1)

Lis pendens of bill to redeem from tax purchaser.

Sec. 238. While, however, as against the State, lis pendens has no force in proceedings for the collection of taxes, yet where the sale has been made and individuals have purchased, the force of lis pendens in bills to redeem from sales is effective.

Where a bill was filed by the assignee of a mortgage whose assignment had never been recorded, for the purpose of setting aside a satisfaction of the mortgage by the mortgagee after the assignment, and to redeem from a tax sale, it was held that the lis pendens of the bill as against the holder of the tax claim was effective and that the purchase at the tax sale was affected with the notice of the suit and was bound by the decree. In that case the purchaser at the tax

(1) Merrick et al. v. Hutt, 15 Ark. 343.

sale was the tenant of the defendant, the mortgagee.(1)

Lis pendens in partition where complainant in bill conveys.

SEC. 239. If, after a plaintiff commences a suit for the partition of lands and the defendants have been served, he shall sell and convey the lands or his interest in them to other parties pendente lite, the defendants are in no wise bound to notify the purchaser of the pendency of the suit or of proceedings taken therein subsequent to the time of conveyance.

Purchasers are bound to know of the pendency of suits commenced by their grantors, and are bound by the results of them.(2)

Where one joint plaintiff sells to another pending suit.

SEC. 240. Where two plaintiffs sue jointly on a contract, and pending the suit one of the plaintiffs sells his interest to his co-plaintiff, it is discretionary with the court to allow the purchaser to prosecute the suit as sole plaintiff.(3)

Lis pendens in cases against executors and administrators.

SEC. 241. Proceedings against executors and administrators in the progress of the settlement of estates are binding upon those dealing with them pending such suits. Where the purchases are made or transactions had before final decree, they are a lis pendens. Where they occur after decree, the property is still bound by the decree. It is immaterial whether it is because the judgment is regarded as notice or as res adjudicata. The result is the same.

---

(1) Hawes *v.* Howland, 136 Mass. 267.

(2) Baird *v.* Corwin, 5 Harris, 462.

(3) Harvey *v.* Myer et al., 9 Ind. 391.

Where lis pendens would apply before decree, res adjudicata will apply after decree.

So it was held in South Carolina, where an executrix had fraudulently sold property belonging to the estate, and pending a bill against her, had delivered the property, that the sale was fraudulent and the property subject to the debts of the estate. But the purchaser was refunded what he had actually advanced upon the property.

In that case the court questions the doctrine that the notice of lis pendens ends with the final decree. It is believed that the doubt as to whether the notice of the lis pendens is ended when the decree is entered is solved by the application of the principle of res adjudicata to purchases made of parties to decrees and their privies after such rendition.(1)

Purchase from the court subject to lis pendens until purchase paid.

Sec. 242. Where land is sold and conveyed under a decree of court, by virtue of which a lien is retained upon the premises sold to secure the purchase money, the case as against the purchaser continues to pend for the purpose of enforcing the lien of the purchase money. Such purchasers under decrees are subject to the lis pendens of the suits until the purchase money is paid, and cannot set up a limitation against the payment of the purchase money.(2)

Where conveyance before suit not pendente lite.

Sec. 243. But where a conveyance of property is made before suit is commenced to a purchaser without

(1) Watlington v. Howley et als., 1 Desau. (S. C. R.) 166.   (2) Spence et al. Ex parte, 6 Lea, 391.

notice, the party acquiring such interest or title cannot be made subject to the pending suit.

Lord Bacon's rule itself states that "No decree bindeth any that cometh in bona fide by conveyance from the defendant before the bill exhibited, and is made no party neither by the bill nor order."(1)

The meaning of that part of the rule in respect to being made a party is that no suit is then commenced against a party who shall have made such a conveyance, not that the grantee or his assigns shall not be made a party afterwards. All of the cases hold to the rule that purchasers before suit without notice for value shall not be affected by the pendency of suits afterwards brought. The only cases where ante litem grantees and their assigns can be successfully brought within the force of lis pendens are where there was actual notice of the equity subsequently sought to be enforced by a bill, where the conveyance was fraudulently made without consideration to avoid creditors, or where the grantee did not become a bona fide owner of the property upon some other ground of infirmity.

And it may be said generally that where, although possession of real estate is acquired pendente lite, yet

(1) Mitchell v. Peters, 18 Iowa, 121; Parsons v. Hoyt, 24 Iowa, 155; Fitzgerald v. Cummings et al., 1 Lea, 239; Bailey et al. v. McGinnis et al., 57 Mo. 371; Shaw v. Padley, 64 Mo. 522 ; Haughwout et al. v. Murphy, 7 Green, 531 ; Powell v. Wright, 7 Beavan, 444; Ensworth v. Lambert, 4 Johns. Ch. 605; Scarlett et al. v. Graham et al., 28 Ill. 319; Fergus et al. v. Woodworth et al., 44 Ill. 381; Alwood v. Mansfield et al., 59 Ill. 508; Bennett v. Hotchkiss et al., 20 Minn. 168; Johnson v. Robinson, 20 Minn. 171.

And so where the conveyance was prior to the action, the purchaser is not bound by lis pendens, although his grantor subsequently becomes a party to the suit. Farmers' Nat'l Bk. of Salem v. Fletcher, 44 Iowa, 253; Macey v. Fenwick's Admrs., 9 Dana, 200; Fenwick's Adm. v. Macey, 2 B. Mon. 470.

under a title disconnected with and independent of
that of the defendant in the pending suit, the rule lis
pendens will not be applied.

If not applied where the conveyance is from the defendant, certainly it could not be where the conveyance or possessory right is acquired from a stranger to the defendant and not a party to the suit.

It is a universal rule that in order to apply the rule
lis pendens, the party against whom it is invoked must
take from a party to the suit as well as acquire the
interest pending the suit.   And so where several persons are the owners of a tract of land as tenants in
common, and the interest of one of them passes to a
purchaser under execution sale, and he brings ejectment against the execution debtor alone and recovers
judgment, neither the other tenants in common, nor
their grantees who purchase and enter upon the land
pending suit, can be dispossessed by the sheriff by
virtue of the writ of restitution issued upon the judgment rendered against the one alone.

This principle is not in conflict with the doctrine
that if a party to a suit conveys land pending the litigation and the grantee enters upon the land with or
without notice of the pending suit, he is bound by the
judgment and is liable to be dispossessed by the writ
of restitution issued thereon, although not a party.

Ante litem equitable owners.

Sec. 244. We have seen in determining this question
of fact that the registry or recording laws of the several States are to be taken into the account.(1)

And so if a claimant had contracted for the purchase
of real estate out of possession, but had not recorded

(1) Fessler's Appeal, 75 Pa. St. 483;   Parks v. Jackson, 11 Wend. 442.

his contract, and one occupying such position with reference to the recording laws as to require that instruments relating to the conveyance of real estate should be recorded in order to be effective against him should commence a suit involving the title to the property purchased, the object of which would be necessarily to defeat the purchase, the contracting claimant, although his contract were dated and executed prior to the commencement of the suit, would not have acquired a right to the property before the suit became effective upon it and would be treated as a pendente lite purchaser.

But if the contract had been recorded prior to the commencement of the suit, his right would have been perfected or established before the suit took effect upon the property, so that he might subsequently require his vendor, notwithstanding the suit, to comply with the contract and vest in him the legal title, and so would be a bona fide purchaser for value and without notice.

Thus numerous examples might be given illustrative of this proposition. If the claimant as against the whole world had, at the time lis pendens became effective as to him, acquired an equitable right to the subject matter of litigation so that, as against the defendant, he could enforce in the courts a legal title to the property, or if such legal title had vested in him bona fide, and without notice of the pending suit before, as against strangers, the suit became effective upon the property, he would fall within the class of ante litem claimants; but on the other hand, if such equitable right or legal title was not acquired or perfected as against the public, until after the suit had

become effective upon the property, he would be a pendente lite purchaser and become subject to the judgment or decree finally to be entered in the pending
case.

Ante litem mortgagees as well as grantees unaffected.

SEC. 245.   And this is equally true of mortgages.
Mortgagees, as well as grantees under deeds and bills
of sale made by persons holding titles and not parties
to the pending litigation, are unaffected by the subsequent lis pendens.

And the same reasons for it that exist in cases where
absolute conveyances are made, also exist for the application of the rule to mortgagees.   Parties are only
required to examine the records of suits involving the
persons with whom they deal and from whom they acquire title and their grantors.   They cannot be held
bound to search for suits involving other persons than
those ocurring in the chain of title under which they
become purchasers.   This may be illustrated by the
case of Stuyvesant v. Hone, which was a bill filed by
a junior mortgagee of a mortgage made pending a suit,
asking the aid of a court of equity to enforce the familiar doctrine requiring the mortgagee of several tracts
pledged to secure the same indebtedness to proceed to
foreclose against the several tracts in the inverse order
of alienation.

The first mortgage was executed before the suit and
covered several tracts, only one of which was embraced
in the junior mortgage.   Pending the suit to foreclose
the second mortgage, of which the first mortgagee had
no actual notice, a portion of the property included in
the first mortgage but not in the second was released
without diminishing the indebtedness, thereby leaving

the property to which the second mortgagee was forced to look for his security so heavily incumbered as to materially impair the value of the junior mortgage. The right of the junior mortgagee to the relief sought, depending upon notice lis pendens, the court held that the senior incumbrancee could not be charged with constructive notice lis pendens of the suit for foreclosure.(1)

Where a plaintiff sues for undivided interest.

SEC. 246.   Where a plaintiff brings suit for an undivided interest in real estate and pending the suit buys in and takes conveyance of the remaining interests,

---

(1) Stuyvesant *v.* Hone, 1 Sandf. Ch. 419; Stuyvesant *v.* Hall, 2 Barb. Ch. 151.

The case of Stuyvesant *v.* Hone et als., 1 Sandf. 419, is a somewhat complicated illustration of the application of the rule that lis pendens does not affect one who has paramount title superior to that of all the parties to the suit, but applies only to those who derive their title to the subject matter of the suit from a party to it after its commencement.

In that case a tract of land was mortgaged to S. H subsequently acquired a lien on it which became known to S. H, without notice to S or making him a party, proceeded in chancery to enforce his lien and the lands were sold by the master to T. The lands were subsequently subdivided into fifty-six building lots, a part of the lots were mortgaged by T to H and the residue were discharged from the lien by the sale of the master. The transfers between H and T were duly recorded. S had no knowledge of any of these proceedings. Afterwards H proceeded to foreclose T's mortgage in chancery and at the commencement of the suit filed notice of lis pendens under the statute, it being in a State where lis pendens statutes were in force. S having no notice of this suit during its pendency released to T from his mortgage forty-two of the fifty-six lots, retaining fourteen lots subject to his mortgage, which were a part of those lots mortgaged by T to H. It was held, first, that S was not chargeable with constructive notice of the first chancery suit of H or of his sale under his decree; second, that the recording of the conveyance to T and of T's mortgage was not notice to S, and that on releasing S was not bound to search the records for conveyances or incumbrances; and third, that neither of the foreclosure suits of H or the lis pendens filed affected S with H's proceeding or his rights under T's mortgage.

and no special objection is made in the trial court on account of the purchase having been made pending the suit, it was held, on an appeal to the Supreme Court, that the judgment would not be disturbed on that ground.

In order to have invoked the judgment of the Supreme Court upon the question of the legality of admitting the evidence of a pendente lite purchase, the defendant ought to have made special objection in the trial court. In that case the alienation did not affect unfavorably the subject matter of litigation, because the remaining interests were brought by the purchase and conveyance within the jurisdiction of the court, and there was no attempt to evade jurisdiction.

So likewise where, pending a suit involving the title to lands, one of the defendants delivered to a co-defendant a deed from the plaintiff to the latter defendant, which had remained undelivered and without effect up to that time, and the court afterwards entered a decree in the case in favor of the plaintiff, disregarding the fact of the delivery and existence of the deed, it was held that the parties to the suit were concluded by the decree.

However erroneous a decree may be as between the parties and their privies it is binding and in full force until reversed.(1)

No lis pendens after final decree and before bill of review.

SEC. 247. Lis pendens ends with a decree of dismissal of a bill even where it is brought by infants and does not exist when subsequently a bill of review is filed to reverse the decree. A statute allowing infants

(1) Moore et al. *v.* Worley et al., 21 Iowa, 441.
24 Ind, 81; McGregor *v.* McGregor,

to file a bill of review within five years after they reach their majority does not change this rule.

A bill filed by infants was dismissed on final hearing. A bill of review was subsequently filed and the decree of dismissal reversed. A purchase was made of the property involved in the litigation after the dismissal of the bill and before the bill of review was filed. The court held in that case that the purchase was not pendente lite. The court say: "A decree which puts an end to the suit has not heretofore been considered less final because it was subject within a limited time to be reviewed upon a bill of review.

The argument for complainants is that the statute giving the infants a day after they come of age to file a bill of review is to be taken as part of the decree itself and considered as if the privilege was contained on its face and that the legal effect thereof is that it remains a matter pendente lite until the rights reserved by the decree are extinguished. I do not consider it at all important to determine in this case whether the statute is to be so blended with the decree as to form a part of it, for if the decree had in terms reserved to the complainants the right to showing cause against it after they arrived at age, it would not have had the effect of continuing the cause until that period."

* * * "Nothing is reserved or left for further determination by the court, but the whole controversy between parties is disposed of and a final end put to that particular cause; and I cannot perceive that the decree, being against infants, at all changes its character or alters its effect as to third persons."(1)

(1) Ludlow's Heirs *v.* Kidd's Exr. et als., 3 Ohio, 541.

The case of Earl et al. *v.* Couch, 3 Met. (Ky.) 454, seems in conflict with the above case. In that case a bill had been filed involving slaves

Intruders pendente lite not entitled to be made parties.

SEC. 248. In determining whether it is necessary to admit a party to a pending suit, it becomes material to determine whether there is a lis pendens or not.

As to the applicant to be made a party, he is not entitled as a matter of right to be made a party, for he is an intruder and is already represented by the party from whom he acquired his interest; but if lis pendens does not exist, and he has an interest, he is entitled to be made a party.(1)

Amendment not required where a purchase pendente lite.

SEC. 249. Where a purchase has been made of the subject matter of the litigation pending the suit, it is unnecessary to amend the pleadings setting up the fact of purchase.

The pendente lite intermeddler must stand in the shoes of his grantor, and has no right to demand to be made a party. There is no new issue which can be

and after decree in the trial court and during the period of infancy of one of the parties to the suit and before the time within which a bill of review could be filed, the slaves were sold. Upon a bill of review he decree was subsequently reversed. It was held that the purchaser of the slaves took pendente lite. The court cites in support of that view two other cases decided by the same court, to-wit: Clarey et al. v. Marshall's Heirs, 4 Dana, 96; Debell v. Foxworthy, 9 B. Mon. 228. The reasoning of the Ohio case is the more satisfactory.

(1) Carter v. Mills, 30 Mo. 437.

In the case of Parks v. Jackson, 11 Wend. 442, it was held that a purchaser of land by contract who by the terms of his contract has the right to take possession and has a day for payment of the purchase money and who enters into possession according to his contract and makes valuable improvements, pays the purchase money and obtains a deed in pursuance of his contract, is not affected by lis pendens, although the purchase money was paid and deed obtained subsequent to the commencement of the suit against his vendor to avoid the title which was conveyed as fraudulently obtained. Such a purchaser, having entered into contract in good faith and without notice previous to the filing of the bill, would not be affected by the result of the suit.

tried or formed by reason of the pendente lite purchase. It is therefore not necessary to amend the bill or other pleadings setting up the fact of purchase.

The effect of the lis pendens is to overreach and annul all conveyances without bringing the party before the court or introducing any proof with respect to the transfer. There is no new issuable fact to be tried or triable. The law executes itself.

It might be well in practice, however, to recite in decrees or judgments such alienations for the purpose of connecting the record of the suit with the transfers, if recorded. To support such recitals evidence is admissible under the original pleadings.(1)

When complainant's interest compulsorily assigned.

SEC. 250. But on the other hand where a complainant's interest is involuntarily assigned by reason of his bankruptcy, insolvency, or other like cause, the assignee is entitled to supply the defects of the suit, if it has become defective merely, and to continue it so as to enforce the interest or right which has passed to him as the assignee.

If the person succeeding to the interest of the complainant shall take no steps to perfect the case, the defendant by proper application to the court may compel the perfection of the cause, if he so desire, and upon such application the court will enter a nisi rule that unless such assignee, within a day named, shall proceed to perfect the cause the suit will be dismissed.

The court, however, will give a reasonable time within which the assignee may perfect the cause.(2)

(1) Keller v. Miller, 17 Ind. 206.
(2) Zane v. Fink et al., 18 W. Va. 693; Story's Eq. Pl. 156, 351, 342, 349, 330, 329; Beames' Pleas in Eq. 299; Williams v. Kinder, 4 Ves. 387; Wheeler v. Malins, 4 Madd. 171;

Assignee may waive right.

SEC. 251. But where, after a compulsory or otherwise involuntary assignment shall have occurred, and the assignee shall proceed in the cause without taking steps to be brought before the court, whether the interest assigned be that of a complainant or defendant, the right to have the cause perfected or the defect arising from the assignment removed will be waived and the cause may proceed for such purposes as are possible or within the power of the court to grant in the absence of such assignee.(1)

Where litigation collusive intervention admitted.

SEC. 252. When collusive litigation is in progress, which may result in injury to one interested in the property in litigation, whether such person acquire his interest prior to or pending suit, he ought to be admitted so as to litigate the questions involving his interest and defeat contemplated fraud.

A judgment was obtained in April against a party whose lands were covered by two mortgages, and during the same month a levy was made under which the land was sold in June and purchased by M, who was surety for the defendant for the debt merged in the judgment. In May actions were commenced to foreclose the mortgages and notices of lis pendens were then filed.

Randall v. Mumford, 18 Ves. 427, note 1; Porter v. Cox, 5 Mad. 80; Bades v. Harris, 20 Eng. Ch. & 1 Young & Collier, 230; Solomon v. Solomon, 13 Sim. 516; 2 Dan'l's Ch. Pr. 957; Sharp v. Hullet, 2 S. & S. 496; Deas v. Thorne et al., 3 Johns. 543; Sedgwick v. Cleveland et al., 7 Paige, 287; Garr v. Gomey, 9 Wend. 649.

In Anderson v. Wilson et al., 100 Ind. 408, it is said, "The fact that Voorhies, pending the proceedings in the cross-bill, was adjudged a bankrupt, would not defeat the jurisdiction of the court."

(1) Gillespie et ux. v. Bailey et al., 12 W. Va. 70.

The mortgagor answered, alleging the sheriff's sale and disclaiming any further interest. M thereupon filed his petition, charging the two mortgages to be fraudulent, and asking to be allowed to intervene as a party.

In deciding the case the court in a majority opinion say: "It appears that the mortgages which are sought to be foreclosed in these actions between son and father in the one case, and between wife and husband in the other, are pretensive and fraudulent, and made to hinder, delay and defeat the creditors of the mortgagor; and it is very manifest that no such defense will be set up, for the defendant, in the actions for foreclosure, has answered, saying that he had no further interest therein since the purchase of the mortgaged premises by the petitioner at the sheriff's sale." * * *

"Unless there be some way by which the petitioner could be protected against such a result a gross fraud would be practiced upon him through the forms of law, provided the allegations in his petition be true."(1)

Where Appellate Court remands with instructions.

SEC. 253.   Various cases have arisen involving the rights of third parties where courts of last resort upon cases appealed or writs of error to such courts have remanded cases, with directions to the court below as to the judgments or decrees which the inferior court should enter.

It is uniformly held in such cases that where a case has been decided by the Appellate Court and remanded with directions as to the proceedings to be had in the court below, none of the parties to the litigation have a right to raise any question in the inferior

(1) Ex parte Mobley, in re McAfee v. McAfee, 19 S. C. 337.

court touching the correctness of the decision of the
Appellate Court, or to raise any new issues to be decided by the inferior court.

The decision of the Appellate Court in such cases
is a final determination of the rights of the parties to
the litigation. All that remains for the inferior court
to do is in the nature of merely ministerial duty.

Hence it was decided in Arkansas, in a case where
one of the parties had died pending a case, that the
determination of the Appellate Court was legally executed without bringing in new parties or making the
personal representatives of the deceased parties to the
case when re-docketed in the inferior court.

In that case one of the parties had conveyed pending the litigation to one of the heirs of the deceased
party, and it was held that it was not necessary to
bring in the grantee of the deceased party, but that
the decree of the inferior court executing the mandate
of the Appellate Court was binding upon the heirs of
the deceased party as well as upon his grantee.(1)

(1) Ashley et al. *v.* Cunningham et al., 16 Ark. 173; Cunningham *v.* Beebe et al., 13 Ark. 673; Fortenberry *v.* Frazier et al., 5 Ark. 202; Doe ex dem. Hawley *v.* Porter et al., 5 Eng. 190; Sheller's Exrs. *v.* May's Exrs., 6 Cranch, 266; Ex parte Tobias Watkins, 3 Pet. 193.

CHAPTER XII.

THE APPLICATION OF LIS PENDENS TO ANTECEDENT LIENS.

General statement.

Sec. 254. There are various species of liens, more
or less connected with pending causes in court, to
which the application of the rule lis pendens gives
efficiency to the date of the lien prior to the commencement of the lis pendens. In such cases when
the jurisdiction of the court attaches—when lis pendens commences—it may be said to energize and give
life to the lien back to the anterior date when the lien
attached.

Among these are various creditor's liens, the liens
of attorneys and solicitors for fees, the liens for the unpaid purchase money of real estate, of proceedings by
attachment, of mechanic's and material men for labor
performed and material furnished, of mortgages and
trust deeds, of ancillary proceedings in aid of suits at
law in personam, and proceedings in bankruptcy.

So also actual notice brought to the knowledge of
one prior to the purchase of equitable and legal rights,
anterior to the origin of res litigiosa, may under certain circumstances have the effect of a lis pendens as
against the person acquiring such knowledge and bind
the conscience, enabling courts to enforce the rights
acquired against such persons, as though there were an
actual lis pendens.

Attorney's lien for compensation and costs.

Sec. 255. A lien may be defined to be "a charge imposed upon specific property for the performance of
an act."

Bouvier's definition is a better one, that "a lien is a

hold or claim which one person has upon the property of another as a security for some debt or charge."(1)

By the common law of England, and also by the laws of most of the States of the Union, attorneys at law and solicitors in chancery have a lien upon certain property of their clients as security for their compensation.

This lien extends to a fund recovered by their aid, whether in legal or equitable proceedings. It is of two kinds. The first is termed a special or charging lien and is imposed upon the property of the client on account of labor bestowed or money expended in regard to that particular property.

The other lien which is allowed an attorney is a more general one, extending not only to the property of the client upon which the labor has been performed, but to all property of a client held by an attorney for such sum as will be due him on account of professional services.(2)

Particular or charging lien.

SEC. 256. In England the particular or charging lien was early recognized by the common law as being founded upon principles of equity and justice.(3)

It is analogous to the lien of the mechanic for the labor which he bestows upon specific pieces of property. The courts have always been careful to protect and enforce such liens.

Now in England the subject has been covered by statute. 23 and 24 Vict., C. 127, Sec. 28, provides that "in every case in which an attorney or solicitor shall be employed to prosecute or defend a suit, matter

(1) Civil Code of Cal., Sec. 2872; 2 Bouv. Law Dic. (tit. "lien") 88.
(2) Weeks on Attorneys, 369;
McDonald v. Napier, 14 Ga. 89.
(3) Weeks on Attorneys, 369.

or proceeding in any court of justice, it shall be lawful for the court or judge before whom any such suit, matter or proceeding has been heard or shall be depending, to declare such attorney or solicitor entitled to a charge upon the property recovered or preserved, and upon such declaration being made such attorney or solicitor shall have a charge upon and against, and have right to payment out of the property, of whatsoever nature, tenure or kind the same may be, which shall have been recovered or preserved through the instrumentality of any such attorney or solicitor, for the taxed costs, charges and expenses, or in reference to such matter or proceeding."

The act also declares any conveyance or act done for the purpose of defeating the lien to be void.(1)

Although a particular lien, it applies to all documents or papers in the hands of the attorney relating to the employment.(2)

It also extends to articles to be exhibited to witnesses on the trial,(3) or to money or other property recovered by their aid.(4)

The plaintiff can not release or discharge this lien.(5)

The lien attaches to money paid or payable into court in a cause, and to money paid to the client by

(1) 23 and 24 Vict. C. 127, Sec. 26.

(2) Hollis *v.* Claridge, 4 Taunt. 807; Spark *v.* Spicer, 1 Ld. Raym. 322, 738; Gist *v.* Hawley, 33 Ark. 233; Read *v.* Dapper, 6 Term R. 361; Randle *v.* Fuller, 6 Term R. 456.

(3) Friswell *v.* King, 15 Sim. 191.

(4) Wilkins *v.* Carmichael, 1 Doug. 104; Welsh *v.* Hole, 1 Doug. 238; Barker *v.* St. Quinten, 12 Mees.

& W. 441; Turwin *v.* Gibson, 3 Atk. 720; Bawtree *v.* Watson, 2 Keen, 713; Skinner *v.* Sweet, 3 Madd. 244; Mitchell *v.* Oldfield, 4 T. R. 75; Ormerod *v.* Taite, 1 East. 464; Irving v. Viand, 2 You. & J. 70; Barnesley *v.* Powell, 1 Amb. Ch. 102.

(5) Hutchinson *v.* Howard, 15 Ves. 544.

way of compromise, although the verdict and judgment are against the client receiving it.(1)

The equitable lien of a solicitor upon property which has been saved by his services is chargeable against it for his fees, and the lien will follow the property into the hands of a purchaser who knows the services were performed.(2)

It was so also at common law in England.(3)

This lien in the United States.

SEC. 257. The particular or charging lien is recognized by the Supreme Court of the United States and in many of the States.

In some of the States statutes have been passed regulating the extent of this lien. In others it has been denied. In some States the lien is limited to the costs and disbursements allowed by statute.(4)

(1) Baylie v. Brickall, 2 Hun. & M. 371; Bouser v. Bradshaw, 4 Giff. 260; Davies v. Lowndes, 3 Mau. & Gr. (3 Com. B.) 808; Hopewell v. Amwell, 2 Halst. 4; Heacht v. Chipman, 2 Aiken, 162; Talcott v. Broneson, 4 Paige, 501; Quested v. Lallis, 10 Mees. & W. 18; Clark v. Smith, 1 Dowl. & L. 960; Wright v. Burrough, 3 Com. B. 344; Worrall v. Johnson, 2 Jacob & W. 218; Abbott v. Rice, 3 Bing. 132; Lann v. Church, 4 Madd. 391.

Where fees are taxed as costs they can only be paid to the attorney. Crotty v. Mackenzie, 52 How. Pr. 54; Marshall v. Meech, 51 N. Y. 140; Pulver v. Harris, 56 N. Y. 73; Lesher v, Roessner, 3 Hun. 217; Ackerman v. Ackerman, 14 Abb. Pr. 229; Bishop v. Gracia, 14 Abb.

Pr. (N. S.) 69.
(2) 3 Moak Eq. 622.
(3) Smith v. Winter, 18 Week R. 447; Barker v. St. Quinten, 12 Mees. & W. 441.
(4) Wylie v. Cox, 15 How. (U. S.) 415; Sexton v. Pike, 8 Eng. 193; Cooley v. Patterson, 52 Me. 472; Waters v. Grace, 23 Ark. 118; Andrews v. Morn, 12 Conn. 444; Carter v. Davis, 8 Fla. 183; Benjamin v. Benjamin, 17 Conn. 110; Newpert v. Cunningham, 50 Me. 231; Cooley v. Patterson, 52 Me. 472; Stratton v. Hussey, 62 Me. 286; Pierce v. Bent, 69 Me. 381; Power v. Kent, 1 Cow. 172; Martin v. Hawks, 15 Johns. 405; Rooney v. Sar. Co., 18 N. Y. 368; Bowling Green Sav. Bank v, Todd, 52 N. Y. 489; Walker v. Sargent, 14 Ver.

Attorney's general lien.

SEC. 258. Attorneys have a general lien in those
States where the common law on that subject is in
force, or statutes have been enacted substantially adopting the common law, for all the costs and charges due
them in the particular cause in which the papers and
documents came into their possession, as well as for
other costs and charges due to them for other professional business and employment in other causes, upon
such papers and documents.(1)

This general lien is not so much favored by the
common law as the special or charging lien,(2) except
in cases of bankruptcy or lunacy, where it attaches to
the fund or the body of the estate.(3)

The general lien does not attach to papers and doc-

247; Heacht v. Chipman, 2 Aik. 162;
Baker v. Cook, 11 Mass. 735; Bank
v. Culver. 54 N. H. 327; Hill v.
Brinkley, 10 Ind. 102; Frissell v.
Haile, 18 Mo. 18; Irwin v. Work-
man, 3 Watts, 357; Newbaker v.
Alricks, 5 Watts, 183; Walton v.
Dickerson, 7 Pa. 376; Du Bois' Ap-
peal, 38 Pa. St. 231; Exparte Kyle,
1 Cal. 331; Mansfield v. Dorland,
2 Cal. 517; Russell v. Conway, 11
Cal. 103; Cozzens v. Whitney, 3 R.
I. 79; Currier v. Railroad, 37 N. H.
223; Wells v. Hatch, 43 N. H. 246;
Dodd v. Brott, 1 Minn. 270; Hum-
phrey v. Browning, 46 Ill. 485;
Warfield v. Campbell, 38 Ala. 532;
Stewart v. Flowers, 44 Miss. 519,
et seq.; Martin v. Harrington, 57
Miss. 208.

In some States the lien is regulated by statute. Baker v. Cook,
11 Mass. 735; Citizens' Bank v. Culver, 54 N. H. 327.

In other States the lien is totally

denied, but the solicitor may de-
duct his fees from funds of his
client in his hands. Hill v. Brinkley, 10 Ind. 102; Frissell v. Haile,
18 Mo. 18; Irwin v. Workman, 3
Watts, 357; Walton v. Dickerson, 7
Pa. 376; Du Bois' Appeal, 38 Pa.
231; Newbaker v. Alricks, 5 Watts,
183; Humphrey v. Browning, 46
Ill. 476; Martin v. Harrington, 57
Miss. 208.

(1) Story on Agency, 383; Hooper
v. Welsh, 43 Vt. 171; Bowling
Green Sav. Bank v. Todd, 52 N. Y.
489; Exparte Sterling, 16 Ves. 258;
Exparte Pemberton, 18 Ves. 282;
Stevenson v. Blakelock, 1 Man. &
Sel. 535.

(2) Scarfe v. Morgan, 4 Mees. &
W. 285; Lucas v. Peacock, 8 Beav.
177; White v. Royal Ex. Ass. Co.,
1 Bing. 21.

. (3) Lann v. Church, 4 Madd. 391;
Barnesley v. Powell, 1 Amb. 102;
Exparte Price, 2 Ves. Ser. 407.

uments which have come into the hands of the attorney or solicitor otherwise than in the course of his employment.(1)

So it has been held that papers received by a solicitor as prochien ami of an infant are not subject to this lien;(2) or where they have been left for a specific purpose.(3)

But if the property is allowed to remain with the attorney after the specific purpose for which they were left has been fulfilled, the lien will attach.(4)

When attorney's lien attaches.

SEC. 259. The rule established by the weight of authority seems to be that the lien of an attorney for his compensation and costs upon property or money recovered by his client in the course of litigation, attaches upon the entry of judgment in favor of his client.(5)

(1) The general lien for services attaches, both in England and America, to papers placed in his hands professionally by his client. Wharton on Agency, Sec. 625; Warburton v. Edge, 9 Sim. 508; Exparte Sterling, 16 Ves. 258; Cowell v. Simpson, 16 Ves. 275; Exparte Nesbit, 2 Scholaler & L. 279; Friswell v. King, 15 Sim. 191; Kemp v. King, 2 Moody & R. 437; Champertown v. Scott, 6 Madd. 93; Ogle v. Story, 1 Moody A. M. 474; Dennett v. Cutts, 11 N. H. 163; Howard v. Oscola, 22 Wis. 453; Stewart v. Flowers, 44 Miss. 513; White v. Harlo, 5 Gray, 463.

The courts will interpose to protect the attorneys in the preservation of their liens and the collection of their fees when litigants collude or clients fraudulently attempt to defeat the lien. Jones v. Bonner' 2 Ex. 229; Rooney v. R. R., 18 N. Y. 368; Talcott v. Broneson, 4 Paige, 501; Swaine v. Senate, 5 Bos. & P. 99; McGregor v. Comstock, 23 N. Y. 237; Roberts v. Carter, 38 N. Y. 107; Mackey v. Mackey, 43 Barb. 58; Read v. Dapper, 6 Term R. 361; Gould v. Davis, 1 Cromp. & J. 415; Brunsden v. Allard, 2 El. & E. 19; Exparte James, 3 Harl. & C. 294; Jones v. Turnbull, 2 Mees. & W. 601; Griffin v. Eyles, 1 H. Black. 122.

(2) Montague on Lien, 59.

(3) Balch v, Symes, 1 Turn. & R. 92; Lawson v. Dickinson, 8 Mod. 306; In re Paschal, 10 Wall. 493.

(4) Exparte Pemberton, 18 Ves. 282.

(5) Hobson v. Watson, 34 Me. 20; Getcheell v. Clark, 5 Mass. 309;

But courts will not allow clients to defeat the prospective lien of their attorneys, pending the suit, by releasing the property from such lien.(1)

The lien of an attorney upon judgments recovered in favor of clients will not be divested by the fact that they were allowed to become dormant and were afterwards revived by other attorneys.(2)

In cases of arbitration resulting in an award, the lien will attach upon the judgment as in other cases.(3)

It will be seen that by the Act of 23 and 24 Vict., C. 127, Sec. 28, where the suit is stopped by the parties before any property has been recovered or preserved, no lien attaches.(4)

Attorney's lien may be waived.

SEC. 260.   Liens secured by law to an attorney to reimburse him for costs and expenses incurred in the business of his client, and to secure payment to him of his fees for services rendered, may be lost by waiver and in different ways.

The lien will be lost by parting with the possession of the deeds or other papers upon which it may have attached.(5)

But if the papers are improperly taken away from him the lien is not lost.(6)

Henchey v. Chicago, 41 Ill. 136; Shank v. Shoemaker, 18 N. Y. 489; Foot v. Tewksbury, 2 Vt. 97; Sweet v. Bartlett, 4 Sandf. 661; Coughlin v. N. Y. C. R. R., 71 N. Y. 443.

(1) Johnson v. Storey, 1 Lea, 114.
(2) Wright v. Burrough, 3 C. B. 344; 4 Dow. & L. 226; Abbot v. Rice, 3 Bing. 132; Jenkins v. Stevens, 60 Ga. 216; Hutchinson v. Howard, 15 Ves. 544.

(3) Ormerod v. Taite, 1 East. 464.
(4) 23 & 24 Vic., C. 127, Sec. 28; Pinkerton v. Easton, L. R. 16 Eq. Cas. 490; Foxon v. Gascoigne, L. R. 9 Ch. App. 654; Sec. 256, *ante.*
(5) Clark v. Gilbert, 2 Bing. (New Cases) 353; Weeks on Attorneys, 375; Nichols v. Poole, 89 Ill. 491.
(6) Dicas v. Stockley, 7 Car. & P. 587.

So the lien is suspended by taking other security for the debt which is the subject of the lien.(1)

So also where an attorney secured satisfaction of the judgment upon which his lien attached, in perfecting his client's title to land attached in the action, his lien is waived.(2)

Contract between attorney and client.

SEC. 261.   The courts have frequently upheld contracts between attorneys and their clients, whereby they were to be paid out of judgments or properties recovered in suits wherein their services were to be rendered, and whereby they were secured liens upon the subject matter of litigation.(3)

Fees secured by special statute.

SEC. 262.   Where statutes provide for compensation or a lien for compensation for the fees of attorneys in the proceeding, and a suit has been commenced under the statute, in which attorneys have earned fees and are secure by reason of their lien in the collection of further fees as compensation for their services, and the parties are duly served with process, or otherwise, in court, the case is a notice lis pendens of the existence of the attorney's fees, and the purchaser of the property is chargeable with notice of such lien.

(1) Balch v. Symes, 1 Turn. & R. 92; Weeks on Attorneys, 375; Cowell v. Simpson, 16 Ves. 275.

(2) Cowen v. Boone, 48 Iowa, 350.

(3) Vaughn et als. v. Vaughn et als., 12 Heisk. 475; Hunt v. McClanahan, 1 Heisk. 510; Creighton v. Ingersoll, 20 Barb. 541.

In the case of the Peoria, Decatur & Evansville R'wy Co. v. Duggan, it was held that the Illinois statute making railroads liable for reasonable attorney's fees for prosecuting claims against the road is notice to the company that the attorney's fee will be claimed, and that no further notice to the railroad company is necessary in order to charge the road. Peoria, Decatur & Evansville R'wy Co. v. Duggan, 109 Ill. 537.

Thus it has been held in a partition suit, where by
statute such a lien was secured, where a levy was
made pending the partition suit and the property was
sold on execution, that the purchaser was chargeable
with the notice of the attorney's lien.(1)

Maintenance and champerty.

Sec. 263. Maintenance is an officious intermeddling
in a suit that in no way belongs to one, by maintaining or assisting either party with money or otherwise
to prosecute or defend it.(2)

This was an offense at common law and punishable
by fine and imprisonment, and by English statute a
forfeiture of a certain amount of money.(3)

The reason assigned for these rigorous laws was that
maintenance leads to oppression.(4)

In some States, however, maintenance is not recognized as an offense.(5)

The term champerty is derived from the Latin
campum partitione, to divide land, and may be defined to be the wrongful maintenance of a suit in
consideration of some bargain to have the thing in
dispute, or some part of it, whereupon the champertor
is to carry on the suit at his own expense.(6)

(1) Ferney v. Wilson, 16 Vroom,
(N. J.) 283; Hopper v. Ludlam, 12
Vroom, (N. J.) 182; Rowe v. Dawson, 1 Ves. Sr. 331; Rodick v. Gan-
dell, De G., Mc. & G. 763; Bower
v. Hadden & Co., 3 Stew. Eq. (N. J.)
171; Lyon v. Bower, 3 Stern Eq.
340; Ely v. Cooke et al., 28 N. Y. 365;
Williams v. Ingersoll, 89 N. Y. 508.

(2) 4 Blackst. 134, 135, 149; Perine v. Dunn, 3 Johns. Ch. 508; Bris-
tol v. Dann, 12 Wend. 142.

(3) 32 Hen. VIII, Chap. 9; 1 Edw.
III, Chap. 14; 1 Rich. II, Chap. 4.

(4) Lambert v. People, 9 Cow. 578;
Lathrope v. Bank, 9 Met. 489; Rush
v. Larne, 4 Litt. 412; Thalhimer v.
Brinkerhoff, 3 Cow. 623.

(5) Matherson v. Fitch, 22 Cal. 86;
Stanley v. Jones, 7 Bing. 369.

(6) Thalhimer v. Brinke, 20 Johns.
384; 4 Blackst. Com. 135; Stanton v.
Haskin et al., 1 McArthur, 561; Hol-
loway v. Low, 7 Port. 488; Brown

In New York and many other States the laws of maintenance and champerty, as they existed in England, are not in force and are only in force as regulated by statute, while in most other States there are statutory regulations on the subject.(1)

The rigor of the common law doctrine has been greatly relaxed by modern decisions.(2)

Contingent fees as well as fees payable out of property in suit are now generally sustained by the courts and are not held champertous.

The distinction is made between an agreement to accept a part of the property in payment for services merely, and such an agreement where costs also are to be advanced in consideration of property in suit.

In the former case the contract would not be held champertous, while in the latter it would.

Lis pendens of attorney's or solicitor's fees.

SEC. 264. The question has sometimes arisen as to whether, where the claim of an attorney or solicitor for fees are involved in the litigation of his client, and the suit is progressing in the name of the client, the claim is a lis pendens so as to bind strangers who deal with the property pendente lite.

Where the fees are fixed by contract, and are in-

v. Beauchamp, 5 T. B. Mon. 416; Thurston v. Percival, 1 Pick. 416; Barnes v. Strong, 1 Jones's Eq. 100; Wheeler v. Pond, 24 Ala. 472; Douglas v. Wood, 1 Swan. 393.

(1) Sedgwick v. Stanton, 14 N. Y. 289; Voohies v. Dorr, 51 Barb. 580; Low v. Hutchinson, 37 Me. 196; Newkirk v. Cohen, 18 Ill. 449; Stoddart v. Mix, 14 Conn. 12; Davis v. Sharron, 15 B. Mon. 64; Miller v. Guest, 6 Tex. 275; Danforth v. Streeter, 28 Vt. 490; Wright v. Meek, 3 Green, 472; Key v. Vatier, 1 Ohio, 158.

(2) Child v. Trist, 1 McArthur, 1; Stanley v. Jones, 7 Bing. 369; Stanton v. Haskin et al., 1 McArthur, 561.

volved in the proceedings, there is no doubt as to the lis pendens in regard to them.(1)

If not so fixed by contract, the question whether attorney's fees do or do not constitute a lis pendens would probably depend upon whether the attorney or solicitor has a lien upon the subject matter of the suit in the forum where the property is situated and the services have been or are being performed.

As we have seen, in some States such lien is established by statute law. In some cases also courts of chancery have the inherent power, and have exercised it in accordance with the equitable jurisdiction of that court, of declaring and enforcing a lien for amounts due solicitors for services, or services and advances in the litigation.

In all such cases where an attorney or solicitor has filed in the cause a proper pleading or other paper having the force and effect of a pleading, or where the existence of the lien is recognized by the general pleadings in the case, such liens for attorney's or solicitor's fees are a lis pendens, and the purchaser of the judgment or decree will take it charged with the attorney's liens. As before remarked, the rule as to the lien of attorney's and solicitor's fees is not uniform in the United States.(2)

(1) Peoria, Decatur & Evansville Ry. Co. v. Duggan, 109 Ill. 537.

(2) Hunt v. McClanahan, 1 Heisk. 503.

In Illinois, Vermont, New Hampshire, Pennsylvania, Indiana, Missouri and other States no lien exists except by contract. Humphrey v. Browning, 46 Ill. 477; Forsythe v. Beverage, 52 Ill. 268; LaFramboise v. Grow, 56 Ill. 201. In this latter case, the question of the lis pendens of a claim for solicitor's fees was involved, and the court say: "The appellant having parted with her interest in a lawful manner in the subject matter of the suit pendente lite, did the solicitor acquire any lien for fees and costs expended? The answer to this inquiry will make it necessary to examine the nature and extent of the lien

Bill to enforce attorney's lien.

SEC. 265. There can be no doubt that the court of chancery has jurisdiction to enforce the liens of attorneys and solicitors for professional services by them performed upon property whereon such liens exist, in all cases where there is not a full and adequate remedy at law.

The Supreme Court of Georgia have held that such a bill may be filed in chancery to enforce the lien of an attorney upon real estate recovered by his services for his client.(1)

There can be no doubt that in all cases where attorneys have common law or statutory liens upon real estate, and there is no other adequate remedy, the court of chancery will entertain bills to enforce such liens.

No reason can be perceived why the same remedy may not be sought under similar circumstances to enforce liens upon personal property anywhere in the United States where such liens exist.

for attorney and solicitor's fees, and in what cases allowed." * * * * "If, then, the solicitor had any lien at all, it must be at the common law or under our statute. At common law the attorney undoubtedly has a lien upon the judgment obtained for his clients for his taxable fees and costs. But it has been held in this State that no such lien exists, for the reason that we have no statute giving costs to attorneys.

The amount of attorney's fees here rests entirely in the contract between the attorney and client, and he must recover for his serv-ices in the ordinary mode by some appropriate action for the purpose."

(1) Wilson v. Wright, 72 Ga. 848.

In Georgia the law is well established that attorneys have a lien at common law as in England, and also by statute upon lands recovered by suit in which the attorney's services were employed.

Wilson v. Wright, Survivor, *ante*, 72 Ga. 849; McDonald v. Napier, 14 Ga. 89; Smith et al. v. Goode et al., 29 Ga. 185; Williams et al. v. Walker et al., 31 Ga. 195; Twiggs et al. v. Chambers, 56 Ga. 281; Moses v. Bagly et al., 55 Ga. 283; Code of 1863, Sec. 1989.

Attorney's lien upon fund in court.

SEC. 266.   While an attorney is usually confined in his lien for compensation for services to property which he has in his possession, yet, where in a court of equity there is a fund whose existence is mainly due to his services and to which he has to look for compensation, he is in equity the owner of the fund to the amount of his fee, and the court may enforce his right by awarding to him a proper compensation out of the fund.

A court of chancery has full power to fix the amount of a counsel fee to be allowed by it without the intervention of a jury.

The Chancellor will also often order such compensation to the counsel of a necessary party who is decreed to have no interest, on the equitable ground that being a necessary party he was compelled to litigate and had sufficient reason.   In such a case it is a charge which the fund ought in equity and good conscience to bear.(1)

Lis pendens of attachment proceedings.

SEC. 267.   The lien of an attachment in a suit at law, if not technically speaking a lis pendens, is in all respects, so far as affects the property attached, analogous, in its efficiency upon the property involved, to lis pendens in chancery.

---

(1) McKelvey's App. 19 Reporter, 572; Daly v. Maitland, 7 Norris, 384; Imler v Imler, 13 Norris, 372; Freeman v. Shreve, 5 Norris, 135.

In McCain v. Portis et al., 42 Ark. 402, it is said that the purchaser of a fund in court during the pendency of the suit, purchases with notice of the attorney's lien upon the fund for his fee for services rendered in reference to it, and that it is not necessary for the attorney to file with the clerk a notice of his lien on the judgment to protect himself against the purchaser of the judgment. Turwin v. Gibson, 3 Atk. 720; Skinner v. Sweet, 3 Mad. 245; Lann v. Church, 4 Mad. 391; Maule Exparte in re Dark, 5 Mad. 463.

If subsequent to the time when the attachment lien takes effect upon the property the defendant sells it, the purchaser takes the property subject to the determination of the attachment. If the attachment is afterwards dissolved or in any wise defeated, the purchaser pendente lite will take it unaffected by the plaintiff's claim. If the attachment lien shall be followed by a jüdgment, in pursuance of which the title of the defendant in the attachment shall be divested, the purchaser's title will fail.

In other words, the purchaser of the attached property will be barred of his claim upon the property in like manner as if the divestiture had taken place by virtue of a decree in chancery in a suit wherein there was a lis pendens in force at the time of the purchase.

But in such case the courts hold, in analogy to the exception to the rule lis pendens, that the attachment proceedings will not apply to negotiable paper, that such paper is not subject to attachment, and in this ruling, municipal bonds, in negotiable words, are treated as commercial paper, except in Pennsylvania.(1)

Action in aid of suit.

SEC. 268. It must not be inferred, however, from the preceding section that where, although the contention is merely in regard to a moneyed demand, an auxiliary proceeding in rem is resorted to in the same case (as an attachment in aid of a suit at law) there will be no lis pendens, or what is equivalent, lien which may ripen into a title by virtue of the result of the litigation. Such would be the result of such an aux-

---

(1) Winston v. Westfeldt, 22 Ala. 760; Diamond v. Lawrence Co., 37 Penn. St. 353; Day v. Zimmerman, 68 Penn. St. 72.

iliary proceeding in accordance with express statutory provisions, wherever the legislatures have enacted laws upon the subject.

The like remark will also apply to all proceedings in rem, although the real contention may be over the existence or extent of the indebtedness. Of such a character is a proceeding to enforce a mechanic's lien where the indebtedness or the amount in dispute is denied; a proceeding for partition where the plaintiff's title is disputed, and a suit to foreclose a mortgage where the contention is that the debt is barred by the statute of limitation, or has been paid, or never was valid.

In all such cases, if specific property is pointed out by the auxiliary or collateral proceedings, as well as where they are involved in the main action and where the title to property or right to a lien thereon is to be judicially determined in the case, the rule lis pendens is applied.

The lis pendens of bankruptcy proceedings.

SEC. 269.   It may be stated in a general way that proceedings in bankruptcy, both under the English bankrupt laws and the several bankrupt laws which have been in force in the United States, become at some stage of their progress a lis pendens.

The least reflection will lead to the conclusion that no efficient bankrupt law could be devised which would not of necessity become a lis pendens at some stage of the proceedings in bankruptcy.

The object of all efficient bankrupt laws must be to arrest the agency of the bankrupt in the further management and control of his estate, and enable the court through its agents, officers and servants to administer the estate and distribute the assets among the creditors of the bankrupt, subject to such exemptions as may be provided by law.

The efficiency of any system of bankrupt laws must necessarily depend upon the attachment, at some early stage in the administration of the bankrupt's estate, of the jurisdiction of the court to the entire property of the bankrupt. That is in what lis pendens consists.

In every system of bankrupt law it must occur that by some interlocutory adjudication or appointment the title of the bankrupt becomes vested in some agent of the court for the purpose of the administration of the property, and thereby that the bankrupt shall become disabled and disqualified from treating with his estate.

Such was the effect of the English bankrupt laws. Mr. Newland, in his work on Contracts, says : " In analogy to the case of lis pendens, it seems that the commission of bankruptcy, whereon the person who is the object of it is declared a bankrupt and a bargain and sale is executed by the commissioners, creates notice."(1)

In Hitchcock v. Sedgwick, speaking of one who deals with the property of the bankrupt, it is said: "He was not in the case of an innocent purchaser; when the commission was sued out, he was bound to take notice."(2) The same is the case in bankruptcy proceedings in the United States, whether under the act of 1841 or that of 1867. It may be safely averred that the same must be equally true of any efficient bankrupt law which may be hereafter enacted.

Actual notice equivalent to notice lis pendens.

Sec. 270. It is well settled that actual notice will

(1) Newland on Contracts, 507. (2) Hitchcock v. Sedgwick, 2 Vern. 160.

take the place of constructive notice lis pendens. It was said in Baker v. Pierson,(1) where no notice lis pendens had been filed, that "a purchaser from a party to the suit pending the litigation, with full knowledge of the litigation, is bound by it;" and that it is not necessary that a "notice of lis pendens should be filed to bind one who has actual notice." That "it is not required in the absence of actual notice to charge a party with constructive notice."

And so also the Supreme Court of California have held under the lis pendens statute of that State.(2)

It is not perceived why the proposition may not be stated as of general application, that full, complete, actual notice from a litigant of the contemplated commencement and pendency of the suit, and also of what will be or is involved therein and what is claimed in respect thereto, should be held sufficient to bind the party acquiring the knowledge with the force of a lis pendens.

As this state of case could not occur, however, except in those States where lis pendens statutes are in force after the jurisdiction of the court had attached and the proceedings constituted constructive notice, the intermeddler, with such actual notice before lis pendens became operative in the case, would have to be made a party.(3)

It was said in the case of Meade v. Lord Orrery: "Now to be sure, notice in a court of equity is extremely material; for if a person will purchase with notice of another's right, his giving a consideration

(1) Baker v. Pierson, 5 Mich. 461.   (3) Saunders v. DeHew, 2 Vern.
(2) Sampson v. Ohleyer, 22 Cal.   271.
209.

will not avail him, for he throws away his money voluntarily and of his own free will."(1)

Lis pendens applied to mechanics's liens.

SEC. 271. The class of liens known as mechanic's liens, because usually they are for labor performed or materials furnished by mechanics, are peculiarly dependent upon the power of jurisdiction of the courts, or lis pendens for their efficiency and enforcement. Usually the acts of the legislatures, by which alone in this country such liens exist, provide that the lien shall not be enforceable unless a suit be commenced within a limited time prescribed by such statutes.(2)

By express provision therefore in all mechanic's lien laws, although they vary in their terms as to the periods within which the suits shall be brought, there are express limitations whereby force, efficiency and permanency are to be given to the lien by the inauguration of lis pendens.

(1) Meade *v.* Lord Orrery, 3 Atk. 235.

In Hart *v.* Hawkins, 3 Bibb. 502, it is held that extra-judicial proceedings do not operate as constructive notice, but where as in that case a purchaser was acquainted with the nature of such extra-judicial proceedings and subsequently became a purchaser, although not from a party to a pending suit, it was held that the knowledge or notice so acquired, while not constructive notice, was express notice and would affect the purchase the same as constructive notice of lis pendens.

So likewise it was held in Dickerson et al. *v.* Campbell et al., 32 Mo. 544, that the clerk of a court in which a suit for specific performance was pending was chargeable with notice of the nature of plaintiff's demand, independent of the doctrine by which purchasers pendente lite are affected with constructive notice of the suit, so as to charge him as the purchaser of the property involved in the judgment. This latter case probably rested upon the presumption that a clerk was bound to know the nature of the proceedings occurring in his court.

So also in Davenport *v.* Muir, 3 J. J. Marsh. 310, it was ruled that verbal notice of the pendency of a suit was sufficient to charge a purchaser.

(2) Kneeland on Mechanic's Liens, Sec. 215.

Thus lis pendens is made necessary by express provision of statutes, of which this species of liens is the
creature; such liens are to be reinforced and vivified
by a suit in which there shall be a lis pendens.

When such a suit is inaugurated the power of jurisdiction will relate back to the commencement of the
mechanic's lien, and the court in its final decree will
give permanent force and efficiency to the lien as thus
aided by lis pendens.

Lis pendens applied to vendor's liens.

SEC. 272. So also, where the vendor of real estate
or other property in respect to which a lien for the
unpaid purchase money at common law or by statute
exists, the lis pendens of a suit is necessary to give
ultimate efficiency to the lien.

While not the creature of the statute in the sense in
which mechanic's liens which are conditioned as
stated in the last section, still the lien would become
extinct and of no force by reason of the running of
statutes of limitation or by reason of the staleness
of the claim by lapse of time, without a suit commenced within the period of limitation and prosecuted
to a decree declaring the lien.

Upon the inauguration of lis pendens in such a case
the jurisdiction of the court, the lis pendens of the
cause, will give efficiency to the lien back to the date
of its initiation, and the final decree will so declare it.

If a bill is filed to enforce a vendor's lien, and pending the bill the defendant should execute a mortgage
on the same premises, the mortgagee and his assignee
will take subject to the decree in the pending case.(1)

(1) Montgomery et al. v. Birge,   et al., 36 Ark. 217.
31 Ark. 4)3; Hale v. Warner, Admr.   It is held in Smith v. Connor et ux.

Lis pendens of bill to enforce vendor's lien.

Sec. 273. Where a bill was filed to enforce a vendor's lien on an interest in two tracts of land for a small amount, a judgment was rendered and sale made thereon in satisfaction of the lien. Plaintiff became the purchaser and the sale was confirmed.

While the vendor's lien was in force, but before the bill was filed to enforce it, the land had been sold on an execution issued upon a judgment at law, which judgment was a junior lien to that of the complainant in the pending suit, and a sale was made upon the execution pending the chancery case. The execution purchaser afterwards filed a petition offering to satisfy the vendor's lien.

It was held that he was a pendente lite purchaser, but as the amount was small and there was some irregularity in the proceedings to enforce the vendor's lien, he was allowed to satisfy the complainant's claim.(1)

Lis pendens in foreclosure cases.

Sec. 274. So also in like manner the lis pendens of proceedings by bill in chancery or by scire facias or other statutory remedy for the foreclosure of mortgages, the lis pendens of the cause when it attaches enables the court to give efficiency to the lien back to a period anterior to the inauguration of the proceedings and

et al., 65 Ala. 371, that a purchaser of land pending a bill to enforce a vendor's lien thereon is chargeable with constructive notice of the proceedings, and that it is not necessary that he should be brought in as a party.

(1) Bush v. Williams, 6 Bush. 405.

It is said in Wagner v. Smith, 13 Lea, 560, which was a suit commenced to enforce a vendor's lien, that equity fastens on the land by the lis pendens of such a bill, and that no creditor can intervene in that proceeding and defeat the vendor's lien.

Mills v. Haines et al.,3 Head, 332.

to the time when the mortgage lien first took effect upon the mortgaged property, and by the final decree to give efficiency to the lien as of its date of commencement.

The same may be said as to the power of jurisdiction or lis pendens of causes in the case of all other liens existing antecedent to the commencement of such proceedings, as creditor's bills, bills to aid in the enforcement of judgments at law, and the like.

In a case in Wisconsin the application of the rule lis pendens was somewhat complicated. A, owning the land in fee, mortgaged it to B and subsequently made a second mortgage to C. Afterwards C purchased of B the first mortgage. To enable him to make the loan for which A gave the second mortgage C borrowed from D certain moneys and left with him as collateral security the first mortgage which had been assigned to him by B. D, who had loaned this money to C upon this collateral, filed a bill to foreclose the first mortgage and also filed a notice of lis pendens under the Wisconsin statute. Pending the suit C conveyed to E, E to F, and F to G, who was E's wife. A receiver was appointed in the case before C's conveyance to E. The parties stipulated as to the terms of the decree which was entered and the premises were sold. There having been no redemption G, E's wife, was put out of possession by writ of assistance. She had not been a party to the suit, and an action of trespass was brought by her against the officer. Pending the chancery suits two tax deeds were issued to one H. H had conveyed to C, C to E, E to F, and F to G, E's wife. These tax titles were set up by the plaintiff as paramount title.

It was held that E, having received conveyance from C, who was a party to the chancery suit, was bound by the decree which was rendered in the foreclosure case, and that C having obtained the tax titles while interested and claiming the lands, these titles were invalid in his hands.(1)

Lis pendens of creditor's bill.

Sec. 275. Where a bill has been filed by creditors to set aside the satisfaction of a judgment in favor of the complainants, caused by the improper sale of lands, and for the further purpose of subjecting the same lands to the payment of the complainants' judgment, the pendency of the bill will give the complainants a lien superior to that of a subsequent judgment creditor of the common debtor, and that, too, although the land may have been previously sold under execution and conveyed.(2)

(1) Newton *v.* Marshall et al., 62 Wis. 8; Warner *v.* Trow, 36 Wis. 195.

The case of Coe, Admr. *v.* Manseau, 62 Wis. 81, was one commenced by C to foreclose mortgage, and notice of lis pendens was filed under the statute. After judgment of foreclosure, but before the sale, the mortgagor conveyed to F and F conveyed to C, the complainant. The last conveyance was not recorded. It was held that the foreclosure proceedings were not constructive notice of C's interest to one who subsequently commenced an action to foreclose tax certificates. The mortgage interest of C had merged in the title acquired under the deed from F.

(2) Mays et al. *v.* Wherry et al., 3 Cooper, 81.

It is held in like manner in the case of Tabb *v.* Williams, 4 Jones' Eq. 352, that a creditor's bill filed to reach equitable assets constitutes a lien upon the judgment debtor's property in all cases where they can be reached in a court of chancery, and that it is not necessary to enjoin or restrain the holder of such property from paying it to the cestui que trust (he being also a party,) for the court, it is said, will make all proper orders for the protection of its funds, and has the power to do so by virtue of the lis pendens.

The filing of a creditor's bill without the service of a summons does not create lis pendens or an equitable levy.

Hirshizer et al. *v.* Tinsley et al., 13 Mo. App. R. 489.

In the case of Miller *v.* Wolf

Pending bill of discovery lien on assets.

SEC. 276.   When a bill of discovery is filed to reach indebtedness of a judgment debtor evidenced by promissory notes made by a third party, also made defendant to the bill, the lien of the creditor upon the assets so sought to be reached would attach from the time of the service of process on the defendants, and the court would subject such assets to the payment of the indebtedness unless payment were made before service.(1)

et al., 63 Iowa, 233, it is held that a mere creditor has no interest in his debtor's real estate, and that a verdict without a judgment rendered thereon gives no interest of which a purchaser is bound to take notice.

(1) Miers et al. *v.* Z. & M. Turnpike Co., 13 Ohio, 197; Bank of M. *v.* Carpenter's Admrs., 7 Ohio, 253. The facts in the case of Robertson *v.* Stewart et al., 2 B. Mon. 321, were that Stewart and Spring had filed a bill of discovery against a judgment debtor and Robertson to reach funds in the hands of Robertson who had given his notes to the judgment debtor, and subsequently Slocumb, who was also a judgment creditor of the same debtor, also filed a bill of discovery to reach the same indebtedness, but alleging a specific liability on the part of Robertson, and also alleging a general indebtedness to the defendant debtor. It turned out that the indebtedness of Robertson was more than sufficient to satisfy the debt of Stewart and Spring, but not sufficient to satisfy Slocumb's debt into a few hundred dollars.

Robertson sought a reversal of the decree in favor of Slocumb upon the ground that Slocumb had a first lien on the fund. It was held that Robertson should have guarded against a possible double liability, by cross bill, and that, not having done so, the decree in the case of Stewart and Spring, satisfying their debt out of the fund, would not be disturbed.

So in Webb *v.* Read, 3 B.Mon. 119, a creditor's bill was held to be a lis pendens against funds in the hands of the third party, who was made party to the suit. Scott *v.* McMillan, 1 Lit. 302.

In Ballet *v.* Stewart et al., 3 B. Mon. 115, the court decide that several creditors may unite in a creditor's bill to subject the property and fund of a common debtor to the lien of their claims, and distribute the same pro rata, and that such a bill will become a lis pendens after service.

In Miers et al. *v.* Zanesville, 13 Ohio, 197, it is said that the petition creditor, pursuing his claim by bill of discovery, acquires a preference over general creditors. See also Bk.

When creditor's bill no lis pendens.

SEC. 277. It has been held that although the filing of a creditor's bill generally creates a lien upon the equitable assets of the defendant, yet that where no answer is filed nor receiver appointed under the bill during the lifetime of the defendant, there is no lien or lis pendens created against equitable assets of the

of Muskegon *v.* Camp's Admrs., 7 Ohio, 253.

In Jackson, etc. *v.* Andrews, 7 Wend. 152, which was a case where a bill in chancery was filed by a creditor to avoid a conveyance of land as having been made fraudulently, and the grantee pendente lite had sold to a third person, it was held that the title of the latter would fail with that of his grantor in the suit.

In Gibbon's Admr. *v.* Dougherty et als., 10 Ohio State, 365, it appeared that the debtor owed one W, and the complainant filed his bill against the debtor and W, and procured service upon W. At the time of the filing of the bill W had recovered a judgment against the debtor, which was set aside at a subsequent term and a new judgment rendered. After the rendition of the new judgment a supplemental bill was filed, setting up the facts as to the latter judgment. After the rendition of the last judgment the common debtor paid W. It was held that W was bound by the lis pendens of the complainant's bill, notwithstanding he had already paid the complainant's debtor and that the payment was made pendente lite.

In Jennings *v.* Bond, 2 Jones & Lat. 720, it is said that a suit by

judgment creditor for an account of the real and personal estate of his debtor and payment of his debts, is a sufficient lis pendens to affect an incumbrancer on the life estate of a defaulting executor in lands the fee of which was subject to the judgment, with notice of an equity to have the life estate applied to answer the default of the executor.

It is also said in the same case that the registration of a title deed of the person sought to be affected does not affect the lis pendens where the question is not between a registered and an unregistered deed.

In Robertson *v.* Stewart et al., 2 B. Mon. 323, it is also held that the filing of a creditor's bill and service upon one holding in his hands funds belonging to the principal debtor, creates a lien upon the funds from the time of service, and that if two creditors file separate creditor's bills against a common debtor, and he answers the bills disclosing more property in his answer to the junior than to the prior bill, still the latter is a prior lien upon the funds by reason of the prior lis pendens, and will reach the additional property disclosed in defendant's answer to the bill last filed.

estate. It is said that such a suit is not sufficiently advanced for the accomplishment of that result.(1)

Lis pendens of mortgage foreclosure.

SEC. 278. Although a defendant to a suit for the foreclosure of a mortgage is not served until after the term to which the writ is returnable, yet a purchaser from a mortgagor after such service upon the defendant is a pendente lite purchaser and bound by the foreclosure, although not a party.(2)

Creditor's bill against funds.

SEC. 279. Where a creditor's bill was filed and service of process had against a defendant to subject funds in his hands to the satisfaction of a judgment against a party whose funds were so held by the defendant, it was held that there was a lien created upon the funds so held from the service of process, and that the defendant holding the funds was liable to the complainant for their amount.(3)

Bill of discovery when judgment not a lien.

SEC. 280. Where the judgment itself was not a lien upon real estate, but the statute of a State had authorized the filing of a bill of discovery based upon it, it was held that the lien of the debt attached upon the commencement of the pendency of the bill, and a levy made pendente lite upon an execution issued upon a judgment which became a lien after the commencement of the lis pendens, and upon which execution real estate might be sold without the aid of equity, was subject to the pending bill.(4)

---

(1) Jones *v.* Smith, Walk. Ch. 115.

(2) Stokes *v.* Maxwell et al., 59 Ga. 79; Cooley *v.* Brayton, 16 Iowa, 19; Knowles *v.* Rablin et al., 20 Iowa, 101.

(3) Robertson *v.* Stewart et al., 2 B. Mon. 223.

(4) Newgate *v.* Lee et al., 9 Dana, 21. The judgment upon which the

When mortgage and notes are assigned pendente lite.

SEC. 281. Where a bill was filed in 1861 for specific performance of a contract relating to the release of a mortgage and the surrendor of the notes secured thereby, to be cancelled against the holder of the mortgage and notes, and he in February, 1862, pending the suit, assigned them, and subsequently a cross-bill was filed in the same case bringing in the assignees as parties, it was held that they took the mortgage and notes pendente lite and subject to the decree which should be entered in the case.(1)

When purchaser under mortgage pendente lite.

SEC. 282. A bill was filed to foreclose a senior mortgage which contained a power of sale. The mortgagee in a junior mortgage on the same premises was made defendant, and his interest alleged. Pending his own suit, the complainant, being the mortgagee in the senior mortgage sought to be foreclosed in the case, sold under his power and conveyed to a stranger to the suit. Thereupon the junior mortgagee filed his cross-bill in the original case and made the purchaser a party. It was held that the purchaser at the mortgage sale took subject to notice of lis pendens and was bound by any decree which should be entered in the case.(2)

When purchaser pending creditor's bill pendente lite.

SEC. 283. A creditor's bill based upon a judgment

bill was based in this case was rendered by a justice of the peace, and was not a lien on real estate, nor could real estate be sold upon execution issued upon it. The legislature of the State, however, had passed a statute giving equity jurisdiction to a court of chancery to subject real estate to the satisfaction of judgments, which was broad enough to embrace judgments before justices of the peace.

(1) Sumner et al. *v.* Waugh et al., 56 Ill. 536.

(2) Hurd et al. *v.* Case, 32 Ill. 48.

which is afterwards reversed in the Supreme Court, a second judgment rendered and a supplemental bill filed setting up the judgment, is a lis pendens binding the property from the filing of the original bill.

A creditor's bill was filed based upon a judgment rendered in September, 1831, to subject a lot to the payment of the judgment. In June, 1832, the judgment upon which the bill was based was reversed in the Supreme Court. In March, 1833, another judgment was recovered. After the cause had been remanded, in June, 1833, a supplemental bill was filed in the chancery case setting up the second judgment. The case had been regularly continued upon the docket up to the time of filing the supplemental bill. Before the first judgment and the filing of the original bill the judgment debtor had conveyed the lot to his children, and they, after the first judgment had been reversed and before the second one was rendered, had conveyed, and their grantee had conveyed, to one Myers.

In 1835, Myers having been brought into court by the supplemental bill, a decree was entered for the sale of the lot, the sale was made and the title accrued thereunder.

It was held that Myers took his title pendente lite, and that the title which accrued under the decree in the chancery case was valid.(1)

A purchaser on execution pending suit.

SEC. 284.   Where a bill in chancery is filed against a judgment debtor, attacking his title to real estate, and while lis pendens is in full force, an execution is

(1) Stoddard's Lessee *v.* Myers, 8 Ohio, 203.

issued upon a judgment at law, and the real estate involved in the chancery suit is sold thereon, the purchaser upon execution becomes a pendente lite purchaser, and will be bound by the result of the litigation.

If the title of the defendant in execution is established in the chancery case, the purchaser at the execution sale will acquire a valid title, but if in the chancery case the judgment debtor shall be decreed to have no title, or if his title shall be in any wise impaired, the title acquired at the execution sale will be in like manner annulled or impaired.(1)

Lis pendens of bill to set aside deed.

Sec 285.   Where a bill was filed to set aside a conveyance under which a judgment debtor holds, and after the bill had become a lis pendens, as against the judgment debtor, the property was sold on execution pendente lite, it was held that the purchaser acquired no title to the land at the judicial sale; that he did not become a bona fide purchaser for value, as to the plaintiff, but was a pendente lite purchaser.(2)

Prior right to fund waived by negligence.

Sec. 286.   Where a general creditor's bill had been filed and allowed to pend for eight years without reaching any results, and a junior creditor by the exercise of superior diligence discovered a fund sufficient to satisfy his claim, the right of the first complainant filing the general creditor's bill to enforce his lis pendens against this fund was considered as waived.(3)

(1) Salter *v.* Salter, 6 Bush. 626; Carr *v.* Fearington et al., 63 N. C. 563; Freeman *v.* Hill, 1 Dev. & Bat. Eq. 389; Polk *v.* Gallant, 2 Dev. & Bat. Eq. 395.

(2) Rider *v.* Kelso, 53 Iowa, 369.

(3) Myrick *v.* Selden, 36 Barber, 22.

Payment to credit of court pending suit.

SEC. 287.   Where a bill was filed against a debtor,
and also against a third party, who was owing the
principal debtor amounts payable in installments *in
futuro*, he cannot safely pay to either party the several amounts of the installments before they become
due and pending the suit.

Should he make payment to the principal debtor,
he will be held bound to the complainant by reason of
the lis pendens of the suit and lien upon the fund.
The only safe way to make payment in such case is to
pay the money into the court to the credit of the
cause, in which case the court will order the evidences
of debt surrendered.(1)

**Pendency of partition cases does not withdraw lands
from execution.**

SEC. 288.   The pendency of a suit for the partition
of lands does not withdraw the lands which are sought
to be partitioned from the reach of an execution at
law against the interest of a part owner.

An execution against such part owner may be levied
upon his interest in the lands, and the lands sold
pending the partition case.   But in such case a pendente lite purchaser must accept such interest as the
court in the pending case may allow to him whose interest was purchased at the execution sale.(2)

When no lis pendens in favor of second mortgagee.

SEC. 289.   Where there were two mortgages upon
the same premises, and a bill was filed by the first
mortgagee to foreclose the prior mortgage, and the
second mortgagee was made a party defendant to the

(1) Mills *v.* Pitman, 1 Paige, 490.   Bush. 437.
(2) Hawes, etc. *v.* Orr, etc., 10

suit, and had come in and answered but had filed no cross-bill, nor sought in the pleadings affirmative relief, it was held that there was no lis pendens in the case in favor of the second mortgagee.

In that case, after the second mortgagee had filed his answer, but before the cross-petition which was finally filed by him in the case became a lis pendens, the mortgagor made another mortgage, and it was held that the latter mortgage was not subject to the lis pendens of the cross-petition filed by the second mortgagee.(1)

Lis pendens in Tennessee where proceedings by attachment allowed in chancery.

SEC. 290.   In Tennessee attachment proceedings are allowed by statute to be taken in chancery, and are required to be immediately levied.

Where a bill was filed in that State, an attachment was taken out in the same case, but was not immediately levied, nor was the lien of the attachment perfected thereunder immediately.

After the bill was filed and service had, but before the attachment lien was perfected under the statute, there was a conveyance of the property by a party to the suit.

It was held that although the lien of the attachment had not been perfected at the time of the purchase, yet that as it was afterwards perfected without unreasonable delay the purchase was pendente lite.(2)

---

(1) Hart, etc., *v.* Hayden, etc., 79 Ky. 346; Hull et al., etc., *v.* Grogan, etc., 78 Ky. 12.

By Secs. 39 and 194 of the Civil Code of Kentucky it is provided that there shall be no lis pendens in that State until a summons is is-

sued, or a warning order is made by the court.

(2) Sharpe *v.* Hunter et al., 16 Ala. 765; Vance *v.* Cooper, 2 Cold. 497; Burrough et al. *v.* Brooks et al., 3 Head, 392.

Estoppel and lis pendens.

SEC. 291. It sometimes occurs that litigants assume such an attitude with respect to conflicting interests in the property involved in litigation that the facts tending to an estoppel by conduct add strength to the force of lis pendens, which otherwise might not bar an interest.

In an Indiana case, G brought suit to foreclose a senior mortgage, making the junior mortgagee a party, and pending the suit became the assignee of the junior mortgage also.

Without amending the bill and setting up the purchase of the junior mortgage, the case resulted in a foreclosure of the senior mortgage. At the sale under the decree a stranger to the suit purchased the property for the amount of the decree, and no redemption having been made the purchaser took out a deed.

Subsequently the complainant filed a bill to redeem from the first mortgage, based upon the ownership of the junior mortgage. The court denied the right of redemption.

The year allowed by statute in that State had been allowed to expire. The attitude also which the complainant had assumed with respect to the junior mortgage, both by the pleadings in the case and also by his conduct at the sale, were held to be an estoppel and conclusive against his right to redeem.(1)

(1) Gordon *v.* Lee, 102 Ind. 125.

CHAPTER XIII.

DOCTRINE OF LIS PENDENS APPLIED UNDER REGISTRY LAWS.

What recording laws are.

SEC. 292. It is undoubtedly within the legislative power of the State to enact laws declaring what effect shall be given to the recording or registration of conveyances, placing limitations upon the time within which they shall be recorded or registered, declaring what shall be the effect of non-registration, and to prescribe what instruments may be admitted to record or registration.

Such laws, however, may not be retroactive, for that would be to impair the obligation of existing contracts. They can affect only registration or non-registration after their enactment. Acts of legislatures of the various States of the Union, declaring what instruments may be admitted to the public records, where and by whom they shall be recorded, and what effect shall be given to the recording or registration, and the non-recording or registration of such instruments are known as the Recording or Registry Laws.

Character of recording laws.

SEC. 293. The character of recording or registry laws in force in the different States, while having many features in common, differs materially in other respects.

They all determine some place where the record shall be kept, who shall record them, and define what instruments may be admitted to record.

They differ in other material respects. In some States recordable instruments may be filed for record or registration at any time after execution, while in others they must be filed within a limited time, and can not be admitted to record thereafter.

This period of limitation varies greatly in the different States. In most of the States recordable instruments are declared valid as between grantor and grantee whether recorded or not, while in some of them they are declared void if not recorded within the period of limitation.

As to what instruments, liens, or legal or equitable claims of claimants recording or registering conveyances shall affect with notice the statutes of the different States vary materially.(1)

(1) A brief synopsis of the recording laws of the States and Territories of the United States may not be out of place in this connection. There is no limitation upon the time when recordable instruments may be filed for record or registration in the following States and Territories: Arkansas, California, Colorado, Dakota, District of Columbia, Idaho, Illinois, Iowa, Kansas, Louisiana, Massachusetts, Michigan, Minnesota, Mississippi, Missouri, Nebraska, Nevada, North Carolina, New Hampshire, New Jersey, New Mexico, New York, Rhode Island, Tennessee, Texas, Utah, Vermont, Virginia, W. Virginia and Wisconsin.

The statutes of these States gen-

Construction of recording acts.

SEC. 294. As we have seen, most of the recording acts declare what legal effect shall be given to recording or registration, but in some of the States it is left to the courts to declare what effect shall be given to the registration or record of recordable instruments. Most of the statutes declare that conveyances shall be valid between the parties thereto and those acquiring knowledge of their existence, whether recorded or not. Such would clearly be the law were the statute silent on the subject.(1)

Upon the question as to whether other classes than those who are bona fide purchasers without notice shall be protected against unrecorded instruments, the statutes themselves, as we have seen, vary, and the

erally declare that conveyances shall have no effect upon subsequent purchasers in good faith without notice, until the conveyance shall be filed for record or registration with some designated officer in some designated place. In these respects the statutes differ but slightly. They also provide that after record or registration they shall be notice to all subsequent purchasers of the contents of such record, and that conveyances to such subsequent purchasers shall be void.

The scope of the effect given to the recording in these States varies. In California an unrecorded conveyance is good as against an attaching creditor.

In the following States and Territories recordable instruments must be filed for record or registration within a limited time: In Alabama, within three months; in Connecticut, within a "reasonable time;" in Delaware, within one year; in Florida, within six months; in Georgia, within twelve months, except as to mortgages, which must be recorded within thirty days; in Indiana, within forty-five days of execution and transfer; in Kentucky, where deed made by resident of the State, within sixty days; where made by a non-resident, within four months; in Maryland, within six months from date; in Ohio, the law formerly was that the conveyance must be recorded within six months, and it is believed to be so now; in Oregon, within five days; in Pennsylvania, if within the city of Philadelphia, "immediately;" if in other parts of the State, within six months; if out of the State, within twelve months ; in South Carolina, within forty days.

(1) 4 Kent's Com. 448.

decisions of the courts in the various States, as we would naturally suppose, also vary.(1)

It is held, in Virginia,(2) that a creditor who became such after the execution of an unrecorded deed would not be affected by it, even though he had knowledge of the existence of the deed, while in California and Mississippi such creditor would not be protected.(3)

Courts have held that mortgagees and trustees are to be regarded as purchasers within the meaning of recording and registration laws, and that purchasers under mortgages and trust deeds, executed to persons without notice, will be protected although having notice.(4)

It has also been held that where the first grantee or mortgagee purchased with notice, one purchasing from him without notice will be protected.(5)

But in order that a purchaser, mortgagee or trustee should be protected under these rulings, the transaction must be a real one, done in good faith, for a proper consideration, and not designed to interfere with or postpone the rights of others.(6)

Some courts have held that it is not sufficient to afford this protection that an agreement to purchase shall have been entered into, even though accompanied by possession and payment of the purchase money.(7)

(1) Thornton on Registration, 34.

(2) Guerrant v. Anderson, 4 Rand. 212.

(3) Dixon et al. v. Lecoste, 1 S. & M. 70.

(4) Harrison v. Forth, Prec. Finch, 51; Lowther v. Carleton, 2 Atk. 139; Brandlyn v. Ord, 1 Atk. 571; Bennett v. Walker, West, 130; Mertins v. Joliffe et als., 1 Amb. 313; Bumpus v. Platner, 1 Johns. Ch.

213; Curtis v. Jones's Exr., 6 Munf. 42; Trutt v. Bigelow, 16 Mass. 406; Boydton v. Rees, 8 Pick. 329.

(5) Southall v. M'Keand, 1 Wash. (Va.) 336; Conn. v. Bradish, 14 Mass. 296; Leaving et al. v. Brickerhoff et al., 5 Johns. Ch. 329.

(6) Sugden on Vend. 511.

(7) Moore v. Mayhow, 1 Ch. Cas. 34; Tourvill v. Naish, 3 P. Wms. 306; Sugden on Vend. 530.

On the other hand, the courts have held that where the purchase money has been all paid, and the equitable title completed, and the party thus has the best right to call in the legal title, he is entitled to the benefit of protection against unrecorded instruments, as having fairly and substantially complied with the rule.(1)

Notice may be express or implied. Express notice is the actual knowledge of a given fact, regularly and formally communicated. Implied notice is a conclusion of law, from violent presumption, which the courts will not allow to be controverted.(2).

When notice has been expressly communicated at any time before the purchase is completed by the payment of the money, and (as most authorities hold) before the execution of the deed or, if the knowledge of the existence of the deed is traced to the party, without a formal communication of it, the notice is express, positive and effectual.(3)

Circumstances which establish satisfactorily the fact of the knowledge are sufficient evidence of this character of notice. A knowledge of the unrecorded deed is not required to be precise, but notice which is sufficient to reasonably put a party upon inquiry, and which by ordinary diligence would lead to the discovery of the fact, is sufficient.(4)

A deed is deemed to be recorded from the hour it is deposited with the recording officer for that purpose, without regard to when it is actually spread upon the record.(5)

(1) Mut. Ass. Soc. etc. v. Stone et al., 3 Leigh, 235.

(2) Coote on Mort. 373.

(3) 4 Kent's Com. 163–4 and 5.

(4) Coote on Mort. 378; McMeechan v. Griffing, 3 Pick. 149.

(5) Thornton on Registration, 38; Hiester's Lessee v. Fortner, 2 Binn. 40; Harvey et al. v. Alexander et. al., 1 Rand. 219, 241; Currie v. Donald, 2 Wash. (Va.) 64.

This, however, will only apply to recordable instruments.   If the instrument is not recordable, although
spread upon the record, it will not be notice, but will
be as though not recorded at all.(1)

Though the record be burned or otherwise destroyed,
in contemplation of law the constructive notice continues.

It is incompetent to prove *aliunde* any fact which
the law requires to appear on the record or in a filed
deed. So it can not be proven by parol that there was
a privy examination of a femme covert.(2)

The admission of a recordable instrument to record
is a ministerial act, and one over which, when the law
is properly complied with, the courts can have no control, neither can they have control of the recording officer.(3)

Lis pendens does not affect recording.

SEC. 295.   It is often said by the courts that lis pendens does not affect recording or registry laws.(4)

That is true. Lis pendens does not affect the recording laws in the same sense that it does not affect
other positive legislative enactments.   It would, however, doubtless be competent for the legislatures of
the States, in enacting lis pendens statutes, to modify
or qualify the recording acts by provisions relating to
statutory lis pendens.

The same legislative power in such cases enacts
both laws, and within the limitations of the State constitutions undoubtedly may frame them with reference
to each other.

(1) Elliott et al. *v.* Piersol, 1 Peters, 328.

(2) Ross *v.* McLung, 6 Peters, 283.

(3) Dawson *v.* Thurston, 2 Hen.
& Munf. 132.

(4) Wyatt *v.* Barwell, 16 Ves. 435.

But when courts say that lis pendens does not affect the recording laws, they refer to the common law rule lis pendens, which is the creature of the courts, and not to rules enacted by positive statute.

The courts may not enact or repeal laws. They can only enforce them.

Even the court of chancery has no power to modify an established rule of the common law, or a provision of an express statute, where it is so clear as not to admit of construction. The chancery courts are as much bound to follow the law as the law courts.

Recording laws modify application of lis pendens.

Sec. 296. But while lis pendens may not modify the recording or registry laws, the converse of the proposition is not true. The application of the recording laws in cases where the rule lis pendens is applied modify the results of the application of that rule.

Thus in the leading case of Norton v. Birge,(1) where the conveyance which the bill was filed to remove was executed by Nott to Nock before the suit was commenced, but was not recorded until long afterwards, it was contended on the part of Nock that the doctrine of lis pendens never was applied to any case except where the conveyance was made after the suit was commenced by a party to it, and that the recording or non-recording of conveyances had no effect upon the question of the lis pendens. But the court held otherwise, and gave force and effect to the recording laws; declaring that under the facts of that case Nock must be deemed to have taken the conveyance pendente lite, that although he took his deed ante litem his failure to record the deed and use the

(1) Norton v. Birge, 35 Conn. 263.

diligence which he should have used to ascertain the rights of the complainant in that case placed Nock in the category of pendente lite claimants.

How lis pendens affected by the registry laws.

SEC. 297. The recording or failure to record instruments under which parties have sought to acquire interests in the subject matter of litigation, either ante litem or post litem, becomes quite material when we come to consider how those rights or supposed rights are affected by lis pendens.

Where the property involved is contained in an unregistered mortgage, which by the statutes of the State is required to be registered before becoming effective as against bona fide purchasers and creditors, the filing of the bill to establish such unregistered mortgage will not constitute constructive notice lis pendens to such subsequent purchaser or creditor. In such cases the courts give force to the registry laws and hold the superior equity in the pendente lite purchaser or creditor, because the law has appointed a place where mortgages must be registered in order to be notice to purchasers, and if there be no registry there the purchaser is not held to constructive notice by any other means.

The registration in such a case, it is said, is the only thing that can operate as constructive notice. This position is fully sustained by the case of McCutchen et al. *v.* Miller.(1) The same doctrine is held by

(1) McCutchen et al. *v.* Miller, 31 Miss. 83.

While this position seems to be fully warranted by the authorities, it would be hardly consistent with well established principles to hold that where the original mortgage is made a part of the bill by being attached to it as an exhibit or otherwise incorporated into the bill and made a part of it, and it appears to have been regularly exe-

the courts where the conveyance is a deed instead of a mortgage.

Mr. Freeman, in his valuable work on Judgments, at Sec. 201, says: "That a person holding title to real estate by virtue of an unrecorded conveyance, is bound by a judgment against his grantor;"(1) thus applying the provisions of the registry law in determining the question whether there is effective lis pendens or not.

The Connecticut case of Norton v. Birge,(2) and the case of Hoyt v. Jones,(3) fully sustain this position.

A creditor with notice not protected.

SEC. 298. But a creditor of the grantor in an unrecorded deed with a notice of the deed cannot proceed and procure a prior lien upon his debt which will avail against the unrecorded deed.

The notice of the deed as to such creditor is equivalent to recording.

cuted and acknowledged in conformity with law, and where recording is not made a prerequisite to its validity, and the court has acquired full jurisdiction of the suit, to hold that a purchaser would not be bound to take constructive notice of the rights of the mortgagee.

Probably a copy would not suffice, because the record of a copy would not be noticed; but it is difficult to perceive why the original mortgage, brought to the attention of the public by the proper allegation in the pending bill, ought not to be held equivalent to the record of it in the recorder's office, and thus charge an intermeddler with the results of the suit. This view would not proceed upon the ground that the lis pendens affected the recording law, but upon grounds entirely independent of them.

In Wyatt v. Barwell, 19 Ves. 435, the court held that lis pendens is not notice for the purpose of postponing a registered deed. Wallace v. The Marquis of Donegal, 1 Drury & W. 487; Houldtich v. Wallace, 1 Drury & W. 498.

But it is said that where a second purchaser had actual notice of the first purchase, although the deed were not recorded, the second purchase will be postponed. 1 Story's Eq. Jur. 406; Murray v. Finster, 2 Johns. Ch. 155.

(1) Freeman on Judgments, 201.
(2) Norton v. Birge, 35 Conn. 262.
(3) Hoyt v. Jones, 31 Wis. 397.

So, where a purchaser has acquired a title regular in all respects, except that his conveyance is not recorded, a creditor of his grantor with full knowledge of his title cannot commence an action by attachment, file a notice of lis pendens under a lis pendens statute, and thus obtain a lien superior to the title of such purchaser, and thereby destroy and cut off the unrecorded conveyance.(1)

Holder of unrecorded deed in the category of a pendente lite purchaser.

SEC. 299. And so the case of Hoyt *v.* Jones,(2) which was twice ably argued in the Supreme Court of Wisconsin, where a deed was made on the 15th day of July, 1854, but was not recorded until the 11th of November, 1858, the next day after the initiation of lis pendens, was another illustration of the rule that the holder of an unrecorded deed of which a litigant has no notice is in the category of a pendente lite purchaser.

The bill in that case was filed to enforce a lien upon the land, and subject it to the payment of a debt of the apparent owners of the recorded title.

Wilcox commenced the suit against Mygatt et als., to cancel a conveyance from Wilcox to Mygatt and other conveyances from Mygatt and his assigns. Wallace Mygatt had conveyed to Edward G. Mygatt in July, 1854, but the deed was not recorded, as above stated, until Nov. 11, 1858. The suit became a lis pendens under the laws of Wisconsin, Nov. 10, 1858, the day before the deed was recorded.

It was held in that case that the claimant under

(1) Lamont *v.* Cheshire et al., 65 N. Y. 30.

(2) Hoyt *v.* Jones, 31 Wis. 389, 403.

the deed, although the defendant had conveyed more than four years before the suit became a lis pendens, but had not recorded his deed until the day after the lis pendens had attached to the property, had not acquired such a perfected right as to be regarded as an ante litem purchaser.

The court, in the course of its opinion in the case last above mentioned, say that "under the registry law and so far as it may be necessary to protect the titles of subsequent purchasers in good faith who are within it, it is sufficient if the court has *apparent* jurisdiction to operate upon the title. It is by the title as it *appears* on record that purchasers and suitors, having no different knowledge or information, are governed; and it is no more necessary, for the purpose of the title so shown by the record, that the court should lay its hand upon the *actual* title, in order that a subsequent purchaser under the judgment may be protected, than it is that the grantor in the common case should have actual seizin and title of the land to protect the purchasers under his conveyance.

The fact is, the grantor has no title, and yet, by default of the true owner to record his deed, the registry law operates to give the grantee a good title.

So it may be, technically, with respect to the jurisdiction of the court, and yet its judgment operates, or may operate under the registry law, to secure a valid title to the purchaser, who afterwards buys on the faith of it, the true owner keeping all evidence and knowledge of his paramount right still covered up and concealed."(1)

(1) Freeman on Judgts. Sec. 201.

Unrecorded deed attacked by bill.

SEC. 300. It was held in a Virginia case(1) that a bill in chancery would lie to prevent the recording of a deed which would prejudice the rights of the complainant were it to be spread upon the record.

In the case referred to, an insolvent debtor in consideration of an extension of time for payment procured from his creditors, or in order to procure such extension, promised that he would give no preference against him. The promise was made while a secret deed of preference was already executed. The deed was not recorded, and the insolvent merchant continued his business with open doors. The creditor from whom the extension had been procured upon this promise, hearing by some means of the unrecorded deed, filed his bill seeking to invalidate the unrecorded conveyance. The court granted the relief prayed.

The court say in that case: "It is clear that deeds, whether bona fide or not, may be assailed before they are recorded. Being null and void as to creditors, if the creditors institute suit before registration and the suit is continued to a successful issue, the suit takes precedence of registration, even though the deed be not fraudulent, and so far as the deed is in conflict with the prayers of the bill it is null and void.

A deed may be free from fault on the part of the grantor, or, if fraudulent as to him, may be free from fault as to the grantee, and still being void as to creditors until recorded, if assailed by a suit commenced before that event, though it may stand for all other purposes, it is null and void as to the purposes of that

(1) Shufeldt v. Jenkins, 22 Fed. R. 371.

suit, if the suit be sustained by the court in which it is brought.

It was on this theory that the suit in this case was brought. It was originally founded on the theory of setting aside a deed to hinder, delay and defraud creditors. An allegation to that effect was indeed presented marginally in the bill as an afterthought; but the bill went primarily upon the theory that the deed operated as a fraud upon the complainants, and, if assailed by suit before its registration, might be set aside as null and void."

The same subject further considered.

SEC. 301. This question was exhaustively discussed by the late Justice Dickey in a dissenting opinion in an Illinois case.(1)

In that case a bill was filed to set aside a conveyance made without consideration. The bill was filed on the 4th day of March, 1869, but service was not had on the defendant, the grantee in the deed above referred to, until the 5th of March.

On the same day on which the decree was entered, and just before the case had proceeded to a decree in favor of the complainant, a deed was placed upon the record purporting to have been executed by the defendant to a third party prior to the suit.

The case was determined by a majority of the court upon the ground that the suit did not pend until the 5th of March, after the alleged deed was made. Justice Dickey dissented, and one of the grounds of his dissension was that the defendant's grantee having held under an unrecorded deed without notice to the complainant before his suit became a lis pendens, was

(1) Grant et al. *v.* Bennett et al., 96 Ill. 513.

in the category of a pendente lite purchaser, following the authority of Norton v. Birge, above referred to.

In the course of his opinion he says: "I deny that the law enables him, (as the holder of a deed from Miss Newcomb, made before lis pendens began, but unrecorded at that time, and of which complainant had no notice,) to avoid or defeat the legal effect of the lis pendens by recording such deed pendente lite, and before the final decree is made." * * * * "I hold that rights and equities of all in the very same property, and derived from a party defendant in the suit, must ultimately rest upon the basis of the strength of their respective rights and equities when the lis pendens began." * * * * "This precise question came in judgment and was expressly decided in Norton v. Birge, 35 Conn., 250.

* * * * In that case a conveyance was delivered before the suit began, but not put on record until after the suit was instituted. It was there held that the grantee stood in relation to the pending suit just as he would have stood if the conveyance had been taken during the pendency of the suit." * * * * "The decision rests upon the idea that the rights and interests in question were in fact acquired from a party to the suit after the institution of the suit, although the deed was delivered before suit began,—and this, because the deed, though delivered, not being recorded, was void as against complainant and therefore as against him passed no interest until it was filed for record, and no interest as against the complainant was acquired until the time of such filing for record, and therefore in so far as concerns the complainant, these rights and interests were acquired by the defendant

after the institution of the suit; and by the terms and true meaning of the rule, lis pendens does not apply to the rights and interests thus acquired."

This position of Justice Dickey, urged with so much earnestness and ability, was nowhere met in the opinion of the majority of the court, and is clearly sustained by the cases of Norton *v.* Birge(1) and Hoyt *v.* Jones,(2) *ante.*

Not an exception to the rule lis pendens.

SEC. 302. Mr. Freeman, in his valuable work on Judgments, Sec. 201, speaking of the decision in Norton *v.* Birge as an exception to the rule lis pendens says: "Lis pendens applies only to the rights and interests acquired by a party thereto *after* the institution of the suit."

In this that learned author is in error, an error naturally fallen into from the loose language of some of the decisions. It is not an exception, but is of the very essence of the rule lis pendens itself, as shown by Justice Dickey in the case of Grant et al. *v.* Bennett et al.,(3) *ante.*

Under the recording laws the unrecorded deed, as to all persons acquiring an interest securing a lien without notice, is null and void. It is as though no conveyance were made. By the registry laws it only becomes effective by filing for record or registration. If at the time it is so filed for record there is a pending suit, the holder of such a deed previously withheld from the record is a pendente lite purchaser.

He stands upon no better ground than he would

---

(1) Norton *v.* Birge, 35 Conn. 250.

(2) Hoyt *v.* Jones, 31 Wis. 397.

(3) Grant et al. *v.* Bennett et al., 96 Ill. 513.

have occupied if his deed were executed at the moment of its recording. The question is, whether at the time the law determines lis pendens commences, it had become effective upon the property involved.

If the recording laws make the deed void as to such claimant before record, the lis pendens had become effective upon the property. This is the substance of the ruling in both the cases of Norton v. Birge(1) and Hoyt v. Jones,(2) and the reasoning of those courts, as well as that of Justice Dickey, seems to me unanswerable.

(1) Norton v. Birge, 35 Conn. 250.   (2) Hoyt v. Jones, 31 Wis. 397.

CHAPTER XIV.

LIS PENDENS STATUTES.

English lis pendens statute.

SEC. 303. The lis pendens statutes adopted by several States of the Union undoubtedly originated indirectly from the English lis pendens statute of 2nd & 3rd Victoria, which was passed in 1839.

This statute was probably passed to remedy the difficulty arising from the practice, which had existed more or less before that time, of issuing the subpœna in chancery before the bill was filed, procuring service of it and thus creating lis pendens before there was anything on the record to show what the suit was about.

This act provided in substance that no lis pendens should be in force as against third persons without express or actual notice thereof, until a memorandum

containing the name, place, residence and description
of the person whose property was intended to be
affected by it, together with the court, title of the
cause and date of the filing, was left with the senior
master of the Court of Common Pleas, whose duty it
was made forthwith to enter these particulars in alphabetical order in a book provided for that purpose.(1)

Lis pendens statute of New York.

SEC. 304.　　Soon after the adoption of the English
statute to which we have referred in the last section,
the legislature of the State of New York passed a lis
pendens statute which has been amended and modified
at various times, and in such modified form is now in
force in that State.

This statute,(2) which may be found as sections

---

(1) Chap. II, Sec. 7, 2nd & 3rd
Victoria.

"And be it enacted, that no lis
pendens shall bind a purchaser or
mortgagee with express notice
thereof, unless and until a memorandum or minute containing the
name and the usual or last known
place of abode, and the title, trade
or profession of the person whose
estate is intended to be affected
thereby, and the court of equity
and the title of the cause or information and the day when the bill
or information, was filed shall be
left with the senior master of the
said Court of Common Pleas, who
shall forthwith enter the same particulars in a book as aforesaid in
alphabetical order, by the name of
the person whose estate is intended
to be affected by said lis pendens,
and said officer shall be entitled for
any such entry to the sum of two

shillings and sixpence, and the provisions hereinbefore contained in
regard to the re-entering of judgment every five years, and the fee
payable to the officer thereon, shall
extend to every case of lis pendens
which shall be registered under the
provisions of this act."

(2) The New York statute reads:
"SEC. 1670. In an action brought
to recover a judgment affecting the
title to or possession, use or enjoyment of real property, the plaintiff
may when he files his complaint or
at any time afterwards before final
judgment file in the clerk's office of
each county where the property is
situated a notice of the pendency
of the action, stating the names of
the parties and the object of the
action and containing a brief description of the property in that
county affected thereby. Such a
notice may be filed with the com-

1670 and 1671 of the revised statutes of that State now in force, provides in substance that in an action brought to recover a judgment affecting the title to or possession, use or enjoyment of real estate, the plaintiff may file with his complaint at the time of commencing it, or at any time afterwards before final judgment in the county clerk's office of the county where the real estate is situated, a notice of lis pendens which shall state the names of the parties and the object of the suit.

The statute requires that the notice be filed before the service of the summons in case of personal service and that in such case the summons must be served upon the defendant within sixty days after the filing of the notice, or in case personal service is not obtained and the defendant is brought in by publication, then it must be filed before the expiration of the time of publication. Section 1671 declares the effect of

plaint before the service of the summons, but in that case personal service of the summons must be made upon a defendant within sixty days after the filing, or else before the expiration of the same time, publication of the summons must be commenced or service thereof must be made without the State pursuant to an order obtained therefor as prescribed in chapter fifth of this act."

"SEC. 1671. Where a notice of the pendency of an action may be filed as prescribed in the last section the pendency of the action is constructive notice from the time of so filing the notice only to a purchaser or incumbrancer of the property affected thereby from or

against a defendant with respect to whom the notice is directed to be indexed as prescribed in the next section. A person whose conveyance or incumbrance is subsequently executed or subsequently recorded is bound by all proceedings taken in the action after the filing of the notice to the same extent as if he was a party to the action."

"SEC. 1672 provides that notice must be filed with clerk and by him recorded."

"SEC. 1673 provides that where defendant sets up by answer counterclaims and seeks affirmative relief he must file a like notice of his claim." N. Y. Annotated Code, Banks & Bro. 1884; Ch. 14, Art. 9, Sec. 1670.

such a notice to be constructive notice to purchasers and incumbrancers of the property affected thereby, from the time of filing of the notice only, from a defendant mentioned in the notice as filed, and that conveyances and incumbrances subsequently executed or recorded should be affected by the lis pendens of the suit. The statute also provides for the recording of the notice of lis pendens and that where defendants set up counterclaims and seek affirmative relief they may file like notices of lis pendens and with like effect as to their counterclaims.(1)

Wisconsin statute.

SEC. 305. The legislature of the State of Wisconsin at an early day followed very closely the lis pendens statute of New York, referred to in the last section, in adopting a statute for that State, and this statute as amended and modified still remains in force.

Section 3187 of the statutes now in force in that State provides, like the New York statute, for the filing of a notice of lis pendens at the time of filing of the complaint, or at any time thereafter before judgment, with the register of deeds of the county or counties where the property involved, or any part of it, is situated, containing the names of the parties and other items with respect to the case, and also provides for the filing of counter lis pendens notices by defendant who may seek to set up and claim affirmative

(1) Prior to 1862 in New York lis pendens was of no force as against purchasers or incumbrancers until service of summons. Barter v. Tomlinson, 38 Barb. 641; Farmers' Loan, etc., v. Dickson, 17 How. Pr. 477.

By an amendment of the lis pendens act in 1862 the action is deemed pending from the time of the filing of the notice lis pendens, provided publication or service should be had within 60 days thereafter.

relief, and also declaring the legal effect of such lis pendens notices to be that every purchaser or incumbrancer whose conveyance or incumbrance is not recorded or filed shall be bound by the proceedings in the suit to the same extent and in the same manner as parties to the suit.

Section 761 of the statutes of that State requires that the register in each county shall keep a separate book in his office, in which shall be entered all writs of attachment, certificates of sales and notices of lis pendens affecting real estate, and that memoranda of notices of lis pendens shall be entered on the margin of the record of mortgages which may be in process of foreclosure.(1)

(1) The Wisconsin statute, now in force, reads as follows:

"SEC. 3187. In an action affecting the title to real property, the plaintiff, at the time of filing the complaint, or any time afterwards before judgment, may file in the office of the register of deeds of each county where the property, or any part thereof, is situated, a notice of the pendency of the action, containing the names of the parties, the object of the action and a description of the property in that county affected thereby. If the action be for the foreclosure of a mortgage, such notice must be filed twenty days before judgment and must contain the date of the mortgage, the names of the parties thereto, and the time and place of recording the same. The defendant may, at the time of filing his answer, or any time afterwards before judgment, where he sets up an affirmative cause of action therein and demands an affirmative judgment affecting the title to real property, file in such register's office a like notice. From the time of such filing, in either case, the pendency of such action shall be constructive notice thereof to a purchaser or incumbrancer of the property affected thereby ; and every purchaser or incumbrancer whose conveyance or incumbrance is not recorded or filed, shall be deemed a subsequent purchaser or incumbrancer, and shall be bound by the proceedings in the action to the same extent and in the same manner as if he were a party thereto."

Section 761 of the statute requires that a separate book of register, properly arranged, shall be kept, in which shall be entered abstracts of writs of attachment, certificates of sale of real estate, and notices of lis pendens affecting real estate, giving the essential de-

California statute.

SEC. 306.   Following also the legislation of the State of New York, the State of California at an early day passed a lis pendens statute, which as amended and modified is now in force.   Section 409 of the statutes of this State provides that the plaintiff, in actions affecting the title to or possession of lands at the time of filing the complaint, or the defendant at the time of filing answer, where affirmative relief is claimed, or at any time afterwards, may record in the recorder's office of the county in which the lands sought to be affected are situated a notice of lis pendens, containing the names of the parties, the object of the suit or defense, and the description of the property.   The statute declares the effect of such filing and record to be that purchasers and incumbrancers from the time of the filing of such notices for record shall be deemed to have constructive notice of the lis pendens, as against parties designated by their real names in such notices only.   As we shall show in the succeeding chapter, this statute has been construed by the Supreme Court of California, in numerous cases, so that it has become an important part of the law of that State.(1)

tails of such papers, and that a memorandum of notices of lis pendens shall also be entered on the margin of the record of mortgages being foreclosed. R. S. Wis., 1878, Ch. 138, Sec. 3187, and Ch. 37, Sec. 761.

(1) The California statute reads as follows:

" SEC. 409. In an action affecting the title or right of possession of real property, the plaintiff, at the time of filing the complaint, and the defendant, at the time of filing his answer, when affirmative relief is claimed in such answer, or at any time afterwards, may record in the office of the recorder of the county in which the property is situated a notice of the pendency of the action, containing the names of the parties, and the object of the action or defense, and a description of the property in that county affected thereby. From the time of filing such notice for record only

Michigan statute.

SEC. 307. Section 6619 of the statutes now in force in the State of Michigan provides, in like manner, for the filing of lis pendens notices. That section directs that in order to render the filing of a bill in chancery constructive notice to a purchaser of real estate, it shall be the duty of complainant to file with the register of deeds of the county in which the lands to be affected are situated a notice of lis pendens, which shall contain the title of the cause, the general object of the suit, and a description of the lands to be affected by it.

The law makes it the duty of the register to record such notices in a book to be kept for that purpose, upon the payment of the fees provided by law, and further declares that copies of such notices duly authenticated by the register shall be evidence of their contents in all courts and places.(1)

Minnesota statute.

SEC. 308. Chapter 75, Section 34, of the statutes of

shall a purchaser or incumbrancer of the property affected thereby be deemed to have constructive notice of the pendency of the action, and only of its pendency against parties designated by their real names." 3 Deering's Code and Stat. of Cal., 1885, Tit. 5, Sec. 409.

(1) The Michigan statute is as follows:

" SEC. 6619. To render the filing of a bill constructive notice to a purchaser of any real estate, it shall be the duty of the complainant to file for record, with the register of deeds of the county in which the lands to be affected by such constructive notice are situat-ed, a notice of the pendency of such suit in chancery, setting forth the title of the cause and the general object thereof, together with a description of the lands to be affected thereby; and it shall thereupon become the duty of the register to record such notice in a book kept for that purpose, upon the payment of the same fees as is provided by law for recording deeds. A copy of such record, authenticated by the register, shall be evidence of such notice, and the filing of the same, in all courts and places."

Howell's Annotated Stats. of Mich., 1882, Tit. XXIX, Sec. 6619.

Minnesota now in force provides that in all actions in which the title to, liens upon, or interest in real estate is sought to be affected and which is involved or brought in question by either party to a suit, the plaintiff or defendant, or both, may at the commencement or at any time during the pendency of such suit file for record in the office of the register of deeds of each county in which the real estate involved or some part thereof is situate a notice of lis pendens, which shall contain the names of the parties, the object of the suit and a description of the property.

The statute further provides that when any pleading in such suit is amended so as to extend the claim to other property, the party so filing such notice shall file a new notice.

It is made the duty of the register of deeds to record such notices in a book, in the same manner as mortgages are recorded, and it is declared by the statute that from the time of filing such notices and from such time only, shall the pendency of the suit be notice to purchasers and incumbrancers of the rights and equities of the parties filing the same.

It is further provided that such notice may be discharged and annulled by an entry to that effect on the margin of the record thereof made by the party filing the same, or his attorney, in the presence of the register of deeds, or it may be done by an instrument in writing executed in the manner provided by law for the execution of deeds and conveyances, to be entered by the register upon the margin of the record of the notice.(1)

(1) The Minnesota statute, Chap. 75, Sec. 34, reads as follows:

"SEC 34. In all actions heretofore or hereafter commenced, in which the title to, or any lien upon, or interest in real property shall be af-

Indiana statute.

SEC. 309. The lis pendens statute now in force in the State of Indiana is embraced in Secs. 324, 325 and 331 of the statutes now in force in this State. Section 324 provides that there shall be kept in the offices of the clerks of the several circuit courts of the State a book to be known as the "Lis Pendens Record," which shall be a public record.

Section 325 provides that when any person shall have commenced a suit, whether as plaintiff by complaint or as defendant by cross-complaint, to enforce any lien upon, right to, or interest in, real estate, upon any claim not founded upon an instrument executed by the person in whose name the legal title to the real estate shall be, or not founded upon a judgment of a court

fected, involved or brought in question by either party, any party to such action may, at the commencement or any time during the pendency thereof, file for record in the office of the register of deeds of each county in which the real property so affected, involved or brought in question, or some part thereof, is situated, a notice of the pendency of the action, containing the names of the parties, the object of the action, and a description of the real property in the county affected, involved or brought in question thereby. And when any pleading in such action is amended by altering the description of the premises affected, involved or brought in question, or so as to extend the claim against such premises, the party filing such notice shall file a new notice. And the register of deeds shall record all such notices in the same book and in the same manner as mortgages are recorded. From the time of the filing such notice, and from such time only, the pendency of the action shall be notice to purchasers and incumbrancers of the rights and equities of the party filing such notice, to the real property in such notice described.

The said notice may be discharged, and the effect thereof annulled, by an entry to that effect on the margin of the record thereof by the party filing the same, or his attorney, in presence of the register of deeds, or by an instrument in writing executed in the manner provided by law for the execution of deeds of conveyance; and such register shall thereupon enter a minute of the same on the margin of the record of such notice."

Gen. Stat. Minn., 1878, Ch. 75, Sec. 34.

of record in the county where the land is situate; that it shall be the duty of such complainant or cross-complainant to file with the clerk of the circuit court in each county where the real estate sought to be affected is situated, a notice of lis pendens, containing the title of the court, the names of all parties to the suit or proceeding, a description of the real estate to be affected and the nature of the lien, right or interest sought to be enforced, which notice, upon payment of the proper fees prescribed by the act, shall be immediately recorded by the clerk in the "Lis Pendens Record," and that he shall note upon the record the day and the hour of filing the same.

Section 331 provides further that until such lis pendens notice shall have been filed, such suit or proceeding shall not operate as constructive notice of the pendency of such suit or proceeding, nor have any force or effect as against bona fide purchasers or incumbrancers of the same.(1)

(1) The Indiana statute reads as follows:

" Sec. 324. There shall be kept in the office of the clerk of the several circuit courts of this State a book to be called the ' Lis Pendens Record,' which shall be a public record."

" Sec. 325. Whenever any person shall have commenced a suit, whether by complaint as plaintiff, or by cross-complaint as defendant, to enforce any lien upon, right to, or interest in, any real estate, upon any claim not founded upon an instrument executed by the party having the legal title to such real estate, as appears from the proper records of such county, and record-ed as by law required; or not founded upon a judgment of record in the county wherein such real estate is situated, against the party having the legal title to such real estate, as appears from such proper records,—it shall be the duty of such person to file with the clerk of the circuit court in each county where the real estate sought to be affected is situated, a written notice containing the title of the court, the names of all parties to such suit, a description of the real estate to be affected, and the nature of the lien, right or interest sought to be enforced against the same; which notice shall, upon the payment of the proper fees, be immediately re-

Missouri statute.

SEC. 309a. A lis pendens statute is also in force in the State of Missouri. It provides in substance for the filing for record with the recorder of deeds of the county in which any real estate to be affected is situated, a notice of lis pendens in writing in any civil action based on any equitable right, claim or lien, stating the names of the parties, the character of the suit, the description of the real estate involved and the term of the court to which it is made returnable. It declares in terms that such notice shall be binding upon all purchasers or incumbrancers from the time of the filing of such notice and imposes the duty upon the recorder to make an index showing all lis pendens notices, as required by the laws of that State in the case of the record of deeds.(1)

corded in said "Lis Pendens Record" by the clerk, who shall note upon the record the day and hour when said notice was filed and recorded."

"Sec. 331. Until the proper notices required by this act have been filed with the proper clerk, the bringing of suits for the purposes mentioned in section seventy-three (Sec. 325) and the seizure of real estate under attachments, and the levy thereon under execution, in the cases mentioned in section seventy-four (Sec. 326), shall not operate as constructive notice of the pendency of such suits, or of the seizure of or levy upon such real estate, nor have any force or effect as against bona fide purchasers or incumbrancers of the same." R. S. Ind., 1881,Secs. 324, 325 and 331, pp. 58 and 59.

(1) The following is a copy of the Missouri statute referred to:

"Sec. 3217. In any civil action, based on any equitable right, claim or lien, affecting or designed to affect real estate, the plaintiff shall file for record, with the recorder of deeds of the county in which any such real estate is situated, a written notice of the pendency of the suit, stating the names of the parties, the style of the action and the term of the court to which such suit is brought, and a description of the real estate liable to be affected thereby; and the pendency of such suit shall be constructive notice to purchasers of incumbrances, only from the time of filing such notice.

The recorder shall note the time of receiving such notice, and shall record and index the same in like

South Carolina statute.

SEC. 310. A like statute is also in force in the State of South Carolina. Sec. 153 of the statutes of this State provides, in like manner, that in actions affecting real estate the plaintiff at the time of the filing of the complaint or afterwards, or whenever a warrant of attachment shall be issued under the statute of this State, or at any time afterwards, the plaintiff or defendant, when the latter sets up an affirmative cause of action, may file with the clerk of each county where the property is situated a notice of the pendency of the action or defense, stating the names of the parties, the object of the suit and the description of the property affected thereby.

That if the action be for the foreclosure of a mortgage, the notice must be filed twenty days before decree, and must contain the date of the mortgage, the parties to it, and the time and place of its record.

The statute also declares the legal effect of the filing of such notice of lis pendens to be constructive notice to all purchasers and incumbrancers of the property affected thereby, and that every person whose conveyance or incumbrance shall be subsequently executed, or subsequently recorded, shall be deemed a subsequent purchaser or incumbrancer and be bound by the proceedings involving the property the same as if made a party thereto, and that the action shall be deemed to pend from the time of the filing of such notices, provided that the lis pendens shall have no

manner as deeds to real estate are required to be recorded and indexed." R. S. of Mo., 1879, p. 542, Ch. 48, Art. 5, Sec. 3217.

In Turner v. Babb, 60 Mo. 342, the Supreme Court of that State decided that "purchasers of incumbrances" should read "purchasers or incumbrancers."

force unless followed by the first publication of summons or by an order therefor, or by the personal service of the defendant within sixty days after the filing, and making further provision as to the cancellation of notices lis pendens, in cases where actions shall be discontinued, by the noting of the fact on the margin of the proper records.(1)

(1) The South Carolina statute, Sec. 153 of the Code of Civil Procedure, reads:

"Sec. 153. In an action affecting the title to real property, the plaintiff, at the time of filing the complaint, or at any time afterwards, or whenever a warrant of attachment under Chapter 4 of Title 7, Part 2, of this Code of Procedure, shall be issued, or at any time afterwards, the plaintiff, or a defendant, when he sets up an affirmative cause of action in his answer and demands substantive relief, at the time of filing his answer, or at any time afterwards, if the same be intended to affect real estate, may file with the clerk of each county in which the property is situated, a notice of the pendency of the action, containing the names of the parties, the object of the action, and the description of the property in that county affected thereby; and if the action be for the foreclosure of a mortgage, such notice must be filed twenty days before judgment, and must contain the date of the mortgage, the parties thereto, and the time and place of recording the same. From the time of filing only shall the pendency of the action be constructive notice to a purchaser or encumbrancer of the property affected thereby; and every person whose conveyance or encumbrance is subsequently executed or subsequently recorded shall be deemed a subsequent purchaser or encumbrancer, and shall be bound by all proceedings taken after the filing of such notice to the same extent as if he were made a party to the action. For the purpose of this section, an action shall be deemed to be pending from the time of filing such notice: Provided, however, that such notice shall be of no avail, unless it shall be followed by the first publication of the summons, or an order therefor, or by the personal service thereof on a defendant within sixty days after such filing. And the court in which the said action was commenced may, in its own discretion, at any time after the action shall be settled, discontinued, or abated, as is provided in Section 142, on application of any person aggrieved, and on any good cause shown, and on such notice as shall be directed or approved by the court, order the notice authorized by this section to be cancelled of record by the clerk of any county in whose office the same may have been filed or recorded; and such cancellation shall be made by an endorsement to that effect on the

West Virginia statute.

SEC. 311.　A like lis pendens statute exists in West Virginia. Section 13 of the statutes of this State now in force provides that the pendency of any action, suit, attachment, or other proceeding, whose object is to affect real estate by charging it with the payment of any debt or liability otherwise than expressly provided by law, shall not bind or affect a purchaser of such real estate for a valuable consideration and without notice, until a memorandum setting forth the title of the cause, the court in which it pends, the object of the proceeding and the location and quantity of land sought to be affected, as near as may be, shall be filed with the clerk of the County Court in the county in which the land is situated, and it is made the duty of every such clerk to record the memorandum without delay in a book to be provided for that purpose, and to index the same in the name of both of the parties to the suit.

This statute differs from those of New York, Wisconsin, California and South Carolina only in that it does not declare the force and effect of recording the notice of lis pendens. This is left as a matter of legal inference without a statutory declaration of it.(1)

margin of the record, which shall refer to the order, and for which the clerk shall be entitled to a fee of twenty-five cents." Code of Civ. Prac. S. C., 1882, Sec. 153, Part 2, Tit. 5.

(1) The West Virginia statute reads as follows:

"SEC. 13. The pendency of an action, suit, attachment or proceedings to subject real estate to the payment of any debt or liability, upon which a previous lien shall not have been acquired in some one or more of the methods prescribed by law, shall not bind or affect a purchaser of such real estate, for a valuable consideration, without notice, unless and until a memorandum setting forth the title of the cause, the court in which it is pending, the general object of the suit, attachment or other proceedings, the location and the quantity of

New Jersey statute.

Sec. 312.   Sec. 57, Chap. 7, of the chancery practice act of New Jersey provides that neither the filing of a bill in chancery, nor any proceeding taken thereon prior to final decree in the case, shall be deemed constructive notice of the pendency of the suit to any bona fide purchaser or mortgagee of lands sought to be affected by such suit, until the complainant in the bill, or his solicitor, shall have first filed a written notice of lis pendens in the office of the clerk of the Court of Common Pleas in the county where the land is situated, and that such notice shall state the title of the cause, the general object of the suit and a description of the lands, with a provision that the act shall not be construed to apply to any bill filed for the satisfaction or foreclosure of any duly registered mortgage.(1)

North Carolina statute.

Sec. 313.   The lis pendens statute in force in

the land, as near as may be, and the name of the person whose estate therein is intended to be affected by the action, suit, attachment or proceedings, shall be filed with the clerk of the County Court of the county in which the land is situated. The clerk of every such County Court shall without delay record the said memorandum in the deed book, and index the same in the name of both the parties." Warth's Amended Code W. Va., 1884, Chap. 139, Sec. 13.

(1) The New Jersey statute reads: "That neither the filing of a bill in chancery, nor any proceedings had or to be had thereon, before a final decree, shall be deemed or taken to be constructive notice to any bona fide purchaser or mortgagee of any lands or real estate to be affected thereby, until the complainant in such bill, or his solicitor, shall have first filed in the office of the clerk of the Court of Common Pleas of the county in which such lands or real estate lie, a written notice of the pendency of such suit, setting forth the title of the cause and the general object thereof, together with a description of the lands or real estate to be affected thereby; *provided*, that nothing in this section contained shall be construed or taken, to apply to any bill filed or to be filed for the satisfaction or foreclosure of any duly registered mortgage." R. S. N. J. 1877, Chancery Pr. Sec. 57.

North Carolina, as section 229 of the civil code, provides that in actions affecting the title to lands the plaintiff at the time of filing complaint, or at any time afterwards, or whenever a warrant of attachment shall be issued or afterwards, or the defendant, when he seeks to set up an affirmative cause of action and demands relief thereon, may file with the county clerk of the county in which the property is situated a notice of lis pendens, which shall state the names of the parties, the object of the suit and the description of the property sought to be affected, and, in case the suit shall be for the foreclosure of a mortgage, that the notice of lis pendens must be filed twenty days before decree and must contain the date of the mortgage, the parties thereto, and the time and place of its registration.

The statute further provides that from the time of filing such notice it shall be constructive notice to all purchasers and incumbrancers of the property affected; and that every person who shall receive any conveyance or incumbrance of or upon the property involved which shall be executed or registered subsequently to such filing shall be deemed subsequent purchasers and incumbrancers, and shall be bound by the proceedings in the case as though they were parties thereto, and that for the purposes of the act the suit shall be deemed to pend from the time of the filing of the notice, provided that the lis pendens shall be invalid unless it shall be followed within sixty days by the filing of the first publication of notice of summons or by an order therefor, or by personal service on the defendant.

The statute also invests the court with power to

annul and cancel notices of lis pendens where such suit shall be settled, discontinued or abated, and directs that in such cases a minute of the cancellation be indorsed by the clerk on the margin of the record, with a reference to the order of the court.(1)

(1) The North Carolina statute reads:

"Sec. 229. From the time of the service of the summons in a civil action, or the allowance of a provisional remedy, the court is deemed to have acquired jurisdiction, and to have control of all subsequent proceedings. A voluntary appearance of a defendant is equivalent to personal service of the summons upon him. In an action affecting the title to real property, the plaintiff, at the time of filing the complaint, or at any time afterwards, or whenever a warrant of attachment shall be issued, or at any time afterwards, the plaintiff, or a defendant when he sets up an affirmative cause of action in his answer and demands substantive relief, at the time of filing his answer, or at any time afterwards, if the same be intended to affect real estate, may file with the clerk of each county in which the property is situated, a notice of the pendency of the action, containing the names of the parties, the object of the action, and the description of the property in that county affected thereby; and if the action be for the foreclosure of a mortgage, such notice must be filed twenty days before judgment, and must contain the date of the mortgage, the parties thereto, and the time and place of registering the same. From the time of filing only shall the pendency of the action be constructive notice to a purchaser or incumbrancer of the property affected thereby; and every person whose conveyance or incumbrance is subsequently executed or subsequently registered shall be deemed a subsequent purchaser or incumbrancer, and shall be bound by all proceedings taken after the filing of such notice; to the same extent as if he were made a party to the action. For the purposes of this section an action shall be deemed to be pending from the time of filing such notice; *Provided*, that such notice shall be of no avail unless it shall be followed by the first publication of notice of the summons or by an order therefor, or by the personal service on the defendant within sixty days after such filing. And the court in which the said action was commenced may, in its discretion, at any time after the action shall be settled, discontinued or abated, on application of any person aggrieved, and on any good cause shown, and on such notice as shall be directed or approved by the court, order the notice authorized by this section to be cancelled of record by the clerk of any county in whose office the same may have been filed or recorded; and such cancellation shall be made by an indorsement to that effect on the margin of the record,

Dakota statute.

SEC. 314.   Section 101, chapter 9, of the statute of the Territory of Dakota provides that, in actions affecting title to lands, the plaintiff at the time of filing complaint or procuring a warrant of attachment or afterwards, or a defendant setting up an affirmative cause of action, may severally at the time of filing their respective pleadings file with the register of deeds of any county where the land sought to be affected is located, a notice of lis pendens, naming the parties, the object of the suit, and the description of the property.

The statute provides that if the action be for the foreclosure of a mortgage, no such notice need be filed.

It also declares that the notice of lis pendens from the time of its filing shall be constructive notice to purchasers or incumbrancers of the property affected, and that all persons who shall receive a conveyance or an incumbrance which shall be executed or recorded subsequent to such filing shall be deemed subsequent purchasers or incumbrancers and bound by the proceedings in the case which may be taken after the filing of such notice the same as if they were parties to the action.

The statute requires that the lis pendens shall become invalid unless followed by a first publication of summons or an order therefor, or by personal service on the defendant within sixty days after such filing.

It also gives power to the court to cancel and annul all notices of lis pendens upon settlement, discontinuance, or abatement of the cause, and directs the

which shall refer to the order, and for which the clerk shall be entitled to a fee of twenty-five cents."   1

N. C., Civ. Code of 1883, Ch. X, Sec. 227.

clerk in such case to make proper entry and reference to the order on the margin of the proper records.(1)

Virginia statute.

Sec. 315.   Section 5 of chapter 182 of the statutes of the State of Virginia provides that no lis pendens or attachment against the estate of a non-resident shall

(1) The Dakota Statute, Code of Civil Procedure, Chapter IX, Section 101, reads:

"Sec. 101. In an action affecting the title to real property, the plaintiff, at the time of filing the complaint, or at any time afterwards, or whenever a warrant of attachment of property shall be issued, or at any time afterwards, the plaintiff, or a defendant when he sets up an affirmative cause of action in his answer, and demands substantive relief, at the time of filing his answer or at any time afterwards, if the same be intended to affect real property, may file with the register of deeds of each county in which the real property is situated, a notice of the pendency of the action, containing the names of the parties, the object of the action, and the description of the real property in that county affected thereby; but if the action be for the foreclosure of a mortgage, no such notice need be filed. From the time of filing only shall the pendency of the action be constructive notice to a purchaser or incumbrancer of the property affected thereby; and every person whose conveyance or incumbrance is subsequently executed, or subsequently recorded, shall be deemed a subsequent purchaser or incumbrancer, and shall be bound by all proceedings taken after the filing of such notice to the same extent as if he were a party to the action For the purpose of this section an action shall be deemed to be pending from the time of filing such notice; *Provided, however,* that such notice shall be of no avail unless it shall be followed by the first publication of the summons or an order therefor, or by the personal service thereof on a defendant within sixty days after such filing. And the court in which the said action was commenced, may, in its discretion, at any time after the action shall be settled, discontinued, or abated, as is provided in section number eighty-five, on application of any person aggrieved, and on any good cause shown, and on such notice as shall be directed or approved by the court, order the notice authorized by this section to be cancelled of record by the register of deeds of any county in whose office the same may have been filed or recorded; and such cancellation shall be made by an indorsement to that effect on the margin of the record, which shall refer to the order, and for which the register of deeds shall be entitled to a fee of twenty-five cents." Vol. 1, Levises' Dakota Code, 1883, Ch. 9, Sec. 101.

be effective without actual notice, until a memorandum shall be left with the county clerk, or in case of a corporation with the clerk of such corporation in which the land is situate, which memorandum shall state the title of the cause, its general object, the court in which it is pending, a description of the lands, and the name of the person whose estate is intended to be affected thereby.

The act makes it the duty of such clerk to forthwith record the memorandum in a " deed book," and index the same in the name of the person whose lands are affected.

It will be perceived that this legislation differs from that in other States, in that it only relates to lands or property belonging to non-residents of the State.(1)

Application of general principles.

SEC. 316.   It will be seen from this review that the general principles and application of the common law doctrine of lis pendens have more or less practical use in those States where the legislatures have passed lis pendens statutes. These States chiefly provide the method in which the lis pendens may be brought into force. They provide also when it shall commence. Where, however, in pursuance of these statutes valid

(1) The Virginia statute, Chap. 182, Sec. 5, Code of 1873:

"No lis pendens or attachment against the estate of a non-resident shall bind or affect a purchaser of real estate, without actual notice thereof, unless and until a memorandum setting forth the title of the cause, the general object thereof, the court in which it is pending, a description of the land, and the name of the person whose estate is intended to be affected thereby shall be left with the clerk of the court of the county or corporation in which the land is situate, who shall forthwith record the said memorandum in the deed book, and index the same by the name of the person aforesaid." Code of Va., 1873, Chap. 182, Sec. 5.

lis pendens is created, its application in the trial of causes, in the disposition of the res litigiosa, is precisely the same in those States where lis pendens statutes exist, as where the principles of lis pendens are applied in accordance with the rules of the common law and where no such statutes are in force.

Comparison of lis pendens statutes.

SEC. 317. It will thus be seen by a comparison of the lis pendens statutes of the various States where they have been adopted, and with the English statute of 2nd and 3rd Victoria, that with few exceptions they are essentially the same in provision. The controlling features of them all are; first, that the notice must be filed or recorded in some public office; second, that the notice must contain the names of the parties, the title to the suit, and a description of the property involved in litigation; and third, that after the filing or recording of the notice in this manner, the suit shall become a lis pendens.

In some of these statutes the last element is explicitly declared, while in others it is left as a legal inference, or arises from the negative declaration that the lis pendens shall not become effective unless the other provisions of the law are complied with. But this being the express object of this class of legislation, no other construction can be placed upon these statutes than that the filing of the notice of lis pendens creates constructive notice of the proceedings in the suit, in accordance with these statutes.

In some of the States the scope of the lis pendens statutes is greater, and in others less. Thus in the State of Virginia the statute is only intended to apply to the property of non-residents, while in most of the other States it applies as well between residents of the same States.(1)

The common law principles of lis pendens remain in force even in those States where lis pendens statutes have been enacted, except so far as the subject has been controlled by express legislation. The common law is abrogated only so far as these statutes have expressly changed it.

We shall discuss in a subsequent chapter the constructions which the Supreme Courts of the different States, whose legislatures have adopted lis pendens statutes, have placed upon them.

There are some of the other States where statutory law has more or less modified the common law on this subject.

(1.) Chap. XV. *post.*

CHAPTER XV.

CONSTRUCTION OF LIS PENDENS STATUTES BY THE COURTS.

Lis pendens commences from time of filing or recording notice.

SEC. 318. There are numerous decisions in those States where lis pendens statutes are in force, to the effect that upon the filing or recording, as the law may require, of a notice of lis pendens, the filing of the pleadings in the case, and service of the subpœna, cease to have effect as a lis pendens, either as to the time of commencement or scope of it.

The common law governing the case up to the time of the passage of the lis pendens act is abrogated, so far as relates to the commencement and scope of lis pendens, by the adoption of these statutes.

The rule otherwise existing that the lis pendens shall commence from the time of the filing of the bill and service of the subpœna, is set aside by the direct declaration of the legislature that it shall commence from the time of the filing or recording, as the case may be, of the notice.

That other rule existing where these statutes are not in force, namely, that the scope of the lis pendens shall be governed by the allegations in the bill or other pleading, is abrogated by the legislative declaration that the notice shall specify the object of the litigation and the property upon which it is to operate. Under the lis pendens acts the res litigiosa is brought into efficiency and force by the filing or recording of the notice, provided proper jurisdiction be obtained in the case, so that, as a rule under these statutes, it commences with the filing or recording of the notice, and its scope is measured by the terms of the notice itself.(1)

(1) Ettonborough v. Bishop, 11 Green, 263; Beekman v. Montgomery, 1 McCarter, 107; Head v. Fordyce, 17 Cal. 151; Richardson et al. v. White et al., 18 Cal. 106; Ault v. Gassaway, 18 Cal. 205; Gregory v. Haynes, 13 Cal. 594; Gregory v. Haynes, 21 Cal. 446; Calderwood v. Tevis et al., 23 Cal 337; Haynes v. Calderwood, et al., 23 Cal. 409; Hurlbutt v. Baleenop, 27 Cal. 50; Horn v. Jones, 28 Cal. 204; Conkey v. Dike, 17 Minn. 462. Lebanon Savings Bank v. Hollenbeck et al., 29 Minn. 322; Heim et al. v. Ellis, 49 Mich. 241; Arnold et al. v. Casner et al., 22 W. Va. 444; Philips et als. v. Williams, 5 Gratt. 259; Cirode v. Buchanan, 22 Gratt. 220; Newton v. Marshall et al., 62 Wis. 8; Warner v. Trow et al., 36 Wis. 196; Zane v. Fink et al., 18 W. Va. 693; Kellogg et al. v. Fancher et al., 23 Wis. 28.

Lis pendens in ejectment.

SEC. 319. In those States where lis pendens statutes are in force, unless the lis pendens acts specially include the action of ejectment, the courts have held that a notice of lis pendens filed in ejectment cases will have no effect, but that the lis pendens acts do not apply to actions of ejectment, but are intended to apply only to proceedings in chancery, the purpose of which is to turn equitable estates into legal ones, or to enforce liens upon legal estates.(1)

The effect of actual notice.

SEC. 320. In the States where notices of lis pendens may be filed, actual notice will operate to subject the party to the rule lis pendens, although no notice of lis pendens may be filed under the statute.

The object under the various statutes of the filing or recording of notices of lis pendens is to afford constructive notice of the pendency of the action.

Actual notice ought certainly to be as effectual as constructive notice under these statutes. No good reason can be perceived why a party, taking an interest in property involved in the suit with notice of the action and that the property is involved, should not be bound by the judgment, although no notice of lis pendens be filed.(2)

(1) People v. Wilson, 26 Cal. 127; Long et al. v. Neville, et al., 29 Cal. 131; Sheridan v. Andrews, 3 Lans. 133; Sherman v. Bemis, etc., impl., 58 Wis. 344.

White v. Perry, 14 W. Va. 66, holds that notice of lis pendens filed in a common law case does not constitute a lis pendens.

It was held in Thompson v. Merrick, 4 Hun. 164, that a notice of lis pendens filed in an ejectment suit was of no force or effect, unless the parties sought to be affected thereby acquired such interest or title from a party to the suit.

Montgomery v. Byers et al.,21 Cal. 108; Baker v. Pierson, 5 Mich. 456.

(2) Sharp v. Lumley, 34 Cal. 615; Sampson v. Ohleyr, 22 Cal. 201.

Where no notice of lis pendens is filed.

SEC. 321.   In those States where lis pendens statutes have been adopted, in case the notice of lis pendens is not filed in suits or proceedings contemplated by the statutes, persons having no actual notice of the suits will not be bound by lis pendens.

The lis pendens acts limit the method of creating the lis pendens,—they abrogate the common law upon the subject, and if the statutory mode be not followed, there can be no lis pendens as to third parties.(1)

In condemnation proceedings.

SEC. 322.   Where lis pendens statutes exist, notice of lis pendens must be filed in all proceedings to condemn lands, unless the party have actual notice of the

(1) Bensley *v.* The Mountain Lake Water Co., 13 Cal. 307; Corwin *v.* Bensley, 43 Cal. 263; Jorgenson et al. *v.* Minneapolis & St. Louis R'y Co., 25 Minn. 206; Arnold *v.* Casner, 22 W. Va. 459; Burroughs *v.* Reiger et al., 12 How. Pr. R. 171; Tate *v.* Jordan, 3 Abb. Pr. R. 392.

That the filing of notice is necessary in States where lis pendens statutes are in force, see also Todd, etc., *v.* Outlaw, 79 N. C. 235; Coot on Morts. 383, and Adams's Eq. 157.

In the case of Abadie *v.* Lobero, 36 Cal. 391, which was a suit to foreclose a mortgage, there was no notice of lis pendens filed under the statute. There was a default, and between the time of the default and the entry of the judgment the defendant conveyed the property involved in the mortgage.

It was held, *first*, that if the purchase was made without notice the purchaser was not bound by the judgment, even if a final judgment gives constructive notice to parties dealing with the subject matter of the suit; *second*, that the action was pending from the time the court acquired jurisdiction until final judgment, but not thereafter; and *third*, that a purchaser from a grantee acquiring thereafter judgment, is in no worse condition than his grantor.

The reason of these conclusions is, that the adoption of the lis pendens statute abrogated the common law on the subject of lis pendens; that no notice of lis pendens being filed in the case, there was no lis pendens except as between the parties to the suit; that the rendition of the judgment put an end to the lis pendens as between the parties, and that therefore the purchaser after the judgment was in no sense bound by lis pendens.

suit or proceeding and unless there be some provision in the constitution of these State which will prevent the application of the provisions of the statute.

In the States of New York and California there are provisions in the constitutions of the States which compel the treatment of condemnation cases as "special" cases, and make the application of a general statute impossible. The courts of these States, however, hold that in such cases actual notice must be given.(1)

Proceedings to enforce tax liens.

SEC. 323. But, in proceedings to enforce the collection of taxes and tax liens, it is held that it is not necessary to file notices of lis pendens.

The assessment of lands for taxation, and the lien which it creates, are public matters of record of which all purchasers are bound to take notice, and when a purchaser buys land which is subject to an existing lien for taxes, he must see to it at his peril that the taxes are paid, and if he neglects this duty, he takes the hazard of the judgment against the land, the lien of which, by operation of law and by relation, will ante-date his purchase.

Notice of lis pendens is therefore unnecessary in this class of actions.(2)

The object of filing notice of lis pendens.

SEC. 324. The object of filing notices of lis pendens is to enable parties to ascertain therefrom the persons and property affected by the bill and the general

(1) Bensley *v.* The Mountain Lake Water Co., 13 Cal. 319; Curran *v.* Shattuck, 24 Cal. 434; Visscher *v.* Hudson R. R. R. Co., 15 Barb. 37; Ex parte Ransom, etc., 3 Code R. 148; N. Y. Cent. R. R. Co. *v.* Marvin 1 Kern. (11 N. Y.) 276.

(2) Reeve *v.* Kennedy, 43 Cal. 654; Wright *v.* Walker, 30 Ark. 44; Bigelow on Equity, 189.

nature of the matter in controversy, leaving them to an examination of the court records to ascertain the details and particulars thereof.

Where such a notice of lis pendens is filed, parties, privies and intermeddlers are bound by what appears in the bill and proceedings thereunder.

While the contents of the bill or other pleading would not of itself constitute a lis pendens in States where express statutes on the subject have been passed, yet the court may construe the scope of the lis pendens in connection with the pleadings, but the notice itself gives shape to the nature of the notice of lis pendens and will limit and determine its character.(1)

Notice before bill filed.

SEC. 325. No effect can be given to the filing or recording of notices of lis pendens before the bill is filed.

The notice of lis pendens, so far as relates to its creation, takes the place of the service of the subpœna at common law. The rule of the common law requires that the bill shall be filed before lis pendens could commence. Although the subpœna were served before the bill was filed, yet there would be no lis pendens until the bill were afterwards filed, when lis pendens would commence from the filing of the bill.

And so where notices of lis pendens are filed while there is no bill on file, they have no effect as constructive notice to third parties until the bill is afterwards filed, when the efficiency of the lis pendens commences.(2)

(1) Alterange v. Christiansen, 48 Mich. 67.

(2) Houghton v. Mariner, 7 Wis. 251; Olson v. Paul, 56 Wis. 30;

Erroneous description in notice.

Sec. 326. Where a notice of lis pendens misdescribes the property sought to be affected by the suit and there has been a default taken, the default should be set aside upon application and a showing of the error.

Otherwise the judgment of the court would have no effect upon the property against which the proceeding was intended to have been brought.(1)

Surplusage in the notice.

Sec. 327. Where a notice of lis pendens is otherwise sufficient, unnecessary and redundant language, although erroneous in its statement of facts, will not vitiate the notice or affect the validity of the lis pendens.

The unnecessary language may be regarded as surplusage, and treated as expunged.

If enough shall remain after the rejection of such language to make the notice a substantial compliance with the statute, it will be held sufficient.(2)

Flood v. Isaac, 34 Wis. 423; Butler v. Tomlinson, 38 Barb. 642; Farmer's Loan, etc. v. Dickson, 17 How. Pr. 47i; Benson v. Sayre, 7 Abb. Pr. 472, note; Stern v. O'Connell, 35 N.Y. 104; Gordon et al. v. Tyler et al., 53 Mich. 629.

To the effect that notice of lis pendens in States where lis pendens statutes are in force, is inoperative unless a complaint or bill is filed, and does not become so until such filing, see also Weeks v. Tomes, 16 Hun. 349; Burroughs v. Reiger et al., 12 How. Pr. R. 171; Leitch v. Wells, 48 Barb. 637.

It is held in Gordon et al. v. Tyler et al., *ante*, 53 Mich. 637, that notices of lis pendens under the lis pendens statute of that State, and affidavits to bring in absentee defendants by publication, may be filed so soon as the bill in the suit to which they are incident is filed. It would seem that if filed before, they would be ineffective, at least until the bill were filed.

(1) Spraggon et al. v. McGreer, 14 Wis. 439.

(2) Drew v. Vequindre, 2 Doug. (Mich.) 93; Watson v. Wilcox, 39 Wis. 643.

Notice broader than attachment.

SEC. 328. In those States where proceedings by attachment are embraced within the scope of the lis pendens statutes, the filing of notices of lis pendens covering property other than that which is seized or to be seized by the attachment, will not be good or efficient, so far as relates to the additional property. As to such property it will be void.

The reason of this is manifest. The final judgment can be no broader than the attachment writ and pleadings in the case, and no efficiency or force could be given to the judgment as to the additional property contained in the notice. Besides, if such a practice were allowed, it would greatly embarrass the handling of property by tying it up pending litigation, without any beneficial results.(1)

In another case it was held that a notice of lis pendens under the lis pendens statute of New York, in an attachment case, was without effect, and that an action by attachment did not fall within the purview of the lis pendens statute of that State.

The attachment itself creates the lien from the time it is levied, and the lien by lis pendens was not necessary for the debt involved in the attachment.(2)

Actions not embraced in statute.

SEC. 329. The filing or recording of a notice of lis pendens in an action not embraced in or contemplated by the statute creates no lis pendens. The purpose of lis pendens statutes is to restrict, and not to enlarge, the operation of the common law rule of lis pendens.

(1) Fitzgerald v. Blake, 42 Barb. 513.

(2) Burkhardt v. Sandford et al., 7 How. Pr. R. 329.

If, therefore, there would be no lis pendens in any particular action at common law, there can be none by reason of the filing or recording of a notice of lis pendens under lis pendens statutes.(1)

Loss or destruction of the notice.

SEC. 330. The loss or destruction of the notice of lis pendens after it has been filed, or of its record after it has been recorded, will not affect the efficiency of the lis pendens. if the statute has been complied with.

In contemplation of law the notice or its record, as the case may be, will be considered in force, although it may not be physically in existence.

The same rule will apply in such cases as applies in the loss or destruction of the record of deeds and other instruments legally admitted to record, where the public records have been destroyed. The courts have always given efficiency to such records after such destruction as constructive notice of their contents, although they had ceased to be physically in existence.(2)

When suit and cross-suit treated as one.

SEC. 331. With respect to the filing of notices of lis pendens, the suit and cross-suit will be regarded as one cause, and where the statute in respect to the filing notice of lis pendens has been complied with on the part of the complainant, but has not been complied with on the part of one of several defendants, by their filing notice in the cross-claim, lis pendens is created as against the co-defendants in favor of the

(1) White v. Perry, 14 W. Va. 66; Harmon v. Byram's Admr. et al., 11 W. Va. 521; Styvesant v. Hone et al., 1 Sandf. Ch. 427.

(2) Hiem et al. v. Ellis, 49 Mich. 243; Boyd v. Weil et als., 11 Wis. 60.

one whose cross-claim was intended to be a lis pendens.

That is to say, a lis pendens will exist as between all the parties to the suit. It might be held otherwise as to third parties having no knowledge of the cross-claim.(1)

No power to strike notice from files.

SEC. 332. Where the legislature has prescribed the substance and manner of the filing or recording of lis pendens notices, and the provisions of the statute have been complied with, the parties filing such notices acquire rights thereby over which the courts have no power.

It is therefore beyond the power of the courts to strike from the files lis pendens notices which were filed under the statute and in conformity with its terms, and that even in cases where an injunction has been issued and subsequently dissolved.

Nor can the court modify or change the character of the statutory rights secured by the notice.(2)

As to unrecorded mortgages.

SEC. 333. After the filing of a notice of lis pendens involving real estate, the holder of an unrecorded mortgage can acquire no rights as against the lis pendens by recording his mortgage, unless the party filing the notice prior to such filing had knowledge of the mortgage.

So where a suit was commenced and a notice of lis pendens had been filed involving real estate, and one holding a mortgage on the same property made by a party to the suit subsequently recorded it, and during

---

(1) S. C. Hall Lumber Co. v. Gastin et al., 54 Mich. 634.

(2) Pratt v. Hoagg, 12 How. Pr. 215; Mills v. Bliss, 55 N. Y. 139.

the pendency of the suit caused a sale to be made on his mortgage, it was held that a purchaser under the mortgage foreclosure during the progress of the suit was barred by its lis pendens, and acquired no rights by the purchase.(1)

Proof of filing notice, etc.

SEC. 334. Although it is proper that it should appear in the record that proof was made in the trial court that a notice of lis pendens was filed, yet an appellate court will not hold the judgment or decree void or reverse it because the record fails to show that such proof was made. It is irregular, but not void.

The usual presumption in such cases will be entertained, where the trial court is a court of general jurisdiction, in the absence of a showing to the contrary, that the proof was in fact made.(2)

Besides, proof of the filing of notices of lis pendens is no part of the record, and unless made so by a bill of exceptions or certificate of evidence, such proof is not required to be filed.

But, on the other hand, when the decree recites it, the fact cannot be contradicted.(3) The record as to that fact will be treated as absolute verity.

Proof and correction of record of notice.

SEC. 335. Proof of the filing of notice of lis pendens or a correction of the record of it may be made

(1) Ostrom v. McCann, 21 How. Pr. R. 431.

(2) Boyd v. Weil et als., 11 Wis. 66; Manning v. McClurg et al., 14 Wis. 350; Potter v. Rowland, 8 N. Y. 448; Best v. Davis, 18 Wis. 386; Weber v. Fowler, 11 How.Pr.R.458; The Farmers' & Millers' Bank of Milwaukee v. Eldred, etc., 20 Wis. 196; Gage v. McLaughlin et al., 34 Wis. 551; Webb v. Meloy et al., 32 Wis. 319.

(3) Mitchell v. Robinson, etc., 52 Wis. 155; Catlin v. Pedrick et al., 17 Wis. 89.

at any time before judgment, and as against a purchaser at a judicial sale, if no liens have intervened, the notice lis pendens may be filed nunc pro tunc.

The purchaser at the judicial sale purchases upon the credit of the record of the proceeding and it is the duty of the court and the parties, third persons having acquired no rights pending the suit, to make his title good. In such cases there is no question arising as to third parties; it is simply in respect to the duty of the complainant or person enforcing such claim against the property and the court, while yet having jurisdiction to make the buyer a good title. Public policy requires this.

In such case a purchaser will not be compelled to take his deed and pay his money until the law has been complied with, with respect to the filing or recording of the notice of lis pendens.(1)

Amendment of bill and notice.

SEC. 336. Where a bill to foreclose a mortgage and a notice of lis pendens under the statute were filed and afterwards the bill was amended by bringing in new parties defendant, but no amended notice of lis pendens was filed, it was held that the complainant could not proceed to decree unless he filed an amended notice of lis pendens.

In such case the lis pendens would not commence as to the new defendants until the amended notice was filed.(2)

What interest in real estate necessary.

SEC. 337. Where the question arose under a lis pen-

---

(1) Sage v. McLaughlin et al., 34 Wis. 557; Waring v. Waring, 7 Abb. Pr. 472.

(2) Clark v. Havens, Clark's Ch. R. 563; Curtis et al. v. Hitchcock, 10 Paige, 399.

dens statute as to what interest was embraced under the statute, which provides that the action in which a notice of lis pendens may be filed shall relate to real estate, it was held that any interest in real estate will authorize the filing of the notice, and that a leasehold estate or tenancy is such an interest affecting lands as will give validity to a notice of lis pendens filed in a case involving such an interest.

So also the question arose where a petition was filed in New York, under the lis pendens act of that State, by a tenant in common against his co-tenants, the object of which was to procure a sale of premises of which they were tenants in common and for an accounting of rents and profits arising from the use of the premises prior to the time of the filing of the petition, and thereafter a notice of lis pendens was filed in the case under the statute.

The question was, whether that was a case relating to real estate within the meaning of the New York statute where a notice of lis pendens would be efficient, and it was held that it was.

A bill for the partition of real estate clearly relates to real estate within the meaning of the lis pendens act.(1)

Notice of no effect upon independent holders.

SEC. 338. Under the lis pendens statutes the rule at common law is not changed that the holder of a title independent of and not under the parties to a suit are not affected by the notice.

And so it is held that notice of lis pendens under a lis pendens statute cannot be properly filed against

(1) Ruck v. Lange, 10 Hun. 303;   Prac. R. 281.
Kunz v. Bachman, N. Y. Civ.

grantees or incumbrancers who were such prior to the commencement of the suit and who were not parties to it.(1)

Statute of North Carolina construed.

SEC. 339.   It is said by the Supreme Court of North Carolina, in Todd et al. *v.* Outlaw, that in order to avail a complainant and create a valid lis pendens, the pleadings must specifically set out and claim the benefit of the lis pendens.

It is intimated also in that case that the same court in Badger et al. *v.* Daniel et al., 77 N. C. 251, and Rollins *v.* Henry, 78 N. C. 342, had construed the North Carolina lis pendens act not to apply within the county where the lands were situate and the suit was brought, but only to apply to foreign counties.(2)

Void description in notice of lis pendens.

SEC. 340.   Although the law is that where there is enough in the description contained in a notice of lis pendens to make it good notwithstanding portions which are erroneous and may be treated as surplusage, yet, where the description is of other lands, although by mistake, than those which were intended, the notice of lis pendens will be invalid.

In such cases the same rule will apply to a notice of lis pendens filed or recorded under lis pendens statutes which applies to the record of deeds and other instruments lawfully admissible to record.

In order to constitute such a record notice, there must be enough contained in the description, either to make out a complete legal description or to indicate where such a description may be found.

(1) People, etc., *v.* Connolly, 8 Abb. Pr. R. 131.

(2) Todd et al. *v.* Outlaw, 79 N. C. 285.

Where the land described is another and distinct piece of property, it cannot be treated either as notice of lis pendens or as binding upon property not described in it.(1)

When lis pendens not docketed.

SEC. 341. In a case in Virginia, where a creditor's bill was filed against the heirs and administrators of an estate to subject the estate to the payment of certain debts, and notice of lis pendens had not been docketed as was required by the statute of that State, after the parties were brought into court, and while the case was in progress, one of the heirs sold his interest in the estate to a bona fide purchaser without actual notice of the pendency of the suit.

It was held that the purchaser was not a pendente lite purchaser, and that the lis pendens not having been docketed was not binding upon him.(2)

Effect of notice of lis pendens.

SEC. 342. In a State where a lis pendens statute is in force, if a complainant shall file his notice of lis pendens in a foreclosure case prior to the record of a deed from the mortgagor to a grantee against whom there were judgment liens, the complainant will be protected in his mortgage lien against the judgment, although the mortgage be defective and the bill seek in addition to the foreclosure to cure the defects of the mortgage.

In a case in Minnesota, brought to reform and foreclose a defective mortgage, the complainant filed with his bill a notice of lis pendens, and subsequently a

(1) Rodgers *v.* Kavanaugh et al., 24 Ill. 583; Nelson *v.* Wade, 21 Iowa, 49; Sanger *v.* Craigne, 10 Vt. 555.

(2) Easley et al. *v.* Barkesdale et als., 75 Va. 274.

deed from the mortgagors to a grantee, against whom judgments had been recovered which would be a lien upon lands of such grantee, and the deed was placed of record.

It was held in that case that the lis pendens of the suit would protect the complainant and his mortgage lien as against the lien of the judgments against the grantee of the mortgagors.(1)

The recording acts of that State provided, as they do in most of the States, that deeds shall be constructive notice only from and after recording.(2)

(1) Lebanon Sav. Bk. *r*. Hollenbeck et als., 29 Minn. 322.

(2) General Statute of Minn., 1878, C. 40, Sec. 21.

CHAPTER XVI.

LIS PENDENS AS A DEFENSE.

The plea in abatement, prior action pending.

Sec. 343.   The pendency of a prior action between the same parties and in the same cause may be plead in abatement in a subsequent suit. This is the general rule.

There are numerous exceptions to the rule, which

will be noticed hereafter. In order that the defense may prevail, it must be shown by the pleadings and the proof that the prior action is still pending at the time the defense is interposed.(1)

(1) Moore et al. *v.* Kessler, 59 Ind. 153; Tracy *v.* Reed, 4 Blackf. 56; Bryan *v.* Alfred, 1 Tex. Ct. of App. Sec. 85, Civ. Cas.; Toland *v.* Ticknor, 3 Rawle, 320; Horn *v.* Jones et al., 28 Cal. 194; Loyd *v.* Reynolds et als., 29 Ind. 299; Dawson *v.* Vaughn, 42 Ind. 395.

It was decided in the Earl of Newbury *v.* Wren, 1 Vern. 219, that on account of the superior and more complete jurisdiction of the latter court, the pendency of a bill in Exchequer to foreclose can not be plead in defense of a bill to redeem from the mortgage afterwards filed in the court of chancery.

This decision was placed upon the ground that the two courts were not of concurrent jurisdiction, the the Court of Exchequer being a private court, whose proper jurisdiction concerned only the king's revenue and the king's officers.

In the case of the People *v.* Northern Railroad Co. et al., 53 Barbour, 98, it was held that where parties to the two suits were not the same, and it does not appear that the entire relief sought in the one case can be awarded in the other, a motion to stay one of the suits will not be entertained. It is said, moreover, that such a motion is addressed to the discretion of the court and is not assignable for error.

A railroad was leased to a railroad company. The lessors declared the lease forfeited and took possession of the road. The lessee filed a bill to restrain the lessors from interfering with them in the use of the road. The lessors then filed a bill and enjoined the lessees from using the road, to which bill the lessees filed a cross-bill alleging breaches of the lease on the part of the lessors, and prayed to be reinstated in the possession of the road. Answers were filed to both bills.

The lessors afterwards brought an ejectment for the recovery of the possession of the road on the ground of the forfeiture of the lease.

A plea in abatement was filed to this latter suit, and it was held that pending the equity suit the lessors could not institute another proceeding involving the same question. The plea set up the facts above stated and was held to be good.

Pittsburg & Cornellsville R. R. Co. *v.* Mt. Pleas. & Br. F. R. R. Co., 76 Penn. St. 481.

Where one of the two suits is to foreclose a mortgage securing notes evidencing the debt, and the other is brought upon the notes secured by the mortgage, the pendency of the foreclosure case can not be plead in abatement of the suit on the notes.

Taylor *v.* Hill, 21 La. An. 639.

Morgan *v.* Tamiet, 21 La. An. 266, holds that both suits must be for the same object.

Where the object of the prior suit

It may also be pleaded in bar.(1)

Defense of prior action must be in limine litis.

SEC. 344. The defense of a prior action pending between the same parties, for the same cause and within the same State, must be made in limine litis.

This is specially the case where the defense is set up by plea in abatement. This class of defenses is regarded as dilatory, and is required to be made at the very threshold of the case.(2)

was to recover possession of property, and that of the junior suit was to foreclose a mortgage upon it, the suits are not for the same cause of action, and a plea of prior action pending is not good.

Coles v. Yorks, 31 Minn. 215; Bolton v. Landers, 27 Cal. 104; State of Wis. v. Tonnius, 28 Minn. 175.

In the case of Rochereau & Co. v. Lewis et al., 26 La. An. 581, where one of the suits was brought to recover from the defendants the amount of notes given for rent under a lease, and the other to cancel these same notes and the lease under which they were given, it was held that the defense was good.

In Killen v. Compton et al., 57 Ga. 63, it is held that the defense of a prior action can not be made by motion. Kennon v. Petty, 59 Ga. 175.

(1) 1 Brac. At. 24; Tit. Abatement. For form of plea see 1 Chit. on Pl. 443; also Port Section 85, note; see also, as to when the plea in bar may be interposed, Rogers v. Holt, Phil. Eq. 110; Story's Eq. Pl. Sec. 791; Mitford's Eq. Pl. (by Jeremy) p. 237; see also Gould on Pl., Chap. 5, Secs. 122 and 131.

The case of Watson et al. v. Jones et al., 11 Am. Law Reg. 430, is an authority to the effect that where the defense of a former action pending is set up to defeat a junior action, the case must be the same, the parties the same, or at least such as represent the same interest, there must be the same rights asserted and the same relief prayed for; and this relief must be founded upon the same facts and title or the essential basis of the relief must be the same.

But where, while the cause of action was originally the same, one suit was being prosecuted by a receiver and was under court control, and the other suit in the name of the party to whom the obligation ran or the indebtedness was due, it was held that the defense would not avail.

(2) White v. Gleason, 15 La. An. 479.

In Merritt v. Bagwell, 70 Ga. 579, it is held that a plea in abatement of a former suit must be taken advantage of at the first term to which the writ is returnable. See also Garrigan v. Carter, 51 Ga. 232; Kennon v. Petty, 59 Ga. 175.

Where want of jurisdiction.

SEC. 345. The defense of prior action pending, however, cannot be sustained where the court in the first action has no jurisdiction by reason of the amount claimed, or for want of any other material jurisdictional fact.

Nor can the defense of a prior lis pendens prevail where the suit is in attachment, unless it is averred in the pleadings and shown in the proofs, that the defendant has been personally served, or has entered his appearance so that a judgment in personam may be rendered against him. (1)

Suits not for the same cause.

SEC. 346. Proceedings had under insolvent acts, in pursuance of general assignments for the benefit of creditors, in the probate or other courts having jurisdiction in such matters, in which a creditor has filed claims to be administered upon in such proceedings, are not the same as suits brought to recover specific property drawn into the estate by such assignments, or its value.

In the former cases the claimant seeks to recover the pro rata amount, or other distributive share which may be allotted to him in pursuance of law upon settlement of the estate under the assignment; in the latter case the suit is for a specific thing or a certain amount.

Hence it has been decided that the former proceeding cannot be plead in abatement of a suit of the latter character. They are not brought for the same thing. (2)

(1) Phillips *v.* Quick, 68 Ill. 325.   (2) Lenthold *v.* Young, 32 Minn. 123

Defense of another action pending, what required.

SEC. 347. The defense of another action pending must show that the two actions are between the same parties and involve the same subject matter, and that the former action is still pending in the same State.(1)

The pendency of a prior suit in one State cannot be plead in abatement of a suit between the same parties for the same cause in a court of another State.

As between themselves the States of the Union, though integral parts of the same national sovereignty, are foreign to and independent of each other.

For it is said that a foreign judgment depending on foreign law might be unjust and could not be enforced beyond the jurisdiction; and second, that the remedy may be more effectual in one State than in another.(2)

Suit pending in foreign State.

SEC. 348. In England the pendency of a prior suit in a foreign State was held to be no bar to the second action, and Scotland, Ireland, and other dependencies, were held to be foreign States.(3)

(1) Vance v. Olinger, 27 Cal. 358; O'Connor v. Blake, 29 Cal. 314; Mann v. Rogers, 35 Cal. 315; Larco v. Clements, 36 Cal. 134; Certain Logs of Mahogany, 2 Sumn. C. C. 593; Wadleigh v. Veazie, 3 Sumn. C. C. 165; Moore v. Kessler, 59 Ind. 153.

(2) Davis v. Morton, Galt & Co., 4 Bush. 444; Salmon v. Wootten et als., 9 Dana, 424; Browne et al. v. Joy, 9 Johns. 221; Walsh ·v. Durkin, 12 Johns. 100; 2 Parsons on Cont., 4th Ed. 232; Story's Conflict of Laws, Sec. 610, (note); Conrad, Trustee, v. Buck et al., 21 W. Va. 396; Danl. Ch. Pr. 633; Allen et al. v. Watt, 69 Ill. 655; Cole v. Flitcraft, 47 Md. 312; Phosphate Sewage Co. v. Mollison, 1 App. Mo. Cas. 780.

(3) White v. Whitman, 1 Curtis, 499. In the case of Smith et al. v. Lathrop et al., 3 Am. Law Reg. 107, or 44 Penn. St., p. 326, may be found an extended discussion upon the question as to whether the several States of the Union are foreign States with respect to the pendency of causes in the State Courts, and as to whether a plea of a prior action pending in another State of the Union is a good plea.

As regards each other, the States of the Union are held to be foreign States. The reason for the rule is well expressed in White *v*. Whitman, where Judge Curtis, in delivering the opinion of the court, says: "Though the constitution and laws of the United States require that the judgments rendered in one State shall receive full faith and credit in another, yet in respect to all proceedings prior to judgment, the courts of different States acting under different sovereignties must be considered as so far foreign to each other that a remedy sought by judicial proceedings under one can not be treated as a mere and simple repetition of a remedy sought under another.

There may be real advantages to be gained in respect to the property on which an execution may be levied, or otherwise, by resorting to an action in an-

See also, Bayley *v*. Edwards, 3 Swan.703; Cox *v*. Mitchell,7 Com. B. (N. S.) 55; Scott *v*. Lord Seymour, 31 L. J. & Ex.461; Cowan *v*.Braidwood, 1 Man. & Gr. 382; Russell *v*. Smith, 7 Mees. & W. 810; Sheehy *v*. Life Ass. Co., 3 Com. B. (N. S.) 597; Henley *v*. Soper, 8 Barn. & Cr. 16; 5 H. Lord's cases, 431; Bk. of Australia *v*.Nias, 16 Ad. & Ellis, (N. S.) 717; Buckner *v*. Finley, 2 Peters, 586; Mahoney *v*. Ashlen, 2 Barn. & Ad.478; 22 E. C. L. R. 202; Browne et al. *v*. Joy, 9 Johns. 221; Walsh *v*. Durkin, 12 Johns. 99; Mitchell *v*. Bunce, 2 Paige, 606; Cook *v*. Litchfield, 5 Sand. 342; Williams *v*.Ayrault, 31 Barb. 364; Salmon *v*.Wootten, 9 Dana, 422; Hart *v*. Granger, 1 Conn. 154; McJilton *v*. Love, 13 Ill. 494; Goodale *v*. Marshall, 11 N. H. 99; White *v*. Whitman, 1 Curtis, 494; Lyman et al. *v*. Brown et al., 2 Curtis, C. C. 559; Hatch *v*. Spofford, 22 Conn. 485; Toland *v*. Ticknor, 3 Rawle, 320; Lowry *v*. Hall, 2 W. & S. 133; Irvine *v*. Lumberman's Bk., 2 W. & S. 208; Ralph *v*. Brown, 3 W. & S. 399; McGilvray et al. *v*. Avery, 30 Vt. 538; Maule et al. *v*. Murray et al., 7 Term R. 278; Imlay *v*. Ellfsen, 2 East. 457; Ostell *v*. Lepage, 10 Eng. L. & Eq. 255; De Gex & S. 95; Conrad, Trustee, *v*. Buck, 21 W. Va. 404; Allen et al. *v*. Watt, 69 Ill. 657; Ralph *v*. Brown, 3 W. & S. 399; Blanchard *v*. Stone, 16 Vt. 234; Newell *v*. Newton, 10 Pick. 470; Colt *v*. Partridge, 7 Met. 574; Warder *v*. Arrel, 2 Wash. (Va.) 359, tp. pg.; Hitchcock *v*. Aiken, 1 Caines, 460; Bartlett *v*. Knight, 1 Mass. 430; Duncan *v*. Course, 1 S. C. Const. R. (Mills) 46; 3 Kent. 93; Foster *v*.Vassall,3 Atk.587.

other State, and the same considerations are applicable to a second suit in a Circuit Court of the United States, while one is pending in the State courts."

In other words, in pursuing a defendant under one jurisdiction, there may be advantages which are not available in another, and the policy of the law seems to be to allow the plaintiff, in the exercise of due diligence in the prosecution of his claim, to select and continue in that jurisdiction where his advantages, from one reason or another, may be greater.

The policy of some States may be to favor defendants, of others plaintiffs, in judicial contests over litigated claims. We know, for example, that the young Western States, for the purpose probably of securing an increase of population, sometimes pass laws less oppressive to debtors than those in force in some of the older States of the Union.

If such a debtor should remove to a jurisdiction where he could not be pursued with the same efficiency as in the Eastern or Middle States, it might result in a great disadvantage, if, after having commenced a suit in a jurisdiction of greater efficiency in the collection of debts, the defendant might plead this suit in abatement of a remedy sought in the jurisdiction of his residence; and hence the rule seems well established, that where the suits are pending in different States the prior lis pendens can not be successfully maintained as a defense. Nor can a suit in attachment, pending in another State, be plead in abatement to a subsequent action in personam.(1)

(1) Lyman et al. *v.* Brown et al., 2 Curtis, 559, is a leading case upon the proposition that the States are foreign with respect to each other, and that a plea in abatement, where the cases are pending in different States, is not good.

For a similar reason, to-wit: the

State and Federal Courts.

SEC. 349.   The law is well settled that the pendency of a prior suit in a State court, although between the same parties and for the same cause of action, where the State court is not within the district of the Federal Court, is not a bar to a suit in a Circuit Court of the United States.(1)

superior jurisdiction and remedy in a court of chancery, it was said, in Howell v. Waldron, 2 Ch. Cas. 85: "Legatee infant sueth in a court ecclesiastical, and pending that suit sueth in chancery, the former suit pending being pleaded; the plea was disallowed, for there is no such security for the infant's advantage as here, and possibly not for interest if placed out, and for bringing in account here, etc."

In the case of Seevers v. Clement, 28 Md. 433, the case of White v. Whitman, 1 Curtis, 494 was approved and the court cites Wadleigh v. Veazie, 3 Sum. 166; O'Connor v. Blake, 29 Cal. 314; Lyman et al. v. Brown et al., 2 Curtis, 559; quotes from interveners Gibson in Lowry v. Hall, 2 W. & Serg. 133: "The pendency of a prior suit in a foreign country can not be pleaded in abatement of a suit for the same cause here, as it has been held that the States of the American Union stand in the relation of foreign States as regards this particular matter." See also, Smith et al. v. Lathrop et al., 44 Penn. State, 326; Hatch v. Spofford, 22 Conn. 485.

It was said that the only authority which seemed to favor the other side of this proposition was a case of Ex parte Balch, 3 McLean, U. S. C. C. 221; but it will be found upon

examination that in that case the two pending cases were both in Circuit Courts of the United States, and it is said that such courts are to be treated as in the same common country, and the jurisdiction being the same, the suits will not be treated as pending in foreign countries with respect to each other.

It was held in Hatch v. Spofford, 22 Conn. 484, that a plea that the plaintiff had brought a prior suit in the State of New York, he being, as well as defendant, a citizen of Connecticut, and defendant being served while temporarily there on business, the two suits being the same as to parties and subject matter, and the New York suit being still pending, was not a good plea.   Hart v. Granger, 1 Conn. 154.

Although a complainant may be prosecuting a chancery suit in another State for the purpose of enforcing payment of a debt due him out of property in that State, he may at the same time bring a suit of attachment, in a State other than the one where the first suit is pending.   The plea of prior suit pending will in such case be no bar.   Lockwood & Co. v. Nye et al., 2 Swan. 515.

(1) Stanton v. Embrey, 93 U. S.

The reasons for this rule are the same as those which have led to the establishment of the doctrine that a suit pending in another State or a foreign country is not a bar to a subsequent suit.(1)

Decree in first suit as to second.

SEC. 350. When a second suit is brought between the same parties and for the same cause, and the suit first brought proceeds to decree in favor of the complainant pending the second action, the defendant may insist upon the complainant's acquiescence in the decree, or the dismissal of the bill without prejudice.

In such a case Lord Hardwicke allowed a defendant to show that the question in the second case was litigated in the first.(2)

Plea of pending writ of error.

SEC. 351. So also a defendant may plead in abate-

(3 Otto), 548; Gordon v. Gilfoil, 99 U. S. (9 Otto), 168; Sharon v. Hill, 22 Fed. Rep. 28; Washburn & Moen Mfg. Co. et al. v. H. B. Scutt & Co., 22 Fed. Rep. 710.

In the case of Lloyd v. Reynolds et als., 29 Ind. 299, the facts were that one of the suits was pending in the United States Circuit Court for the District of Indiana, while the other was pending in a State court in the State of Indiana. The parties were not the same altogether, but upon application might be admitted as parties and allowed to intervene.

It was held that lis pendens was not available as a defense. See also Innes v. Lanning, 7 Paige Ch. 585.

While the pendency of an attachment suit in another State is no bar,

a judgment rendered in attachment might be. Williams v. Ayrault, 31 Barb. 364; Cook v. Litchfield, 5 Sandf. 330; Jackson v. Wilson, 9 Johns. 94.

(1) Sec. 348, ante.

(2) Shepherd v. Titley, 2 Atk. 354. In Bishop v. Bishop, 7 Robertson, (N. Y.) 197, while the junior action was pending in the trial court and the prior action in the Appellate Court, a motion was made in the trial court to stay the case until the decision in the prior action.

The motion was denied; the court holding that the proper remedy under the New York Code was a plea of another action pending.

See also Cummins v. Bennett, 8 Paige, 79; Burroughs v. Miller, 5 How. Pr. R. 51, and Hornfager v. Hornfager, 6 How. Pr. R. 279.

ment the pendency of a writ of error which operates as a supersedeas taken from a prior action for the same cause prior to the second suit;(1) but if the writ of error was sued out without being made a supersedeas and after the second suit was commenced, the plea would not be a good defense.

In such case upon a proper application and showing to the court where the second action is pending, it would be proper to grant a stay order in the case until the determination of the writ of error.(2)

As a defense in criminal cases.

SEC. 352. The lis pendens of a prior indictment for the same crime or offense by the same defendant may be plead in abatement of subsequent indictments.(3)

Dismissal in Supreme Court.

SEC. 353. A second lis pendens is ground of dismissal in Supreme Court.

Where a suit was brought in a State court and dismissed, but the dismissing order was appealed from or otherwise taken to the Supreme Court of the State, after dismissal the same plaintiff sued the same defendant in United States Circuit Court for the same cause.

Upon judgment passing in favor of the defendant in the Federal Court and upon bringing the fact to the knowledge of the Supreme Court of the State, the prior suit was dismissed.(4)

(1) Hailiman v. Buckmaster, 3 Gil. 500; Merritt v. Richie, 100 Ind. 416.

(2) 1 Tidd's Prac. 530; Christie v. Richardson, 3 D. and East. 78; Myer v. Arthur, 1 Stra. 419; Gressy v. Kell, 1 Wils. 120; McJilton v. Love, 13 Ill. 487.

(3) State v. Fleming, 66 Maine, 142.

(4) Hartell, Trustee, v. Seacy, 32 Ga. 191.

When pendency of prior suit a bar.

SEC. 354. But where two notes were given for the purchase of a schooner and one of them had been sued in a court of competent jurisdiction, to which the defense had been made that the schooner at the time of sale was rotten and unseaworthy and the sale fraudulent, and the defense was sustained and the defendant had judgment in his favor, and subsequently the same plaintiff, the vendor, brought suit on the second note in another court, and the defendant gave in evidence the record in the former case, it was held that the first judgment was a bar to the recovery.(1)

Two suits presumed vexatious in some jurisdictions.

SEC. 355. The pendency of two suits at one time for the same cause, brought by one plaintiff against the same defendant, is of itself ground for presumption that they are brought for the purpose of vexatiousness and oppression.

The fact that the plaintiff before commencing the second suit gave the defendant written notice that he would discontinue the first suit, will not change the result so as to avoid the abatement of the prior suit.(2)

But this rule is not enforced in other States.(3)

(1) Gardner *v.* Buckbee, 3 Cow. 120; Doty *v.* Brown, 4 Comst. N· Y. Ct. of Appeals, 75.

(2) Gamsby *v.* Ray, 52 N. H. 513; Denning *v.* Goodall, 18 N. H. 251; Parker *v.* Colcord, 2 N. H. 36.

(3) Bacon Abr. Abatement M. This rule is altered by statute in N. H. as to trustees. Gen. Statute of N. H. Ch. 230, Sec. 18. In pursuance of this statute proceedings in one action may be stayed until the other is disposed of. See also Haigh *v.* Paris, 16 M. & W. 144; Binnill *v.* Williamson, 7 H. & N. 391.

The courts say in Gamsby *v.* Ray, page 516: "English authorities, treatises, decisions and forms of pleading are uniform, on the ground that upon a plea of former action pending, vexatiousness is a conclusion of law drawn from the fact of two suits brought by one person against another for one

When suit not deemed vexatious in other jurisdictions.

SEC. 356. Although the doctrine of the common law is well established that the pendency of a prior suit between the same parties and for the same cause of action is ground for abatement of the second suit; yet, as the reason for the doctrine is the prevention of vexatious litigation where it is clear that the second suit is not vexatious, it is said the doctrine should not be enforced.(1)

cause and pending at one time, and is not a matter of fact depending upon the question whether the first action was defective or whether the plaintiff was justified in seeking better security in the second, or whether upon some other special ground it is equitable that the second should be commenced while the first is pending."

(1) Downs *v.* Garland, 21. Vt. 365; Hill *v.* Dunlap, 15 Vt. 645; Gould's Pl. 283; Bank *v.* Tarbox, 20 Conn. 510; Ward *v.* Curtis, 18 Conn. 290; Durand *v.* Carrington, 1 Root, 355; Hixon *v.* Schooley, 2 Dutcher, 461; Frogg *v.* Long, 3 Dana, 157; Adams *v.* Gardiner, 13 B. Mon. 197; Rogers *v.* Haskins, 15 Ga. 270; Langham *v.* Thomson, 5 Tex. 127; State *v.* Dougherty, 45 Mo. 294; Reynolds *v.* Harris, 9 Cal. 338; Ballou *v.* Ballou, 26 Vt. 673; Kirby *v.* Jackson, 42 Vt. 552; Averill et al. *v.* Patterson, 10 N. Y. 500; Jewett *v.* Locke, 6 Gray, 233.

In the case of Gamsby *v.* Ray, 52 N. H. 516, the court say: "That the pendency of a prior suit between the same parties, and for the same cause of action, is ground of abatement of the second suit, is a doctrine of the common law. And the doctrine is founded upon the supposition that the second suit is unnecessary, oppressive and vexatious.

"Such are the reasons assigned in the books for the adoption of the rule. It is based upon the supposition that the first suit was effective and available, and affords an ample remedy to the party, and hence the second suit would be unnecessary, and consequently vexatious.

"This being the reason for the adoption of the rule, there would seem to be no propriety in extending and applying it to cases where the reason does not exist. It would be much more consonant to reason to apply the maxim, that when the reason for the rule ceases, the rule itself should cease.

"Hence it is that courts, in modern times, have somewhat modified the rule, and, instead of regarding the second suit as necessarily vexatious, have gone into the inquiry of whether in fact it was vexatious.

"It is upon this principle that the courts in Connecticut have uni∗formly proceeded, in holding that the second suit is not vexatious, when it appears that the prior suit

When former action not a bar.

SEC. 357. Although it is a general rule, long established and well understood, that the judgment or decree of a court of competent jurisdiction upon a question directly involved in the suit, is conclusive in a second suit between the same parties depending on the same question, notwithstanding the subject matter of the second action be different; yet, where the parties in the former suit were not in position to controvert the conclusion arrived at in the case sought to be set up as a bar, the former adjudication will not be conclusive in the second suit.

And, accordingly, where a bill was filed by the indorsee of promissory notes given under a contract of purchase of real estate against the maker and payee of the notes, who were the contracting parties, to enforce a vendor's lien upon lands, and a demurrer was interposed by the maker of the notes, upon

must have been ineffectual and consequently that it is no ground for abating the second suit.

"This doctrine is laid down in the case from Root's Reports, cited by Judge Gould in his treatise upon pleading, and is recognized by the Superior Court, in 18 Conn. 290, as settled law in that State. And we think the rule thus established in Connecticut is founded in reason, and sustained by authority."

In New York, the rule seems to have been somewhat different. In that State it has been held, and professedly upon English authority, that when the defendant pleads in abatement the pendency of another action, the plaintiff may enter a discontinuance in the first suit before a replication is filed to the plea in abatement, and that without leave of the court, and thereby sustain a replication of nul tiel record. Marston v. Lawrence, 1 Johns. Cas. 397.

This was held to be matter of right; and the court cited, as sustaining the position, Barnes' Notes, 257; 1 Leon, 105, and 1 Sellon's Practice, 304.

So it was held by the court in Hill v. Dunlap, 15 Vt. 645, that if one commences a suit by a process which is defective, he may discontinue it and bring fresh suit, and the second suit will not be considered vexatious, and that the former suit may be discontinued by oral notice." Downs v. Garland, 21 Vt. 362, 365, 366.

which demurrer the court held the complainant's right barred by the statute of limitation and gave judgment accordingly; it was held in an action of ejectment brought to recover the same lands that the adjudication in the former suit was not a bar in the latter as to those parties who did not join in the demurrer.(1)

Practice in New York where another lis pendens.

Sec. 358. It was held in New York that where the defendant pleads the pendency of another suit, the plaintiff may enter a discontinuance in the first suit before a replication is filed to defendant's plea, and thereby sustain a replication of nul tiel record filed in the second suit.(2)

This seems to be the English practice also.(3)

Forcible entry and detainer and distress for rent.

Sec. 359. Although the action of forcible entry and detainer does not involve title to the property, but only involves the right to possession, the defense of a prior action pending may be interposed in that form of action.

This is probably not so much on the ground that the judgment in the cause would be a bar as to avoid vexatious litigation.(4)

So also the defense of prior action pending may be made in a case of distress for rent where the junior action is for the same rent.(5)

In garnishee process.

Sec. 360. Where in an attachment proceeding a

(1) Gudger et als. *v.* Barnes, 4 Heiskell, 570.

(2) Marston *v.* Lawrence et al., 1 Johns. Cas. 397.

(3) Leonard R. (K. R.) 105; 1 Sel-lon, 304.

(4) Bond *v.* White, 24 Kas. 45; Turner *v.* Lumbrick, Meigs. 7.

(5) Chisholm et al. *v.* Lewis & Co., 66 Ga. 729.

defendant is garnisheed and the conditions are such that the defense of the pendency of the attachment suit and garnishment may be interposed, it should be shown by the pleadings and proof whether the whole or what part of the debt has been attached or garnisheed in order to constitute a defense.

Where a foreign attachment is relied upon as a defense, it must be specially pleaded. It cannot be given in evidence under the general issue, or one pro tanto.(1)

Actions different.

SEC. 361. Where the relief sought in the two cases is different, the defense of lis pendens cannot be interposed, although the same question may to some extent be involved in the two actions.

Unless a judgment recovered in a prior action would be a bar to the second suit, it would not constitute a defense.(2)

Where two actions for same cause, when both should be tried.

SEC. 362. Where two actions were brought for the same cause and between the same parties, and in one of them a trial was had and final judgment rendered, and that fact was plead in the other action, it was

(1) Clark *v.* Marbourg, 33 Kas. 471; Updegraff *v.* Spring, 1 Serg. and R. 188.

An attachment in a foreign State cannot be pleaded in abatement of a subsequent action in personam. Wilson *v.* Mech. Savings B'k, 9 Wright, 488.

As to proceeding by foreign attachment in another State, see Embree *v.* Hanna, 5 Johns. 101; Brook *v.* Smith, 1 Salk. 280.

(2) Coles *v.* Yorks, 31 Minn. 213. It is held in Hacket *v.* Lenares et al., 16 La. An. 205, that where the parties are different, the defense of prior action pending is not admissible, although the two suits may have the same object and grow out of the same cause of action and depend in the same court or courts of concurrent jurisdiction in the same State. See also Ingram *v.* Richards, 2 La. An. 839.

held in a California case that although upon final trial of the remaining case upon its merits the determination of the former suit might be held a bar to the latter, yet that a mandamus should issue from the Supreme Court to compel a trial of the second action, on the ground that the plaintiff had the right to have the action tried and determined, so as to enable him to take an appeal, if he saw proper, in the event that the judgment should be against him.(1)

It seems that the prior action was a proceeding in chancery and the junior cause was at law. If the court in both of these cases had the same power to administer the rights of the parties, it is difficult to see why it should have held as it did. It is presumable this was not the case, otherwise this case would seem to be in conflict with other causes.(2.)

There must be service of summons.

Sec. 363. A plea in abatement of a prior action pending for the same cause, should show that summons had been issued and served on the defendant, or that he had voluntarily appeared in the cause.

Otherwise it would not appear that the suit is pending. Non constat, but that the summons would never be issued or served.(3)

Lis pendens no bar to cumulative remedies upon mortgage.

Sec. 364. A holder of bonds or notes secured by mortgage on real estate may have cumulative remedies at the same time.

He may have ejectment to recover the land, a bill

(1) Watson *v.* Dowling, 26 Cal. 194.
127.
(2) Horn *v.* Jones et al., 28 Cal.
(3) Weaver *v.* Conger, 10 Cal. 238.

to foreclose, and an action in personam on the bonds or notes.

The lis pendens of neither action will be a bar to the others.(1)

In some States scire facias to foreclose the mortgage may also be maintained cotemporaneously.(2)

Issue as to debt in plea.

SEC. 365. When a plea in abatement of a prior action pending is interposed, the issue formed upon the plea and the question to be tried is, so far as relates to the debt or cause of action, whether the debt sued for in the second suit was in fact included in the former suit.

It is not whether or not it might have been included.(3)

Where service in first suit after that in second, not a prior suit.

SEC. 366. A foreign attachment cannot be said to be pending so as to constitute a pending suit until the appearance of the defendant has been entered or he has been personally served with a summons.

In a case where such a suit was brought in another State, but before the defendant had appeared or been personally served, another action was brought.

It was held that there was not a prior suit pending, and that the attachment suit could not be plead in abatement of the other suit.(4)

Where one suit is brought for use of another.

SEC. 367. Where one of two suits was brought for

(1) In Booth v. Booth, 2 Atk. 343, it is held that a mortgagee may proceed to foreclose a mortgage and bring ejectment at the same time.

(2) State Bank v. Wilson, 4 Gilm.

62.

(3) Chase v. Ninth Nat'l Bk. of N. Y., 56 Penn. St. 358.

(4) Wilson v. Mechanics' Sav'gs Bk., 45 Penn. St. (9 Wright), 488.

the same cause in the name of the original obligee or
payee, and the other was brought in the same name
but for the use of one who, prior to the commencement of the suit, had purchased the claim in good
faith for value, the defendant cannot plead in abatement the former suit brought in the name of the
original payee or obligee.

The original claimant, having sold his claim, had lost
all interest in it, and there was no right of recovery
in the prior suit or danger that the defendant would
be compelled to pay twice.

In such case a replication that the real plaintiff in
the junior suit had purchased the claim prior to
bringing the suit and was the owner of the debt, is a
good answer to a plea in abatement of the former
action.(1)

Plea of prior action pending in mandamus.

SEC. 368.   Although in an action of mandamus the
name of the State may be used merely nominally, and
the relator be the real litigant, yet where the action
is brought by virtue of an act of the legislature for
the purpose of providing a remedy against usurpation
and intrusion into office, in the name of the State, the
State is regarded as the real party.

Where the two actions were between the same parties, yet in the one case the State was the real litigant, and in the other the relator was the real party
in interest, it was held that a plea in abatement would
not lie, because, although the suits were in the same
name, so far as the plaintiff was concerned, yet it did
not sue in the same capacity or for the same interest

(1) Johnson et al. *v.* Irby et al., 8 Humphrey, 654.

in both cases, and a plea in abatement was disallowed.(1)

Where one suit against the officer and the other against the deputy.

SEC. 369.   Where one of two suits is pending against a deputy sheriff for wrongful acts done under color of his office, and the other is brought for the same cause against the sheriff himself, the lis pendens of the one cannot be plead in abatement of the other.(2)

But where a judgment is rendered in the one, it may be plead in bar in the other.(3)

Character of proof of lis pendens.

SEC. 370.   Upon an issue of fact upon a plea of another action pending, the *onus probandi* is upon the defendant pleading it, and the proof to sustain it must be record evidence.(4)

A record is a memorial of a proceeding or act of a court of record entered in a roll for the preservation of it.(5)

Parol evidence is not admissible for the purpose of proving the pendency of the former suit.(6)

(1) State of La. v. Kreider, 21 La. An. 482; Tapping on Mandamus, Chap. 8, title, "Abatement of Writ," p. 446; Chitt. Pr. 1406 to 1409, 8th edition.

(2) Sevrey v. Nye, 58 Maine, 246.

(3) White v. Philbrick, 5 Greenl. 147; Bucklin v. Johnson, 80 E. C. L. 145; Emery v. Fowler, 39 Maine, 327.

(4) 1 Sand. Pl. and Ev. 19.

(5) 7 Com. Dig. Tit. Record (A.)

(6) Fowler v. Byrd, Hempsted's R. 214; Brush v. Taggart, 7 Johns. 20; Hasbrouck v. Baker, 10 Johns. 220; Jenner v. Joliffe, 6 Johns. 9.

CHAPTER XVII.

LIS PENDENS AS A DEFENSE, CONTINUED.

Pleading and practice in this defense.

SEC. 371. It is proper, before closing this subject, to treat somewhat with respect to the rules governing pleading and practice in this defense—although those are subjects usually treated in special treatises on pleading and practice—because it will often be con-

venient to the practitioner to find in one volume the
law governing the subject.

In most respects the same principles of pleading the
defense of prior action pending for the same cause prevail in chancery as at common law.(1) As we shall
see hereafter, the mode of determining the issue, however, differs.(2)

Where codes have been adopted abrogating the
common law on the subject of pleading, the provisions
of those codes will control on this subject and take
the place of the common law rules.

Under these codes, however, the forms of pleading
are so much liberalized that very little may be said
upon the subject, except to refer the practitioner to
the provisions contained in these codes.

Defense seldom raised by demurrer.

SEC. 372. It is manifest that the facts constituting
the defense of prior action pending seldom appear
upon the face of a bill in chancery. It can not therefore be interposed by demurrer to the bill. Being
also in the nature of a dilatory defense, not involving
the merits of the cause of action, it must be set up by
plea in the nature of a plea in abatement.

Should, however, the complainant set up in the bill
the fact of a prior action pending between the same
parties and for the same cause or otherwise, and seek
to avoid the allegations in the bill with respect to such
prior action by other averments in the bill, the defendant would be at liberty to test the complainant's case
by the interposition of a demurrer.

(1) Beames' Pl. in Eq. 136; Foster v. Vassall, 3 Atk. 589.
(2) Jones v. Segueira, 1 Phill.
82; Wedderburn v. Wedderburn, 2
Beav. 208; S. C. 4 and Myl. and Cr.
585.

The demurrer, however, would necessarily admit all of the material allegations of the bill, well pleaded, and as it would seldom occur that the defense of prior action would be fully and fairly made to appear upon the face of the bill, the defense by demurrer would fall short of being complete.

Of pleas generally.

SEC. 373. A plea, whether in bar or abatement, usually reduces the defense to a single point, thereby showing a bar to the action or other obstruction to the suit, or to the point to which the plea applies. It may be affirmative or negative, but must either allege or deny some leading fact which is a defense.(1)

(1) Metf. Eq. by Jeremy, 295–297; Cooper, Eq. Pl. 223; Story, Eq. Pl. § 652; Chapman v. Turner, 1 Atk. 54; Ritchie v. Aylwin, 15 Ves. 82; Rowe v. Teed, 15 Ves. 378; Whitehead v. Brockhurst, 1 Bro. Ch. 404, and note (1), and 416, note (9), by Belt; S. C. 2 Ves. & B. 153, note; Wood v. Rowe, 2 Bligh, 595, 614.

In Rowe v. Teed, 15 Ves. 377, 378, Lord Eldon, in speaking of the case where matter was brought forward by the answer for the same purposes as a plea, said: "The office of a plea, generally, is not to deny the equity, but to bring forward a fact, which, if true, displaces it; not a single averment, as the averment in this answer that no bill of sale was executed, but perhaps a series of circumstances, forming in their combined result some one fact which displaces the equity.

"There is this difference between law and equity, that here for the sake of convenience, that is, of jus-

tice, the denial of some fact alleged by the bill, in some instances with certain averments, has been considered sufficient to constitute a good plea, though not perhaps precisely within the definition of good pleading at law.

"If each case is to be considered upon its own circumstances, it is desirable that this point should be brought before the court by plea rather than by answer, as an answer prima facie admits that the defendant cannot plead; and with the exception of the cases in which it is settled as general law that the party is not to answer a particular circumstance, as that he is not to criminate himself, the case of a purchaser for valuable consideration, etc., this court does not trust the master, generally, with the determination how much of the answer considered as a plea would be a good defense.

"The master is, therefore, almost under the necessity of admitting

The defense, however, may consist of a variety of circumstances if they all tend to a single point.(1) The plea ought not to contain more than one defense. If it does, it is improper for informality and multifariousness.(2)

If various facts are pleaded in one plea, they must all conduce to a single point on which the defendant means to rest his defense.(3)

Two or more facts which are inconsistent with each other cannot therefore be pleaded in one plea.(4)

But at law and by consent of court in chancery, different pleas may be pleaded in the same cause, although

an exception. And when the propriety of his judgment comes to be argued here, it would be most incongruous that the court, admitting his judgment not to be wrong, should yet give a different judgment, considering the answer as a plea. Another circumstance deserving attention is the great difference of expense in bringing forward the objection by plea rather than by answer.

"There is but one more material general observation to be added to those which are to be found in the cases reported; that generally admitting there are exceptions, the practice of this court requires that the bill and the answer should form a record upon which a complete decree may be made at the hearing. If, for instance, this plaintiff is a part owner of a ship, he has a right to an answer that will enable him, if a certain sum is admitted to be due, to obtain a decree for that sum if he is satisfied with that and does not desire an account.

"With that general observation, in addition to those to be found in the other cases, I conclude that this is not a case in which I can say there is one clear fact, or such a combination of facts, giving as the result one clear ground upon which the whole equity of this bill may be disposed of. First, it is very difficult upon this answer to say there is a positive affirmation that there was no bill of sale. Next, it is argumentative."

(1) Story's Eq. Pl. § 652; Robertson v. Lubbock, 4 Sim. 161; Saltus et al. v. Tobias et al., 7 Johns. Ch. 214; Beames' Pl. in Eq. 10–14; 2 Dan. Ch. Prac. 102–104.

(2) Mitf. Eq. Pl. by Jeremy, 296; Cooper, Eq. Pl. 225; 2 Dan. Ch. Prac. 103, 104.

(3) Story's Eq. Pl. § 553; see 2 Dan. Prac. 102, 104; Rhode Island v. Massachusetts, 14 Peters, 210, 259.

(4) Story's Eq. Pl. § 653; Whitehead v. Brockhurst, 1 Bro. Ch. 405, 413, by Belt, note (9); S. C. 2 Ves. & B. 154, note; see King v. Ray, 11 Paige, 239.

the facts alleged in the different several pleas are inconsistent.(1)

In its discretion a court of chancery will also allow
the practice.(2)

(1) Story's Eq. Pl. § 657; Cooper,
Eq. Pl. 224; London v. Liverpool,
3 Anst. 738.

(2) Story's Eq. Pl. § 657; Mitf.
Eq. Pl. by Jeremy, 245, 296, and
note (n); Cooper, Eq. Pl. 226;
Story's Eq. Pl. § 652; Jones v
Frost, 3 Mad. 8; Saltus et al. v. Tobias et al.. 7 Johns. Ch. 214. See
Didier v. Davison, 10 Paige, 515,
where this subject is carefully considered.

Lord Thurlow, in Whithead v.
Brockhurst, 1 Bro. Ch. 404, 416, note
(9), by Mr. Belt; S. C. 2 Ves. & B.
154, 155, note, gives the reason of
this practice more fully. "The reason," says he, "why a defendant is
not permitted to plead two different pleas in equity, though he is
permitted to plead them at law, is
plain. It is because at law the defendant has no opportunity, as he
has here, of answering every different matter stated in the bill. The
reason of pleading in equity is, that
it tends to the forwarding of justice,
and saves a great expense, that the
matter should be taken up shortly
upon a single point. But that end
is so far from being attained, if the
plea puts as much in issue as the
answer could do, that on the contrary it increases the delay and expense.

"But why, it may be asked, should
not the defendant be permitted to
bring two points, on which the
cause depends, to issue by his plea?
The answer is, because if two, he

may as well bring three points to
issue, and so on till all the matters
in the bill are brought into issue
upon the plea, which would be productive of all the delay and incon-
venience which pleading was intended to remedy."

Mr. Cooper says: "It is said in
a manuscript of Lord Nottingham,
that 'no man shall be permitted to
two several dilatories at several
times, nor several bars, because he
may plead all at once. But after a
plea in disability, as outlawry or
excommunication, or a plea to the
jurisdiction, he may be admitted to
plead in bar, because it was not
consistent with those pleas to plead
in bar at the same time.' This
passage certainly imports that, in
the opinion of Lord Nottingham,
both several dilatory pleas and several pleas in bar might be pleaded,
so that they were pleaded at the
same time. And it may be said
that such pleading is admitted at
law, and ought, therefore, now be
equally so in equity.

"But it should be considered that
a plea is not the only mode of defense in equity, and that, therefore,
there is not the same necessity as
at law for admitting this kind of
pleading." Cooper, Eq. Pl. 226, 227.

Mr. Chancellor Kent, in Saltus et
al. v. Tobias et al., 7 Johns. Ch. 214,
215, refers to the same passage in
Lord Nottingham's manuscript.
See also Beames' Pl. in Eq. 15–17,
where the learned author doubts

In some States this right of double pleading is granted by statute. Where such statutes do not exist, the usual practice is to apply to the court for leave to plead doubly, which is granted in its discretion. The plea in chancery need not be on oath.(1)

Pleas are divisible into two classes with respect to the matter set up in them, viz.: the pure plea and the plea not pure. The pure plea should be founded on new matter not apparent on the bill; it must aver facts *dehors* the bill and not rest on facts stated in the bill. Pleas not pure rely upon matter stated in the record and upon denials or negations of facts appearing on the face of the bill.(2)

Plea in chancery of former action pending may be said to be a plea to the bill or the frame of the bill. This plea differs from the plea to the jurisdiction, in that it does not dispute the original power of the court to take cognizance of the particular matter, but impliedly admits it and objects to the suit as framed or contends that it is unnecessary.

Neither does it deny the validity of the right of action which is asserted as the subject of the suit, but contends that that right ought not to be asserted in that suit. This plea bears some resemblance to those pleas at law which are in abatement of the writ.(3)

the doctrine of Lord Nottingham. Curs. Canc. 187.

But it has been expressly decided that where a plaintiff seeks relief as to more than one subject, the defendant may put in a plea to each subject. Emmott *v.* Mitchell, 14 Sim. 432.

(1) Story's Eq. Pl. Sec. 696; Ur-lin *v.* Hudson, 1 Vern. 332; Beames' Pl. in Eq. 146; Cooper's Eq. Pl. 276; Mitford's Eq. Pl. by Jeremy, 275, by Taylor, 338; Story's Eq. Pl. Sec. 742, note (a.)

(2) Story's Eq. Pl. Secs. 651 to 667.

(3) Beames' Eq. 133; Story's Eq. Pl. Sec. 735.

What allegations the plea must contain.

SEC. 374. The plea of prior action pending, when interposed in chancery, should set forth with certainty the fact of the commencement of the former suit, its nature, character and object, and the relief sought by it.(1)

It should also aver that the second suit is for the same subject matter as that of the first; that the same issue is joined in the two suits, and that the proceedings in the former suit were taken for the same purpose.(2)

(1) 2 Mitf. Eq. by Jeremy, 244 (by Tyler, 337); Beames Pl. in Eq. 142-144; Cooper, Eq. Pl. 274; Foster v. Vassall, 3 Atk. 589, 590.

(2) Behrens v. Sieveking, 2 Myl. and Cr. 602.

Lord Cottenham, in giving judgment in this case, said: "That in order to support the plea, it was necessary to show that the proceedings in which the plaintiffs were alleged to have failed, were taken for the same purpose as the present suit; for the issue might have been the same, while the object was different; and the circumstance that the matter had been tried, as a matter of evidence, could not be conclusive. The defendant had to show that the subject matter was the same; that the right came in question before a court of competent jurisdiction; and that the result was conclusive, so as to bind the judgment of every other court.

"His lordship added that it was in the plea alone that any statement of the bill of proof or of the proceedings taken upon it was to be found; but that the plea left the court in ignorance upon the question, whether the proceedings, which it alleged to have taken place in the Lord Mayor's court, were conclusive, even in that court.

"His lordship thought that the plaintiff could not have taken issue upon the plea, and that no question was stated in the plea upon which his lordship could ask for the opinion of the Recorder."

Moore v. Welsh Copper Co., 1 Eq. Cas. Abr. 39; Mitf. Eq. Pl. by Jeremy, 247 (by Tyler, 337); Cooper, Eq. Pl. 272; Beames Pl. in Eq. 138, 139.

Lord Redesdale says that it has been held that a positive averment that the former suit is depending, is not necessary; Mitf. Eq Pl. by Jeremy, 247 (by Tyler, 337); and he cites Urlin v. Hudson, 1 Vern. 332, which certainly seems to support his statement; although the averment there was, "which suit is still depending for aught he (the defendant) knows to the contrary."

However, it seems very doubtful if this case is sound law. Mr. Beames and Mr. Cooper both ap-

That proceedings have in fact been taken in the former suit, such as an appearance or the service of process requiring an appearance.

The plea should also aver that the former suit is still depending and should show that it is depending in the same court, or some other court of complete jurisdiction, and whose jurisdiction is not inferior to that in which the second suit is pending.(1)

Suit not necessarily between same parties.

SEC. 375. While the general rule is that the suit must be between the same parties, yet it is not necessary to the sufficiency of the plea or of the defense that the parties should be precisely the same. If the complainant institutes a suit and afterwards sells a part of the property involved in the suit to another, who brings his bill, asserting his right to the part of the property so purchased by him, the plea and defense of the former suit depending, with respect to the whole property, and with the original party will be a good plea and defense. The part is included in the whole, and being involved in the former suit, notwithstanding the sale by the complainant subsequent to its commencement, must be adjudicated upon in that suit.

And so, where the part owner of a ship filed a bill against the ship's husband for an account, and afterward joined with the rest of the owners in a bill for the same purpose, and the pendency of the first suit was plead and interposed, it was held to be a good plea and defense to the last suit; for, although the first bill was

pear to doubt it. Beames Pl. in Eq. by Jeremy, 248 (by Tyler, 338); Cooper, Eq. Pl. 272.

(1) Mitf. Eq. Pl. by Jeremy, 246

(by Tyler, 336); Cooper, Eq. Pl. 272; Story's Eq. Pl. 737.

For form of Plea in Equity, see Sec. 393, (note) *post.*

insufficient for want of parties, the defendant was thereby doubly vexed for the same cause.(1)

When same person sues in different right.

SEC. 376. But there are some cases where the plea of former suit will not properly apply, although the two suits may involve the same subject matter. The complainants must sue and defendants be sued in the same right or character.

If the suits are brought in a different right or character, the complainants, although the same persons in fact, may be said to sue in contemplation of law as different persons, and hence the suits cannot, in law, be considered as being brought by the same persons.

In such cases the effect had and relief obtained in the second suit cannot be had and obtained in the former suit.

Thus, where an administrator sued in the capacity of the representative of an estate, and afterwards procured administration *de bonis non*, and in that capacity filed another bill, Lord Redesdale overruled a plea of the pendency of the former bill, assigning as the reason that the first bill, being wholly irregular, the plaintiff could have no benefit from it, and it might have been dismissed upon demurrer.

But Lord Hardwicke assigned a different reason, and founded it upon the position that where the same person sues in different capacities it is the same as if there were different persons.(2)

(1) Mitf. Eq. Pl. by Jeremy, 248 (by Tyler, 337 and 338); Cooper, Eq. Pl. 273; Beames Pl. in Eq. 139 and 140; Story's Eq. Pl. 738; Moore *v.* Welsh Copper Co., Eq. Cas. Abr. 39.

(2) 4 Mitf. Eq. Pl. by Jeremy, 248, 249 (by Tyler, 339); Story's Eq. Pl. 739; Beames Pl. in Eq. 140, 141 and cases there cited; Huggins *v.* York Bldg. Co. 2. Atk. 44; Neve *v.* Weston et ux., 3 Atk. 557; Law *v.* Rigby, 4 Bro. Ch. 60; Gage *v.* Stafford, 1 Ves. Sr. 544; Amb. 103; Cooper Eq. Pl. 274.

Bills filed for self and other creditors.

Sec. 377.   Where a creditor has brought a bill on behalf of himself and of all other creditors of the same defendant debtor, and a creditor other than himself comes in before the master to take the benefit of an interlocutory decree, and proves his debt, but afterwards files another bill in behalf of himself and other creditors, defendants may plead the pendency of the former suit.

In that case the second complainant must be held to have been a complainant to the first suit, although not a party by name, having become a quasi party by going before the master and taking the benefit of the proceedings which had been taken.

It sometimes occurs in such cases that the nominal complainant delays the proceedings to the detriment of a creditor, thus regarded as complaint, although not by name.   To avoid the effect of such wrongful delay, if the complainant in the original suit is unreasonably dilatory in its prosecution, or colludes with the defendant, a creditor may make his application to the court for liberty to conduct the cause.(1)

Plea of pendency of suit in foreign tribunal.

Sec. 378.   We have already seen that the pendency of a suit in a foreign country, although between the same parties, involving the same subject matter and for the same purpose, cannot be interposed as a defense.

(1) Mitf. Eq. Pl. by Jeremy 242, by Tyler 339; Neve v. Weston et ux., 3 Atk. 557; Houldtich v. Donegall, 1 Sim and Stu. 491; Cooper Eq. Pl. 274; Beames Pl. in Eq. 139 and 140; Story's Eq. Jur. 740; Powell v. Wallworth, 2 Madd. 183; Sims v. Ridge, 3 Meriv. 458; Edmunds v. Acland, 5 Madd. 31; Fleming v. Prior, 5 Madd. 423; Hardford v. Storie, 2 Sim. and Stu. 196.

It follows that such a plea would be bad. It is certain that the pendency of another suit for the same matter, in a foreign tribunal would not be a good plea at law, and no reason can be perceived why it should not be held equally bad in chancery.(1)

(1) Foster *v.* Vassall, 3 Atk. 589, 590; Mitf. Eq. Pl. by Jeremy 247, by Tyler 337, note (*t*); Dillon *v.* Alvares, 4 Ves. 357. See Cooper, Eq. Pl. 275; Beames, Pl, in Eq. ; Story's Eq. Pl. Sec. 740.

See Ins. Co. *v.* Brune, 96 U. S. (6 Otto), 588; Scott *v.* Rand et al., 118 Mass. 215; Cole *v.* Flitcraft, 47 Md. 312; Seevers *v.* Clement, 28 Md. 426; Paine *v.* Schenectady Ins· 11 R. I. 411; Grider, etc., *v.* Apperson & Co., 32 Ark. 332.

The question whether the pendency of a prior suit in a state court is a bar to a suit in a circuit court of the United States by the same plaintiff against the same defendant for the same cause of action, seems to be now fully settled in the negative.

See Stanton *v.* Embrey, 93 U. S. 548; Brooks *v.* Mills County, 4 Dillon, 524; Loring et al. *v.* Marsh et al., 2 Cliff. (U. S. C. C.) 311, 312.

In the case of Loring *v.* Marsh, *ante*, Mr. Justice Clifford, said: "Cases may unquestionably be found where it is held that the mere pendency of another suit for the same matter between the same parties in another jurisdiction, may be pleaded in abatement or in bar to a second suit. The decision in Hart *v.* Granger, 1 Conn. 154, was of that class, but the case has recently been distinctly overruled by the court in which it was made.

Hatch *v.* Spofford, 22 Conn. 485.

" The English cases go no further than to hold that the plea of another suit depending will be good, if the first suit was instituted in the same jurisdiction. Such a plea is not a good one in the courts of that country if the first suit is pending in another country, nor in the colonies of the parent country.

Maule et al. *v.* Murray et al., 7 T. R. 278; Imlay *v.* Ellefsen, 2 East.453; Dillon *v.* Alvares, 4 Ves. 357; Foster *v.* Vassall, 3 Atk. 587; Bayley *v.* Edwards, 3 Swanst. 703; Howell *v.* Waldron, 2 Ch. Cas. 85; 2 Dan. Ch. Prac. 721; Story, Eq. Pl. Sec. 741.

"The weight of American authority also is decidedly to the same effect. The undeviating rule in this circuit has been that the pendency of another action for the same cause in a State court is not a good plea in abatement. White *v.* Whitman, 1 Curtis, 494; Lyman et al. *v.* Brown et al., 2 Curtis, 559; Wadleigh *v.* Veasie, 3 Sum. 165.

The same rule is estalished in most of the States. Browne et al. *v.* Joy, 9 Johns. 221; Walsh *v.* Durkin, 12 Johns. 99; McJilton *v.* Love, 13 Ill. 486; Mitchell *v.* Bunce, 2 Paige Ch. 606.

"Much consideration was given to the whole subject in the case of Salmon *v.* Wootten, 9 Dana, 422,

Where prior suit is pending in a United States Court in a different State from that where the other pends in State court.

SEC. 379. The defense of prior action pending will not be good where the prior action is pending in a Circuit Court of the United States, in a State other than that in which a suit between the same parties and for the same thing is pending in a State court.

The same reasons which make the defense not applicable where two suits are pending in different States in State courts, exist where one of the suits is depending in a Federal court, and the other in a State court not within its district. We have seen that in the application of this question, the States are regarded as foreign to each other, and so may, in the latter case, the two courts be regarded as within jurisdictions foreign to each other.

This question was expressly decided in Walsh *v.* Durkin, where a plea in abatement was filed, setting up that another action was pending between the same parties in the Circuit Court of the United States for the district embracing the State of Virginia.(1)

Where the prior suit is pending in a State court and the junior suit in a Federal Court, not embracing in its district the State where the prior suit pends.

SEC. 380. The converse of the proposition discussed in the preceeding section is equally true. Where a prior suit between the same parties and for the same cause is pending in a State court, and the junior suit, wherein the defense of the prior action is interposed,

to which reference is specially made, for a clear and full exposition of the reasons on which the rule is founded."

(1) Walsh *v.* Durkin, 12 Johns. 99; Cook *v.* Litchfield, 5 Sandf. Ch. 330; Story on Conflict of Laws, Sec 601a; Sec. 347, *ante.*

is pending in a Federal Court, within whose jurisdiction or district the State wherein the prior suit pends is not embraced, it will not be a good defense.

It follows that a plea of such prior action pending, filed in a Federal Court, would not be good.

Thus the converse of this proposition, while there are few authorities on the question, would seem to hold good. In most of the States the rule is thoroughly established that a prior suit for the same cause in another State is not a defense to the second suit.(1)

The same reasons lying back of this rule and of that disallowing the plea of the pendency of a prior suit in a State Court in another district, when interposed in a Federal Court, would seem to have force where the prior suit has been commenced in the Federal Court, not embracing the State court within its district.(1)

So far as relates to the right to interpose this defense, the State not embraced within the district of the Federal court will be regarded as a foreign State.

So, the same reasons which are held sufficient to avoid this defense where one of the actions is pending in one of the States of the Union, and the other in another, exist in the case supposed in this section. Although, as organized, the courts may in some sense, have concurrent jurisdiction, yet, process can not be sent from one to the other, and the defendant may be

---

(1) Stanton v. Embrey, 93 (U. S. C. C.) 548; Brooks v. Mills Co., 4 Dillon, 524; Loring et al. v. Marsh et al., 2 Cliff. 311, 322; Hart v. Granger, 1 Conn. 154. The latter case was overruled by Hatch v. Spofford, 28 Conn. 495; White v. Whitman, 1 Curtis, 494; Lyman et al. v. Brown et al., 2 Curtis (C. C.) 559; Wadleigh v. Veasie, 3 Sum. (C. C.), 165; Browne et al. v. Joy, 9 Johns. 221; Walsh v. Durkin, 12 Johns. 99; McJilton v. Love, 13 Ill. 486; Mitchell v. Bunce, 2 Paige Ch. 606. Much consideration was given to the whole subject in Salmon v. Wooten, 9 Dana, 422.

possessed of property in one of the jurisdictions which could not be reached upon process issued in a case brought in the other jurisdiction. The plaintiff, therefore, should have the the right to the use of both jurisdictions in the prosecution of his claim until after judgment or satisfaction of the debt.

The question which we are now considering is quite distinct from the one arising under the comity clause of the Constitution of the United States. After judgments have been rendered, that provision of the Federal constitution gives the record of the judgment and proceedings full faith and credit in those States of the Union where the proceedings were not had. Therefore, after judgment, different reasons and a different rule come in and allow the defendant to plead in bar the judgment in the other jurisdictions.

That is not in conflict with the position which courts have assumed, with respect to the interposition as a defense, of the pendency of the prior action.(1)

Where prior suit pending in a United States Court, and the junior suit in a State Court within the district.

SEC. 381. But where the prior action is pending in a Circuit Court of the United States, and the junior action pends in a State court in a State embraced within the District of the United States Court, and the State and Federal courts have concurrent jurisdiction, a plea in abatement of prior action pending is a good plea

All of the reasons which apply in favor of this defense where the two suits are pending in two State

(1) White v. Whitman, 1 Curtis, et al., 2 Curtis (C. C.), 559; Story (C. C.) 494; Lyman et al. v. Brown on the Conflict of Laws, Sec. 610a.

courts of the same State of concurrent jurisdiction
apply here. The Federal courts are established by
the constitution, as a branch of the general government of this country. Within its territorial limits,
and as to causes within its jurisdiction, the Circuit
Court of the United States should not be regarded as
a foreign court. Its judgments operate directly upon
and bind the persons and property within the State;
its powers are derived from a government exercising
sovereignty over the same territory; and its process is
efficient to enforce its orders, judgments and decrees.

The Circuit Court of the United States for another
district has no such power, authority or efficiency
within the State, and may, as we have seen, be regarded territorially and for some purposes as a foreign
jurisdiction.

Although the Circuit Court of the United States
and the courts of the state embraced within its district, derive their powers from different sources and
are independent of each other, in certain cases, they
exercise concurrent jurisdiction. The plaintiff in
these cases has his election to pursue his remedy in
the Circuit Court of the United States, or to resort
to the concurrent remedy in the courts of the State
within the district.

The law forbids that a defendant should be harassed
at the same time by two suits for the same cause,
where the plaintiff has the same remedy and one of
the same efficiency in both courts.

This is not a case where the prior suit is in an inferior court of special and limited jurisdiction, incapable
of affording the plaintiff the remedy which he needs.(1)

(1) Smith *v.* Atlantic Mut. Fire on the Conflict of Laws, Sec. 610*a.*
Ins. Co., 2 Foster, (N. H.) 21; Story

When prior suit pends in State court within the district of a United States Circuit Court, where junior action pends.

SEC. 382. For the same reasons which sustain the defense of prior action pending, when interposed in the State court and where the prior action is pending in a Circuit Court of the United States within whose district the State court is, this defense may be interposed in a State court having concurrent jurisdiction with the Circuit Court of the United States, where the prior action pends in the Federal court, and the defense is interposed in the State court. It is there a good defense.(1)

Where parties reversed, defense not allowable.

SEC. 383. The defense of prior action pending will not be entertained where the plea shows that, although the parties to the suit are the same and the subject matter of litigation the same, the parties are reversed; that is, where in the one case a party is plaintiff and in the other defendant, and vice versa.(2)

When State and Federal Courts have jurisdiction in rem.

SEC. 384. When a State court and a United States court have concurrent jurisdiction in a proceeding in rem, that court which first acquires and has the right to exercise jurisdiction, and takes possession of the res, has the right to maintain its jurisdiction to render and enforce its judgments and decrees.

This is without regard to the State court being

(1) Smith *v.* Atlantic Mut. Fire Ins. Co., 2 Foster (N. H.), 21; Story on the Conflict of Laws, Sec. 610, *ante.*

(2) Taylor *v.* The Royal Saxon, 1 Wal., Jr., C. C. 311; Certain Logs of Mahogany, 2 Sumner, 589.

within the district or territorial jurisdiction of the Federal court. The proposition is a general one; that where by State or Federal laws a State court has the right and the power to exercise jurisdiction in rem, concurrent with a Federal court; that that court which first exercises its jurisdictional power by seizing the property, shall be respected by the other court in the exercise of its jurisdiction, and shall have the right to proceed to judgment or decree and final execution in respect to the res.(1)

Where one suit at law and the other in equity.

SEC. 385. Hitherto we have supposed that both suits were pending at law or in chancery. The question now presents itself, whether the pendency of a suit at law for the same subject matter is a good de-defense in a court of equity.

The defense is not generally available where one of the suits is a suit at law and the other is a proceeding in chancery. The reason why the defense is not allowable in such case is, that the two suits are not deemed to have the same efficiency in the enforcement of the plaintiff's rights. The remedy at law may be assumed to be of a different character, reached by an application of different rules in some respects and enforced by different processes than that furnished by a court of chancery. Hence it is held that the pendency of the one may not be interposed to abate the other.

The general rule is that the plea is not available in equity.(2) Formerly the principal reason assigned for the rule was, that in equity the complainant has the

(1) The Ship Robert Fulton, 1 Paine, C. C. 621; Story on Conflict of Laws, Sec. 610a.

(2) Beames, Pl. in Eq. 146–148; Cooper, Eq. Pl. 276; Story's Eq. Pl. 363; Story on Conflict of Laws, Sec. 610a.

right to the oath of the defendant to exonerate him of the *onus probandi* at law.(1) But in modern practice under legislative enactments, allowing parties to suits generally to testify in their causes, when called by their adversaries, this technical reason would seem to have lost its force in a large measure.

The practice in chancery is quite prevalent, also, of waiving the oath of the defendant to his answer, by a clause in the bill itself, so that a suit in chancery in this respect ordinarily comes to trial before the court under very much the same circumstances as regards the proofs as a suit at law.

The right, however, to call upon the defendant to answer under oath and to make discovery still remains in practice in some States, and where that right is exercised and the defendant is called upon to answer under oath, the reason for the rule would still remain.

But a more general ground for holding the plea of the pendency of a suit at law ordinarily no bar to the right to bring a bill in chancery is, that it can scarcely ever occur that the measure of remedial justice and the ground of relief are precisely the same in each court, for, if the remedy be complete at law, then the court of equity for that reason can have no jurisdiction of the cause.(2)

On the other hand, where the merits of the chancery case could not be fully tried at law, where the relief

(1) Gilb. For. Rom. 55; Beames, Pl. in Eq. 146–148, Sec. 742.

Yet a plea of this sort is never required to be put in upon oath, because it is examinable by a master, as a matter of record. Mitf. Eq. Pl. by Jeremy, 247; Urlin *v.* Hudson, 1 Vern. 332; Beames, Pl. in Eq. 146; Cooper, Eq. Pl. 275.

(2) Gilb. For. Rom. 55; Beames, Ord. in Chan. 11, 12; Beames, Pl. in Eq. 146–148; Mitf. Eq. Pl. by Jeremy, 249, 450; Cooper, Eq. Pl. 276 Story's Eq. Pl.. Sec. 742; Rindskopf *v.* Platto, 29 Fed. R. 130.

given could not be adequate to that sought in the chancery court, it is manifest that the pendency of the suit at law ought not to stay the progress or bar the chancery suit.

As, however, the defendant should not to be vexed with a double remedy, a court of equity will, upon the coming in of the defendant's answer, put the plaintiff to his election whether he will proceed in the suit at law or in equity; and if he shall elect to proceed in equity, the chancellor will enjoin further proceedings in the suit at law.

If the complainant shall elect to proceed at law, the bill will be dismissed, but if he shall fail in the suit at law, the dismissal of his bill will not be a bar to his bringing another bill.(1)

Both suits must pend in courts of superior jurisdiction.

SEC. 386.   In order that the plea and defense of prior action pending may avail, the first suit must pend in a court of superior or equal jurisdiction with that of the second, and the defense will not be valid unless such is the case.

Thus, where an infant legatee sued an executor in

(1) Mitf. Eq. Pl. by Jeremy, 250, by Tyler, 340; Royle v. Wynne, Cr. and Phill. 252; Story's Eq. Pl., Sec. 742; Hogue v. Curtis, 1 Jac. & W. 449; Browne v. Ponytz, 3 Madd. 24.

But the plaintiff will not be required to elect in such case, unless the suit at law is for the same cause, and the remedy at law is co-extensive and equally beneficial with the remedy in equity. Way v. Bragaw, 16 N. J. Eq. 213.

If the pendency of the prior action is alleged in the bill, the court will take notice of it on demurrer, or on motion, and thereupon require the plaintiff to elect which remedy he will pursue. Sears v. Carrier, 4 Allen, 339.

Lord Bacon's 18th Rule provided that if the suits at common law and in chancery were for the same cause, the plaintiff should be required to elect by a day certain, and in default the case should be dismissed. See Lord Bacon's 18th Rule, Appendix.

the Ecclesiastical Court, and afterwards brought a suit in the Chancery Court, and the pendency of the prior suit in the Ecclesiastical Court was pleaded, it was held not to be available, because there was not the same security for the infant's advantage in the Ecclesiastical Court that there was in chancery.

So, also, where the original suit has been commenced in a court of superior jurisdiction, and the defendant has avoided the effect of the suit by going out of the jurisdiction of the court, the plea will not be good.(1)

Cannot be pleaded to a cross-suit.

SEC. 387. A cross-suit, although between the same parties as an original suit, cannot be met by a plea of this nature.

Thus, where a bill was brought in the Exchequer to foreclose a mortgage, it was held that the defendant might bring a bill to redeem in a Court of Chancery, and the pendency of the former suit was held not pleadable.

We have already seen that such a plea will not lie in a case where the second bill, although brought by the same party, was not brought in the same right.(2)

Where relief sought in one suit broader than in the other.

SEC. 388. There is another class of cases to which the same rule of practice may be applied.

It may occur that two cases are pending at the same time, between the same parties and with respect to the same res or subject matter, and where the cases are both on the common law or the chancery side of

(1) Way v. Bragaw, I. C. E. Green, N. J. 213; Howell v. Waldron, 1 Ch. Cas. 85.

(2) First Story's Eq. Pl. Sec. 400; Lord Newbury v. Wren, 1 Vern. 220.

the court, and yet where the relief sought in one of the cases may be in some respects broader and more comprehensive than that sought in the other.

In this class of cases a strict application of the technical rules would not allow of the sufficiency of a plea in abatement of the pendency of the former suit in the junior action. The usual reasons or grounds, however, of affording relief to the defendant in the junior action exist. They are, first, to prevent a collision between courts; but chiefly, second, to assure the parties a certain and unfluctuating adjudication of their rights and at the same time avoid the vexation of unnecessary suits.

Thus, it was held in the United States Circuit Court for the Western District of Michigan, in a case where it was shown that a former suit was pending between the same parties and involving the same res, but where the extent of the relief sought was less in degree than that before the court, that all further proceedings should be stayed in the case until the determination of the suit first commenced. In that case the court says: "It is quite likely that there is a distinction between those cases where the question is whether the former suit is one pleadable in strict abatement of the second, and those where the pendency of the former suit is presented as a ground for staying proceedings in the second. There would seem to be something of practical substance in that distinction, and, if so, it would furnish ground for holding, with complainant's counsel, that in order to be pleadable in abatement the first suit must be for the same purpose as the second, and substantially the same relief obtainable, and vice versa. I shall be required to hold that when the subject matter has been drawn into another jurisdiction for some purpose which may involve a decision upon its merits, the court should stay the second suit brought for a different purpose, and for relief not obtainable in the first suit, until the determination of the first, when the subject matter is released from the hold of the court, impressed or not by the adjudication which that court has made."(1)

Where prior action determined pleadable in bar.

SEC. 389. Where the prior action has proceeded to judgment or decree, it is not strictly correct to speak of the defense as that of a prior action pending. It is more properly denominated a prior action concluded, or determined. When the action, at the time of the commencement of the second suit, has proceeded to judgment or decree, the defense, when proper to be interposed, is in bar of the right of action, and not merely in abatement of that particular suit.

When plea in bar may be interposed.

SEC. 390. Where a judgment of a court of law of ordinary jurisdiction has finally determined the rights of the parties, that judgment may generally be pleaded in bar of a bill in chancery.(2)

But the plea must aver that the same issue was joined in the former suit as in the bill; that the subject matter of the suits was the same, and that the

(1) Hurd *v.* Moiles, 28 Fed. R. 899.

(2) Story's Eq. Pl, 780; Mitfs. Pl. in Eq. by Jeremy, 253, 254, 255; Cooper, Eq. Pl. 266; Beames' Pl. in Eq. 197, 198; Behrens *v.* Pauli, 1 Keen, 456; Behrens *v.* Sieveking, 2 Mdl. & Cr. 602.

proceedings in the prior case were for the same object and purpose.(1)

The sentence or judgment of a foreign court when rendered upon the same matter put in issue by bill, may be pleaded in bar of the latter, if the court pronouncing the sentence or judgment had jurisdiction.(2)

If the bill seeks to impeach the sentence or judgment at law by alleging fraud or other circumstances as ground for relief, the plea must, in addition to the usual averments, deny fraud or other circumstances, upon which the sentence or judgment is sought to be impeached, and thereby put them in issue by the plea.(3)

Although the court is not one of general jurisdiction, but has a peculiar and exclusive jurisdiction in matters properly cognizable there, its sentence, judgment or decree is conclusive when drawn in question collaterally in another court, whether a court of law or equity.(4)

A decree of a court of equity is generally of as high a dignity and character as a judgment in a law court.(5)

(1) Story's Eq. Pl. 781; Mitfs. Eq. Pl. by Jeremy, 255; Beames' Pl. in Eq. 198 & 199; Williams v. Lee, 3 Atk. 223; Mitchell v. Harris, 2 Ves. Jr. 135.

(2) Story's Eq. Pl. 783; Mitfs. Eq. Pl. 255, 256; Cooper's Eq. Pl. 266, 267; Beames' Pl. in Eq. 200, 201; Story on Conflict of Laws, 584, 618; Bowles v. Orr, 1 Y. & Coll. 464; Henderson v. Henderson, 3 Hare, 100, 113, 115; Ricardo v. Garcias, 12 Cl. & Fin. 368.

(3) Story's Eq. Pl. 784; Mitfs. Eq. Pl. by Jeremy, 256; Cooper, Eq.

Pl. 267; Beames' Pl. in Eq. 203, 204.

(4) Beames' Pl. in Eq. 201; Mitfs. Eq. Pl. by Jeremy, 257; Cooper. Eq. Pl. 268; Gaines v. Chew, 2 How. 619; Griffiths v. Hamilton, 12 Ves. 307; Meadows v. Kingston, Amb. 756.

(5) Story's Eq. Pl. 790; Beames Pl. in Eq. 205; Robinson v. Tonge, 3 P. Wms. 401, note (f), by Cox; Morice v. Bk. of Eng., Talbot 217; Mitfs. Eq. Pl. by Jeremy, 237, 239, 245.

In order to be a bar to the new suit, the decree must be substantially between the same parties, and for the same subject matter. It must either be final, or made so by subsequent order in the case.(1)

The plea of former decree must set forth so much of the former bill and answer as is necessary to show that the same point was then in issue.(2)

A decree in a prior suit against an infant may be pleaded in bar to a new bill brought by him, after he comes of age, for infants like adults are bound by decrees.(3)

If a former bill were dismissed upon the hearing, and it were not in terms directed to be without prejudice, the decree of dismissal may be pleaded in bar to a new bill for the same matter.(4)

But a decree in a former suit dismissing a bill for want of prosecution is not a bar to another bill. In order to be in bar to a new bill, the decree in the former suit must be conclusive upon the rights of the complainant in that bill, or those under whom he claims.(5)

A decree or judgment rendered final in an inferior court, by reason of the equal division of the judges of

(1) Story's Eq. Pl. 791; Mitfs. Eq. Pl. by Jeremy, 237, 238, 245; Cooper, Eq. Pl. 271; Beames' Pl. in Eq. 208, 210; Hunter v. Stewart, 10 W. R. 176, Waine v. Crocker, 31 L. J. (N. S.) Ch. 285; Londonderry v. Baker, 7 Jur. (N. S.), 811; Taylor v. Cornelius, 60 Penn. St. 187.

(2) Story's Eq. Pl. 791; Mitfs. Eq. Pl. by Jeremy, 237, 238, 245; Cooper, Eq. Pl. 271; Beames' Pl. in Eq. 208, 210.

(3) Story's Eq. Pl. 792.

(4) Story's Eq. Pl. 793; Mitfs Eq. Pl. by Jeremy, 239. 240.

(5) Story's Eq. Pl. 793; Mitfs. Eq. Pl. by Jeremy, 238, 239; Beames' Pl. in Eq. 210, 212; Cooper, Eq. Pl. 270, 271; Jones v. Nixon, Younge, 359; Perine v. Dunn, 4 Johns. Ch. 140; Neafie v. Neafie, 7 Johns. Ch.1; Durant v. Essex. Co., 7 Wal. 107; House v. Mullen, 22 Wall. 42; Badger v. Badger, 1 Cliff. 237; Foote v. Gibbs, 1 Gray, 412; Sayles v. Tibbitts, 5 R. I. 79.

the Appellate Court, and an order based thereon, is of equal force and validity between the parties to the suit, as if rendered by the unanimous voice of the court, and may be plead in bar like any other decree.(1)

It follows, of course, that where both actions are at law or in chancery and between the same parties and for the same purpose, the defense of prior judgment or decree is a good defense.

Practice in chancery.

SEC. 391. The usual course in a court of chancery where the plea of prior action pending is interposed, is not to reply to the plea, or to have the plea set down and argued, but to refer it to one of the masters in chancery to look into the two suits, and report whether or not they are both for the same matter. If the master reports that both suits are for the same subject matter, and that the plea is otherwise properly interposed, the plea is allowed, but if he reports otherwise, the plea is overruled.

Of course the report of a master, in a case of this kind, is subject to exception and argument before the court like any other report.

If, on the other hand, the complainant shall set down the plea to be argued, he admits the truth of the plea, and unless upon the face of the plea it shall appear defective in form, it must be allowed.(2)

(1) Durant v. Essex Co., 7 Wal. 107.

(2) Jones v. Segueira, 1 Phill. 82; Wedderburn v. Wedderburn, 2 Beav. 208; Cooper, Eq. Pl. 275; Story's Eq. Sec. 743; Mitford's Pl. by Tyler, 337; Baker v. Bird, 2 Ves. Jr. 672; Murray v. Shadwell, 17 Ves. 353; Carwick v. Young, 2 Swan St. 239.

By the present practice in England, when a bill is filed in one branch of the court, and a second bill in respect to the same matter has been previously filed in another branch, the second suit will be

Examination into the truth of the plea.

SEC. 392. There is said to be an anomaly in the proceeding relative to this plea, as its effect, it is said, is to preclude the complainant from having an examination both as to the truth of the plea, and a decision as to its form, as a plaintiff is generally entitled to it in legal proceedings.

It is said the anomaly consists in this, that if the complainant examine into the truth of the plea by the reference to the master, he waives his right to an opinion of the court on the form of the plea. While, on the other hand, if he set down the plea for the purpose of having a decision of the court upon its form, he thereby admits the truth of the plea and deprives himself of the right of examination before the master as to its truth, as in the latter case unless it should be held by the court defective in form, it must be allowed.(1)

When plea interposed in suit at law.

SEC. 393. We have already seen that the same principles of pleading are involved in a plea of prior action pending when interposed in chancery as at law.(2) The mode of procedure or practice, however, necessarily differs.

In an action at law an issue must be formed upon the plea which usually is triable by a jury, while as

transferred, on motion, to that branch of the court in which the first bill was filed, even when a decree in it has been obtained, and the complainant in the second suit will be required to pay the costs of the application for transfer, if he knew of the institution of the first suit. Orrell v. Busch, Lr. 5 Ch. 467; Lucas v. Siggers, Lr. 7 Ch. 517.

(1) Story's Eq. Pl. 744; Beames' Pl. in Eq. 144 and 146; Beames' Orders in Ch. 176, 177; Mitf. Eq. Pl. by Jeremy, 247 (by Tyler, 338); Cooper, Eq. Pl. 274, 276; Story's Eq. Pl. Sec. 744; Murray v. Shadwell, 17 Ves. 353.

(2) Sec. 371, ante.

we have seen, in chancery, the matter is referred to a master to make examination and report to the court his conclusions upon the facts involved in the plea.(1) There is also more strictness, probably, in pleading this defense, as there is in interposing any other dila‑ tory defense, in the suit at law, than there is in the chancery suit.

The averments, however, necessarily contained in the pleas interposed in both courts, are in substance the same.(2)

When the plea is filed, unless the plaintiff shall de‑ mur to it, a replication forming an issue on it is filed. This may be, that there is no such record as is averred in the plea, or setting up a new assignment, that the suit is for other and different causes of action than that alleged in the plea.(3)

(1) Sec. 382, *ante.*
(2) Sec. 371, *ante.*
(3) Puterbaugh's Pl. and Pr. 160, 161; Swan's Pr. 652 *a;* 1 Esp. 452.

For forms of pleas and replica‑ tions, see Nos. 1, 2, 3 and 4 follow‑ ing this section, pages 433 to 436 inclusive, *post.*

The following forms of pleas of prior suit depending, the one to be used in chancery and the other at law, and also forms of replications at law, may be convenient to the practitioner.

No. 1.   Plea in chancery of a former suit depending.

[Proper title and caption]. The plea of A, of the county of——[or if an infant or under disability, state how and by whom plead], to the bill of complaint of M against him in equity exhibited.

This defendant, by protestation, not confessing or acknowledging all or any part of the matters and things in the said bill of complaint contained to be true, in manner and form as the same are therein set forth, for plea nevertheless to the said bill doth plead and aver: that heretofore and before the said complainant exhibited his present bill in this court, to-wit: on the —day of——, A. D. 18—, the said complainant filed his bill of complaint in this court [or as the case may be], against this defendant, and also against——[or as the case may be], for the same matters and to the same effect, and for the like relief and purpose as against this defendant, as said complainant prays by his present bill, to which said bill this defendant answered [or appeared, as the case may be], and other proceedings thereupon were had; and the said former bill and proceedings now remain depending in this court [or as the case may be], and the said cause is yet undetermined and undismissed. All of which matters and things this defendant doth aver and plead in abatement of the complainant's present bill of complaint, and prays judgment of this court, whether he should be compelled to make any further answer to the said bill, and prays to be hence dismissed with his reasonable costs in this behalf sustained.

G H, Sol. for Defendant.

If the prior suit has gone to judgment or decree, substantially the same form may be used, varying it in the statement of the prior suit, and using the word "bar" instead of "abatement" in the closing part of the plea.

No. 2. Plea of another action pending for same cause.

In the————Court,

————Term, 18————

C D ⎱
ats. ⎰ Assumpsit.
A B

And the said C D, by G H, his attorney, comes and defends, etc., and prays judgment of the said writ, because he says that before the commencement of this suit, to-wit: on the————day of————, in the year 18————, the said A B impleaded the said C D in the said————Court of the said county of————in the State of————aforesaid [as the case may be], in a certain plea of trespass on the case, on the very same promises in the said declaration in this present suit mentioned; as by the record thereof remaining in the court last aforesaid more fully appears. And the said C D further says that the parties in this and the said former suit are the same, and not other or different persons [or if different state the fact], and that the said former suit is still pending in the court last aforesaid. And this he, the said C D, is ready to verify; wherefore he prays judgment of the said writ in this suit, and that the same may be quashed, etc.

G H, Attorney for Defendant.

In the——Court,
   ——Term, 18——

C D }
 ats. }   Assumpsit.
A B }

C D, the defendant in the above cause makes oath and says that the plea hereunto annexed is true in substance and in fact.   C D.

Subscribed and sworn, etc.

No. 3. Replication to plea—nul tiel record.

In the——Court,
   ——Term, 18——

A B }
 vs. }   Assumpsit.
C D }

And the plaintiff says that the said writ, by reason of anything by the defendant in his said plea above alleged, ought not to be quashed, because he says that there is not any record of the said supposed former suit remaining in the said——Court of the said county of——, in manner and form as the said C D has above in his said plea alleged: And this the plaintiff is ready to verify, when, where and in such manner as the court here shall order, etc.

      L M, Attorney for Plaintiff.

No. 4. Replication. New assignment that suit was for different cause of action.

In the——Court,
   ——Term, 18——

A B }
 vs. }   Assumpsit.
C D }

And the plaintiff says that the said writ, by reason

of anything by the defendant in his said plea above
alleged, ought not to be quashed, because he says that
he sued out his said writ against the said defendant,
and declared thereon not for the non-performance of
of the promises in said plea mentioned [or as the case
may be in other form of action], and in respect
whereof the supposed former suit therein also mentioned is so pending as aforesaid, but for the non-performance of other and different promises made by the
defendant to the plaintiff [or as the case may be in
other form of action], in manner and form as he has
above thereof complained against the defendant:
And this the plaintiff is ready to verify; wherefore,
etc., he prays judgment, etc.

L M, Attorney for Plaintiff.

APPENDIX.

Rule 21. No injunctions against suits at law, except on a matter confessed or of record. Plain writing when in contempt, or debts stale, or death before suit.

Rule 22. Injunctions against suits at Common Law when defendant appears not, fails to answer, is attached, takes oath, etc., sues at common law, etc., or is beyond seas granted until, etc. Upon answer without motion, etc., injunction dissolved without special order, etc.

Rule 23. If like suit to stay, etc., in Chancery by *scire facias*, privilege, English bill, suits stayed by order, etc.

Rule 24. If no prosecution for three terms, injunction dissolves without motion.

Rule 25. After arrest for debt principal money brought into Court, except debt shown clearly inequitable, or injunction dissolved.

Rule 26. No injunction for possession before decree, except possession for three years before bill upon same title, and not by lease or otherwise.

Rule 27. Sequestration of the lands when contempt, *non est inventus*, resistance, etc., or rescue, or surrender within the year.

Rule 28. Injunctions against felling timber, ploughing, etc., maintaining inclosures, etc., allowed according to circumstances, but not where defendant claims estate of inheritance, etc.

Rule 29. No sequestration, except as to property in suit.

Rule 30. Where decree for rent of lands, lands sequestrated.

Rule 31. Chancery gives remedy when Provincial Counsel, Court of Requests, or Queen's Court are interrupted.

Rule 32. Decrees in causes in other Courts first read before determined.

Rule 33. Bonds to prove suggestions of bill when re-hearings.

Rule 34. Decrees to correct injunctions against judgments shall not avoid or weaken the judgment.

Rule 35. Registers are to be sworn.

Rule 36. The Court to be informed of last order, or order set aside. Made the duty of registers.

Rule 37. Orders explained in court. Registers to set down orders truly, etc.

Rule 38. Registers keep copy of orders delivered to parties and why.

Rule 39. Opinion of Court on leases not to be omitted in order of reference. Unless directed otherwise registers make full memoranda, etc.

Rule 40. Registers not to regard interlineations of counsel.

Rule 41. Registers careful in draughting decrees and advise Chancellor of important ones.

RULE 42. Decrees to be presented two or three days after term.

RULE 43. Injunctions with orders for possession or stay of suits, etc., to be presented before signing.

RULE 44. Registers to set down grounds in special cases where rules are to be varied.

RULE 45. No references to Masters of demurrers, or questions of jurisdiction.

RULE 46. Orders *nisi* confirming report not less than seven days.

RULE 47. No reference to hear and determine as to examination of witnesses, except in special cases, etc.

RULE 48. Report not to exceed reference.

RULE 49. Not to report synopsis of evidence, but opinion or otherwise if doubtful, etc.

RULE 50. In cases on account the Court will hear and then refer with directions, except both parties agree otherwise.

RULE 51. The like course before two Masters for examination of Court rolls, etc.

RULE 52. In references of answers for defects, points of insufficiency must be shown.

RULE 53. When trust confessed reference presently.

RULE 54. Where no probable cause plaintiff pays cost.

RULE 55. Where pleadings too lengthy parties and counsel fined.

RULE 56. Pleadings with libelous, slanderous, impertinent matter, etc., taken from files, etc., and parties punished, etc., and counsellors, etc., receive reproof, etc.

RULE 57. Demurrers and pleas in abatement first heard.

RULE 58. Demurrer to defective matter contained in bill. Plea sets up foreign matter, etc., without oath, if of record, but otherwise on oath.

RULE 59. Plea of outlawry *sub pede sigilli;* of excommunication, without seal of ordinary.

RULE 60. Demurrer dismissed on demurrer under fifteenth rule.

RULE 61. Upon insufficient answer defendant pays single cost, then double costs, etc. If answer certified sufficient, plaintiff pays costs.

RULE 62. Replication admits answer sufficient.

RULE 63. Answer to direct charge must be direct, and not upon belief; denial not by way of negative pregnant. Traverse not literally in language of bill but in substance.

RULE 64. When hearing on bill and answer, answer must admit bill true in all points.

RULE 65. When defendant does not appear his answer must be read.

RULE 66. No new matter in replication, except in avoidance.

RULE 67. All copies must contain fifteen lines per page subscribed by name of principal clerk.

Rule 68. Interrogatories accompany commission to examine witnesses. Depositions must be compromised in one roll,
or in roll, signed, etc.

Rule 69. If plaintiff do not produce witnesses on commission to examine, no new commission granted except the fault was
defendant's. May examine in court upon former interrogatories, etc.

Rule 70. Defendant not to be examined except by order of court and
upon plaintiff's offer to be concluded.

Rule 71. Decrees of other courts read without special order, depositions not; and then between same parties and cause of
action.

Rule 72. No impeachement of witnesses except by special order.

Rule 73. Examination of witnesses in *perpetam rei memoriam*, except after bill and answer, and giving the names of the
witnesses. Deposition to be used only in case of death,
age, incompetency, or absence from the realm.

Rule 74. Witnesses not examined after publication except by consent
or special order.

Rule 75. Affidavit not taken by Masters, touching merits, etc.

Rule 76. No affidavit taken against affidavit, etc.

Rule 77. Committed for contempt, for force, if words, words of scandal,
etc. For other contempts, attachments, examination on
interrogatories and examination confessed. Committed
if confessed or proved. Contempt discharged for non-
prosecution.

Rule 78. Those in contempt not suffered in court, except the Court
suspend the contempt.

Rule 79. Imprisonments discharged, etc., unless for disobedience to
decree when must first obey decree. May be suspended
temporarily.

Rule 80. Injunctions, etc., not granted upon petition.

Rule 81. No former order to be altered, etc., on petition except for
small stay or until hearing of motion.

Rule 82. No commission for examination of witnesses, etc., upon petition except upon reference to and certification of clerk.

Rule 83. No demurrer overruled upon petition.

Rule 84. No *scire facias* on recognizances not enrolled, nor on one
enrolled, except on examination of the record, with writ,
etc.

Rule 85. Certain writs not awarded without warrant from Lord Chancellor, except certain writs named.

Rule 86. Where rule for rights of privilege. Suitors and witnesses
proved *eundo, redeundo* and *morando*. Interference
with privilege a contempt of court.

RULE 87. *Supplicavit* granted only on certain conditions.

RULE 88. No recognizance, etc., without warrant from Lord Chancellor.

RULE 89. Writs *ne exeat regnum,* how granted in different classes of cases.

RULE 90. Writs, etc., filed in Chapel of Rolls, etc. Depositions of witnesses remain with six clerks.

RULE 91. Writs of injunction enlarged, etc.

RULE 92. All directions to sheriffs to return writs filed in register's office or Pety Bag. All recognizances with the clerks of the Inrollment.

RULE 93. Exceptions only in certain cases where decree may be entered without bill.

RULE 94. Proceedings in suit for commission of sewers.

RULE 95. New commission of sewards not granted except for abuse of first commission or other weighty ground.

RULE 96. Proceedings in petition of bankrupt.

RULE 97. Commission of delegates, how appointed.

RULE 98. Defendants may defend *forma pauperis.* How plaintiffs may proceed thus.

RULE 99. Licenses to clerk for losses from fire or water granted, when and how.

RULE 100. Exemplification, how made.

RULE 101. Reservations of power to amend or add to ordinances.

Bill of review brought only for error on record or new matter.

RULE 1. "No decree(1) shall be reversed, altered, or explained, being once under the great-seal, but upon bill of review; and no bill of review shall be admitted, except it contain, either error in law appearing in the body of the decree, without further examination of

(1) Mitford Ch. Pl. 78, 81; Taylor *v.* Sharp, 3 P. Wms. 371; Lewellin *v.* Mackenworth, 2 Atk. 40; Standish *v.* Radley, 2 Atk. 176; Moore *v.* Moore, 2 Ves. Sr. 596; Perry *v.* Phillips, 17 Ves. 177; Davis *v.* Larner, 1 Dick. 42.

It was more than usual to proceed by way of supplemental bill, in the nature of a bill of review, as a bill of review could only be brought when the decree had been enrolled, and as decrees were seldom enrolled.

matters in fact,(1) or, some new matter(2) which hath risen in time after the decree, and not any new proof which might have been used when the decree was made; nevertheless, upon new proof that is come to light after the decree made, and could not possibly have been used at the time when the decree passed, a bill of review may be grounded(3) by the special license of the Court and not otherwise."(4)

Clerical error corrected without bill.

. Rule 2. "In case of mis-casting (being a matter

(1) Mitford Ch. Pl. 65, 81; Young v. Keighly, 16 Ves. 350; Mitford Ch. Pl. 78; Grice v. Goodwin, Finch, Prec. Ch. 260; Combs v. Proud, 1 Ch. Cas. 54; Slingsby v. Hale, 1 Ch. Cas. 122; Colwell v. Child, 1 Ch. Cas. 86; Lytton v. Lytton, 4 Bro. Ch. Cas. 442; Millish v. Williams, 1 Vern. 166; Fitton v. Lord Macclesfield, 1 Vern. 287; 2 Freem. 88; Bonham v. Newcomb, 1 Vern. 214.

As to when a bill of review could be brought without leave of court, see: Gould v. Tancred, 2 Atk. 533; Gartside v. Ishenwood, 2 Dick. 614; and Mitford Ch. Pl. 78.

(2) Attorney Gen. v. Turner, 2 Amb. 587; Chambers v. Greenhill, 2 Ch. R. 35; seems contra.

Tuthill mentions two cases (Transact. 20) to the effect that "no bill of review admitted upon new matter," but in the same work at page 66 he gives another case of "decree reversed though no new matter."

The new matter should be relevant. Lord Portsmouth v. Lord Effingham, 2 Ves. Sr. 430; Bennett v. Lee, 2 Atk. 528; Mitford Ch. Pl. 79.

(3) The distinction is made where the matter was particularly in issue before the former hearing, though the party have new proof of such matter, and when the new fact was not then in issue. A bill of review would not lie in the former case.

Lord Hardwicke in construing this order in Norris v. Le Neve, 2 Atk. 26, said: "It has not been so strict that the new proof must not come to the party's knowledge till after the cause has been heard; it is very sufficient if it did not come to their knowledge, till after publication, or when by the rules of the court they could not make use of it."

In Patterson v. Slaughter, 1 Amb. 293, speaking of words of the order, he said, "they are dark in themselves," that is, "that came to the knowledge of the party after publication passed."

(4) Leave would not be given, unless upon allegation upon oath, that the new matter could not be produced, or used when the decree was made. Mitford Ch. Pl. 78.

demonstrative) a decree may be explained and reconciled by an order without a bill of review; not understanding by mis-casting any pretended mis-rating or misvaluing, but only error in the auditing or numbering."(1)

Decree first obeyed and performed.

RULE 3. "No bill of review shall be admitted, or any other new bill to change matter decreed, except the decree be first obeyed and performed; as, if it be for land, that the possession be yielded; if it be for money, that the money be paid; if it be for evidences, that the evidences be brought in; and so in other cases which stand upon the strength of the decree alone."(2)

Saving extinguishment of rights until final decree.

RULE 4. "But, if any act be decreed to be done which extinguisheth the party's right at the Common Law, as making of assurance or release, acknowledging satisfaction, cancelling of bonds, or evidences, and the like, those parts of the decree are to be spared, until the bill of review be determined; but such sparing is to be warranted by public order made in Court."(3)

Recognizances to be filed by complainant.

RULE 5. "No bill of review shall be put in, except the party that prefers it enter into recognizance, with

(1) Wallis v. Thomas, 7 Ves. Jr. 292.

(2) Mitf. Ch. Pl. 79; Ruton v. Ascough, Finch. R. 162; Williams v. Mellish, 1 Vern. 117; Bishop of Durham v. Liddell, 2 Br. P. C. 24.

As appears in Savil v. Darcey, 1 Ch. Ca. 42, the House of Lords in 1662, in Baston v. Byron, dispensed with the rule in the text, upon the mere circumstance, that the decree was "for a great sum of money"

(3) Fitton v. Lord Macclesfield, 1 Vern. 264.

sureties, for satisfying of costs and damages for the delay, if it be found against him."(1)

No decree against Act of Parliament.

RULE 6. "No decree shall be made upon pretence of equity against the express provision of an Act of Parliament; nevertheless, if the construction of such Act of Parliament hath for a time gone away in general opinion and reputation, and after, by a later judgment hath been controlled, then relief may be given upon matter of equity, for cases arising before the said judgment, because the subject was in no default."(2)

Imprisonment for breach, strict, but close confinement for wilful disobedience only.

RULE 7. "Imprisonment for breach of a decree is in nature of an execution, and, therefore, the custody ought to be straight, and the party not to have any liberty to go abroad but by special license of the Lord Chancellor; but no close imprisonment is to be but by express order for wilful and extraordinary contempts and disobedience as hath been used."

Fines pronounced in open court for persistent contempts.

RULE 8. "In case of enormous and obstinate disobedience in breach of a decree, an injunction is to be granted *subpœna* of a sum; and upon affidavit or other

(1) This order of Lord Bacon seems to have been repealed by general orders of March 12th, 1700, and Oct. 17th, 1741, substituting a deposit with the register of fifty pounds before any bill of review or supplemental bill in the nature thereof be allowed. See Beames'

Orders of Chancery, pp. 312 and 366.

(2) It was one of the provisions of Oliver Cromwell's ordinance for regulating the court of chancery, "that no decree be made in chancery against an act of parliament."

sufficient proof of persisting in contempts, fines are to be pronounced by the Lord Chancellor in open Court, and the same extracted down into the Hanaper, if cause be, by a special order."(1)

Writ of execution for possession of lands. Mode of execution in such cases.

RULE 9. "In case of a decree made for the possession of land, a writ of execution goeth forth; and, if that be disobeyed, then process of contempt, according to the course of the Court against the person to commission of rebellion; and then a Sergeant at Arms by special warrant; and in case the Sergeant at Arms cannot find him, or be resisted, upon the coming in of the party and his commitment, if he persist in disobedience, an injunction is to be granted for the possession, and in case that also be disobeyed, then a commission to put him in possession."(2)

Contemner not enlarged until decree executed, except as to parts to be performed in futuro.

RULE 10. "Where the party is committed for breach of a decree, he is not to be enlarged until the decree be fully performed in all things which are to be done presently.

But, if there be other parts of the decree to be performed at days or times to come, then, he may be enlarged by order of Court upon a recognizance, with sureties, to be put in for the performance *de futuro*, otherwise not."(3)

(1) Harrison's Pr. 331; Newland's Pr. 193.

(2) If the injunction to deliver up possession be disobeyed, after it is served and oath made thereof, the court in that case granted a commission to some justice of the peace to put the party in possession. West's Symbol (2d Pt.) 189; Boles *v.* Walley, Cary's R. 53.

(3) In Forum Romanum, p. 191, it is said "the ancient way of pun-

Process ad audiendum judicium.

RULE 11. "Where causes come to a hearing in Court, no decree bindeth any person who was not served with process *ad audiendum judicium*, according to the course of the Court, or did appear in person in Court."

Grantee before suit not served nor bound. Grantees pending suit bound by decree.

RULE 12. "No decree bindeth any that cometh in *bona fide*, by conveyance from the defendant before the bill exhibited, and is made no party, neither by bill, nor order: but where he comes in *pendente lite*, and, while the suit is in full prosecution, and without any color of allowance or privity of the Court, there regularly the decree bindeth; but, if there were any intermission of suit, or the Court made acquainted with the conveyance, the Court is to give order upon the special matter according to justice."(1)

Where cause dismissed on hearing not again heard, except on bill of review.

RULE 13. "Where causes are dismissed upon full hearing, and the dismission signed by the Lord Chancellor, such causes shall not be retained again, nor new bill admitted, except it be upon new matter, like to the case of the bill of review."

ishing the contumacy was by imprisonment; but, after the sequestration process obtained, then it was not thought enough to punish the evil conscience of the party by imprisonment, but likewise to compel him, when he appeared to be a prisoner, to make satisfaction." See also 192, Forum Romanum, note.

This section of Lord Bacon's order was further enforced by Lord Clarendon's orders. Beames' Orders of Chancery, p. 208.

(1) This particular ordinance is the subject of the foregoing Treatise on Lis Pendens, and has been presented in all its phases, in the body of this work.

When case dismissed not on hearing, new bill dismissed or retained according to justice.

RULE 14. "In case of other dismissions which are not upon hearing of the cause, if any new bill be brought, the dismission is to be pleaded: and after reference and report of the contents of both suits, and consideration taken of the causes of the former dismission, the Court shall rule the retaining or dismissing of the new bill, according to justice and the nature of the case."(1)

Suits on nuncupative wills, parol leases, long leases, perpetuities, remainders, for brokage, rewards of marriage, wagers, sales of office, etc., contract upon usury, dismissed on motion. Suits under ten pounds regularly dismissed.

RULE 15. "All suits grounded upon wills nuncupative,(2) leases parol,(3) or upon long leases that tend to the defacing of the King's tenures,(4) for the establishing of perpetuities, or grounded upon remainders put into the Crown to defeat purchasers, or for brokage or rewards to make marriages, or for bargains at play and wagers; or for bargains for offices contrary to the

(1) Mitf. Ch. Pl. 195 and 196. A dismission for want of prosecution upon an interlocutory order is not pleadable. Forum Romanum, 201; Brandlyn v. Ord, 1 Atk. 571; Prettyman v. Prettyman, 1 Vern. 309; Anon. 1 Ch. Ca. 155.

(2) The statutes 29 Cas. 2 C. 3 and 4 and 5 Ann. C. 16, materially altered the old laws on the subject of nuncupative wills.

(3) Since the Statute of Fraud, 29 Cas. 2, C. 3, all interest in lands, etc., except leases for three years, had to be in writing. The doctrine

of part performance has been allowed to take cases out of that statute, and there is no case known to have been decided, where that doctrine was not applicable to chattels.

(4) In Hire v. Wordall, Tuth. 121, the reporter states the lease was for 1,000 years, "which is most commonly to prevent the king's right." And in Risden v. Tuffin, Tuth. 122, it is said there is no relief in equity touching leases of one thousand years, because they tend to defraud the Crown.

statute of 2 Edw. 6,(1) or for contracts upon usury(2) or simony, are regularly to be dismissed upon motion, if they be the sole effect of the bill, and if there be no special circumstances to move the Court to allow them a proceeding; and all suits under the value of ten pounds are regularly to be dismissed."(3)

Dismissions at first of cause and not after examination, except for special cause.

RULE 16. "Dismissions are properly to be prayed and had, either upon hearing, or upon plea unto the bill, when the cause comes first into the Court; but dismissions are not to be prayed after the parties have been at charges of examination except it be upon special cause."

Dismissals of course without motion for non-prosecution, after answer for one term. After replication not without motion and order.

RULE. 17. "If the plaintiff discontinue by prosecution, after all the defendants have answered above the space of one whole term, the cause is to be dismissed of course, without any motion; but, after replication put in, no cause is to be dismissed, without motion and order of the Court."(4)

(1) 5th and 6th Edw., 6 C. 16; Earl of Kingston v. Pierrepont, 1 Vern. 5; Law v. Law, Talbot, 140; Harrington v. Du Chatel, 1 Bro. C. C. 124; Bellamy v. Burrow, Talbot, 180; Morris v. M'Bullock, 1 Amb. 435; Thrale v. Ross, 3 Bro. C. C. 57; Ive v. Ash, Finch Prac. Ch. 199; Berrisford v. Done, 1 Vern. 98.

(2) So early as 37 Eliz. the court relieved from usurious contract, on payment of money advanced. Tuth·(Transact.) 134; 1 Forb. Tr. 25, 139, 140, 237.

(3) There were exceptions to the rule, one of which was when the suit was for the benefit of the poor or for charity. Parrot v. Pawlet, Cary, 147.

Another was where the bill was brought to establish a right.

(4) Harrison's Pr. Ch. 313 *et seq.*; Newland's Pr. 106 *et seq.*; Forum Romanum, 114.

If suits at Common Law and in Chancery for same cause, plaintiff must elect.

RULE 18. "Double vexation is not to be admitted: but if the party sue for the same cause at Common Law and in Chancery, he is to have a day given to make his election where he will proceed; and, in default of such election, to be dismissed."

Upon special certiorari plaintiff must give bond to make proof within fourteen days. If not done, it must be upon certificate dismissed.

RULE 19. "Where causes are removed by special *certiorari* upon a bill containing matter of equity, the plaintiff is, upon receipt of his writ, to put in bond to prove his suggestion within fourteen days after the receipt, which, if he do not prove, then, upon certificate from either of the examiners presented to the Lord Chancellor, the cause shall be dismissed with costs, and *procedendo* to be granted."

No injunctions upon private petition.

RULE 20. "No injunction of any nature shall be granted, revived, dissolved or stayed, upon any private petition."(1)

No injunctions against suits at law, except on a matter confessed or of record. Plain writing when in contempt, or debts stale, or death before suit.

RULE 21. "No injunction to stay suits at the law shall be granted upon priority of suit only, or upon surmise of the plaintiff's bill only, but upon matter confessed in the defendant's answer or matter of record, or writing plainly appearing, or when the de-

(1) 1 Turn. Pr. Ch. P. 244, note; Mayor of London *v.* Bolt, 5 Ves. 129; Mason *v.* Murray, 2 Dick. 536; Nicholls *v.* Kearsly, 2 Dick. 645; Harris, Pr. 541.

fendant is in contempt for not answering, or that the
debt desired to be stayed appeareth to be old and hath
slept long, or the creditor or the debtor hath been
dead some good time before the suit brought."

Injunctions against suits at Common Law when defendant appears not, fails to answer, is attached,
takes oath, etc., sues at Common Law, etc., or is
beyond seas, granted until, etc. Upon answer without motion, etc., injunction dissolved without special
order, etc.

RULE 22. "Where the defendant appears not but
sits an attachment; or when he doth appear, and de-
parts without answer, and is under attachment for
not answering; or when he takes oath he cannot answer without sight of evidences in the country; or
where after answer he sues at Common Law by attorney, and absents himself beyond sea; in these cases
an injunction is to be granted for the stay of all suits
at the Common Law, until the party answer, or appear
in person in Court, and the Court give further order:
but, nevertheless, upon answer put in, if there be no
motion made the same term, or the next general seal
after the term, to continue the injunction, in regard
of the insufficiency of the answer put in, or in regard
of the matter confessed in the answer, then, the injunction to die and dissolve without any special order."

If like suit to stay, etc., in Chancery by scire facias,
privilege, English bill, suits stayed by order, etc.

RULE 23. "In the case aforesaid, where an injunction is to be granted for stay of suits at the Common
Law, if the like suit be in the Chancery, either by *scire
facias,* or privilege, or English bill, then, the suit is to
be stayed by order of the Court as it is in other Courts

by injunction; for that the Court cannot enjoin itself."(1)

If no prosecution for three terms, injunction dissolves without motion.

RULE 24. "Where an injunction hath been obtained for stay of suits, and no prosecution is had for the space of three terms, the injunction is to fall of itself without further motion."

After arrest for debt, principal money brought into court, except debt shown clearly inequitable, or injunction dissolved.

RULE 25. "Where a bill comes in after an arrest at the Common Law for a debt, no injunction shall be granted without bringing the principal money into Court, except there appear in the defendant's answer, or by sight of writings, plain matter tending to discharge the debt in equity; but, if an injunction be awarded and disobeyed, in that case no money shall be brought in or deposited in regard of the contempt."

No injunction for possession before decree, except possession for three years before bill upon same title, and not by lease or otherwise.

RULE 26. "Injunctions for possession are not to be granted before a decree, but where the possession hath continued by the space of three years, before the bill exhibited and upon the same title, and not upon any title by lease, or otherwise, determined."

(1) "A suit by English bill by way of distinction from the proceedings in suit within the ordinary jurisdiction of the court, which till the statute of 4 Geo. 2 C. 26 were entered and enrolled more anciently in the French or Norman tongue, and afterwards in the Latin, in the same manner as the pleadings in the other courts of common law." Mitf. Ch. Pl. P. 7.

Sequestration of the lands when contempt, non est in-
    ventus, resistance, etc., or rescue, or surrender
    within the year.

RULE 27. "In case where the defendant sits all the
process of contempt, and cannot be found by the
Sergeant at Arms, or resists the Sergeant, or makes
rescue, a sequestration shall be granted of the land in
question; and, if the defendant render not himself
within the year, then, an injunction for the possession."

Injunctions against felling timber, ploughing, etc., main-
    taining inclosures, etc., allowed according to cir-
    cumstances, but not where defendant claims estate
    of inheritance, etc.

RULE 28. "Injunctions against felling of timber,
ploughing up of ancient pastures, or for the maintaining of inclosures, or the like, shall be granted according to the circumstances of the case: but not in case
where the defendant upon his answer claimeth an
estate of inheritance, except it be where he claimeth
the land in trust, or upon some other special ground."

No sequestration, except as to property in suit.

RULE 29. "No sequestration shall be granted but of
lands, leases, or goods in question,(1) and not of any
other lands or goods, not contained in the suits."

Where decree for rent of lands, lands sequestrated.

RULE 30. "Where a decree is made for rent to be
paid out of land, or a sum of money to be levied out
of the profits of land, there a sequestration of the
same lands, being in the defendants' hands, may be
granted."

(1) Hide v. Pettit, 1 Ch. Ca. 91; Harris, Pr. 132.

Chancery gives remedy when Provincial Counsel, Court of Requests, or Queen's Court are interrupted.

RULE 31. "Where the decrees of the Provincial Counsel, or of the Court of Requests, (1) or the Queen's Court, are by continuancy or other means interrupted, there the Court of Chancery, upon a bill preferred for corroborations of the same jurisdictions, decrees, and sentences, shall give remedy."

Decrees in causes in other courts first read before determined.

RULE 32. "Where any cause comes to a hearing that hath been formerly decreed in any other of the King's Courts of Justice at Westminster, such decree shall be first read, and then to proceed to the rest of the evidence on both sides."

Bonds to prove suggestions of bill when re-hearings.

RULE 33. "Suits after judgment may be admitted according to the ancient custom of the Chancery, and the late royal decision of his Majesty of record after solemn and great deliberation: but, in such suits, it is ordered, that bond be put in with good sureties to prove the suggestions of the bill."

Decrees to correct injunctions against judgments shall not avoid or weaken the judgment.

RULE 34. "Decrees upon suits brought after judgment shall contain no words to make void or weaken the judgment, but shall only correct the corrupt conscience of the party, and rule him to make restitu-

(1) *Curia Requisitionum*, the Court of Requests, a court of equity said to be of the same nature as the court of chancery, but inferior to it.

4 Just. 96, 97; 3 Bl. Comn. 50, note (*h*).

This court was virtually abolished by Stat. 12, Car. I. C. 10. For instances of its proceedings see Troth. (Transact.) 24, 64, 65, 66 68 and 118.

tion, or perform other acts, according to the equity of the case."

Registers are to be sworn.

RULE 35. "The registers are to be sworn, as hath been lately ordered."(1)

The court to be informed of last order, or order set aside. Made the duty of registers.

RULE 36. "If any order shall be made, and the Court not informed of the last material order formerly made, no benefit shall be taken by such order, as granted by abuse and surreption; and to that end, the registers ought duly to mention the former order in the latter."

Orders explained in court. Registers to set down orders truly, etc.

RULE 37. "No order shall be explained upon any private petition, but in Court as they are made; and the register is to set down the orders as they were pronounced by the Court truly at his peril, without troubling the Lord Chancellor by any private attending of him to explain his meaning; and if any explanation be desired, it is to be done by public motion, where the other party may be heard."

Registers keep copy of orders delivered to parties and why.

RULE 38. "No draught of any order shall be delivered by the register to either party, without keeping a copy by him; to the end, that if the order be not entered, nevertheless, the Court may be informed what was formerly done, and not put to new trouble and

(1) It is said that in the 40th of Elizabeth there was but one register, but that in Lord Bacon's time and about 1618 four deputy registers were appointed.

hearing, and, to the end also, that knowledge of orders be not kept back too long from either party, but may presently appear at the office."

Opinion of court on leases not to be omitted in order of reference. Unless directed otherwise registers make full memoranda, etc.

RULE 39. "Where a lease hath been debated, upon hearing of both parties, and opinion hath been delivered by the Court, and, nevertheless, the cause referred to treaty, the registers are not to omit the opinion of the Court in drawing of the order of reference, except the Court doth specially declare, that it be entered without any opinion either way; in which case, nevertheless, the registers are, out of their short note, to draw up some more full remembrance of that that passed in Court, to inform the Court, if the cause come back and cannot be agreed."

Registers not to regard interlineations of counsel.

RULE 40. "The registers, upon sending of their draught unto the counsel of the parties, are not to respect the interlineations or alterations of the said counsel (be the said counsel never so great), further than to put them in remembrance of that which was truly delivered in Court, and so to conceive the order upon their oath and duty, without any further respect."

Registers careful in draughting decrees and to advise Chancellor of important ones.

RULE 41. "The registers are to be careful in the penning and drawing up of decrees, and special matters of difficulty and weight, and, therefore, when they present the same to the Lord Chancellor, they ought to give him understanding which are those decrees of weight, that they may be read and reviewed, before his Lordship sign them."

Decrees to be presented within two or three days after term.

RULE 42. "The decrees granted at the Rolls are to be presented to his Lordship with the orders whereupon they are drawn, within two or three days after every term."

Injunctions with orders for possession or stay of suits, etc., to be presented before signing.

RULE 43. "Injunctions for possession, or for stay of suits after verdict, are to be presented to his Lordship, together with the orders whereupon they go forth, that his Lordship may take consideration of the order before he sign them."

Registers to set down grounds in special cases where rules are to be varied.

RULE 44. "Where any order upon the special nature of the case shall be made against any of these general rules, there the register shall plainly and expressly set down the particulars, reasons, and grounds, moving the Court to vary from the general rule."

No references to Master of demurrers, or questions of jurisdiction.

RULE 45. "No reference upon a demurrer, or question touching the jurisdiction of the Court, shall be made to the Masters of the Chancery, but such demurrers shall be heard and ruled in Court, or by the Lord Chancellor himself."(1)

(1) It seems, that in the Star Chamber it was usual when a plea or demurrer was put into the form or matter of the bill, to refer it to the judgment of the judges or king's counsel, "except the plea and the demurrer be to the jurisdiction of the court, then it was deemed fit to be decided in open court." 2 Coll. Jur. 20; Beames' Orders of Chancery, pp. 173 and 174.

Orders nisi confirming report not less than seven days.

RULE 46. "No order shall be made for the confirming or ratifying of any report, without day first given, by the space of a seven-night at the least, to speak to it in Court."(1)

No reference to hear and determine as to examination of witnesses, except in special cases, etc.

RULE 47. "No reference shall be made to any Masters of the Court, or any other Commissioners, to hear and determine, where the cause is gone so far as to examination of witnesses, except it be in special cases of parties near in blood, or of extreme poverty, or by consent, and generally reference of the state of the cause, except it be by consent of the parties, to be sparingly granted."

Report not to exceed reference.

RULE 48. "No report shall be respected in Court, which exceedeth the warrant of reference."

Not to report synopsis of evidence, but opinion or otherwise, if doubtful, etc.

RULE 49. "The Masters of the Court are required not to certify the state of any cause, as if they would make breviates of the evidence on both sides, which doth little ease the Court, but with some opinion, or otherwise, in case they think it too doubtful to give opinion, and, therefore, make such special certificate, the cause is to go on to a judicial hearing, without respect had to the same."

(1) Mr. Newland, in his Ch. Pr. 173, says that an order to confirm a master's report, "is necessary only where the report is to be the ground of a decree;" therefore his report on the alleged scandal or impertinence of pleadings, or on the insufficiency of an answer need not be confirmed, nor his taxation of costs, nor his report of receiver's account.

In cases of account the court will hear and then refer with directions, except both parties agree otherwise.

RULE 50. "Masters of account, unless it be in very weighty causes, are not fit for the Court, but to be prepared by reference, with this difference, nevertheless, that the cause comes first to a hearing, and, upon the entrance into a hearing, they may receive some direction, and be turned over to have the accounts considered, except both parties before a hearing do consent to a reference of the examination of the accounts to make it more ready for a hearing."

The like course before two Masters for examination of court rolls, etc.

RULE 51. "The like course to be taken for the examination of Court-rolls, upon customs and copies, which shall not be referred to any one Master, but to two Masters at the least."

In references of answers for defects, points of insufficiency must be shown.

RULE 52. "No reference to be made of the insufficiency of an answer, without shewing of some particular point of the defect, and not upon surmise of the insufficiency in general."

Where trust confessed reference presently.

RULE 53. "Where a trust is confessed by the defendant's answer, there needeth no farther hearing of the cause, but a reference presently to be made of the account, and so to go on to a hearing of the accounts."

Where no probable cause plaintiff pays cost.

RULE 54. "In all suits, where it shall appear upon the hearing of the cause, that the plaintiff had not *probabilem causam litigandi*, he shall pay unto t defendant his utmost costs to be assessed by the Court."(1)

Where pleadings too lengthy parties and counsel fined.

RULE 55. "If any bill, answer, replication, or rejoinder, shall be found of an immoderate length, both the party and the counsel under whose hand it passed, shall be fined."

Pleadings with libelous, slanderous, impertinent matter, etc., taken from files, etc., and parties punished, efc., and counselors, etc., to receive reproof, etc.

RULE 56. "If there be contained in any bill, answer, or other pleadings, or interrogatory, any matter libelous or slanderous against such as are parties to the suit, upon matters impertinent, or in derogation of the settled authorities of any of his Majesty's Courts, such bills, answers, pleadings, or interrogatories, shall be taken off the file and suppressed, and the parties severally punished by commitment or ignominy, as shall be thought fit for the abuse of the Court, and the counselors at law who have set their hands shall likewise receive reproof or punishment, if cause be."(2)

(1) In the Star Chamber, if it appeared that the plaintiff had *probabilem causam litigandi*, though the court could not decree against defendant, if he is left suspected, he should have no costs. 2 Coll. Jur. 232.

In Vancouver *v.* Bliss, 11 Ves. 458, it is held that costs in equity are in the discretion of the court upon the circumstances of the case; not controlled by a positive rule, as at law; though prima facie, he who fails is liable to them, and it is said, that, "those parties who depend upon circumstances to govern the discretion of the court in withholding the costs, have it imposed on them to show the existence of those circumstances in a sufficient degree to cut down the prima facie claim of costs."

(2) Rattray *v.* George, 16 Ves. 232.

Demurrers and pleas in abatement first heard.

RULE 57. "Demurrers and pleas which tend to discharge the suit shall be heard first upon every day of orders, that the subject may know whether he shall need farther attendance or not."

Demurrer to defective matter contained in bill. Plea sets up foreign matter, etc., without oath, if of record, otherwise on oath.

RULE 58. "A demurrer is properly upon matter defective contained in the bill itself, and no foreign matter,(1) but a plea is of foreign matter to discharge or stay the suit;(2) as that the cause hath been formerly dismissed, or that the plaintiff is outlawed, or excommunicated, or there is another bill depending for the same cause, or the like; and such plea may be put in without oath, in case where the matter of the plea appears upon record; but, if it be anything that doth not appear upon record, the plea must be upon oath."

Plea of outlawry sub pede sigilli; of excommunication, without seal of ordinary.

RULE 59. "No plea of outlawry shall be allowed without pleading the record *sub pede sigilli;* nor plea of excommunication without the seal of the ordinary."

Demurrer dismissed, on demurrer under fifteenth rule.

RULE 60. "Where any suit appeareth upon the bill to be of the natures which are regularly to be dismissed, according to the 15th ordinance, such matter is to be set forth by way of demurrer."

(1) 2 Coll. Jur. 164; Mitf. Ch.   (2) 2 Coll. Jur. 164; Mitf. Ch.
Pl. 13, 14.   Pl. 14, 15.

Upon insufficient answer defendant pays single costs, then
double costs, etc. If answer certified sufficient,
plaintiff pays costs.

RULE 61. "Where an answer shall be certified insufficient, the defendant is to pay costs; and if a second
answer be returned insufficient in the points before
certified insufficient, then double costs; and upon the
third, treble costs; and upon the fourth, quadruple
costs; and then to be committed also until he hath
made a perfect answer, and to be examined upon interrogatories touching the points defective in his answer;
but if any answer be certified sufficient, the plaintiff is
to pay costs."

Replication admits answer sufficient.

RULE 62. "No insufficient answer can be taken hold
of after replication put in; because it is admitted sufficient by the replication."

Answer to direct charge must be direct, and not upon
belief; denial not by way of negative pregnant. Traverse not literally in language of, but in substance.

RULE 63. "An answer to a matter charged, as the
defendant's own fact must be direct, without saying,
it is to his remembrance, or as he believeth, if it be
laid as done, within seven years before; if the defendant deny the fact, he must traverse it directly, and
not by way of negative pregnant; as, if a fact be laid
to be done with diverse circumstances, the defendant
may not traverse it literally as it is laid in the bill, but
must traverse the point of substance; so, if he be
charged with the receipt of £100, he must traverse
that he hath not received £100, nor any part thereof;
and, if he have received part, he must set forth what
part."

When hearing on bill and answer, answer must admit bill true in all parts.

RULE 64. "If a hearing be prayed upon bill and answer, the answer must be admitted to be true in all points, and a decree ought to be made, but upon hearing the answer read in Court."

When defendant does not appear his answer must be read.

RULE 65. "Where no counsel appears for the defendant at the hearing, and the process appears to have been served, the answer of such defendant is to be read in Court."

No new matter in replication, except in avoidance.

RULE 66. "No new matter is to be contained in any replication, except it be to avoid matter set forth in the defendant's answer."(1)

All copies must contain fifteen lines per page subscribed by name of principal clerk.

RULE 67. "All copies in Chancery shall contain fifteen lines in every sheet thereof, written orderly, and unwastefully, unto which shall be subscribed the name of the principal clerk of the office where it is written, or his deputy, for whom he will answer, for which subscription only no fee at all shall be taken."

Interrogatories accompany commission to examine witnesses. Depositions must be comprised in one roll, or each roll, signed, etc.

RULE 68. "All commissions for examination of witnesses shall be *super interr. inclusis* only, and no re-

(1) Forum Romanum, 108; Goodfellow *v.* Marshall, 1 Ch. Ca. 197.

In that case the plaintiff having put new matter into his replication, the defendant's plea and demurrer were allowed.

Finch. 426; 2 Coll. Jur. 191.

turn of depositions into the Court shall be received,
but such only as shall be either comprised in one roll
subscribed with the name of the commissioners, or
else in divers rolls, whereof each one shall be so subscribed."(1)

**If plaintiff do not produce witnesses on commission to
examine, no new commission granted except the
fault was defendant's. May examine in court upon
former interrogatories, etc.**

RULE 69. "If both parties join in commissions, and,
upon warning given, the defendant bring his commissioners, but produceth no witnesses, nor ministereth
interrogatories, but after seek a new commission, the
same shall not be granted; but, nevertheless, upon
some extraordinary excuse of the defendant's default,
he may have liberty granted by special order to examine his witnesses in Court upon the former interrogatories, giving the plaintiff, or his attorney notice that
he may examine also if he will."

**Defendant not to be examined except by order of court
and upon plaintiff's offer to be concluded.**

RULE 70. "The defendant is not to be examined
upon interrogatories, except it be in very special
cases, by express order of the Court, to sift out some
fraud, or practice pregnantly appearing to the Court, or
otherwise, upon offer of the plaintiff, to be concluded
by the answer of the defendant, without any liberty
to disprove such answer, or to impeach him after of
perjury."

(1) The interrogatories were anciently annexed to the commission.
Forum Romanum, 126.
In the Star Chamber practice all
commissions for the examination
of witnesses were accompanied by
the interrogatories annexed.
2 Coll. Jur. 202.

Decrees of other courts read without special order; depositions not; and then between same parties and cause of action.

RULE 71. "Decrees in other Courts may be read upon hearing, without the warrant of any special order; but no depositions taken in any other Court are to be read, but by special order; and, regularly, the Court granteth no order for reading of depositions, except it be between the same parties, and upon the same title and cause of suit."(1)

No impeachment of witnesses except by special order.

RULE 72. "No examination is to be had of the credit of any witness, but by special order, which is sparingly to be granted."(2)

Examination of witnesses in perpetuam rei memoriam, except after bill and answer, and giving the names of the witnesses. Deposition to be used only in case of death, age, incompetency, or absence from the realm.

RULE 73. "Witnesses shall not be examined in *perpetuam rei memoriam*, except it be(3) upon the ground of a bill first put in and answer thereunto made, and the defendant or his attorney made acquainted with the names of the witnesses that the plaintiff would have examined, and so publication to be of such witnesses, with this restraint nevertheless, that no benefit shall be taken of the depositions of such witnesses, in case they may be brought *viva voce* upon the trial; but

(1) Norcliff *v.* Worsley, 1 Ch. Ca. 234; Terwit *v.* Gresha *v*, 1 Ch. Ca. 73; Cooke *v.* Fountains, 1 Vern· 413; Nevill *v.* Johnson, 2 Vern. 447; Wilford *v* Beasoley, 3 Atk. 500; Lubiere *v.* Genou, 2 Ves. Sr.

579.

(2) White *v.* Fussell, 1 Ves. and Beam. 151; Mill *v.* Mills, 12 Ves. 406, and notes.

(3) Mitf. Ch. Pl. 50; Allan *v.* Allan, 15 Ves. 131.

only to be used in case of death before the trial, or age, or impotency, or absence out of the realm at the trial."

Witnesses not examined after publication except by consent or special order

RULE 74. "No witnesses shall be examined after publication, except it be by consent, or by special order *ad informandum conscientiam judicis*; and then to be brought close sealed up to the Court, to peruse or publish, as the Court shall think good."

Affidavit not taken by Masters, touching merits, etc.

RULE 75. "No affidavit shall be taken or admitted by any Master of the Chancery, tending to the proof or disproof of the title, or matter in question, or touching the merits of the cause; neither shall any such matter be colorably inserted in any affidavit for serving of process."

No affidavit taken against affidavit, etc.

RULE 76. "No affidavit shall be taken against affidavit, as far as the Masters of the Chancery can have knowledge; and if any such be taken, the latter affidavit shall not be used nor read, in Court."

Committed for contempt, for force, if words, words of scandal, etc. For other contempts, attachments, examination on interrogatories and examination confessed. Committed if confessed or proved. Contempt discharged for non-prosecution.

RULE 77. "In case of contempts granted upon force, or ill words, upon serving of process, or upon words of scandal of the Court proved, by affidavit, the party is forthwith to stand committed; but, for other contempts against the orders or decrees of the Court, an attachment goes for the first upon affidavit made, and then the party is to be examined upon interrogatories, and his examination referred, and, if upon his examination he confess matter of contempt, he is to be committed; if not, the adverse party may examine witnesses to prove the contempt; and therefore, if the contempt appear, the party is to be committed; but if not, or if the party that pursues the contempt do fail in putting in interrogatories, or other prosecution or fail in the proof of the contempt, then, the party charged with the contempt is to be discharged with good costs."

Those in contempt not suffered in Court, except the Court suspend the contempt.

RULE 78. "They that are in contempt, especially so far as proclamation of rebellion, are not to be here,(1) neither in that suit, nor any other, except the Court of special grace suspend the contempt."

Imprisonments discharged, etc., unless for disobedience to decree when must first obey decree. May be suspended temporarily.

RULE 79. "Imprisonment upon contempt for matters passed may be discharged of grace after sufficient punishment, or otherwise dispensed with; but, if the imprisonment be for not performance of any order of the Court in force, they ought not to be discharged except they first obey: but, the contempt may be suspended for a time."

(1) In Vowles v. Young, 9 Ves. 173, Lord Eldon, says, "as to the contempt, the general rule is, that the parties must clear their contempt before they can be heard." It is said also in Forum Romanum, 102, "it is to be observed as a general rule, that the contemnor who is in contempt is never to be heard by motion or otherwise, till he hath cleared his contempt and paid the costs."

Injunctions, etc., not granted upon petition.

RULE 80. "Injunctions, sequestrations, dismissions, retainers upon dismissions, or final orders, are not to be granted upon petitions."

No former order to be altered, etc., on petition, except for small stay or until hearing of motion.

RULE 81. "No former order made in Court is to be altered, crossed, or explained upon any petition; but, such orders may be stayed upon petition for a small stay, until the matter be moved in Court."

No commission for examination of witnesses, etc., upon petition, except upon reference to and certification of clerk.

RULE 82. "No commission for examination of witnesses shall be discharged, nor any examinations or depositions shall be suppressed upon petition, except it be upon point of course of the Court first referred to the clerks, and certificate thereupon."

No demurrer overruled upon petition.

RULE 83. "No demurrer shall be overruled upon petition."

No scire facias on recognizances not enrolled, nor on one enrolled, except on examination of the record, with writ, etc.

RULE 84. "No *scire facias* shall be awarded upon recognizances not enrolled, nor upon recognizances enrolled; unless it be upon examination of the record with the writ; nor no recognizance shall be enrolled after the year, except it be upon special order from the Lord Chancellor."

Certain writs not awarded without warrant from Lord Chancellor, except certain writs named.

RULE 85. "No writ of *ne exeat regnum*, prohibition,(1) consultation statute of Northampton, *certiorari* special, or *procedendo* special, or *certiorari* or *procedendo* general, more than one in the same cause; *habeas corpus*, or *corpus cum causa; vi laica removend;* restitution thereupon, *de coronatore et viridario eligendo*, in case of a moving *dc homine repleg. assiz.*, (2) or special patent, *inde ballivo amovend, certiorari super presentationibus fact, coram commissariis seward*, or *ad quod dampnum* shall pass without under the Lord Chancellor's hand and signed by him, save such writs as (of) *ad quod dampnum*, as shall be signed by Master Attorney."

Rule for rights of privilege. Suitors and witnesses protected eundo, redeundo and morando. Interference with privilege a contempt of court.

RULE 86. "Writs of privilege(3) are to be reduced to a better rule, both for the number of persons that shall be privileged, and for the case of the privilege; and as for the number, it shall be set down by schedule: for the case, is to be understood, that besides parties privileged, as attendants upon the Court, suitors and witnesses are only to have privilege *eundo, redeundo, et morando*, for their necessary attendance, and not otherwise; and that such writ of privilege dischargeth

---

(1) Worcester *v.* Bennett, 1 Dick. 143; Anon. 1 Vern. 301; Hill *v.* Turner, 1 Atk. 516; Rotherham *v.* Fanshaw, 3 Atk. 628; Anon. 1 P. Wms. 476; Iveson *v.* Harris, 7 Ves. 251.

(2) Atwood *v*, Atwood, Finch,

Prec. Ch. 492; Treblecock's Case, 1 Atk. 633; Exparte Ashton, 1 Dick. 23.

(3) Bromley *v.* Holland, 5 Ves. 2; Moor *v.* Booth, 3 Ves. 350; Exparte Ledwich, 8 Ves. 598; Sidigier *v.* Birch, 9 Ves. 69.

only an arrest upon the first process; but yet where at such times of necessary attendance the party is taken in execution, it is a contempt to the Court, and accordingly to be punished."(1)

Supplicavit granted only on certain conditions.

RULE 87. "No *supplicavit* for the good behavior shall be granted, but upon articles grounded upon the oath of two at the least, or certificate of any one Justice of Assize, or two Justices of the Peace, with affidavit, that it is their hands, or by order of the Star Chamber(2) or Chancery, or other of the King's Courts."

No recognizance, etc., without warrant from Lord Chancellor.

RULE. 88. "No recognizance of the good behavior and the peace taken in the country, and certified into the Petty-Bag, shall be filed in the year, without warrant from the Lord Chancellor."(3)

Writs ne exeat regnum, how granted in different classes of cases.

RULE 89. "Writs of *ne exeat regnum* are properly to be granted, according to the suggestion of the writ, in respect of attempts prejudicial to the King and State; in which case the Lord Chancellor will grant them, upon prayer of any of the principal secretaries,

(1) This writ is founded on the statute 21 Jac. 1 C. 8, passed about five years after the making of this ordinance. Exparte Gumbleton, 9 Mod. 232; Hilton *v.* Biron, 3 Salk. 248. The Coll. Jur. 193, carries supplicavits so far back as the reign of Hen. VII. and Hen. VIII., where both parties, plaintiff and defendant, were bound over to their good behavior.

(2) The Court of Star Chamber was erected by Stat. 3 Hen. 7, C. 1, and dissolved by Stat. 16 and 17 Car. 1, C. 10, repealing the former act. Lord Coke denies this, 4 Inst. 62.

(3) Howden *v.* Rogers, 1 Ves. & Beam. 129; Dick *v.* Swinton, 1 Ves. & Beam. 137.

without cause shewing; or upon such information as his Lordship shall think of weight: but otherwise also they may be granted, according to the practice of long time used,(1) in case of interlopers in trade, great bankrupts, in whose estate many subjects are interested, or other cases that concern multitudes of the King's subjects; also, in case of duels and divers others."

Writs, etc., filed in Chapel of Rolls, etc. Depositions of witnesses remain with six clerks.

RULE 90. "All writs, certificates, and whatsoever other process *ret. coram Rege in Canc.* shall be brought into the Chapel of the Rolls, within convenient time after the return thereof, and shall be there filed, upon their proper files and bundles, as they ought to be; except the depositions of witnesses, which may remain with any of the six clerks by the space of one year next after the cause shall be determined by decree, or otherwise be dismissed."

Writs of injunction enlarged, etc.

RULE 91. "All injunctions shall be enrolled, or the transcript filed, to the end, that if occasion be, the Court may take order to award writs of *scire facias* thereupon, as in ancient time hath been used."

All directions to sheriffs to return writs filed in register's office or Petty Bag. All recognizances with the clerks of the Inrollment.

RULE 92. "All days given by the Court to sheriffs to return their writs, or bring their prisoners upon writs of privilege, or otherwise, between party and party,

(1) It is not easy to fix the period when this writ was first applied to civil purposes. The earliest in- stance known was in the case of Hasell *v.* Badick, in 32 Elizabeth.

shall be filed either in the Register's office or in the Petty Bag respectively; and all recognizances taken to the King's use, or unto the Court, shall be duly enrolled in convenient time with the Clerks of the Inrollment, and calendars made of them; and the calendars every Michaelmas Term to be presented to the Lord Chancellor."

Exceptions only in certain cases where decree may be entered without bill.

RULE 93. "In case of suits upon the commissions for charitable uses, to avoid charge, there shall need no bill, but only exceptions to the decree and answer forthwith to be made thereunto: and thereupon, and upon sight of the inquisition, and the decree brought unto the Lord Chancellor, by the clerk of the Petty Bag, his Lordship, upon perusal thereof, will give order under his hand for an absolute decree to be drawn up."

Proceedings in suit for commission of sewers.

RULE 94. "Upon suit for the commission of sewers, the names of those that are desired to be commissioners are to be preferred to the Lord Chancellor in writing: then his Lordship will send the names of some Privy Counsellor, Lieutenant of the Shire, Justices of Assize, being resident in the parts for which the commission is prayed, to consider of them, that they be not put in for private respects; and upon the return of such opinion, his Lordship will farther order for the commission to pass."

New commission of sewards not granted except for abuse of first commission or other weighty ground.

RULE 95. "No new commission of sewards shall be

granted while the first is in force, except it be upon discovery of abuse or fault in the first commissioners, or otherwise upon some great and weighty ground."

Proceedings in petition of bankrupt.

RULE 96. "No petition of bankrupts shall be granted, but upon petition first exhibited to the Lord Chancellor, together with names presented, of which his Lordship will take consideration, and always single some learned in the law with the rest, yet so as care be taken, that the same parties be not too often used in commissions; and likewise care is to be taken, that bond with good surety be entered into, in two hundred pounds at least, to prove him a bankrupt."

Commission of delegates, how appointed.

RULE 97. "No commission of delegates in any case of weight shall be awarded, but upon petition preferred to the Lord Chancellor who will name the commissioners himself; to the end, that they may be persons of convenient quality; having regard to the weight of the cause, and the dignity of the Court from whom the appeal is."

Defendants may defend forma pauperis. How plaintiffs may proceed thus.

RULE 98. "Any man shall be permitted to defend *in forma pauperis* upon oath but for plaintiffs, they are ordinarily to be referred to the Court of Requests, or to the provincial counsels, if the case arise in the jurisdictions, or to some gentlemen in the country, except it be in some special cases of commiseration or potency of the adverse party."

Licenses to clerk for losses from fire or water granted, when and how.

RULE 99. "Licenses to collect for losses by fire or water, are not to be granted, but upon good certificate, and not for decays of suretyship, or debt, or any other casualties whatsoever: and they are rarely to be renewed; and they to be directed unto the county where the loss did arise, if it were by fire, and the counties that abut upon it, as the case shall require: and if it were by sea, then unto the county where the port is from whence the ship went, and to some counties adjoining."

Exemplification, how made.

RULE 100. "No exemplification(1) shall be made of letters patent (*inter alia*) with omission of the general words; nor of records made void or cancelled; nor of the decrees of this Court not inrolled; nor of depositions by parcel;(2) nor of depositions in Court, to which the hand of the examiner is not subscribed; nor of records of the Court, not being inrolled or filed; nor of records of any other Court, before the same be duly certified to this Court, and orderly filed here; nor of any records upon the sight and examination of any copy in paper, but upon sight and examination of the original."

(1) An "exemplification" is the copy or example of a matter recorded or inrolled as decrees: letters patent, etc., and is made out or copied from the inrollment thereof, and sealed with the Great Seal. Therefore all decrees, deeds, etc., must be inrolled before they are exemplified. Fisher *v.* Smith, 33 Eliz., and Attorney General *v.* Taylor, Finch, Prec. Ch. 59.

(2) Backhouse *v.* Middleton, 1 Ch. Ca. 173; Kinaston *v.* Derby, 1 Ch. R. 8.

Reservations of power to amend or add to ordinances.

RULE 101. "And, because time and experience may discover some of these rules to be inconvenient, and some other to be fit to be added; therefore, his Lordship intendeth, in any such case from time to time to publish any such revocations or additions."

GENERAL INDEX.

Pages.

VERDICT.
 Without judgment thereon, no lien on real estate........ 324 (note)
VERMONT.
 Commencement of suit in................................... 104
VIGILANCE.
 Maxim, in respect to.....................   82
VIRGINIA.
 Lis pendens statute of.................................. 367–368
VITIUM LITIGIOSA.
 Name given lis pendens in Continental Europe............ 63
WAIVER.
 By involuntary assignee of right to perfect case.......... 298
 Of prior right to funds, lost by negligence............... 329
WEST VIRGINIA.
 Commencement of suit in................................. 105
 Lis pendens statute of.................................. 362
WISCONSIN.
 Lis pendens statute of................................ 352–353
WRIT.
 Of error, a new lis pendens........................... 101–118
 Of error, a good defense in abatement of second suit....... 395–396
 Formerly issued before bill filed....................... 92
 When declaration in ejectment served discloses subject of
  suit... 99
 When alias or pluries issue, original must be returned...... 110
 Issued in blank, in Connecticut......................... 107
 Issue of, necessary to commencement of suit.............. 104
 Of assistance, what steps to be taken in chancery case to se-
  cure.. 241 and note (1)
 Of error, purchase before and after, effect of............. 259
 Time of issue of, commencement of suit in Vermont, when
  afterwards delivered for service...................... 104
 Of error, a new suit................................... 101
 When given to the sheriff with instructions.............. 101–102
 Of restitution, who can be evicted on it................. 290
 Of possession, steps to be taken in procurance and execu-
  tion of, in accordance with Lord Bacon's rules........... 470
 Of *ne exeat regnum*, when granted, according to Lord Ba-
  con's rules.. 445
WRITS.
 Of privilege, Lord Bacon's rule with respect to............ 468–469
 And other process, where filed, under Lord Bacon's rules... 470
 Of *ne exeat regnum* and other writs, when and how issued,
  according to Lord Bacon's rules...................... 468–470

www.ingramcontent.com/pod-product-compliance
Lightning Source LLC
Chambersburg PA
CBHW021543210326
41599CB00010B/297